The Indoor Environment Handbook

The Indoor Environment Handbook
How to Make Buildings Healthy and Comfortable

Philomena M. Bluyssen

Earthscan works with RIBA Publishing, part of the Royal Institute of British Architects, to promote best practice and quality professional guidance on sustainable architecture

publishing for a sustainable future
London • Sterling, VA

First published by Earthscan in the UK and USA in 2009

ISBN: 978-1-84407-787-8

Typeset by Domex e-Data, India
Cover design by Yvonne Booth

For a full list of publications please contact:

Earthscan
Dunstan House
14a St Cross St
London, EC1N 8XA, UK
Tel: +44 (0)20 7841 1930
Fax: +44 (0)20 7242 1474
Email: earthinfo@earthscan.co.uk
Web: **www.earthscan.co.uk**

22883 Quicksilver Drive, Sterling, VA 20166-2012, USA

Earthscan publishes in association with the International Institute for Environment and Development

A catalogue record for this book is available from the British Library

Library of Congress Cataloging-in-Publication Data

Bluyssen, Philomena M.
 The indoor environment handbook : how to make buildings healthy and comfortable / Philomena M. Bluyssen.
    p. cm.
 Includes bibliographical references and index.
 ISBN 978-1-84407-787-8 (hardback)
 1. Buildings--Environmental engineering--Handbooks, manuals, etc. 2. Sick building syndrome--Prevention--
Handbooks, manuals, etc. I. Title.
 TH6024.B58 2009
 729--dc22

                        2009000863

At Earthscan we strive to minimize our environmental impacts and carbon footprint through reducing waste, recycling and offsetting our CO_2 emissions, including those created through publication of this book. For more details of our environmental policy, see www.earthscan.co.uk.

This book was printed in the UK by The Cromwell Press Group.
The paper used is FSC certified inks are vegetable based.

Contents

PART I: HUMANS AND THE INDOOR ENVIRONMENT

PART II: HEALTH AND COMFORT IN THE INDOOR ENVIRONMENT

PART III: MANAGEMENT OF THE INDOOR ENVIRONMENT

List of Figures, Tables, Boxes and Plates

Figures

Tables

Boxes

Plates

The plate section is located at the end of Part II, between pages 162 and 163.

Why this Book?

This book is meant for all students of the world who want to learn about design, construction and maintenance of non-industrial indoor environments (mainly in the Western countries) in which end users can feel healthy and comfortable now and in the future. It is meant for their teachers, who help them learn to design, build and maintain; and it is meant for anyone else who wishes to learn about the subject.

This book shows that management of the indoor environment can be very complex and is more than being able to 'open' a window. We spend more than 80 per cent of our daily lives indoors. Managing the indoor environment so that we feel comfortable and healthy is therefore very important. The book is also an attempt to provide the reader with some fundamental knowledge and insights on current methods and is also an attempt to contribute to a 'new' way of thinking – one contribution to the solution of how to manage the indoor environment.

During my PhD studies at the Technical University of Denmark under the supervision of Professor P. O. Fanger, I was already intrigued by the human mind and how the body reacts and responds to different environmental stresses. Professor Fanger noted that life would be much easier for us investigators of indoor environments if people didn't live in them. A second intriguing fact is the way in which we (occupants of that indoor environment) take this indoor environment for granted, completely contrary to the way in which we manage our car or our television. If a sales person were to inform us that, for the first few months of acquisition, the television we had just bought will only show images of snow, we would not accept this. But then why do we buy a smelly carpet that takes three months to finally become acceptable? Is it that we have not been educated to explain what we expect and want of an indoor environment?

Lately, more and more knowledge of the indoor environment has become available; but, equally, more generalizations have been made. Labelling a building according to its health? This might be a good tool for policy-makers, but, in practice, it doesn't mean a thing. A building is not healthy; it's the person's health that counts.

This book is an attempt to give insights to human needs during interactions with, and reactions to, the indoor environment and the methods available to provide these insights and to manage the indoor environment. Nevertheless, it is merely an attempt – I do not have the illusion that the book provides a complete answer to complex matters. On the other hand, the book is unique in its kind, as far as I can tell, and I wish you a healthy and comfortable time with it.

Philo Bluyssen
July 2009

How to Read this Book

This book is divided into three parts:

1 'Part I: Humans and the indoor environment': here some of the basics on the human body and the indoor environment are explained.
2 'Part II: Health and comfort in the indoor environment': the history and drivers of health and comfort in the indoor environment are presented and discussed.
3 'Part III: Management of the indoor environment': here a 'new' approach towards health and comfort in the indoor environment is introduced.

Each part begins with an introductory chapter that provides a summary of the information presented in the following chapters.

In Part I the reception and perception mechanisms of the human senses are explained, as well as some basics on indoor environmental parameters that create the indoor environment as we perceive it. In order to understand Parts II and III of this book, it is necessary to present this basic knowledge. Chapter 2 describes the characteristics and the mechanisms of each of the components of the human body that have some relation to the perception or reception of the indoor environment, and presents possible diseases and disorders that might be experienced as a result of the indoor environment. Chapter 3 describes the parameters of each of the environmental factors (thermal comfort, visual quality, indoor air quality and acoustical quality) encountered in the indoor environment. It explains the mechanism behind it, and possible strategies to control this environmental factor.

The aim of Part II is to provide an overview of how managing the indoor environment has developed over the years, and which drivers of health and comfort can be identified. In Chapter 5 the (scientific) approaches applied to cope with indoor environmental quality are sketched and discussed. The approaches have developed from a component related to a bottom–up approach. In Chapter 6, drivers of health and comfort in the indoor environment are presented, including economic and social drivers, the basic needs of end users, the requirements of stakeholders and last, but not least, climate change as a very important driver.

In Part III a new approach towards managing health and comfort in the indoor environment is introduced: a top–down approach in addition to the more traditional bottom–up approach, with a focus on individual interactions in the whole building life cycle. In Chapter 8, the top–down approach is presented analogous to the system engineering methodology used in other disciplines. This top–down approach only works well if the interactions taking place at several levels and places are well understood. As a result, in Chapter 9 the interactions occurring in the indoor environment and between people and the indoor environment are described. It is clear that no single parameter of the indoor environment can be evaluated on its own: different environmental parameters interact and influence the perceptions of people.

Finally, in the concluding chapter, a concise summary and some general conclusions are presented.

Acknowledgements

Due to a knee injury that caused me to stay at home and spend considerable time in hospitals over the last two years, and inspired by the discussions I had with family, friends and colleagues, I managed to write this book. In particular, I would like to thank those for believing in me and giving their support to the book: Dr H. J. A. (Hans) Bluyssen, my father, who is officially a retired physicist but, in practice, never really stopped – he helped me with the correctness of the physics of this book; Professor O. C. G. (Olaf) Adan from TNO Built Environment and Geosciences and the Technical University of Eindhoven, my dear colleague and friend, who gave me the courage to even start the book – we discussed the main set-up and he reviewed the first version; Dr N. (Nadia) Boschi from Bovis Lend Lease, my dear and long-time Italian friend and colleague who reviewed the first version with such passion: she also really helped me through the next versions with her encouraging words; Professor Owen Lewis from University College Dublin School of Architecture, Landscape and Civil Engineering, my Irish friend and colleague from the architecture community who gave me very good advice in general; and Professor C.-A. (Claude-Alain) Roulet (retired), my Swiss friend and colleague, with whom I have worked in the European indoor environmental research arena for almost 20 years. My husband Darell Meertins not only loaned his picture, but gave me the opportunity to write the book and supported me on several levels; my eldest son, Anthony, gave me several of his excellent drawings; and my youngest son, Sebastian, I thank just for being himself.

And last, but not least, I would like to thank those individuals who give me permission to use drawings, figures or photos. They are all acknowledged in the book.

List of Symbols, Acronyms and Abbreviations

Symbols

A	surface area (m^2)
A_c	mean body surface area in standing position (m^2)
A_{eff}	effective body surface area (m^2)
AH	absolute humidity grams per cubic metre (g/m^3)
A_s	total absorption surface in space (m^2)
b	width (m)
c	speed of light (m/s)
c_a	specific heat for air (J/kgK)
c_p	specific heat of dry air at constant pressure (J/kg°C)
c_w	specific heat for water (J/kgK)
C	concentration of a compound in the air expressed in ppm, ppb or $\mu g/m^3$
C_e	concentration of pollutant in exhaust air ($\mu g/m^3$)
C_i	concentration of pollutant in indoor air ($\mu g/m^3$)
C_s	concentration of pollutant in supplied air ($\mu g/m^3$)
C_{ev}	heat of evaporation of water (J/kg)
C_g	correction for type of façade
C_t	capital/value at end of period ($)
C_{t-1}	capital/value at beginning of period ($)
CFL_n	cash flow at time n ($)
°C	degree Celsius
d	thickness (m)
d	diameter (m)
D	the damping or attenuation by the wall the sound is transferred through (dB)
D_{nT}	normalized difference in sound pressure level (dB)
D_a	diffusion coefficient through air (m^2/s)
D_m	diffusion coefficient through material (m^2/s)
DR	draught rating (%)
E	heat loss (W) or energy use (MJ)
E	thermal internal energy in Joule (J)
E	illuminance/light level (lumen/m^2) or (lux)
E_i	illuminance indoors (lux)
E_0	horizontal illuminance outdoors in free surroundings (lux)
E_v	ventilation efficiency
f	frequency (Hz) or (s^{-1})
Fij	fraction of radiation leaving the ith surface, which reaches the jth surface directly
g	gravitational acceleration (m/s^2)
h	Planck's constant = 6.63×10^{-34} (J/s)
h_b	mass transfer coefficient in buffer layer (m/s)
h_c	heat transfer coefficient for convection (W/m^2K)

h_d	mass transfer coefficient for diffusion (m/s)
h_{ij}	mass transfer coefficient in layer between i and j (m/s)
h_m	mass transfer coefficient in laminar layer (m/s)
H_{ex}	humidity ratio of expired air (kg water/kg dry air)
H_{in}	humidity ratio of breathed in air (kg water/kg dry air)
I	intensity of light (lumen/sr or candela)
I	given sound intensity (W/m²)
I_0	10^{-12} = minimum hearing intensity (W/m²)
I_t	total energy index (MJ/m²)
I_{clo}	thermal resistance from the skin to the outer surface of the clothed body (clo)
INC_t	income during time period t–1 to t ($)
J/s	joules per second
k	permeability of the skin (s/m)
l	length (m)
L	luminance (lux)
L_b	luminance of background (cd/m²)
L_p	sound pressure level in decibel (dB)
$L_{receiver}$	sound pressure level in the receiving space (dB)
L_{send}	sound pressure level in the sending space (dB)
L_p	sound pressure level perceived at distance r (dB)
L_w	sound pressure level in point (dB)
Lp_{2m}	sound pressure level at 2m for the façade with the highest sound load (dB)
Lp_2	the mean sound pressure level in receiving space (dB)
LAeq,T	energy average equivalent level of the A-weighted sound over a period T (dB)
LAmax	maximum noise level (dB)
m	mass in g or kg
m_w	quantity of water (kg)
$\dot{m}$	mass air flow rate (kg/s)
m/s	metres per second
M	metabolic rate of human body (W)
n	the specific airflow rate or air change rate
OUT_t	payment during time period t–1 to t ($)
p	partial vapour pressure (N/m²)
p	static pressure (N/m²)
p	Guth position index for a lighting system
p^*	saturated vapour pressure (N/m²)
p_a	partial air pressure (N/m²)
P_b	pressure of the barometer (N/m²)
P_s	saturated water vapour pressure at skin temperature (N/m²)
P_w	partial water vapour pressure (N/m²)
P_i	production of pollutant indoors (µg/s)
P_t	profit ($)
PMV	predicted mean vote index
ppm	parts per million
ppb	parts per billion (ppb = 24.45 × µg/m³/molecular weight)
Q	heat transfer (W)
Q	ventilation rate (m³/s)
q_t	heat transfer via conduction through clothing (W)

q_c	heat transfer via convection from clothed body (W)
q_r	heat transfer via radiation from clothed body (W)
q_d	heat loss by water vapour diffusion through skin (W)
q_{sw}	heat loss by sweat evaporation (W)
q_{re}	heat loss by latent respiration (W)
q_l	heat loss by dry respiration (W)
R	perceived odour intensity
R	heat resistance ($°C/Wm^2$)
R	reflectance factor = ability of surface to reflect light (%)
r_d	reflectance of a diffuse reflecting surface
r_c	reverberation radius (m)
R_a	colour index for 8 or 14 R_is
R_i	colour index for one colour
R	sound insulation of the wall (dB)
R_i	sound insulation for surface area I (dB)
$R_{combined}$	combined sound insulation of surface areas i (dB)
RH	relative humidity in percentage (%)
S	surface area of the wall (m^2)
Sh_l	Sherwood number
t	time (s)
T	temperature in Kelvin (K) or Celsius (°C)
T_a	air temperature (°C) or (K)
T_{cl}	temperature of clothing (K)
T_{ex}	temperature of exhaled air (K)
T_{in}	temperature of breathed in air (K)
T_{mrt}	mean radiant temperature (°C)
T_r	radiant temperature (°C)
T_s	absolute surface temperature (K) or skin temperature (K)
Tu	turbulence intensity (%)
T	number of repetitions of the disturbance (for sound) (s)
T_r	reverberation time (s)
T_2	reverberation time in receiving space (s)
T_n	normalized reverberation time (for dwellings 0.5 sec) (s)
U	heat transfer coefficient (W/m°C)
v	velocity (m/s) or (cm/s)
v_m	mean air velocity (m/s)
V	volume (m^3)
V_a	volume of air (m^3)
$\dot{V}$	supplied fresh airflow rate (including infiltration) (m^3/s)
W	external mechanical power (W)
x	distance (m)
Y_m	path through material (m)
y	yield or interest of a project ($)
z	height of gravity field (m)
α_i	absorption coefficient of walls (I = w), ceiling (I = c) and floor (I = f) for sound
β	transfer coefficient for condensation of water (s/m)
δ	dissipation coefficient of sound
δt	time interval (s)

ε	emission coefficient
ε_D	eddy diffusivity (m/s)
σ	standard deviation
σ	Stefan Boltzmann constant (5.67×10^{-8}) (W/m^{2}K^4)
κ	transport coefficient for evaporation of water (s/m)
λ	wavelength of light (nm)
λ_{max}	wavelength at which maximum amount of energy is emitted (nm)
ρ	mass density (kg/m^3)
ρ_a	mass density of air (kg/m^3)
ρ_w	mass density of water (kg/m^3)
ρ	given sound pressure (Pa)
ρ	reflection coefficient of sound
ρ_0	2×10^{-5} = minimum hearing sound pressure (Pa)
ρ	reflectance of light
Φ	amount of moving air/water (kg/s)
Φ	rate of light emission (lumen)
η	dynamic viscosity (n.s/m^2)
η	output of a lighting system
η	mechanical efficiency
η_a	air exchange efficiency
τ	transmission coefficient = the reciprocal of the sound insulation measure
τ_a	time required on average to replace the air present in the space (s)
τ_n	nominal time constant (s)
τ_r	age of air (s)
$<\tau>$	room mean age of air (s)
γ	resistance coefficient
ω	angle (star radials)

Acronyms and abbreviations

ACA	adaptive control algorithm
ACTH	adrenocortico tropine hormone
AD	Anno Domini (after Christ)
ADH	anti-diuretic hormone
AEIF	Environmental Assistance for Railing Interoperability
AHU	air handling unit
ANS	automatic nervous system
ASHRAE	American Society of Heating, Refrigerating and Air Conditioning Engineers
ASHVE	American Society of Heating and Ventilation Engineering
AQG	air quality guideline
AW	water activity
BACnet	Building Automation and Control network
BAL	building automation and control
BAR	gross starting yield
BASE	Building Assessment Survey and Evaluation Study
BAT	best available technology
BOLD	blood oxygen level dependent
BOSTI	Buffalo Organization for Social and Technological Innovation

BPD	Biocides Product Directive
BRE	Building Research Establishment
BRI	building-related illness
BSI	Building Symptom Index
BQA	building quality assessment
CAD	computer-aided design
CD	concurrent design
CDF	*Clostridium difficile*
CDF	Concurrent Design Facility
CE	Conformité Européenne
CEN	European Committee for Standardization
CFC	chlorofluorocarbon
CH_4	methane
CIB	International Council for Research and Innovation in Building and Construction
CIE	International Commission on Illuminance
CME	coronal mass emission
CNS	central nervous system
CO	carbon monoxide
CO_2	carbon dioxide
COPD	chronic obstructive pulmonary disease
CPD	Construction Product Directive
CRA	comparative risk assessment
2D	two dimensional
3D	three dimensional
DALY	disability-adjusted life years
dB	decibel
DBFMO	design, build, finance, maintain and operate
Defra	UK Department for Environment, Food and Rural Affairs
DF	daylight factor
DICL	Danish Indoor Climate Labelling Scheme
DNA	deoxyribonucleic acid
DNP	dinitrophenyl
DNPH	dinitrophenylhydrazine
DOP	dioctylphthalate
DPI	daylight performance index
DR	draught rating
E	energy
EC	European Commission
ECA	European Concerted Action
EDT	early decay time
EEG	electro-encephalography
EL	electroluminescent/electroluminescence
ELF	extreme low frequency
EPA	US Environmental Protection Agency
EPBD	Energy Performance Building Directive
ER 3	Essential Requirement 3 (of the CPD)
ERC	externally reflected component
ESA	European Space Agency

ESA CDF	European Space Agency Concurrent Design Facility
ET	effective temperature
ETS	environmental tobacco smoke
EU	European Union
FID	flame ionization detector
FiSIAQ	Finnish Society of Indoor Air Quality and Climate
fMRI	functional magnetic resonance imaging
GABA	gamma aminobutyric acid
GDP	gross domestic product
GHG	greenhouse gas
GNP	gross national product
GR	glare rating
Hz	Hertz
HHRS	UK Housing Health and Safety Rating System
HLY	healthy life years
HOPE	Health Optimization Protocol for Energy-Efficient Buildings project
HPLC	high performance liquid chromatography
HVAC	heating, ventilating and air conditioning
HWS	hot water supply
IARC	International Agency for Research on Cancer
IAQ	indoor air quality
ICC	International Code Council
IEA	International Energy Agency
IEC	International Electrotechnical Commission
IEQ	indoor environmental quality
Ig	immunoglobulins
IOM	Institute of Medicine
IPCC	Intergovernmental Panel on Climate Change
IPF	individual performance factor
IPPC	Integrated Pollution Prevention and Control Directive
IRC	internally reflected component
IRR	internal rate of return
ISO	International Organization for Standardization
J	joule
kHz	kiloHertz
KPI	key performance indicator
kWh	kilowatt hours
LCA	life-cycle analysis
LCC	life-cycle cost
LCI	lowest concentration of interest
LED	light-emitting diode
LEEC	lamp energy efficiency class
LLMF	lamp lumen maintenance factor
LOAEL	lowest-observed adverse-effect level
LOS	lipo-oligo-saccharide
LPS	lipo-polysaccharide
LSF	lamp survival factor
MALT	mucosal-associated lymphoid tissue

MEG	magneto-encephalography
MHz	megaHertz
MJ	megajoule
MRSA	multidrug-resistant *Staphylococcus aureus*
MS	mass spectrometry
NAE	National Academy of Engineering
NAS	National Academy of Sciences
NCA	US Noise Control Act
NIF	non-imaging forming
NIOSH	National Institute for Occupational Safety and Health
nm	nanometre
NO	nitric oxide
NO_2	nitrogen dioxide
N_2O	nitrous oxide
NOAEL	no-observed adverse-effect level
NPV	net present value
NRC	National Research Council
O_3	ozone
OEL	occupational exposure level
OH	hydroxyl radical
OIE	open information environment
OSHA	Occupational Safety and Health Administration
OWA	organizational workplace analysis
Pa	Pascal
PAH	polycyclic aromatic hydrocarbon
PAP	perceived air pollution
PBAX	private branch automatic exchange
PCB	polychlorinated biphenyl
PCP	pentachlorophenol
PEL	permissible exposure level
PET	positron emission tomography
PM	particulate matter
PMV	predicted mean vote
PNS	peripheral nervous system
ppb	parts per billion
PPC	public–private cooperation
PPD	predicted percentage of dissatisfied
PPF	panel performance factor
ppt	particles per trillion
POE	post-occupancy evaluation
POM	particulate organic matter
PSI	Personal Symptom Index
PTH	parathyroid hormone
PUF	polyurethane foam
PV	present value
PVC	polyvinyl chloride
QALY	quality-adjusted life year
RAST	radio allegro sorbent test

R&D	research and development
RCS	Reuter centrifugal air sampler
REACH	Registration, Evaluation, Authorization and Restriction of Chemicals regulation
REL	recommended exposure level
REN	Real Estate Norm Nederland
RF	radiative forcing
RH	relative humidity
RHE	rotating heat exchanger
RNA	ribonucleic acid
RSP	respirable suspended particle
SARS	severe acute respiratory syndrome
SAW	surface acoustic wave
SBS	sick building syndrome
SC	sky component
SCN	suprachiasmatic nucleus
SEL	sound exposure level
SEM	structural equation modelling
SO_2	sulphur dioxide
STI	Speed Transmission Index
STM	serviceability tools and methods
SVOC	semi-volatile organic compound
TOW	time of wetness
TLV	threshold limit value
TQM	total quality management
TRH	thyrotropin-releasing hormone
TRR	total rate of return
TSH	thyroid-stimulating hormone
TSI	technical specification for interoperability
TVOC	total volatile organic compound
UFP	ultra-fine particle
UGR	unified glare rating
UNEP	United Nations Environment Programme
UNFCCC	United Nations Framework Convention on Climate Change
US	United States
UV	ultraviolet
VDI	virtual desktop infrastructure
VOC	volatile organic compound
VSL	value of statistical life
VVOC	very volatile organic compound
WHO	World Health Organization
WMO	World Meteorological Organization
XAD	styrene-divinylbenzene copolymer
μm	micrometre

Part I

Humans and the Indoor Environment

1

Health, Comfort and Indoor Environmental Control

In this chapter, an introduction to Part I is presented. Possible diseases and disorders related to the human body and caused by indoor environmental stress factors are described (see Chapter 2 for fuller discussion) and general strategies to control environmental factors such as thermal comfort, lighting quality, indoor air quality and acoustical quality are presented (see Chapter 3). These indoor environmental parameters are defined and identified with quantitative indicators, largely expressed according to (assumed) acceptable numbers or ranges. Although many control strategies have been identified for these parameters, it should be emphasized that control strategies that focus on one parameter and numbers only will probably not be optimal because the health and comfort of humans in the indoor environment is not easy to define and is difficult to relate to the even more complicated characterization of diseases and disorders. Knowledge of how the human body and its systems function is of utmost importance.

1.1 Introduction

> From the occupant's point of view, the ideal situation is an indoor environment that satisfies all occupants (i.e. they have no complaints) and does not unnecessarily increase the risk or severity of illness or injury. (Bluyssen et al, 2003a)

The importance of the indoor environment has been recognized since the first century BC, particularly indoor air quality, as is described by Vitruvius in his ten books of architecture (Rowland and Howe, 2007).

Although chemistry was only seen as a separate science during the 17th century, from the Middle Ages until the beginning of the 19th century people began to realize that air in a building should be good and, if not, could result in diseases or at least extreme discomfort (bad smells). The miasmatic theory of disease, now taken over by the germ theory of disease

(micro-organisms are the cause of many diseases), was used to explain the spread of disease such as cholera (Madigan and Martinko, 2005). Miasma (Greek for pollution) was considered to be a poisonous, smelly vapour or mist that is filled with particles from decomposed matter (miasmata) which can cause illnesses. Ventilation thus became an important part of the indoor environment. Discussions on how much ventilation is sufficient to prevent the spread of disease and to provide adequate comfort (no noxious odours) were thus born and are still taking place (Billings, 1893).

During the late 19th century, 'thermal comfort' was introduced as an environmental factor that is part of overall indoor comfort. In addition to poor air quality, poorly ventilated rooms can result in unwanted thermal effects (both through temperature and humidity) (Billings et al, 1898; Janssen, 1999).

Source: drawings by eight-year-old Anthony Meertins

Figure 1.1 *The human being in an indoor environment*

The positive health effects of (sun) light were already acknowledged by the Egyptians, Romans and the ancient Greeks, who worshipped the sun gods. Much later, at the beginning of the 1900s, sanatoria were built for light therapy for people suffering from, among other ailments, skin diseases. During the late 1980s, light therapy, with artificial light, began to be used to cure winter depressions. Artificial lighting has been an applied science since around the 1890s, when the development of the first electrical lamps made the extension of the working day into the dark hours possible (*Encyclopaedia Britannica*, 1991a).

With regard to sound, the ancient Greeks and Romans realized that good auditory conditions for an audience listening to speech or music, whether indoors or outdoors, are important. They placed audiences on steep hillsides in order to reduce distance and to concentrate sound. However, not all noise was welcome: like bad air, it can be something that we would rather do without. Noise or unwanted auditory experience became an important aspect of practical acoustics during the 1970s. It was considered a form of environmental pollution, and noise control developed into a major branch of acoustical engineering.

By now, the indoor environment had begun to be described by environmental factors or (external) stressors, such as:

- indoor air quality: comprising odour, indoor air pollution, fresh air supply, etc.;

- thermal comfort: moisture, air velocity, temperature, etc.;
- acoustical quality: noise from outside, indoors, vibrations, etc.;
- visual or lighting quality: view, illuminance, luminance ratios, reflection, etc.

These various factors have slowly become incorporated within the building process through environmental design. However, aesthetic quality and spatial and ergonomical quality are also part of the indoor environment. In fact, historically, these parameters received the most attention when designing a building. This book merely focuses on environmental parameters, without downgrading the dimensions and aesthetics of shapes and spaces. As Hawkes (2008) writes: 'The interaction of light and air and sound with the form and materiality of architectural space is of the very essence of the architectural imagination.' And note the way in which Pallasmaa (2005) describes the essence of architecture, which comes even closer to the meaning of this book: 'Architecture is the art of reconciliation between ourselves and the world, and this mediation takes place through the senses.'

The human senses, the so-called 'windows of the soul' (*Encyclopaedia Britannica*, 1991b), are basically the instruments we have to report or indicate whether we feel comfortable (and also how we feel our health is affected) in terms of acceptability with respect to heat, cold, smell, noise, darkness, flickering light, etc. With respect to health effects, not only are the human senses involved, but the entire human body and its systems. Indoor environmental (external) stressors that can cause discomfort and health effects are represented by environmental factors and psycho-social factors, such as working and personal relationships, as well as factors such as sex, whether we smoke, genetics, age, etc.

1.2 Disorders and diseases

External stress factors influence all three systems of the human body (the nervous system, the immune system and the endocrine system) and can result in both mental and physical effects. Given that diseases and disorders of the human body could be caused by or related to an 'unhealthy indoor environment', the following division of diseases and disorders can be made:

- Diseases/disorders that are stress induced by external stress factors and that are 'handled' by the cooperation between the nervous system and the endocrine system, but can be influenced by the status of the immune system, such as:

- direct noticeable comfort-related complaints by the human senses (e.g. smell, noise, heat, cold, draught, etc);
- systemic effects (e.g. tiredness, poor concentration, etc.);
- psychological effects (e.g. not being in control, depression, anxiety, etc.).

- Diseases/disorders that are induced by external noxious effects and are 'handled' by the cooperation between the immune system and the endocrine system, but where the handling can be influenced by the nervous system, such as:
  - irritation, allergic and hyper-reactive effects (e.g. irritation of the mucous membranes of the skin and respiratory tract, asthma, rashes on skin caused by allergic reactions to certain pollutants, sunburn, hearing loss, damage of eyes caused by too bright light, etc.);
  - infectious diseases (e.g. Legionnaires' disease);
  - toxic chronic effects that gradually increase or appear (e.g. cancer).

Besides the effects of external stress factors, the performance of the human senses (internal stress factor) can also have a major influence on the first category of complaints. Degradation of the eyes, ears, olfactory bulb, etc. which usually occurs with age is an example of this. Degradation of the immune system functions also increases with age. And, lastly, genetics can also be of influence, such as colour blindness or being anosmic (not being able to smell normally).

Table 1.1 provides an overview of the possible diseases and disorders related to the different parts of the human body involved in responding to indoor environmental stress factors. Psychological or mental effects are not included in this overview because they are difficult to pinpoint. Not being able to cope with a certain situation (consciously or unconsciously) can cause a whole range of different diseases and disorders, mostly indirectly related to environmental factors and affected by psycho-social and personal factors. Together with systemic effects, they are, in fact, a category of their own, influenced by all the human systems and vice versa.

1.3 Indoor environmental parameters and control

Over the years, control of indoor environmental factors has merely focused on the prevention or cure of different related observed physical effects in a largely isolated way – trying to find separate solutions for thermal comfort, lighting quality, sound quality and air quality.

Thermal comfort can be controlled via so-called heating, ventilating and air-conditioning (HVAC) systems. Heating can be provided through convection, conduction, radiation and air-conditioning systems. Regulation of relative humidity can be provided through (de)humidification systems via an air-conditioning system or locally. In addition, one can adjust one's clothing and type of activities.

Table 1.1 *Diseases and disorders related to the human body (parts) caused by indoor environmental stress factors*

Level	Skin	Eyes	Ears	Nose	Respiratory tract
Discomfort	Warm, cold, sweat, draught	Too much light, too little light, blinding, glare, reflection	Disturbance, hearing and understanding problems	Smell, irritation	Cough; shortness of breath
Systemic effects		Tiredness	Tiredness		Chest pain; wheezing
Allergic or irritant reaction	Contact dermatitis: dry, itchy, red skin	Redness, itching, dry feeling		Runny nose, sneezing, blocked nose	Asthma and bronchitis; hypersensitivity reactions
Infectious diseases	Infection (bacterial, viral or fungal)	Rare: dry-eyes syndrome	Inflammation of the inner ear	Blocked nose, runny nose and stuffy nose; temporary loss of smell	Infection (bacterial, viral or fungal – e.g. bronchitis)
Toxic chronic effects	Radiation-related disorders (such as sunburn)	Damage to the eye by UV light; cataract forming (as a result of long-term infrared light)	Severe and permanent loss of hearing	Permanent loss of smell	Damage and/or tumours

The best way to control exposure to pollutants (air quality) is to perform source control (i.e. to minimize the emission of either primary or secondary pollutants to the air that we are exposed to). Besides source control, there are three other ways to control the exposure, directly or indirectly: ventilation, air cleaning and activity control (e.g. designating smoking areas in a non-smoking building). What is often underestimated now is the contribution of ventilation systems to the indoor air pollution encountered in the indoor environment. Design and maintenance of such systems are important matters (see section 5.1.3 in Chapter 5). Furthermore, the detection and interpretation of the thousands of pollutants in the indoor air is difficult and complex: besides the fact that these pollutants interact with each other (indoor chemistry), they also cause interactions with the sensations and perceptions of the human body. Therefore, providing guidelines for levels of permissible concentrations will always be questionable unless a direct relation has been found.

Comfortable light does not cause blinding (through lighting systems or direct sunlight), or flickering or stroboscopic effects and glare (e.g. from computer screens), and produces good colour impressions, with no reflection and an equal distribution of light. Positioning and intensity of lighting systems, surface area treatment (e.g. mat surface area and colours), solar screens and solar reflecting glazing are means to achieve this. Comfortable light also signifies controllability and healthy light (day–night rhythm). The latter can be provided by offering the right variation on light intensity and colour temperature at the right time (see section 5.1.2 in Chapter 5). With automatic or manual dimming or intensifying of light, an appropriate integration of artificial light and daylight can be achieved. Transparent parts in the enclosure of the space play a pivotal role in the human need, on the one hand, for visual contact with the outdoors (visual comfort) and daylight entrance, and thermal comfort on the other. For thermal comfort, in particular, (one-sided) direct sun radiation can be perceived as uncomfortable, even though air temperature may be at a comfortable level. Furthermore, the issue of energy is inherently involved, particularly in relation to the influx of solar energy and the demand for cooling. Therefore, a great effort is made to develop so-called integrated systems.

Control strategies can be performed to prevent noise from entering a space or approaching a person, or to make the space perform better acoustically. With respect to the latter, besides the reverberation time and the speech–background noise ratio, speech audibility is influenced by the speaker, the communication channel and the listener. Speech intelligibility can therefore be augmented by improving the speech–background noise ratio, by shortening reverberation time, and by improving the clarity and loudness of speech. By introducing absorbing material and/or decreasing volume, the reverberation time can be shortened. Introduction of absorption material also decreases the sound pressure level and suppresses echoing. Prevention or reduction of noise entering a space can be established by preventing/closing sound leaks, preventing or reducing contact sound transmission, and/or applying active (noise) control.

Besides the level and duration of noise disturbance, the positive or negative feelings that people have towards the type of noise and vibrations are also significant. Health effects, for example, reported from exposure to traffic noise during the night are very serious (see section 5.1.4 in Chapter 5).

Table 1.2 provides an overview of indoor environmental parameters and factors that may be controlled, and issues of concern.

1.4 Link with Parts II and III

Part I describes how indoor environmental parameters, thermal comfort, air quality, acoustical quality and lighting quality are currently defined and identified according to quantitative indicators, mostly expressed according to (assumed) acceptable numbers or ranges. Many control strategies for these parameters have been identified in order to minimize or prevent possible diseases and disorders of the human body and its components (with the focus largely being on one parameter at a time). Part II will show that although these control strategies are currently being applied, people still show symptoms of being ill as a result of the indoor environment (e.g. sick building syndrome is a well-known phenomenon). How the human body and its systems receive, perceive and respond to certain environmental conditions is a very important question to answer. Part III will show that not every individual

Table 1.2 *Indoor environmental factors, parameters, control and issues of concern*

	Thermal comfort	Lighting quality	Acoustical quality	Air quality
Parameters	Temperature (air and radiant) Relative humidity Air velocity Turbulence intensity Activity and clothing	Luminance and illuminance Reflectance(s) Colour temperature and colour index View and daylight Frequencies	Sound level(s) Frequencies Duration Absorption characteristics Sound insulation Reverberation time	Pollution sources and air concentrations Types of pollutants (allergic, irritational, carcinogenic, etc.) Ventilation rate and efficiency
Control	Heating, cooling and air-conditioning systems Design of building (insulation, façade, etc.)	Luminance distribution Integration Artificial and natural lighting Daylight entrance	Acoustical control Passive noise control Active noise control	Source control Ventilation systems Maintenance Air cleaning Activity control
Issues	Dynamic effects Adaptation Integration systems (façade, floor and ceiling) Energy use	Daylight entrance relation to thermal comfort and energy use Health effects and control	Long-term health effects Vibrations and annoyance Degree of annoyance with type of noise	Interpretation and detection Secondary pollution (indoor chemistry and micro-organisms) (Fine) dust Energy use

receives, perceives and responds in the same way due to physical, physiological and psychological differences, as well as to differences in history, context and local situation. In addition to 'human drivers' and the influence of time on, and the interactions between, the environmental aspects, external drivers such as economics and regulatory issues need to be considered.

Since a strategy is, most of the time, better than no strategy at all, the control strategies that are presented in this Part I are worthy of being followed. Just be aware not to blindly adopt only one of them!

2

Human Reception and Perception

In this chapter, the characteristics and mechanisms of each of the components of the human body that relate to the reception and perception of the indoor environment are described: the human senses such as the skin, eye, ear and respiratory tract, and the human systems (nervous, endocrine and immune). Possible diseases and disorders that might be experienced due to the indoor environment are presented, as well as measurement techniques to identify diseases and disorders.

2.1 The human senses and human systems

2.1.1 Human senses

The human senses are essentially the instruments we have to report or indicate whether we feel healthy and/or comfortable, knowingly (consciously) or unknowingly (unconsciously). Through sensory receptors, via nerves (the spinal cord and cranial), these senses can provide information to the brain, which is processed and used to send messages with prescribed actions to the relevant parts of the human body. The most obvious senses that most of us are aware of are the sense of sight by the eyes (see section 2.3), the sense of hearing by the ears (see section 2.5), the sense of smell by the nose (see section 2.4), the sense of taste in the mouth (tongue), throat and larynx, and the sense of touch and the awareness of temperature and pain by parts of the skin (see section 2.2). But the human senses also comprise senses that we normally are not so aware of (*Encyclopaedia Britannica*, 1991b) (see Table 2.1):

*   kinaesthetic (motion) sense: the sense organs in muscles, tendons and joints that give us the awareness of the position of our legs and arms and the perception of the active or passive movement of a limb; they play an important role in the regulation of reflex and voluntary movement;

*   sense of balance or equilibrium in the human inner ear (see section 2.5);
*   receptors within the circulatory (cardiovascular) system, sensitive to carbon dioxide in the blood or changes in blood pressure;
*   the receptors in the digestive tract that appear to mediate such experiences as hunger and thirst (although not exclusively: some parts of the brain may also participate).

All of these sense organs have the same basic features – namely:

*   They contain receptor cells that are specifically sensitive to one class of stimulus (e.g. light is the stimulus for visual experience) (see Table 2.1). Nevertheless, other stimuli can also activate the receptor if they are sufficiently intense (e.g. one may see pressure when a thumb is placed on a closed eye and one experiences a bright spot opposite the touched place).
*   The sensitive receptor cells are often localized in the body at a receiving membrane or surface (such as the retina of the eye). Sensory inputs (stimuli) enter through the eyes (vision), ears (audition), mouth (taste), nose (olfaction) and body sensors (touch and internal organ configurations).
*   The sensory cells connect with secondary ingoing nerve cells that carry the nerve impulse (action potential) along (some are very short, such as in

Table 2.1 *Types of sensory receptors found in or on the human body and senses (besides these sensory receptors, the human body also has motor and integration receptors)*

Receptor	Where	Sensitive to/detect stimuli	Function
Mechano-receptor	Skin, muscles, joints and visceral organs	Mechanical deformation by indentation, stretch and hair movement	Touch, muscle length, tendon and limb position Hearing and balance Blood pressure
Chemo-receptor	Olfactory bulb (nose) Taste buds in mouth Internally (e.g. blood)	Chemicals	Smell (odour) and taste Blood levels (oxygen, carbon dioxide, glucose, osmopolarity)
Thermo-receptor	Free nerve endings in skin	Warmth and cold	Internal temperature (hypothalamus)
Noiciceptor	Free nerve endings in skin	Noxious stimuli	Pain
Photoreceptor	Retina in eye	Light energy	Vision

Source: Kapit et al (2000)

the eye, and some are very long, such as in the skin).

• From such nerves, higher-order neurons make complex connections with pathways of the brainstem and deeper parts of the brain (e.g. the thalamus) that eventually end in specific areas in the cerebral cortex of the brain (see Figures 2.1 and 2.2). Vision goes to the occipital lobe in the back, smell to the frontal lobe (visual cortex: for early vision), audition to the temporal lobes on the sides, and touch (tactual function) to the parietal lobes towards the top of the brain. Associations between stimuli are developed by memory in various cortical sites.

• Conscious and unconscious actions are then coded and sent back to the relevant parts of the human body, where they are executed.

As mentioned above, the sensory receptors all start by transforming the information to the nerves that carry the nerve impulse (action potential) along the nervous system to the brain (see Box 2.1). Depending upon the type of receptors, the type of nerve fibres carrying the signal and the location in the cortex to which the signal is sent, the brain knows which kind of information it receives (pain, cold, smell, touch, etc.).

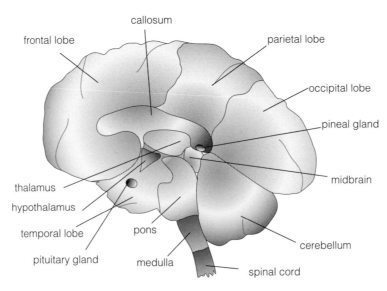

Source: adapted from several sources

Figure 2.1 *Lobes of the cerebral cortex and other components of the brain*

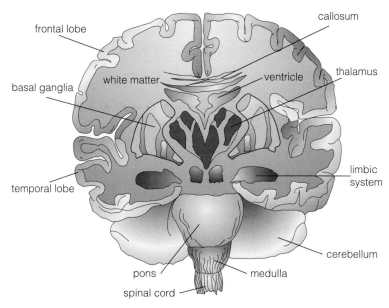

Source: adapted from Kapit et al (2000)

Figure 2.2 *Cross-section of the human brain*

Box 2.1 The human brain

The brain comprises the *forebrain*, which consists of:

- the lower diencephalons structure, with:
  - the hypothalamus for regulating the internal environment (homeostasis: body temperature, blood sugar, hunger and satiety) and sexual behaviour, the diurnal cycles through its biological clock, and the activities of the endocrine system and hormones;
  - the thalamus, involved in integrating sensory signals and relaying them to the cerebral cortex, participating in motor control and in regulating cortical excitation and attention;
- the higher telencephalon, which has two nearly symmetrical hemispheres, connected by the corpus callosum, with:
  - the cerebral cortex (see Figure 2.1): a network of nerve cells with:
    - the frontal lobe: for intellectual functions, such as reasoning and abstract thinking, aggression, sexual behaviour, olfaction, articulation of meaningful sound (speech) and voluntary movement (the primary motor cortex is part of this lobe);
    - the parietal lobe: body sensory awareness, including taste, the use of symbols for communication (language), abstract reasoning (e.g. mathematics) and body imaging (the primary somatic sensory cortex is part of this lobe);
    - the occipital lobe: concerned with receiving, interpreting and discriminating visual stimuli and associating these with other cortical areas (e.g. memory);
    - the temporal lobe: the part that is limbic is concerned with emotions (love, anger, aggression, compulsion, sexual behaviour); the non-limbic part is concerned with interpretation of language and awareness and discrimination of sound (hearing centres and some speech centres);
    - the insular lobe: invisible externally;

- the basal ganglia: work with the motor areas of the cortex and cerebellum to plan and coordinate gross voluntary movements;
- the limbic system or lobe: centre of emotional behaviour (oldest part of the cortex).

The brain also comprises the *brainstem*, which consists of:

- the midbrain: with somatic motor centres involved in the regulation of walking, posture and reflexes for head and eye movements;
- the pons: with the inhibition control centres for respiration (it interacts with the cerebellum);
- the medulla: the lowest of the brain's areas with the centres for respiration, cardiovascular and digestive functions;
- the cerebellum: involved in movement coordination.

Even though the functions of the brain are localized at specific brain areas, these regions are well connected and the brain often works as a whole – for example, for the functions of learning, memory and consciousness.

Source: Kapit et al (2000); Kapit and Elson (2002)

Behaviour or response as a consequence of the perceived sensory information can be divided into conscious (lifting your arm, walking away, etc.) and unconscious (sweating, increased respiration, blinking your eyes, etc.) actions. Emotions can be categorized under the latter.

More detailed information on the human senses can be found in sections 2.2 to 2.6 (based on information acquired from *Encyclopaedia Britannica*, 1991b).

2.1.2 Human systems

The human body has several systems that regulate, control and produce responses and symptoms to external and internal processes and experiences, of which the human brain regulates virtually all human activity: the nervous system, the endocrine system and the immune system.

Our body's health in relation to environmental stimuli is controlled (fought against) by the immune system; our emotions and perceptions are controlled by our limbic system and other parts of the brain (central nervous system); and our instincts (such as hunger, the need for sleep, thirst and breathing) are controlled by the brainstem and the cerebellum. Additionally, the endocrine system provides boundary conditions for 'control' of environmental stimuli by our immune as well as our limbic system.

The nervous system

The receiving and sending of information all takes place via the nervous system. Responsibilities of the nervous system are sensory and motor functions, instinctive and learned behaviour, and regulation of activities of the internal organs and systems. The nervous system can be divided into two parts: the central nervous system (CNS) and the peripheral nervous system (PNS). The PNS comprises nerves, sensory receptors (see section 2.1.1) and motor effectors, while the CNS comprises the lower and higher centres in the brain and the spinal cord. The PNS has an autonomic part (involuntary) and a somatic part (voluntary).

The autonomic nervous system (ANS) (or visceral nervous system) is part of the PNS and acts as a control system, maintaining homeostasis in the body. These maintenance activities are primarily performed without conscious control or sensation, although sometimes the conscious mind is involved, such as with breathing. This explains the fact that when the CNS is damaged, a vegetative life is still possible, where cardiovascular, digestive and respiratory functions are adequately regulated. The sensory neurons of the ANS monitor the levels of carbon dioxide, oxygen and sugar in the blood, arterial pressure and the chemical composition of the stomach and gut content.

The CNS performs actions with the sensory, motor and association (integrative) centres in the brain. The lower centres of the CNS are in direct contact with the PNS via sensory and motor nerves. Synapses of the CNS are responsible for the integrative functions of the CNS. Billions of neurons (the excitable cells of the nervous tissue) generate and conduct action potentials (pulses). Trillions of synapses and neural circuits make the release of so-called neurotransmitters possible (see Figure 2.3 and Table 2.2). A CNS neuron may receive thousands of synapses from other neurons and make hundreds of synapses upon other neurons. They can inhibit (suppress) or excite a neuron, depending upon the level that is reached (by spatial or temporal summation of the synaptic interaction). Synapses can be fast responding, which is good for relay but not for integration of responses, and synapses can be slow responding (long time delay between arrival of impulse and response). The latter often involve neuromodulators and neuropeptides, and many work in arousal, attention and neural plasticity (learning and memory).

The endocrine system

The endocrine system is an information signal system much like the nervous system, the difference being that the nervous system uses nerves to conduct information, whereas the endocrine system mainly uses blood vessels as information channels. This makes the effects, in general, take and last much longer. Endocrine glands located all over the human body release specific chemical messengers (hormones) into the bloodstream. These hormones regulate the many and varied functions of an organism through binding with the appropriate receptors (e.g. mood, growth and development, tissue function, and metabolism), as well as sending messages and acting on them.

The endocrine system comprises endocrine glands and organs with partial endocrine function (see Figure 2.4); locally produced hormones are also involved.

Two groups of secreted hormones can be distinguished: the slow-acting but long-lasting (i.e. steroid hormones of the adrenal cortex and gonads, amine hormones from the thyroid gland, and

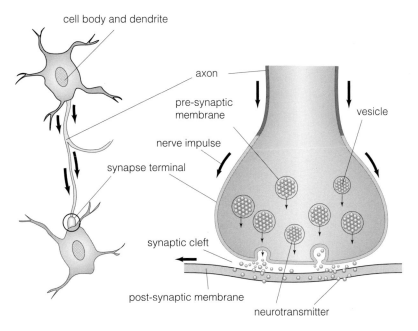

Note: When an impulse arrives at the synaptic terminal it opens, the vesicles with pre-synaptic cell membranes fuse and release neurotransmitters, which diffuse across the synaptic cleft to the postsynaptic membrane (in some cases, ion channels are involved as well).

Source: adapted from Kapit et al (2000)

Figure 2.3 *Synapses: Sites of transmission of nerve impulses via axons*

Table 2.2 *Neurotransmitters found in central nervous system (CNS) synapses*

Type of neurotransmitter synapses	Involved in
Acetylcholine synapses	Regulating sleep, wakefulness, memory, learning and motor coordination
Biogenic amine synapses:	
• Dopemina	Motor coordination (basal ganglia), central inhibition (olfactory bulb), cognition, personality (frontal lobe)
• Serotonin	Regulating moods, appetite, pain, pleasure, sex
• Histamine	Vasodilatation and increased permeability of blood vessels
• Norepinephrine	Fight-flight response
Amino acid synapses:	
• Aspartate and glutamate	Excitatory transmission; motor and sensor relay
• Gamma aminobutyric acid (GABA) and glycerine	Inhibitory transmission
Over 80 neuropeptides, such as:	Co-transmitters and modulators
• Substance-P	Slow pain relay
• Beta endorphin	Pain inhibition
• Oxytocin, gastrin, scretin and angiotensin	Hormones as elsewhere in body
Gaseous compounds:	
• Carbon monoxide (CO)	–
• Nitric oxide (NO)	Smooth muscle relaxing factor in blood vessels, intestine and penis

Source: adapted from Kapit et al (2000)

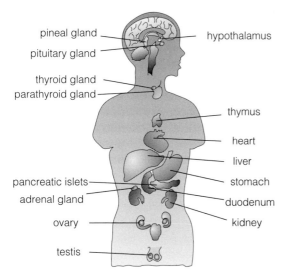

Source: adapted from Kapit et al (2000)

Figure 2.4 *The endocrine system: On the left are the endocrine glands and on the right are the organs with partial endocrine function*

hormones derived from vitamin D₃) and the fast-acting and not long-lasting hormones (e.g. peptide hormones of the hypothalamus and the pituitary gland, and catecholamine hormones of the adrenal medulla). In general, the long-lasting hormones bind with nuclear receptors and via deoxyribonucleic acid (DNA), and messenger ribonucleic acid (RNA) initiates the synthesis of new proteins (this takes hours to days), or they first connect to another hormone. Fast-acting hormones bind with plasma membrane receptors, releasing intercellular messengers that activate cellular enzymes (within seconds to minutes).

There are three main chemical groups of hormones – amines, peptides and steroids – of which the first two overlap with the neurotransmitters found in the CNS.

The *pituitary gland*, often named the 'Master gland', is vital to the complex functioning of the whole hormonal system. It is the main link between the nervous and the endocrine system. The pituitary gland (hypophysis) is divided into three lobes of which the anterior lobe is the true gland. Its secreted growth hormone promotes tissue and body growth by stimulating cells to multiply and make more proteins. The posterior lobe is, in fact, an extension of the hypothalamus; its hormones are mainly involved in maintaining the water balance (e.g. affects kidneys by making them produce less and more concentrated urine). And the intermediate lobe comprises only a few cells with no known functions (Kapit et al, 2000; Parker, 2003).

The *adrenal glands* are divided into two layers: the adrenal cortex and the adrenal medulla, which produce several of the fast-acting hormones to help the body cope with all kinds of stress (mental and physical).

While the main hormone of the *thyroid gland* (thyroxin) increases metabolism, another hormone (calcitonin) works together with a hormone from the *parathyroid gland* (parathormone) to regulate the levels of calcium in the blood (the parathyroids are small glands embedded in the thryroid tissue). This is important for strong bones and teeth and healthy nerves. Hormones from the pancreas control the glucose level in blood and cells: the body's energy source (Kapit et al, 2000).

The *pineal gland* has links with the hypothalamus and the pituitary gland, as well as with the nerves that carry signals from the eyes to the brain and with the brain's biological clock. It produces melatonin, the sleep hormone, which makes one sleepy (see section 5.1.2 in Chapter 5).

Another interesting gland to mention in more detail is the *thymus*, which is most active during childhood and early adolescence, but shrinks with age after the body is fully grown. The thymus works as a lymph gland of the lymphatic system and has a major role to play in the immune system (Parker, 2003). One of its hormonal roles is to process cells from the bone marrow to make specialized cells of the immune system so that they can fight infection. The cells become white blood cells known as T-lymphocytes. Hormones produced by the thymus help other white blood cells: the B-lymphocytes (see the following sub-section on 'The immune system').

Locally produced hormones, which act on the same cell as it is released from cells in the tissue environment, are the prostaglandins and related substances (thromboxane and leukotines). They may induce vasodilatation and bronchiole dilation by causing relaxation of the bronchiole smooth muscle, an effect with therapeutic value in the respiratory disorders of asthma. Some are produced during inflammatory responses (e.g. in arrhythmic disorders of joints) (Kapit et al, 2000).

Table 2.3 presents some hormones of different glands and their effects.

Three control mechanisms exist to regulate the excretion of hormones:

1 *Simple hormonal regulation* in which the blood hormone level and physiological parameter are regulated and interact according to predetermined and set limits to maintain hormone secretion. Only one gland is involved (e.g. regulation of blood sugar by insulin and glycagon from pancreatic islets).

2 *Complex hormonal regulation* in which the activity of one gland is controlled by the hormones of another. An example is the control of the thyroid, adrenal cortex and gonads (testes and ovaries) by the pituitary gland.

3 *Complex neurohormonal regulation* in which interaction between the brain (hypothalamic hormones) and the endocrine system (production of hormones by anterior pituitary gland) takes place. Environmental factors (e.g. light, sound, temperature and odour) and brain activities exert control over the endocrine system, and hormone secretions exert control over the neuron system via feedback effects from the target glands (see Figure 2.5).

In the latter system two sources of stimuli are used in the control: other brain areas mediating exogenous (environmental) stimuli and stresses, as well as endogenous rhythms, and feedback signals from the target hormones in the plasma. This results in a dynamic control, adjusting its operation to the needs of the body. For example:

- Long-term changes in environmental temperature can result in an adjustment of the basal metabolic rate and heat production by altering thyroid secretion via increasing the thyrotropin-releasing hormone (TRH) by the hypothalamus, which initiates release of the thyroid-stimulating hormone (TSH) by the pituitary gland, which in turn stimulates the thyroid gland.
- In response to various stresses, there may be an increase in the secretion of anti-stress glycocorticoids from the adrenal cortex through the increase of corticotropin by the hypothalamus, which increases the secretion of the adrenocortico tropine hormone (ACTH) or cortisol from the pituitary gland, in turn affecting the adrenal cortex.

The immune system

The immune system is a collection of layered protection mechanisms of increasing specificity against disease. It starts with physical barriers (mechanical, chemical and biological), followed by the natural or innate immune system, and, finally, by the acquired or adaptive immune system. The lymphoid system, comprising the primary organs (bone marrow and the thymus), the secondary organs (spleen, lymph nodes

Table 2.3 *Hormones and their effects for the main glands*

Hormone	Effect
	Pituitary gland – anterior lobe
Growth hormone	Promotes tissue and body growth
Beta-endorphin	Pain inhibition
Melanocyte stimulating hormone	Affects melanocytes in skin, which produces melanin (makes skin coloured)
Prolactin	Involved in breast milk flow and child birth
	Pituitary gland – posterior lobe
Anti-diuretic hormone (ADH)	Regulates overall water balance of body
Aasopressin	Moderates vasoconstriction
Oxytocin	Involved in breast milk flow and child birth; involved in trust between people and circadian homeostasis (body temperature, activity level, wakefulness)
	Pineal body
Melatonin (sleep hormone)	Antioxidant and causes drowsiness
	Thyroid gland
Amine hormones: thyroxin (tetra-iodothyronin) and tri-iodothyronin)	Increases metabolic rate by increasing oxygen consumption and heat production in many body tissues (important for adaptation to external cold and heat); influences cardiovascular functions by increasing heart rate and contractibility and vascular responsiveness to atecholamines, resulting in increased blood pressure
Calcitonin	Decreases plasma calcium levels (opposite of PTH); stimulates absorption of calcium and its deposition into bone (important for growing children)
	Parathyroid glands
Parathyroid hormone (PTH)	Acts on bone and kidney to elevate plasma calcium level, critical for normal nerve and muscle function; vitamin D_3 obtained in diet or produced in skin in the presence of UV light is converted to calcitrol in the kidneys (kidney hormone), which increases intestinal absorption of calcium and enhances PTH action on bone cells
	Thymus
Hormones and hormone-like substances known as factors (e.g. thymosin)	Effects on both the immune (involved in the production of T-lymphocytes and antibodies produced by B-lymphocytes) and reproductive system
	Pancreatic islets
Insulin and glucagon	Regulates carbohydrate metabolism in tissues and ensures maintenance of optimal plasma glucose levels; a rise releases insulin, while a decline releases glucagon
Somatostatin	Regulates insulin and glucagon secretion locally; may inhibit growth hormone from the pituitary
	Adrenal glands – cortex
Sex steroids	In females, stimulate formation of red blood cells and have mainly anabolic effects; can be converted to testosterone (much less potent than from testes)
Aldosterone (a mineralcorticoid)	Involved in the regulation of plasma salts (sodium and potassium), blood pressure and blood volume; very important for life
Cortisol (glucocorticoid)	Regulates metabolism of glucose, especially in times of stress, and increases blood glucose; important in defending the body against noxious and traumatic stresses; normally daily (diurnal) cycle regulated by the hypothalamus
	Adrenal glands – medulla
Catecholamines: epinephrine or adrenaline and norepinephrine or noradrenaline	Prepares for stressful situations, such as fight-flight response (increased heart rate and blood pressure; vasoconstriction of blood vessels to skin and visceral organs; vasodilatation of blood vessels to heart and muscles; bronchiole dilation; increased glycogen breakdown and lipolysis of fat; increase arousal, alertness and excitability; dilation of pupils)
Dopamine	Increases heart rate and blood pressure
Endorphine	Anti-stress analgesic (anti-pain) effects
	Local
Prostaglandins and related substances (thromboxane and leukotines)	May induce vasodilatation and bronchiole dilation; some cause vasodilatation in blood vessels; role in hypothalamic temperature regulation; are produced during inflammatory responses; some act in conjunction with endocrine hormones

Source: Kapit et al (2000); Parker (2003)

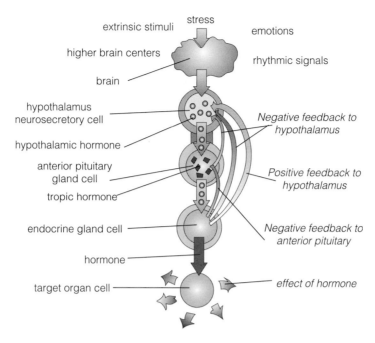

Note: The feedback of the hormones from these target glands regulates the pituitary and hypothalamus, in this way controlling levels of pituitary hormones and neurohormones.

Source: adapted from Kapit et al (2000)

Figure 2.5 *Complex neurohormonal regulation: Neurohormones of the hypothalamus regulate hormones of the pituitary, which regulate target glands*

and lymphoid tissue) and the white blood cells, helps the body in this defence (see Box 2.2 and Figure 2.6). The lymphoid tissues and organs are collections of lymphocytes and related cells, supported by fibres and cells. *Lymphocytes* are among the principal cells of the immune system. From their generative organs (bone

---

Box 2.2 Components of the lymphoid system

Primary organs:

- Bone marrow: some of lymphocytes become B-lymphocytes. The larger ones enter circulation to function as natural killer cells; others migrate via blood to the thymus.
- Thymus: where the B-lymphocytes become T-cells and differentiate further, re-entering circulation and migrating to secondary lymphoid organs.

Secondary organs: where antigens activate lymphatic operation:

- Spleen: processes blood, produces antibodies and performs phagocytosis (a type of eating) with cellular and humoral responses.
- Lymph nodes: processes lymph in a similar way as spleen does with blood.

Mucosal-associated lymphoid tissue (MALT): unencapsulated follicles and collections of lymphocytes and/or phagocytic cells (also found in nodes and spleen).

Source: Mygind (1986); Kapit and Elson (2002)

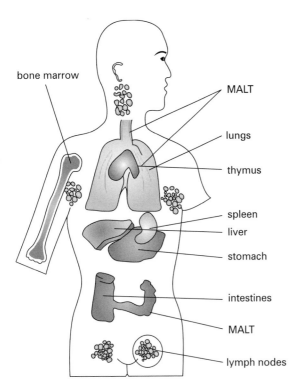

bone marrow

MALT

lungs

thymus

spleen

liver

stomach

intestines

MALT

lymph nodes

Note: MALT = mucosal-associated lymphoid tissue.

Source: adapted from Kapit and Elson (2002)

Figure 2.6 *Components of the lymphoid system*

marrow and thymus), they are transported in the lymph vessels and lymphoid tissues and organs.

Physical barriers, such as the skin, prevent pathogens (e.g. bacteria and viruses) from entering the body. Other systems act to protect body openings such as the lungs, intestines and the genitourinary tract. In the lungs, coughing and sneezing eject pathogens and other irritants from the respiratory tract. Tears and urine are also a way to mechanically expel pathogens, while mucus secreted by the respiratory and gastrointestinal tract serves to trap and entangle microorganisms. Chemical barriers, such as antimicrobial peptides and enzymes in saliva, tears and breast milk, also protect against infection. Biological barriers can be found in the genitourinary and gastrointestinal tracts.

If a pathogen breaks through the barriers, *the innate immune system* provides an immediate, but non-specific and short-lasting response. Upon an injury of the epithelium (the 'skin' of an organ), the following occurs:

- Microbes enter the body, release toxins (antigens) and create local infection.
- The mast cells in the tissue release granules containing heparin (prevents blood coagulation) and histamine (causes vasodilatation and increased permeability of local blood vessels to blood proteins and blood cells) within the tissue space, and basophiles (type of white blood cells) do the same in blood.
- Blood proteins and fluids leak into the injured site causing oedema (swelling).
- Gradually the fluid in the swelling clots traps the microbes and prevents further penetration.
- *First line of defence*: tissue macrophages attack microbes and destroy them by phagocytosis (leading to digestion by lysosomal enzymes) (see Figure 2.7).
- *Second line of defence*: if infection persists, neutrophils (type of white blood cells) migrate to the injury site and phagocytize the microbes.
- *Third line of defence*: if still not enough, agranular monocytes (type of white blood cells) move to the site, grow and begin to phagocytize microbes and the dead neutrophils.

Box 2.3 provides descriptions of the cells and substances encountered in the immune system.

If pathogens successfully avoid the innate response, a third layer of protection, the *adaptive immune system*, is activated. Afterwards, the acquired immunity is adapted and/or improved. When a new attack is made by the same pathogen, the adaptive immune system should respond faster and more vigorously. This system works slowly and specifically, based on two types of lymphocytes:

1   *Humoral immunity or active immunity*: anti-body mediated responses are carried out by B-lymphocytes, which recognize the presence of certain types of antigens (genetically). Upon activation by antigen, they develop and form memory and plasma cells, which secrete antibodies. These antibodies attach to antigen and facilitate its phagocytosis (elimination) by phagocytes. The formation and proliferation of plasma cells are controlled by the release of cytokines from helper T-lymphocytes. Antibody production takes days to weeks. Antibodies can also activate the complement

---

Box 2.3 Cells and substances in the immune system

Lymph is plasma including white blood cells that is transported through the lymphatic vessels and feeds the human cells. It is part of our blood, but does not use the blood vessels for transportation. Lymph or, in fact, the white blood cells that are produced in the lymph nodes, can also destroy (eat) harmful substances such as infections.

White blood cells (leukocytes) comprise two types of cells, the granulocytes (with cytoplasmic granules: neutrophils, eosinophils and basophils) and the agranulocytes (without granules: monocytes, macrophages and lymphocytes).

Lymphocytes:

* B-lymphocytes: formed in bone marrow;
* T-lymphocytes: differentiated B-lymphocytes migrated via the blood to the thymus:
    * helper T-lymphocytes: bind and interact with B-cells and macrophages, releasing cytokines (lymphokines and interleukins) to regulate their functions as well as those of the T-cells; cytokines can also be released from injured tissues and control the migration of white blood cells in the natural and acquired immunity;
    * cytotoxic T-lymphocytes: bind to and destroy infected cells and form memory cells;
    * suppressor T-cells: inhibit activity of other T- and B-cells;
    * memory T-cells: antigen-stimulated lymphocytes circulate in the blood and lymph for years; when the organism is re-exposed to the antigen, the immune response can take place faster and stronger.

Antibodies – protein molecules (immunoglobulins, Ig):

* IgA type: secretory immunoglobulins released into secretions of gastrointestinal and respiratory mucosa and milk;
* IgE: participate in allergic reactions;
* IgD: exist on the surface of B-cells;
* IgG and IgM: function against bacterial and viral infections.

The *complement system* is a biochemical cascade that attacks the surfaces of foreign cells. It contains over 20 different proteins and is named for its ability to 'complement' the killing of pathogens by antibodies. Complement is the major humoral component of the innate immune response.

Source: Mygind (1986); Kapit and Elson (2002)

---

system. Passive immunity refers to antibody transfer across placenta and via milk, while artificial immunity refers to vaccination of memory cells.

2   *Cellular immunity:* cell-mediated responses are carried out by T-lymphocytes (the cytotoxic). Antibodies are not involved. Upon recognition of the infected cell (host cell), cytotoxic T-lymphocytes bind to antigens on the host cell and release cytoplasmic granules that contain perforin, which makes the host cell swell and die. Microbes are released and phagocytized by macrophages (see Figure 2.7). Abnormal body cells (tumour and cancer) produce endogenous antigens and are also

recognized and attacked in the same way. The recognition is based on the differentiation between 'self' (specific protein complex on cell membrane – genetics) and 'non-self' (with antigen), which is acquired during their stay in the thymus.

2.1.3 Possible diseases and disorders

Considering the diseases and disorders to the human body that can originate from an 'unhealthy indoor environment', the following divisions can be made (diseases and disorders to the individual human senses and the respiratory tract are treated subsequently):

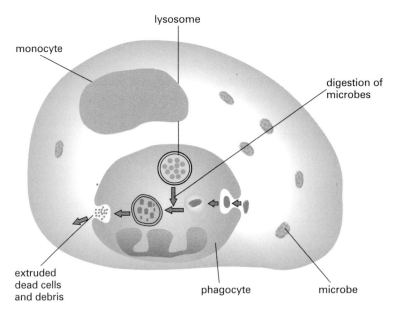

Source: adapted from Mygind (1986); Kapit et al (2000)

Figure 2.7 *Phagocytosis of microbes: Monocytes migrate to the site, transform into macrophages and swallow bacteria and digest them within their lysosomes*

- direct noticeable comfort-related complaints by the senses, such as smell, noise, heat, cold, draught, etc.;
- systemic effects, such as tiredness, poor concentration, depression, etc.;
- irritation, allergic and hyper-reactive effects, such as irritation of mucous membranes of the skin and respiratory tract, asthma, rashes on the skin caused by allergic reactions to certain pollutants, sun burn, hearing loss, damage of the eyes caused by too bright light, etc.;
- infectious diseases such as Legionnaires' disease;
- toxic chronic effects that slowly increase or appear (such as cancer).

Allergy and infectious diseases are different reactions of the human body. Allergy is the reaction of the body to (in itself) un-harmful substance, while with an infectious disease, it is the reaction of the body to a substance that can cause harm (Mygind, 1986). In both, inflammation-like reactions (e.g. swelling, pain, redness and/or heat) occur and both are hypersensitivity reactions of the immune system, which can be divided into four classes based on the mechanisms involved and the time course of the hypersensitive reaction:

1   Type I hypersensitivity is an immediate reaction, often associated with allergy. Symptoms can range from mild discomfort to death.
2   Type II hypersensitivity occurs when antibodies bind to antigens on the patient's own cells, marking them for destruction. This is also called antibody-dependent hypersensitivity.
3   Type III hypersensitivity reactions are triggered by immune complexes (aggregations of antigens, complement proteins and antibodies).
4   Type IV hypersensitivity, also known as cell-mediated or delayed-type hypersensitivity, usually takes between two and three days to develop. Type IV reactions are involved in many autoimmune and infectious diseases.

The main response of the immune system to tumours is to destroy the abnormal cells. However, tumour cells are often not detected; some tumour cells also release products that inhibit the immune response; immunological tolerance may also develop against tumour antigens, so the immune system no longer attacks the tumour cells. Paradoxically, sometimes tumour growth is promoted.

Diseases of the endocrine system are common, including diseases such as diabetes mellitus, thyroid disease and obesity; but for the indoor environment, too much stress (mental or physical) is of the greatest important. Stress can cause short-term illness and long-term health problems, both physically and mentally. Hormones play an important role in the response. For brain-related diseases and disorders, the same can be said. We know that common brain disorders such as Alzheimer's disease (loss of memory and cognitive disorders associated with loss of cholinergic synapses), Parkinson's disease (motor disorders caused by loss of dopamine synapses), schizophrenia (mental and cognitive dysfunctions associated with hyperactivity of dopamine synapses) and epilepsy (seizures associated with the function of GABA synapses) are all related to the functioning of the CNS synapses. Synapses are obviously crucial for the mental and physical state our body is in.

2.1.4 Measurement of human reception and perception

An indication of the quality of the environment that people are exposed to is seen in the prevalence of symptoms, complaints, measurable contaminants in body fluids, the prevalence of exposure to specific sources, or through investigations of the brain. Questionnaires given to occupants of investigated buildings, medical examinations and biological monitoring of body fluids of exposed people, and the response of visitors of the investigated buildings, all belong to this group of techniques. There are no absolute tests for lethargy, headaches and dry throat. Objective measurements have been used to validate dry eyes, blocked nose and asthma symptoms. Sensory evaluation techniques can be applied to evaluate indoor air quality (through the human nose) or the emission of certain products, such as construction and furnishing products and heating, ventilating and air-conditioning (HVAC) system components. And last, but not least, non-invasive brain imaging techniques are used to investigate people's behaviour.

Many *questionnaires* have been used to investigate the working conditions of the office environment. A questionnaire generally comprises questions about the indoor environment and the symptoms that might be caused by the indoor environment, such as sick building syndrome (SBS) symptoms. Because there is considerable variation in the range of symptoms covered,

whether symptoms are defined as work related or not, and in the type of response scales used, comparisons of prevalence between studies can therefore be misleading. In the European Audit project a standardized questionnaire was used to investigate 56 buildings for the first time in nine European countries (Bluyssen et al, 1996a). This questionnaire formed the base for other questionnaires in several European projects, such as the questionnaire developed for the European TOBUS project (see Annex A) (Bluyssen and Cox, 2002).

Telephone interviews are another form of questionnaire. Jenkins et al (1990) conducted telephone interviews with 1780 respondents (11 years and older), in which a 24-hour recall diary of activities and locations, and the use and proximity of potential pollutant sources were determined. With this information it is possible to determine exposure estimates by population subgroups (age, gender, employment, status, income, etc.), which can lead to more effective strategies for risk estimation.

A diagnosis of allergy and hyper-reactivity can be established through several tests (Mygind, 1986). Exercise-induced asthma as a measure of bronchial hyper-reactivity can be used to confirm the diagnosis in suspected asthmatics (examined in a symptom-free period). Bronchial provocation with metacholine or histamine can be used as a test for non-specific hyper-reactivity (in a symptom-free period). The number of blood eosinophils can depict the severity of an allergic inflammation and the size of the organs involved (eosinophilia is highly characteristic of allergy and allergic-like diseases, but is not pathognomonic). And the level of serum IgE can predict the development of allergy in the first years of life. Skin testing is another test for allergens, and is a measure of the mast-cell fixed IgE antibody. The radio allegro sorbent test (RAST) is a laboratory test for determining circulating IgE-antibody (when a confirmatory test is indicated, RAST is preferable to skin testing).

A diagnosis of eye irritation has been made through photography of eye redness (Kjaergaard, 1992), reflex-induced tear production and eye-blinking frequency (Nielsen, 1985). Promising objective measures are foam formation (the appearance of foam at the eyelid or corner of the eye), tear fluid cytology, time interval registration from the conclusion of a blink to the occurrence of tear film fracture (breakup time), and lissamine green stinging of conjuctival epithelial damage (Johnson, et al, 1990; Kjaergaard, 1992).

Respiratory tract irritation to certain pollutants can be tested through respiratory frequency and volume (Johnson et al, 1990). And for sensory irritation of the nose (nasal potency), several techniques are available (Rohr, 2001), of which nasal resistance and nasal peak inspiratory flow seem to give promising results.

Besides using *human subjects* as measuring instruments for sensory evaluation of air quality (see Annex B), *animals* are useful for investigating problems related to the irritation of the respiratory tract in humans, such as the identification of target organs and systems, the clarification of mechanisms of toxicity and the assessment of carcinogenicity. However, bioassays used are not particularly sensitive and higher exposure concentrations then typically found indoors are necessary to elicit a response by the reflex-induced decrease in respiratory rate (Nielsen, 1985).

Analysing the *body fluids* of a person in order to detect previous exposure to pollutants is also a way of determining indoor air quality. Breath, blood, hair, faeces and urine samples have been investigated. Breath measurements can reflect long-term repeated exposure, as well as short-term peak exposures to volatile organic compounds (VOCs) (Wallace, et al, 1990). Urine samples have been taken to detect nicotine and cotinine as markers for exposure to tobacco smoke, but also to measure the chromium content as an index of exposure (Coniglio, et al, 1990). Blood collection is an invasive and more complex procedure than breath or urine sampling.

In addition, in order to investigate responses directly in the *brain*, two types of non-invasive brain imaging techniques are currently used simultaneously (Taylor, 2006):

1   techniques that detect an increased flow of blood arising from increased nerve cell activity, such as positron-emission tomography (PET) machines and functional magnetic resonance imaging (fMRI);
2   techniques observing more directly the electrical or magnetic activity across the brain due to nerve cells producing electric fields and concomitant magnetic fields as part of their interaction with each other, such as electro-encephalography (EEG) and magneto-encephalography (MEG).

According to Taylor (2006), blood-flow-based machines have greater spatial accuracy (down to a millimetre or so). But the MEG and EEG techniques provide a far better temporal sensitivity, with sensitivity

to changes over one millisecond compared to one second for fMRI or many seconds for PET.

2.2 The human skin

2.2.1 Components of the skin

The largest part of the human body is the skin, with a mean surface area of around 1.8 square metres. The skin comprises two pressure senses (for light and deep stimulation), two temperature sensitivity senses (warm and cold) and a pain sense (nociceptor). These senses are not located all over the body, but can be found on specific spots. The spots for pain are most prevalent, followed by those for touch, then for cold and, last, for warmth. Besides these senses, three different systems for secreting chemicals to the skin surface can be found – namely, eccrine glands, sebaceous glands and apocrine glands.

Nerve terminals are various: one can distinguish between the most common free nerve endings and the encapsulated endings (see Figure 2.8). Some nerve endings respond to only one stimulus; others show combined sensitivity. The nerve fibres (axons) are diverse: they range in size from 10 to 15 microns in diameter to only tenths of microns, the fatter one conducting the impulses more rapidly. When axons of different size form a single bundle (a nerve), they are called a mixed nerve.

In order to perceive pressure through hearing or seeing, the skin requires in the order of 100 million times more energy than the ear and 10,000 million times more energy than the eye. Adaptation to pressure and thermal sensation is well known: continued presentation of warm or cold stimulus leads to reduction or disappearance of the initial sensation and an increase in threshold values.

Pain sense (nociceptor)

All nociceptors are free nerve endings that have their cell bodies outside the spinal column. Nociceptors can detect mechanical, thermal and chemical stimuli, and are found in the skin and on internal surfaces.

There are different kinds of pain. Some pain shows cyclic fluctuations of intensity, such as headaches and toothaches as a result of blood circulation or degree of inflammation. Some pain is sharper (cutaneous pain) than others – in deep tissues of body (somatic pain) or organs (visceral pain). And certain areas of the body do

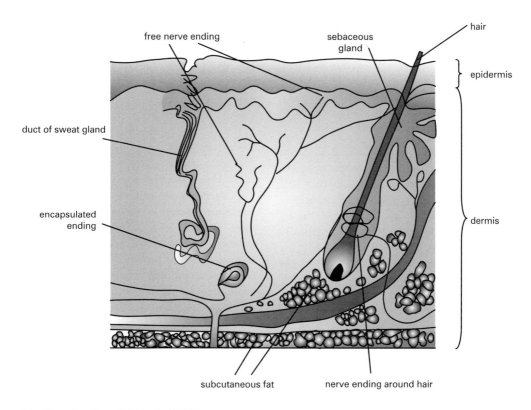

free nerve ending

sebaceous
gland

hair

epidermis

duct of sweat gland

dermis

encapsulated
ending

subcutaneous fat

nerve ending around hair

Source: adapted from *Encyclopaedia Britannica* (1991b)

Figure 2.8 *Cross-section of the human skin: A human hair, glands, free nerve endings and fat in layers of the skin (the dermis and epidermis)*

not respond to pain stimulation or only slightly (e.g. the inside of the cheek). Deep internal surfaces have only a few pain receptors, which propagate sensations of chronic, aching pain if tissue damage in these areas occurs. Nociceptors do not adapt to a stimulus. In some conditions, excitation of pain fibres becomes greater as the pain stimulus continues, leading to a condition called hyperalgesia.

Temperature senses

Cold and warm receptors are different from each other: a cold receptor does not respond to a warm sensation and the same is true for a warm receptor to a cold sensation. A cold receptor responds to a temperature range of approximately 15°C to 34°C, while a warm receptor responds to a range of 38°C to 43°C. But neither shows a response to mechanical sensation.

Glands

The secretion of the eccrine glands (thermoregulatory sweat glands) consists of 99 per cent water and 1 per cent electrolytes, amino acids, vitamins and miscellaneous compounds. They are distributed throughout most of the skin surface, but are most numerous in palms and soles, while the sebaceous glands can be found all over the human body (most occur in the forehead, face and scalp), except for the palms and foot soles. They secrete lipid materials such as triglycerides and esters, resulting in a slightly pleasant odour. The apocrine glands (genital and axillary areas) secrete protein (10 per cent), cholesterol (1 per cent) and steroids (0.02 per cent).

Bacteria present in the axillae, scalp and feet break down the secretions and the breakdown products cause the particular smells for these areas: cheesy smell (methanethiol) from feet, the smell of unwashed hair (γ-decalactone) or the sweat smell of the axillae (mix of musky, urine and sour smell caused by androstenol, androstenone and isovaleric acid, respectively).

2.2.2 Mechanisms

Thermal balance

To keep the human body in thermal balance, heat transmission should be equal to heat production. The human body is capable of coping with temporary heat production and heat losses through small changes in body temperature. This is called the thermal storage capacity of the body. However, if these differences in heat balance take too long, actions are required.

Temperature control takes place in the hypothalamus, and two parts can be distinguished:

1   the anterior hypothalamus, which takes care of the regulation of temperature when the body is overheated (i.e. vascular dilatation and sweating); and
2   the posterior hypothalamus, which defends the body against cold (i.e. vascular narrowing and trembling).

This temperature regulation is influenced by the core temperature, the temperature of the central parts or vital organs of the human body, and skin temperature.

The human being has an average core temperature of 37°C, which can easily increase during sport or physical labour to 38°C to 39°C. After ending the activity, the temperature will go back to approximately 37°C. This core temperature is required for certain processes in the body (e.g. beating of the heart, breathing and functioning of the intestines). For a person in thermal balance, skin temperature lies around 34°C.

The different nutrients (proteins, carbohydrates and fats) present in the body are transported by the blood to the cells where required. The energy released by partial combustion of these nutrients is called metabolism (the unit is the watt). The lungs breathe in the required oxygen for these combustion products, which is transported by the blood in the lungs to the cells. Carbon dioxide (CO_2) produced is transported via the blood and the lungs and exhaled to the air. Metabolism can be measured through the amount of oxygen that is assimilated and the amount of CO_2 released by the body.

The type and amount of clothing a person wears also influences the heat balance of the human body.

The influence of clothing on this balance can be expressed by the thermal resistance of clothing.

In order to describe the heat balance of the human body, several models have been developed. The simplest one is the Fanger model, based on a stationary heat balance and extensive experiments with people (Fanger, 1982):

$$\text{energy supply + energy produced} = \text{energy removed.} \qquad [2.1]$$

The energy produced is called metabolism. The transmitted energy is the labour performed and the heat losses through radiation, convection, conduction and evaporation. The energy supply is equal to zero if the surrounding temperature is less than the skin temperature and no radiation source with a higher absolute temperature than the surface temperature of a dressed person is present. Physical activity (metabolism), clothing resistance and environmental parameters (air temperature, mean radiation temperature, air velocity and air humidity) are inputs to the Fanger model (see section 3.2.3 in Chapter 3).

When these parameters are estimated and/or measured, the thermal sensation of the whole body can be predicted by calculating the predicted mean vote (PMV) index. The PMV is an index that is used to predict the mean thermal sensation of a large group of people at a seven-point thermal perception scale, from cold (–3) to warm (+3). The predicted percentage of dissatisfied (PPD) – the percentage of people who will be warm or cold in a certain environment – can be calculated using the Fanger comfort equation (see Figure 2.9 and section 5.1.1 in Chapter 5).

Secretion of chemicals by glands

While the eccrine glands respond to physical activity, the sebaceous glands are controlled by hormones and the apocrine glands secrete continuously. With the sebaceous glands the entire cell disintegrates to secrete its substances, and with the apocrine glands the sweat already present in the tubule (duct of the sweat gland) is squeezed out (emotional stress increases the production of sweat). The eccrine glands are controlled by sympathetic cholinergic (alkaline amino) nerves, which are controlled by a centre in the hypothalamus. From sensing the core temperature and from input from temperature receptors in the skin, the

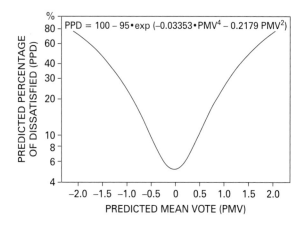

Source: adapted from Fanger (1982)

Figure 2.9 *Predicted percentage of dissatisfied (PPD) as a function of predicted mean vote (PMV)*

hypothalamus adjusts the sweat output, together with other thermoregulatory processes.

Sensation of pain

Pain is a sensation transmitted from sensory nerves through the spinal cord to the sensory area of the brain where the sensations are perceived. Pain can be perceived simultaneously with nociception, the system which carries information about inflammation, damage or near-damage in tissue to the spinal cord and brain. However, it is independently perceived. Nociception transmits somatic information without conscious awareness, while pain is a perception of sensorial information.

2.2.3 Possible diseases and disorders

Possible diseases and disorders of the skin can be caused by infection (bacterial, viral or fungal), inflammation (allergic reaction), radiation-related disorders (such as sunburn) and psychological reasons (e.g. anxiety). Itching, rashes, hives, blisters or redness may be the symptoms.

Dermatitis, which means inflammation of the skin, is usually used to refer to eczema, a term broadly applied to a range of persistent skin conditions. These include dryness and recurring skin rashes characterized by redness, skin oedema, itching and dryness, with possible crusting, flaking, blistering, cracking, oozing or bleeding. Some common types of eczemas include the following:

- *Atopic eczema* is believed to have a hereditary component and often runs in families whose members also have hay fever and asthma. An itchy rash is particularly noticeable on the face and scalp, the neck, the insides of elbows, behind the knees and on the buttocks.
- *Contact dermatitis* comprises two types: allergic (resulting from a delayed reaction to some allergen, such as poison ivy or nickel) and irritant (e.g. resulting from direct reaction to a solvent). Some substances act both as allergen and irritant (e.g. wet cement), while other substances cause a problem after sunlight exposure, resulting in phototoxic dermatitis. Contact eczema is curable provided the offending substance is avoided.
- *Xerotic eczema* is dry skin that becomes so serious that it turns into eczema, affecting primarily the limbs and trunk. The itchy, tender skin resembles a dry, cracked river bed. It is very common among older people and worsens in dry winter weather.

2.3 The human eye

2.3.1 Components of the eye

The eyeball comprises two pieces: a small transparent segment occupying one sixth of the cornea with a radius of 8mm, and a large one (the sclera segment) with a radius of 12mm. The eyeball is covered with six muscles for its movements and is kept moist by secretions from the tear glands, situated under the upper lids extended inward from the outer corner of each eye. The iris is visible through the cornea, which determines the colour of the eye. In the centre lies the pupil, which appears dark because light passing into the eye is reflected back (see Figure 2.10).

From inside to outside the eye is enclosed with three coats (see Figure 2.11): the retina, the innermost layer; the second coat, which consists of the choroids (nourishing the retina through its vessels), the ciliary body and the iris; and the last layer, which comprises the cornea and the sclera. Behind the iris lies the lens, followed by the vitreous body (a clear jelly filling). The posterior chamber (the space between the rear surface of the iris and the ciliary body, zonule and the lens) is much smaller than the anterior chamber (the space between the cornea and the forward surface of the iris and the lens). Both chambers are filled with a clear aqueous fluid and are connected through the pupil.

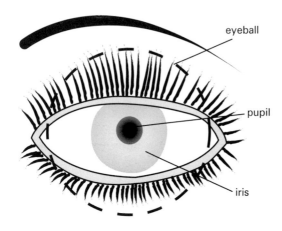

Source: inspired by several sources

Figure 2.10 *The eye: Only the 'white' part of the eyeball (cornea), the iris and the pupil can be seen from the outside*

The retina is the part of the eye that receives the light and converts it into chemical energy. The largest sensitivity is around 550 nanometres (nm) (yellow-green) for daylight and 500nm (blue-green) at night. It is, in essence, an outgrowth of the forebrain, and transmits messages from the eye to the higher brain regions. The light-sensitive cells, the rods (approximately 75 million to 150 million) and the cones (approximately 7 million) transmit the light effects to the bipolar horizontal cells (neuron cells), which connect to the ganglion cells, the innermost layer of neurons, that carry the messages out of the eye along axons, comprised of the optic nerve fibres.

In the fovea, a localized region of the retina, light has an almost free passage to light-sensitive cells. This region of the retina is for accurate vision. In the central region of the fovea there are only cones present; towards its edges, rods also occur and the proportion of rods increases in the successive areas (parafovea), approximately 1250 micrometres (μm) from the centre of the fovea. Surrounding the parafovea, in the perifovea (outermost edge circa 2750μm from the centre), even fewer cones are present. The yellow spot covers the whole central retina (i.e. the fovea, the parafovea and the perifovea) and is characterized by its yellow pigment. The blind spot on the retina corresponds to the optic papillae, the region in which the optic nerve fibres (approximately 1 million) leave the eye.

2.3.2 Mechanisms

Light enters the eye via the aperture in the iris: the pupil. Through the lens, which is a flexible body that can change its surface area curve (accommodation), and the jelly bodies before and after the lens (vitreous body), which adsorb part of the light, the rest of the light falls on the light-sensitive layer (the retina), which transforms the light to a signal that is transported via the optic nerve to the brain for interpretation.

Protection

Besides dosing the amount of light falling into the eye, the blinking of the eye has two functions: it protects the eye from external effects such as small objects (flies and dust); and it prevents the eye from drying out through smearing the eye with a fluid that is produced by the tear glands.

Normally, blinking is an involuntary act; it occurs without thinking, but it can be carried out voluntarily. A sudden full closure can be triggered as a reflex response – for example, as protection from bright light, often causing the muscles of the face to contract as well (e.g. forehead folds and eyebrows towards the bridge of the nose).

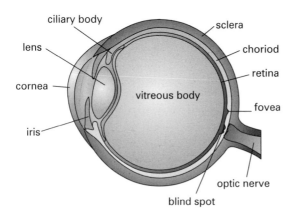

Source: ISO/SBR 2007

Figure 2.11 *Horizontal section of the eye: Incoming light passes the cornea, the pupil, and the lens and enters the vitreous body, where in the back it hits the retina (part of the retina, the fovea, is sensitive to light)*

Besides the normal secretion of tears, tears can be secreted by reflex in response to a variety of stimuli (e.g. irritative stimuli to the cornea, conjunctiva and nasal mucosa; hot or peppery stimuli to the mouth and tongue or bright lights). And tear flow occurs in association with vomiting, coughing, yawning and emotional upset (psychic – mentally induced – weeping, not a reflex).

Light entering the eye

The amount of light entering the eye is restricted by the aperture in the iris: the pupil. In a dark room, the pupil is large (perhaps 8mm in diameter). When the room is lighted, the pupil immediately constricts. A bilateral effect occurs if only one eye is exposed and both pupils contract nearly to the same extent.

Constriction and accommodation occur together when a person looks at a near object (the near reflex). Additionally, for near response, convergence (turning in) of the eyes is important. Dilation occurs as a result of a strong psychical stimuli and when any sensory nerve is stimulated (e.g. in extreme fear and pain).

The cornea admits light with a wavelength between 295nm and 2500nm. The lens protects the retina against short-wave light (350–400nm) by transforming this into long-wave light. The vitreous body adsorbs wavelengths larger than 1600nm. Light with wavelengths between 400nm and 800nm can, in principle, reach the retina.

Reception

Two types of receptors are located in the retina: rods and cones. Rods give only achromatic, or colourless, vision, and cones permit wavelength discrimination. There are three types of cones in the retina, each containing a different pigment. The absorption spectra of the three pigments differ; one is maximum sensitive to short wavelengths (blue), one to medium wavelengths (yellow-green) and the third to long wavelengths (yellow). They cover most of the visible spectrum (380nm to 760nm; see section 3.3.1 in Chapter 3) and it is not entirely accurate to refer to them as the 'blue', 'green' and 'red' receptors because the 'red' receptor actually has its peak sensitivity in the yellow.

In order to receive a light impulse, only a very small portion of energy is required: the rods are then the first to respond. A quantum defined as the product of

Planck's constant (6.63×10^{-34} joules per second) multiplied by the frequency of light is the minimum amount of light energy that can be used. For visible light, the energy carried by a single photon is around a tiny 4×10^{-19} joules (J); this energy is sufficient to excite a single molecule in a photoreceptor cell of an eye, thus contributing to vision.

Photons show wave-like phenomena, such as refraction by a lens and destructive interference when reflected waves cancel each other out. However, as a particle, it can only interact with matter by transferring the amount of energy (E):

$$E = hc/\lambda \ [J] \qquad [2.2]$$

where:

- h = Planck's constant (J/s);
- c = the speed of light (m/s);
- λ = wavelength (m).

Cones are only affected by higher energy levels, but are very sensitive to differences in brightness (contrast). The sensitivity of the eye under dark conditions (scotopic vision) is determined by the rods, the only active receptors in the dark. Sensitivity to light is highest for light with a wavelength of approximately 509nm (see Figure 2.12) and it decreases towards the red as blue light. For fotopic vision (sensitivity of the

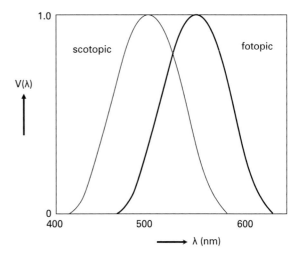

Source: adapted from Boer and Rutten (1974)

Figure 2.12 *Light sensitivity curve under dark (scotopic vision) and light (fotopic vision) conditions*

eye during the day), this sensitivity curve is slightly shifted to the right (the maximum lies around 555nm).

Adaptation

After five minutes in a dark room, the cones increase in sensitivity, while after ten minutes, the rods increase their sensitivity to the point that they are more sensitive and determine the sensitivity of the whole eye. After 30 minutes the rods have reached maximal adaptation. When the light stimulus is weak and the eye has adapted to the dark, the rods are used because their threshold is then much lower than that of the cones.

The phenomenon of simultaneous contrast, where a patch of light appears much darker if surrounded by a bright background than by a black one, is caused by the inhibitory effect of the surrounding retina on the central region, induced by the bright surrounding. Many colour-contrast phenomena have a similar cause: if a blue light is projected on a large white screen, the white screen rapidly appears yellow (missing its blue light) caused by the inhibition of blue sensitivity in the periphery.

When a visual stimulus is repeated rapidly, the sensation becomes a flicker. At a certain speed (the critical fusion frequency), the sensation becomes continuous and the subject is unaware of the changes in the illumination. At high levels it may require 60 flashes per second, and at low levels (night) only 4 flashes are required to reach this critical fusion frequency. This difference in the number of flashes occurs because cones inhibit activity, which leaves the eye ready to respond to the next stimulus, more rapidly than rods.

Transformation and interpretation

The image of the external world on the retina is essentially flat or two dimensional; the simultaneous precision of different aspects of the two eyes and our own experience provides us with a three-dimensional character. But even with one eye, a person can make estimates of the relative positions of objects in all three dimensions. Another important parameter for depth is perspective: the changed appearance of an object when it is viewed from different angles. The perception of depth in a two-dimensional pattern depends to a large extent upon experience, but also upon light and shade, overlapping contours and the relative sizes of familiar objects.

The information gathered by the receptors at the retina undergo selection, summation, coding, etc. before

it is transported to the brain. This process takes place in the ganglia, the bipolar cells and synapses (see Figure 2.13). In the retina, connections can be made between ganglia and also between ganglia and the brain through the synapses.

2.3.3 Possible diseases and disorders

Diseases and disorders of the eye can have several origins. They can be genetic, psychological, a result of ageing, internal malfunction, external factors, or due to both internal and external factors.

Genetic

Colour blindness is primarily a genetic-originated disorder, and is the inability to perceive differences between some or all colours. The most common form is the inability to discriminate reds, yellow and green from each other. Complete colour blindness (only seeing black, grey and white) is not very common, as is the problem with differentiating blues from yellows.

Psychological

Eyestrain, or asthenopia, the term used for symptoms of fatigue and discomfort following the use of the eyes, is often related to psychological factors. But it may also result from intensive close work by people with normal eyes and it may indicate abnormalities of muscle balance or refractive errors.

Ageing

With age, several of the eye's functions begin to deteriorate. The extent to which the pupil dilates, for example, decreases with age. Because of the smaller pupil size, older eyes receive much less light at the retina and therefore need extra light when performing a detailed task.

The refractive power of the eye is increased by altering the shape of the lens to focus the image on the retina. With age this power decreases: the distance at which an ageng person can see an object in focus increases. In some eyes, old or young, distant objects are not brought into focus on the retina but on a plan in front of the retina. This condition is called myopia or short sightedness. In the case of long sightedness, hypermetropia, the focus point for near objects lies behind the retina. With astigmatism (cylindrical

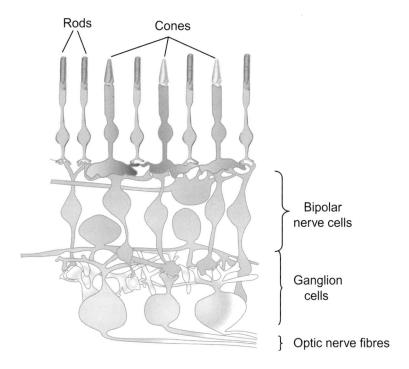

Rods   Cones

Bipolar
nerve cells

Ganglion
cells

Optic nerve fibres

Note: The synapses are located at the regions where the cells touch each other.

Source: adapted from Boer and Rutten (1974)

Figure 2.13 *Connections among neural elements in the retina: Via the rods and the cones (the receptors of light in the fovea), the information of the received light is coded, added, etc. by the ganglia, the bipolar cells and synapses, and is transferred via the optic nerve fibres to the brain*

disorder), the refractive power of the eye varies along different axes, and vision at all distances is distorted. Most refractive errors can be easily corrected by spectacles, contact lenses or laser techniques.

The sensation of small, black objects floating in front of the eye is due to cells and fragments of debris in the vitreous cavity of the eye. Almost everyone has them; a sudden increase may indicate degenerative changes in the vitreous gel, which are not serious. The appearance of many 'floaters' may be associated with inflammation or bleeding in the eye. The number of floaters gradually increases with age.

Internal malfunctions

Dry eyes are a medical condition in which the eye fails to produce tears. It is usually caused by a deficiency in vitamin A.

Inflammations of the cornea, sclera, uvea and iris are called keratitis, scleritis, uveitis and iritis, respectively. These are all usually associated with infectious diseases within the body and can be painful, causing redness and mistiness of vision, sensitivity to light and watering of the eye.

Inflammation of the cornea by a fungal infection (keratomycosis) or bacterial infections is possible after a corneal injury or other lesion, especially in concurrence with vegetable/organic matter, such as a wheat plant (it implants the fungus directly into the cornea during the injury). Few bacteria have the power to penetrate the intact surface layers of the cornea; the same is true of fungi.

External factors

Most foreign bodies that enter the eye remain near the surface, and cause pain and a flow of tears, which usually washes out the foreign body. If it becomes embedded in the cornea it may have to be removed surgically. Many small foreign bodies nestle in the under surface of the upper lid so that every time the eye blinks the foreign body rubs on the cornea, causing pain and irritation. Small foreign bodies with a high speed may penetrate the interior of the eye with very few symptoms, and their presence may not even be recognized when inflammatory changes occur. Allergic reactions can consist of redness and itching of the conjunctiva (allergic conjunctivitis).

Ultraviolet light is strongly absorbed by the cornea and is the cause of snow blindness, characterized by intense pain and a substantial flow of tears some time after exposure. Usually the eye recovers without damage. However, long-term exposure to infrared radiation may cause cataract formation.

A cataract may be the result of injury through exposure to radiation, or as a result of the ingestion of toxic substances. The lens relies for its nutrition on the aqueous fluid secreted by the ciliary body and, if the latter is severely damaged as the result of long-term uveitis or a tumour, the metabolism of the lens suffers and a cataract develops. The symptoms are gradually yellowing and opacification of the lens, vision loss and eventually blindness. Extraction of the cataract is the cure, although the refractive power of the lens has to be replaced by a spectacle or contact lens.

Internal and external factors

The dry eyes syndrome is an eye disease caused by decreased tear production or increased tear film evaporation causing an unstable tear film. Typical symptoms of keratoconjunctivitis are dryness, burning and a sandy-gritty eye irritation that gets worse during the day. Other symptoms are pain, redness, a pulling sensation and pressure behind the eye, causing increased discomfort and sensitivity to bright light. Both eyes are usually affected. There may also be a stringy uncomfortable discharge from the eyes due to the irritation.

Ageing is one of the most common causes of dry eyes, but it can also be caused by thermal or chemical burns, or (in epidemic cases) by adenoviruses. People wearing contact lenses are at risk (the soft contact lenses, which float on the tear film that covers the cornea, absorb the tears in the eyes).

Most people who have dry eyes experience mild irritation with no long-term effects. However, if the condition is left untreated or becomes severe, it can produce complications that can cause eye damage, resulting in impaired vision or (rarely) in the loss of vision.

2.4 The human nose

2.4.1 Components of the nose

The human perception of indoor air quality normally involves two human senses: the common chemical sense (somesthesia) and olfaction. Indoor air pollutants that can reach and activate the olfactory epithelium (in the nose) are perceived as odorous. Indoor air pollutants that activate the trigeminal nerve (in mucous membranes of the nasal and mouth cavities, over entire facial and forehead skin) are called irritants. The latter can cause irritation of mucosal membranes in the eyes, nose or throat, dryness of the eyes, nose and throat, facial skin irritation and dryness of the skin.

To be perceived, a molecule is, in general, volatilized from its source, inhaled into the nasal cavity and dissolved in the protective mucous layer (epithelium). The nose comprises two nostrils with smelling organs (see Figure 2.14).

In each nostril one patch of yellowish tissue (the olfactory epithelium) is located in the dome of the nasal cavity. Two types of nerve fibres – the olfactory sense and the trigeminal nerve, whose endings receive and detect volatile molecules – are embedded in this tissue. The trigeminal nerve endings (part of the common chemical sense) are located all over the nasal respiratory lining, not only in the olfactory epithelium. While the olfactory organ is sensitive to the odorant aspect of a chemical, the trigeminal nerve endings are sensitive to the irritant aspect of a chemical in the air. On being stimulated by pollutants, the olfactory nerve endings and the trigeminal nerve endings send signals to the brain where the signals are integrated and interpreted. The result of this process is called perceived air quality.

The biological principles for receptor activation of odour and irritation are fairly well understood, while for the information processes at higher centres of the brain, this is less clear (ECA, 1999). How these basic processes relate to the more complex psychological

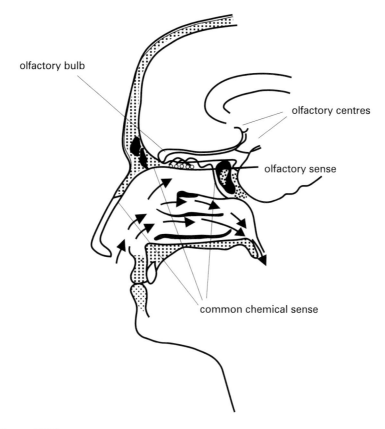

Source: adapted from Bluyssen (1990)

Figure 2.14 *The human nose, comprising the common chemical and olfaction senses*

responses to odorant/irritant stimulation, such as perceived air quality, annoyance and symptom reporting, is uncertain.

Inorganic gases (such as NO_x and SO_x) and biological pollutants (except for some products that are excreted by micro-organisms) are, in general, not odorous, except for some, such as ammonia and sulphur dioxide. Particulate matter can only partly reach the nose. On the other hand, virtually all organic vapours stimulate olfaction (Gardner et al, 1990). Under normal conditions, most non-volatile chemicals cannot reach the human olfactory epithelium and therefore are unable to stimulate olfaction. However, such molecules, when presented as aerosols, can reach the sensory tissue and can then stimulate a response. Odorants are typically small hydrophobic organic molecules with a mass range of 34-300 Dalton. Most odorants contain a single polar group. A majority of odorants contain oxygen.

2.4.2 Mechanisms

Olfaction

The olfactory epithelium comprises between 10 million and 25 million olfactory receptor cells, covering a total area of about 4 square centimetres (VDI, 1986). Each cell ends in a swollen bulb with a network of hair-like outgrowths (cilia) that rate out into the nasal cavity. The fibres from specific epithelium areas are bunched together and end in a glomerule of the olfactory bulb. The olfactory bulb is connected to the brain by a fibre tract. Via the latter, the axons of the bulb are connected with different brain centres, which together are called the olfactory brain.

The sense of smell depends initially upon the interaction between the stimulus and the olfactory epithelium. It is believed that the molecule must be bound by a receptor on the cilia. The 'binding' process causes olfactory nerve impulses to travel from the sensory cell to the olfactory lobe of the brain. The brain interprets the incoming signals by associating them with a previous olfactory experience. This is how the nose distinguishes between perceived air qualities (Geldard, 1972).

Several theoretical ideas about this process have been developed during the last decades. These ideas can be divided into two main categories: theories that are based on chemical reactions between the perceived molecules and the tissues in the olfactory cleft, and theories that are based on physical interaction between molecules in the nostrils and the sensitive tissue surface or other physical processes.

The first category comprises a few theories. Kistiakowsky (cited in Geldard, 1972) stated that the olfactory response may be set off by a system of reactions that are catalysed by enzymes. A smelling molecule would inhibit the action of one or more of the enzymes. Another theory is that the primary factor determining the odour of a substance might be the overall geometric shape of the molecule. Amoore (1964) proposed the stereo-chemical theory, which provides a mechanism based on a 'lock-and-key' principle.

In the second category, even more theories are available. For example, Dyson (cited in Geldard, 1972) claimed in his Raman shift theory that only substances with shifts of wavelengths between 140nm and 350nm, when monochromatic light is shining through them, are detected. Dravniek (in Harper et al, 1968) suggested a hypothetical mechanism based upon a change in coupling between electron donor/acceptor pair of large molecules which occurs when a substance is absorbed. The altered charge transfer balance would then be monitored by the appropriate nerve fibres. And Mozell (cited in Harper et al, 1968) supported the hypothesis that differential sensitivity to substances may be largely a matter of how molecules spread themselves across the olfactory mucosa. The nasal epithelium may act like a gas chromatograph.

Latest research indicates that there are around 1000 genes that encode 1000 different odour receptors (Axel, 1995). Genes provide the template for proteins, the molecules that carry out the functions of the cell. Each type of receptor is expressed in thousands of neurons. Mammalian DNA contains around 100,000 genes, which indicates that 1 per cent of all our genes are devoted to the detection of odours, demonstrating the significance of this sensory system for the survival and reproduction of most mammalian species. This is in contrast with the human eye. Humans can discriminate among several hundred hues using only three kinds of receptors on the retina. These photoreceptors detect light in different but overlapping regions of the visible spectrum, so the brain can compare input from all these types of detectors to identify a colour.

Mammals can detect at least 10,000 odours; consequently, each of the 1000 different receptors must respond to several odour molecules, and each odour must bind to several receptors. The results shown by Axel (1995) suggest that each neuron features only one type of receptor. The problem of distinguishing which receptor was activated by a particular odour is then reduced to the problem of identifying which neurons fired. In all other sensory systems, the brain relies on defined spatial patterns of neurons as well as the position of the neurons' ultimate targets to define the quality of a sensation. It was found that the olfactory epithelium is divided into four broad regions according to the types of receptors found in each zone, but with a random distribution of receptors within each region, and with no precise spatial pattern of neurons in the epithelium. The results also showed that the glomeruli in the olfactory bulb are differentially sensitive to specific odours. Since the positions of the individual glomeruli are topologically defined, the olfactory bulb provides a two-dimensional map that identifies which of the numerous receptors has been activated in the nose. A given odour will activate a characteristic combination of glomeruli in the olfactory bulb; signals from the glomeruli are then transmitted to the olfactory cortex. Buck and Axel (1991) have shown that each olfactory receptor neuron remarkably only expresses one kind of olfactory receptor protein and that the input from all neurons expressing the same receptor is collected by a single dedicated glomerulus of the olfactory bulb. In the glomeruli, not only the nerve processes from the olfactory receptor cells are found but also their contacts with the next level of nerve cells: the mitral cells. Each mitral cell is activated by only one glomerulus, and the specificity in the information flow is thereby maintained. Via long nerve processes, the mitral cells send the information to several parts of the brain. These nerve signals in turn reach defined micro-regions in the brain cortex. Here the information from several types of odorant receptors is combined into a pattern characteristic for each odour. This is interpreted and leads to the conscious experience of a recognizable odour. Buck and Axel (1991) received the Nobel prize for their work in 2004 (see Figure 2.15).

Although no specific receptors have yet been identified, it is believed that about 100 to 300 receptor classes exist. This makes it difficult to predict odour sensations from the chemical structure of an odorant and to establish an objective classification system for odorants.

To summarize the biological process of the olfactory sense:

- An odorant molecule binds to a protein receptor site in the membrane of the receptor cell (at the cilia).
- A receptor is activated by the stimulus (odorous molecule) and, in turn, activates other proteins, which trigger an enzyme cascade (second messenger system), which results in an electric potential.
- Axons of the receptor cells form bundles (glomeruli). Between 30 and 50 of such bundles carry olfaction information to the olfactory bulbs.
- Several hundred primary olfactory axons converge on a single mitral cell, located on an olfactory synapse of the olfactory bulb.

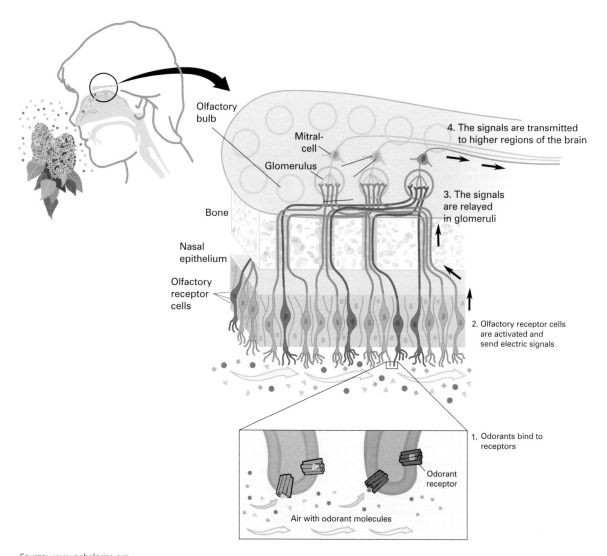

Source: www.nobelprize.org

Figure 2.15 *Odorant receptors and the organization of the olfactory system by Buck and Axel (1991)*

Somesthia

It should not be forgotten that the perceived air quality of a substance is the interaction of the perception of the olfactory organ and the common chemical sense (somesthia or trigeminal nerve endings). Cain (1989) stated that the difference in the time course between olfactory and common chemical sensations suggests that different processes of stimulation occur even when stimulated with the same substance. Sensations of the common chemical sense grow during inhalation, but also between inhalations and for relatively long durations, while sensations of the olfactory sense do not build over time. Cain (1989) gave three possibilities for explaining the initial buildup of the common chemical sensation:

1   an integration of sensation of purely physiological origin (i.e. neural);
2   an accumulation of incident stimuli at the neural receptor (the majority of trigeminal nerve endings lie somewhat below the surface of the epithelium, so the stimuli may reach the receptors by diffusion; the olfactory receptors are only separated from the atmosphere by a thin layer of mucous); or
3   a repetitive damage to some structure, such as an epithelial cell which might repetitively secrete endogenous chemicals to serve as the actual stimulus for the common chemical sense (this sensation might increase with cumulative damage and might continue after cessation of the stimuli because of low-level inflammation).

It is now believed that nociceptors on the free nerve endings from the sensory branches of the trigeminal nerve are principally responsible for their chemical sensitivity (Silver and Finger, 1991). Chemosthesis is thus closely related to the somatic sensory system, particularly pain.

Many airborne substances are complex stimuli. They are combinations of many chemicals, which can interact at one or several levels before or during the perception: chemical or physical interaction in the gas mixture, interaction of molecules at the receptor surfaces (olfactory and trigeminal systems), peripheral interaction in the nervous system, and, finally, interaction in the central nervous system. Therefore, effects such as masking, neutralization and counteraction are not surprising in gas mixtures (Berglund et al, 1976).

Only a few volatile organic compounds (VOCs) lack the potential to cause irritation. Biological assays to learn the potency of irritants are numerous – for example, the recording of the negative mucosal potential from the nasal epithelium or the recording of cortical evoked potentials; measurement of neural mediators or modulators; measurement of the products of inflammation; and measurement of reflexes (Cain and Cometto-Muniz, 1993).

The two types of sensations, trigeminal and olfactory, can be separated by making use of anosmics (individuals who lack the sense of smell), compared to individuals with normal olfaction and nasal irritation. In order to determine the relevant physiochemical determinants of potency, these two groups of people were exposed to single chemicals (Cain and Cometto-Muniz, 1993). The study showed that a general relationship between odour and irritation thresholds might be present. It was found that the threshold level (odour/irritation) decreases as the length of the carbon chain increases.

Predicted versus 'real' perception

The olf and decipol theory (Fanger, 1988) (see also Annex B) is based on the assumption that the pollutants in buildings all have the same relation between exposure and response. Besides the questionable use of the term 'perceived air quality', which can involve many other dimensions of dissatisfaction and acceptability (e.g. odour intensity, stuffiness, perceived dryness and degree of unpleasantness) (Bluyssen, 2004a), the main item that is discussed with this method is the assumption that all pollutants have the same relation between exposure and response (i.e. that the calculated olf values from separate sources can be added).

According to Stevens' law, perceived odour intensity of one single compound increases as a power function of concentration (Stevens, 1957):

$$\text{perceived odour intensity} = bC^a \qquad [2.3]$$

where:

- C = concentration (g/m^3);
- a, b = constants.

The perceived intensity of a mixture of two compounds may, in theory, be as strong as the sum of the perceived intensities of the unmixed compounds (complete addition), more intense than the sum of its compounds (hyper-addition), or less intense than the sum of its compounds (hypo-addition). There are three kinds of hypo-addition:

1 *Partial addition*: the mixture is perceived as more intense than the stronger compound perceived alone.
2 *Compromise addition*: the mixture is perceived as more intense than one compound perceived alone, but less intense than the other.
3 *Compensation addition*: the mixture is perceived as weaker than both the stronger and the weaker compound.

According to Berglund et al (1976), stimulation is proportional to the number of molecules as long as just one type of molecule is present. The odour interaction for mixtures of constituent odorants is governed by a strongly attenuating function: hypo-addition (Berglund et al, 1976). The concentration of numerous compounds may be less important to the perceived air quality than the addition or subtraction of a few specific compounds to the gas mixture (Berglund and Lindvall, 1990).

Reviewing previous addition studies of perceived air quality (in decipol), it was observed that, for the majority of the comparisons between predicted (by using the addition assumption) and measured pollution loads of combinations of sources, the predicted pollution loads are frequently higher than the measured pollution loads (Bluyssen and Cornelissen, 1999), thus implying hypo-addition as well. The same was found for perceived air qualities.

Olfactory adaptation, which is similar to visual adaptation to light, makes it even more difficult to predict or model perceived odour intensity or perceived air quality. With continuous exposure, the perceived odour intensity will decrease with time and the odour threshold will increase with time. Recovery or readaptation will occur within less than a minute after removal from odour (VDI, 1986).

In conclusion, modelling of perceived quality or intensity of indoor air is not possible yet, based on single compounds, although some predictions have been made with mixtures of several compounds. Indoor air comprises thousands of compounds, of which some are odorous, some are not, and others are irritants. Besides the combined odours and irritant effects of the thousands of compounds, qualitative character is even more complex. The 'sensory' print is, in general, different from the 'chemical' print.

Human nose versus electronic nose

The development of instruments, such as an artificial nose or an electronic nose, that can evaluate air quality as the human nose does is an ongoing activity. Many attempts have been made, some successful for the purpose they are designed for, others not. The reason is not only related to the still incomplete knowledge of the perception mechanism (information processes in brain), but also to the fact that the nose is able to detect very low concentrations.

Table 2.4 presents the lowest odour detection level that could be found in the literature for a number of compounds that are emitted by the human body

Table 2.4 *The lowest human odour detection levels for some compounds, emitted by the human body*

Compound	Molecular weight	Chemical structure	Odour detection level	
			$\mu g/m^3$	ppb*
Acetaldehyde	44	CH_3CHO	0.2	0.111
Benzaldehyde	106	C_6H_5CHO	0.8	0.185
Butyric acid	88	$CH_3CH_2CH(OCCH_3)CO_2C_2H_5$	1	0.278
Coumarin	146	$C_9H_6O_2$	0.007	0.0012
Dimethylsulfide	62	$(CH_3)_2S$	2.5	0.986
Dimethyldisulfide	94	CH_3SSCH_3	0.1	0.026
N-decanal	156	$CH_3(CH_2)_8CHO$	0.25	0.039
Ethanethiol or ethylmercaptan	62	C_2H_5SH	0.1	0.039
Hydrogen sulphide (inorganic)	34	H_2S	0.7	0.503
Methylmercaptan or methanethiol	48	CH_3SH	0.04	0.020
Phenylacetic acid	136	$(C_6H_5CH_2CO)_2O$	0.03	0.0054

Note: * ppb = 24.45 × µg/m³/molecular weight.

Source: Bluyssen (1990)

(Bluyssen, 1990). From this table it can be concluded that the human nose is able to detect certain compounds at a particle per trillion (ppt) level. It must be noted that not every nose has the same sensitivity (i.e. the same compound can be detected by some people at a much lower level than others).

Furthermore, the results of Cain and Cometto-Muniz (1993) indicate that complex chemical environments may enable chemosensory and particularly irritative detection when single VOCs lie far below their individual thresholds. This means that in gas mixtures, the nose may detect even far below single thresholds – that is below the parts per trillion (ppt)–parts per billion (ppb) range.

It should be understood that the use of human subjects to evaluate perceived air quality (the so-called sensory evaluation of air) is only one way of measuring air quality. Compounds such as carbon monoxide cannot be smelled by a human being but can, nevertheless, threaten one's health. These compounds should therefore be measured in another way.

2.4.3 Possible diseases and disorders

The sense of smell (olfaction) can be out of order, temporarily or permanently. This is called anosmia. Hyposmia is a reduction in the ability to smell, while hyperosmia is an increased ability to smell. Some people may be anosmic for one particular odour; this is called 'specific anosmia' and may be genetically based.

The linings of the mucous membrane in the nose are the other segments that are exposed to diseases and disorders, such as nasal congestion and increased mucus production. The latter is, in general, a symptom of many common illnesses, such as the common cold.

Nasal congestion is the blockage of the nasal passages, usually due to membranes lining the nose becoming swollen from inflamed blood vessels. It is also known as nasal blockage, nasal obstruction, blocked nose, runny nose and stuffy nose. Most common causes for nasal congestion are an allergic reaction, a common cold or influenza, allergic reaction to pollen or grass, and sinusitis or sinus infection. One should furthermore be aware that it is possible for retrograde infections from the nasal area to spread to the brain due to the special nature of the blood supply to the human nose and surrounding area.

2.5 The human ear
2.5.1 Components of the ear

The human ear provides us with two different human senses: the sense of hearing through the cochlear nerve and the sense of equilibrium through the vestibule nerve. The human ear comprises an external, middle and inner ear, and is connected to the nasal cavity via the Eustachian tube (see Figure 2.16).

The inner ear contains the sensory organs of hearing and equilibrium. The middle ear is a narrow air-filled space within the temporal bone, separated from the outside by the tympanic membrane (eardrum) and crossed by a chain of three tiny bones: the auditory ossicles (the malleus or hammer, the incus or anvil, and the stapes or stirrup). The external ear comprises the auricle or pinna and the external auditory canal, which ends at the eardrum. It is covered with skin, just as the eardrum membrane. Fine hairs directed outward together with sweat glands producing earwax prevent unwanted objects from entering the canal.

The inner ear, as a whole, is called the labyrinth because of its complicated galleries and chambers. In fact, there two labyrinths, one inside the other: the membrane labyrinth in the bony labyrinth. The bony labyrinth (see Figure 2.17) comprises a central chamber (the vestibule), three semicircular canals (superior, lateral and posterior) and the spirally coiled cochlea, which resembles the shell of a snail.

The cochlea is, in fact, a tube that turns around a hollow pillar, the modiolus, which contains the fibres and ganglion cells of the cochlear nerve. Each of the semicircular canals contains a narrow membranous semicircular duct, which end in an elongated sac: the utricle. The utricle is connected to another sac, the saccule, also located in the vestibule. The space within the bony labyrinth that is not occupied with the membranous labyrinth is filled with a watery fluid: the perilymph (similar in composition to fluid in the eye and the cerebrospinal fluid). The membranous labyrinth is filled with another fluid, called the endolymph.

2.5.2 Mechanisms
Hearing

During hearing, sound waves in the air are directed by the pinna in the auditory canal. Sound or noise

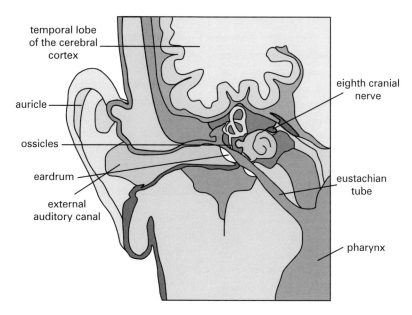

Note: The Eustachian tube takes care of the pressure equilibrium between the nasal cavity and the middle ear.

Source: adapted from *Encyclopaedia Britannica* (1991b).

Figure 2.16 *Section through the right ear: A sound enters the external auditory canal, setting the eardrum and the ossicles in motion, which transmit these vibrations to the fluid of the inner ear see (see Figure 2.17), where nerve impulses are transmitted via the eight cranial nerve to the brain*

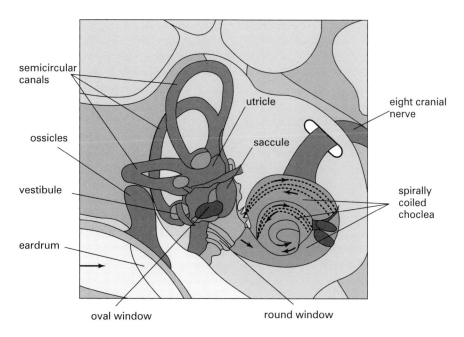

Source: adapted from *Encyclopaedia Britannica* (1991b).

Figure 2.17 *The inner ear: The bony labyrinth comprises a central chamber (the vestibule), three semicircular canals (superior, lateral and posterior) and the spirally coiled cochlea*

reaching the eardrum is partly absorbed and partly reflected (acoustic impedance). The part that is absorbed sets the drum and the ossicles in motion. The impedance (a type of resistance) depends upon the mass and stiffness of the drum and the ossiclar chain, and on the frictional resistance that they offer.

The central part of the eardrum vibrates and its motion is transmitted to the auditory ossicles, which intensify the vibrations and transmit them to the fluid of the inner ear. It is in the coiled cochlea that the vibrations of this fluid are converted by the hair cells of the organ of Corti into nerve impulses that are transmitted to the brain.

The cochlea is divided into three scalae: the scala vestibule, the scala tympani and the scala media or cochlear duct, which lies in between. The organ of Corti is a neuroepithelium comprising sensory cells in orderly rows and their supporting cells on the surface of the basilar membrane in the cochlear duct. The length of the basilar membrane (and the organ of Corti that covers it) is about 35mm in humans. Total outer hair cells have been estimated at 12,000 and the inner hair cells at 3500, with almost 30,000 fibres (indicating some overlap, especially with the outer hair cells). Each ear is represented in both the right and the left cortex. For this reason both ears can continue to function normally, even if the auditory cortical area of one side is destroyed.

Most neurons of the auditory pathway show a 'best frequency' (i.e. a frequency to which an individual neuron responds at minimal intensity). In general, pitch tends to be coded in terms of neurons that are responding, loudness in terms of the rate of response and the total number of active neurons. It appears likely that in humans, both pitch and loudness are distinguished at lower levels of the auditory pathways and that the cortex is reserved for the analysis of more complex acoustic stimuli, such as speech and music, for which the temporal sequence of sound, is equally important. At the cortical level, the 'meaning' of sounds is recognized and behaviour is adjusted in accordance with their significance. The localization of sounds depends upon the recognition of very small differences in intensity and in the time of arrival of the sound at the two ears.

A fundamental characteristic of sound is its frequency – that is, the number of cycles per second expressed in Hertz (Hz) of the causative vibration. Low-frequency sound is heard as a low pitch and high frequency as a high pitch. The human ear is sensitive to frequencies between 20Hz and 20,000Hz, with some variation from person to person. The ear is most sensitive to frequencies of 3000Hz to 5000Hz. The normal human ear is remarkably sensitive and can recognize sound already at about 10^{-25} kilowatt hours (kWh) of sound energy. Hearing becomes painful at about 10^{-11} kWh. Human ears differ from person to person and vary even in the same person with age and environmental conditions.

Equilibrium sense

The inner ear also contains the equilibrium organ that acts independently of hearing, activated by acceleration in space and by the rotation of the body. The vestibular system is concerned primarily with controlling the position of the head and the posture of the body. The semicircular canals control angular acceleration, and the utricle and saccule control linear acceleration. These organs are closely related to the cerebellum and to the reflex centres that control the movements of eyes, neck and limbs.

The utricle and saccule each contain a single sensory patch, a macula, which is covered by neuro-epithelium. This epithelium consists of sensory cells, called hair cells, and supporting cells. The utricle and saccule with their macula respond to gravitational forces; therefore, they are also called gravity receptors.

The sensory end organ of each semicircular duct is located in the expanded end, or ampulla. The sensory epithelium on the crista contains the same types of cells as the maculae – hair cells with stereocilia (hairs). If these hairs are stimulated (sudden movement of the fluid) without actual rotation according to the visual response (swimming of the visual field), dizziness, disorientation and nausea can be the result (sea sickness). Unusual stimulation (such as ear infections which cause irritation of vestibular nerve endings) of the vestibular receptors and semicircular canals can also cause sensory distortions in visual and motor activity. Static pressures, such as gravitational forces, are detected by hair cells in the two sacs of the vestibule, permitting perception of the orientation of the head.

Together with the visual and visceral senses, the equilibrium sense is sensitive to low frequencies (vibrations), while the auditory sense is more sensitive to higher frequencies (hearing). There are large differences between people in terms of vibration perception thresholds. The vibration dose value appears to predict relative annoyance. The perception of vibration depends upon mechanical aspects (frequency, duration and amplitude of the vibrations), human factors (age, health and sensitivity) and position and activity of the person (Esposito, 2005).

2.5.3 Possible diseases and disorders

The mucous membrane that covers the middle ear and mastoid bone (the facial nerve passes through this bone) is subject to the same allergic reactions and infections that can affect the nasal passages. Because the brain cavity lies just above and behind the middle ear and mastoid air spaces, and is only separated by a thin plate of bone, an infection, if severe and untreated, may lead to meningitis (inflammation of the covering of the brain) or brain abscess. Paralysis of the facial nerve and infection from the middle ear to the labyrinth of the inner ear are other possible complications.

An acute head cold together with inadequate ventilation through the Eustachian tube can lead to filling of the middle ear cavity with a yellow fluid. This can cause impairment of hearing, an allergic reaction of the membranes of the Eustachian tube, and an enlarged adenoid blocking the Eustachian tube. Finding and removing the cause and then removing the fluid, if it does not disappear, is the cure. If it becomes chronic, inflammation of the inner ear can occur and, later, loss of both equilibrium and hearing in the affected ear.

The effects of exposure to noise depend upon intensity and duration. A single exposure to an extremely intense sound, such as an explosion, may produce a severe and permanent loss of hearing. Repeated exposures to sounds in excess of 80 to 90 decibels may cause gradual deterioration of hearing by destroying the hair cells of the inner ear, and possible subsequent degeneration of nerve fibres. A gradual decline of the hearing function usually starts after the age of 60.

Motion sickness, arising when sensory information concerning body orientation and movement is inconsistent, can include breathing problems, yawning, a sensation of warmth, disorientation, nausea and vomiting. Vertical oscillation of the body at low frequencies (e.g. when a building is vibrating from the wind) is one of the causes. The effects are most distinct between 0.125Hz and 0.25Hz, while sickness rarely occurs with frequencies above 0.5Hz. (Esposito, 2005).

2.6 The human respiratory tract

2.6.1 Components of the respiratory tract

The human respiratory tract can be divided into the upper and lower airway system. The upper airway system comprises the nose and the paranasal cavities (sinuses), the pharynx (throat) and also, partly, the oral cavity. The lower airway system consists of the larynx, the trachea, the stem bronchi and all the airways in the lungs, such as the intrapulmonary bronchi, the bronchioles and the alveolar ducts (see Figure 2.18).

The nose adjusts the temperature and water-vapour content of the air and removes a large proportion of foreign gases and dust; the nasal mucocilliary systems clear foreign material deposited on it. The nasal cavity is lined with respiratory mucosa (mucous membrane), containing mucus-secreting glands and venous plexuses (networks of blood vessels).

In the lowest part of the pharynx, directly above the larynx, food and air cross each other: air from the nasal cavity into the larynx, and food from the oral cavity to the esophagus behind the larynx. The larynx has two functions: as air canal to the lungs and controller of its access, and as the organ of phonation. Below the larynx lies the trachea, a tube about 10cm to 12cm long and 2cm wide, stiffened by horseshoe-shaped rings. The interior is lined by typical respiratory epithelium containing mucous glands. At the lower end, the trachea divides into an inverted Y into the two stem (or main) bronchi: one for the left and one for the right lung. The right main bronchus has a larger diameter, is oriented more vertically, and is shorter than the left main bronchus, causing foreign bodies passing beyond the larynx to slip into the right lung. The structure of the stem bronchi is similar to the trachea.

The conducting airways comprise the trachea, the two stem bronchi, the bronchi and the bronchioles. They warm, moisten and clean the inspired air and distribute it to the gas-exchanging zone of the lung. They are lined with typical respiratory epithelium with ciliated cells and numerous spread-out mucus-secreting goblet cells. In the bronchioles the goblet cells are replaced with Clara cells, another type of secreting cells. The epithelium is covered by a layer of fluid, in which the cilia produce a synchronized, rhythmic beat directed outwards through which foreign bodies are cleared and ingested. This is called the mucocilliary escalatory clearance mechanism.

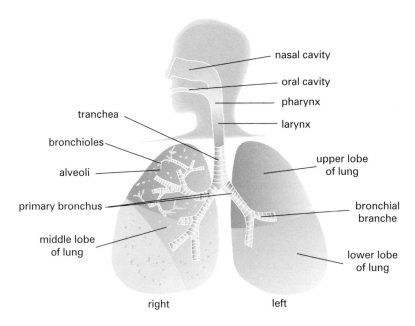

nasal cavity

oral cavity

pharynx

larynx

tranchea

bronchioles

alveoli

upper lobe
of lung

primary bronchus

bronchial
branche

middle lobe
of lung

lower lobe
of lung

right   left

Source: adapted from *Encyclopaedia Britannica* (1991b).

Figure 2.18 *The respiratory tract: The upper airway (the nose and the paranasal cavities, the pharynx and partly also the oral cavity) and the lower airway system (the larynx, the trachea, the stem bronchi and all the airways in the lungs, such as the intrapulmonary bronchi, the bronchioles and the alveolar ducts)*

The last conductive airway generations in the lung are the terminal bronchioles, with the first gas-exchanging alveoli. After several generations (splitting up approximately 16 times) of such respiratory bronchioles, the alveoli are packed so densely that an airway wall is missing: the airways consist of alveolar ducts and, finally, end in alveolar sacs (see Figure 2.19).

The right lung is larger than the left lung (56 per cent versus 44 per cent of total lung volume) and has three lobes, while the left lung has two lobes, each separated by a sloping gap. These lobes are subdivided into smaller units: the pulmonary segments (approximately ten per lung). The inside of the thoracic cavities and the lung surface are covered with watery membranes – the parietal pleura and the visceral pleura, respectively, with fluid in between, connecting at the helium (the only place where the lung is secured to surrounding structures). The pleural cavity is larger than the lung volume because of the pleural recesses. During inspiration, the recesses are partly opened by the expanding lung.

The gas-exchange region for oxygen and carbon dioxide begins with the first alveoli and comprises air, blood and tissue, the latter providing the supporting framework that is known as the pulmonary parenchyma.

2.6.2 Mechanisms

Breathing

The diaphragm is the major muscle of breathing, assisted by a complex assembly of other muscle groups. Breathing is an automatic and rhythmic activity produced by networks of neurons in the hindbrain, and can adjust to changes in internal and external environment (e.g. changes in metabolic rate and disturbances such as an asthmatic attack).

Feedback by chemo receptors is one way in which breathing is controlled: chemo receptors in the arterial blood, monitoring the changes in partial pressure of oxygen and carbon dioxide, and central chemo receptors in the brain, which respond to the partial pressure of carbon dioxide in their immediate environment.

Receptors in the respiratory muscles and in the lung can also affect breathing patterns. The receptors in the airways and alveoli are stimulated by rapid lung inflation

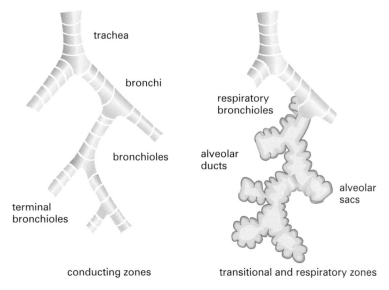

trachea

bronchi

respiratory
bronchioles

bronchioles

alveolar
ducts

alveolar
sacs

terminal
bronchioles

conducting zones

transitional and respiratory zones

Source: adapted from *Encyclopaedia Britannica* (1991b).

Figure 2.19 *Airway branching: The last conductive airway generations in the lung are the terminal bronchioles, with the first gas-exchanging alveoli: After several generations of such respiratory bronchioles, the airways consist of alveolar ducts and, finally, end in alveolar sacs*

and by chemicals such as histamine and prostaglandins. The most important function of these receptors (irritant receptors) is to protect the lung against noxious material. When stimulated, these receptors constrict the airways and cause rapid shallow breathing, which inhibits the penetration of injurious agents into the bronchial tree. Stimulation also causes coughing.

Defences

The smaller the particles that exist in the air that is breathed in, the further they can enter the respiratory tract. It is said that particles smaller that 200μm can reach the throat; particles smaller that 10μm can reach the larynx; while particles smaller that 5μm can reach the alveoli. Fibrous particulate matter can be inhaled. Most inhaled fibrous material is cleared by the mucocilliary escalatory clearance mechanism, which results in ingestion. Other inhaled particles are retained in the lungs, where they accumulate. Some fibres, through uncertain routes, migrate to the pleura and stay there. Fibre transportation from the lung also occurs via the haematogenous and lymphatic systems, with eventual accumulation of fibres in virtually every organ of the body.

The alveolar macrophage cells in the airway and the alveoli of the lungs can ingest and destroy bacteria and viruses and remove small particles. They secrete chemicals that attract white blood cells to the site and, hence, initiate an inflammatory response in the lung. Particles are removed to the lymphatic system of the lung and are stored in adjacent lymph glands. Soluble particles (i.e. small lead particles emitted by an automobile exhaust) are removed to the bloodstream and are excreted by the kidney (this takes approximately 12 hours).

2.6.3 Possible diseases and disorders

The respiratory tract can suffer from many diseases and disorders, most of them caused by infection (bacterial, viral or fungal), inflammation (allergic reaction), damage or tumours. In most cases they are caused by an external pollutant that is breathed into the lungs, causing an immediate or long-term effect.

Symptoms can be a cough, shortness of breath (dyspnoea) or chest pain. Coughing with sputum is the most important manifestation of disease in major airways – for example, bronchitis. An irritating cough without sputum may be caused by an extension of a malignant disease to the bronchial trees from nearby organs. The presence of blood in the sputum is an important sign and can result from an infection, but can also indicate the presence of inflammation, capillary damage or tumour. Shortness of breath may vary in severity as a result of something harmless such as walking upstairs, but can also indicate something more serious when it is continuously present, such as emphysema (swelling in the lung). It can also occur acutely when a foreign body is inhaled into the trachea or with the onset of a severe attack of asthma. Dyspnoea is also an early symptom of congestion of the lung as a result of the impaired function of the left ventricle of the heart. Chest pain may be an early symptom, but is mostly related to pneumonia due to an inflammation of the pleura. Severe chest pain may be caused by the spread of a malignant disease or a tumour, such as mesothelioma, arising from the pleura itself. Other symptoms are:

- wheezing caused by airway obstruction (as in asthma);
- swelling of the fingertips and sometimes toes (a feature of bronchiectasis – chronic inflammation and dilation of the major airways – diffuse fibrosis of the lung and lung cancer);
- swelling of the lymph nodes that drain the affected area, particularly the small nodes above the collarbone in the neck; this should always lead to suspicion of intrathoracic disease;
- a general feeling of malaise, unusual fatigue or minor symptoms as a first indication of disease.

Whether the cause is an infection or an allergic reaction is not always clear because the symptoms might be similar. Asthma and bronchitis are examples of this.

With *asthma*, a contraction of the smooth muscle of the airways occurs and, in severe attacks, obstruction from mucus that has been accumulated in the bronchial tree occurs. Two forms of asthma can be distinguished: first, extrinsic asthma, caused by an identifiable antigen and intrinsic asthma, occurring without an identifiable antigen or specific antibody. Extrinsic asthma is caused by being in contact with any of the proteins to which sensitization has occurred, such as pollens, mould spores, animal proteins of different kinds and proteins from a variety of insects (i.e. cockroaches and mites). Intrinsic asthma may develop at any age, while extrinsic asthma commonly manifests itself during childhood. Intrinsic asthma may

be triggered by infections, which are assumed in many cases to be viral. In people with asthma, symptoms may occur at much lower concentrations of histamine or acetylcholine (both normally occurring smooth muscle constrictors). Affected individuals may develop airway obstructions when inhaling cold air or during exercise.

Acute bronchitis is generally caused by a viral infection, but may also be caused by acute exposure to irritant gases, such as ammonia, chlorine or sulphur dioxide. The bronchial tree is reddened and congested and minor blood streaking of the sputum may occur. Bronchiolitis refers to inflammation of the small airways. It normally clears spontaneously.

Hypersensitivity pneumonitis can be induced by several pollutants or agents. The lung is sensitized by contact with a variety of agents. The response consists of acute pneumonitis, with inflammation of the smaller bronchioles, alveolar wall oedema and a greater or lesser degree of airflow obstruction due to smooth muscle contraction. Examples are farmer's lung, caused by spores from mouldy hay (*Thermophilic actinomyces*) and the bird fancier's lung – allergic responses to proteins from birds (particularly in the excreta of pigeons and parakeets). Humidifier fever, caused by exposure to moulds growing in the humidifier system, an influenza-like illness, is another example (the agent is not known).

There are a number of pollutants whose health effects have been given specific names, such as the following:

- *Legionellosis* is an infectious disease caused by bacteria belonging to the genus Legionella. Over 90 per cent of legionellosis cases are caused by *Legionella pneumophila*, an aquatic organism that thrives in warm environments (25°C to 45°C with an optimum around 35°C) and may grow in air-conditioning systems or on shower heads. Legionellosis can take two distinct forms:
  - *Legionnaires' disease*: the more severe form of the infection, which produces pneumonia and is named after the outbreak of pneumonia among US veterans attending a convention in Philadelphia in 1976;
  - *Pontiac fever*: caused by the same bacterium, producing a milder respiratory illness without pneumonia, resembling acute influenza;
- *Silicosis*: inhalation of silica dust leads to the development of masses of fibrous tissue and

nodules (swellings) of dense fibrosis, which, by contracting, distort and damage the lung.

- *Hay fever*: allergy to grasses and pollen causing conjunctival infection and oedema of the nasal mucosa, leading to attacks of sneezing.
- *Asbestosis*: the microscopically fibres of asbestos may cause significant health damage when inhaled. Fibrous materials are not metabolized after entering the body; but there is leaching of chemical constituents varying with fibre type and size. Some fibres become coated with an iron-protein matrix and form an 'asbestos body' when asbestos is the core material. Some structural and compositional changes occur after fibres are taken up in tissue, particularly in the lungs. The mechanism by which asbestos and other fibrous materials produce fibrosis appears to be different from that of silica, which acts by causing secondary lysosomal release of enzymes of macrophages that lead to a fibrotic tissue reaction. Fibrotic process of either the lung parenchyma or the visceral pleura develops only after considerable time (> 20 years), when earlier exposure has been intense. The latency period for asbestosis, mesothelioma or lung cancer is 20 to 30 years (WHO, 2006).

And then there are specific pollutants that, depending upon the exposure time and exposure concentration, can cause different diseases and disorders when inhaled, such as the following:

- *Radon and its progeny* attach to an aerosol and reach the lungs by inhalattion of the nose and sore throat, lower airway and pulmonary effects (cough, chest tightness) and pulmonary oedema, inflammation, pneumonia; with very high and *long exposures*, it leads to death.
- Inorganic gases (such as SOx and NOx) can cause severe airwtion of the nose and sore throat, lower airway and pulmonary effects (cough, chest tightness) and pulmonary oedema, inflammation, pneumonia; with very high and long exposures, it leads to death.

- *Inorganic gases* (such as SO_x and NO_x) can cause severe airway symptoms.
- *Micro-organisms*, such as bacteria, viruses and fungi, can produce health effects including infection, disease and allergic reactions.
- *Particulate matter* (PM) can cause a wide range of health effects. While PM from different sources has different effects on the human body, DNA damage refers to all (i.e. these particles may cause cancer).
- *Lead*: through inhalation or ingestion, lead can have toxicological effects on the nervous system, in particular (e.g. causing damage to the developing brain of young children) (WHO, 2006).

Some recent health issues, such as severe acute respiratory syndrome (SARS) caused by the SARS coronavirus, multidrug-resistant *Staphylococcus aureus* (MRSA), caused by the bacterium with the same name, and *Clostridium difficile* (CDF), caused by a species of bacteria of the genus *Clostridium*, are not discussed here because the detailed description of those important health issues would take too much space. Hospitals seem to have a greater risk for contracting the latter two diseases in particular.

Last, but certainly not least, an important disease of our time is chronic obstructive pulmonary disease (COPD), caused by noxious particles or gases, which trigger an abnormal inflammatory response in the lungs (WHO, 2008). COPD is a chronic disease of the lungs in which the airways become narrowed, leading to a limitation of the flow of air to and from the lungs, causing shortness of breath. The limitation of airflow is poorly reversible, usually gets worse over time and is not curable, but is preventable. It is frequently diagnosed in people aged 40 or older because it develops slowly. The primary cause is tobacco smoke; other risk factors include indoor and outdoor air pollution, occupational dusts and chemicals, and frequent lower respiratory infections during childhood. More than 3 million people died of COPD in 2005 (equal to 5 per cent of all deaths globally that year), and it is predicted that in the next ten years this death rate will increase by 30 per cent if no measures are taken.

3

The Indoor Environment

The parameters of each of the environmental factors (thermal comfort, lighting quality, indoor air quality and acoustical quality) encountered in the indoor environment are described. This chapter describes the mechanisms behind these parameters, the measurement techniques available and strategies to control these environmental factors.

3.1 Indoor environmental factors

There are four basic environmental factors in the indoor environment (see Figure 3.1) that directly influence the perception of that indoor environment through the senses, but also have an effect on the physical and mental state (comfort and health) of occupants:

1   thermal comfort or indoor climate, comprising parameters such as moisture, air velocity and temperature;
2   visual or lighting quality, determined by view, illuminance, luminance ratios, reflection and other parameters;
3   indoor air quality: a complex phenomenon comprising odour, indoor air pollution, fresh air supply, etc.;
4   acoustical quality, influenced by outside and indoor noise, as well as vibrations.

In addition, ergonomics, such as the dimensions and sizes of the space, tools, furniture, etc., play an important role in total body perception. Although significant, this will not be discussed in this book.

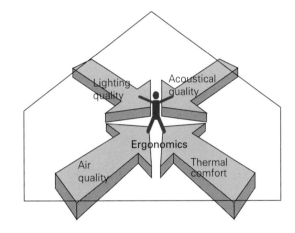

Source: Bluyssen

Figure 3.1 *Basic environmental factors in an indoor space*

3.2 Thermal parameters

3.2.1 Parameters and definitions

Parameters of the indoor environment that determine/influence the thermal comfort of an individual in that indoor environment (see Figure 3.2) can be described according to:

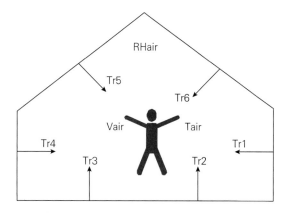

Source: Bluyssen

Figure 3.2 *Thermal parameters of the thermal comfort factor: Tr is the radiant temperature of a surface, RHair is the relative humidity of the indoor air, Vair is the air velocity and Tair is the air temperature*

- air temperature (T_a) and mean radiation temperature (mean of T_{r1} to T_{r6});
- air velocity (v_a) and turbulence intensity; and
- relative humidity (RH_a).

Temperature

The temperature of a system is determined by the average energy of microscopic motions of a single particle in the system per degree of freedom. In simple terms, temperature is a measure of the motion of molecules. For a solid, these microscopic motions are principally the vibrations of the constituent atoms about their sites in the solid. For an ideal monatomic gas, the microscopic motions are the translational motions of the constituent gas particles. For multi-atomic gas, vibrational and rotational motion should be included as well.

Temperature can be measured with the Celsius scale, while the thermodynamic temperature is usually measured with the Kelvin scale, which is just the Celsius scale shifted downwards so that 0 K = −273.15°C, or absolute zero.

The mean radiation temperature is the temperature of a uniform enclosure with which a black sphere at the test point would have the same radiation exchange as it does with the real environment. If this environment is comprised of i black surfaces with temperature T_i, the mean radiation temperature T_{mrt} is defined as:

$$T_{mrt} = (\Sigma F_{si} T_i^4)^{1/4} \ [°C] \qquad [3.1]$$

where F_{si} = fraction of radiation leaving the black sphere, which reaches the ith surface directly.

A black body is an object that absorbs all electromagnetic radiation that falls onto it. No radiation passes through it and none is reflected. It is this lack of both transmission and reflection to which the name refers. These properties make black bodies ideal sources of thermal radiation – that is, the amount and wavelength (colour) of electromagnetic radiation that they emit is directly related to their temperature.

Air velocity

Velocity is defined as the rate of change of position (displacement per unit of time) expressed in metres per second (m/s). It is a vector physical quantity; both speed and direction are required to define it. The average velocity (v) of an object moving through a displacement (δx) in a straight line during a time interval (δt) is described by the formula:

$$v = \delta x/\delta t \ [m/s]. \qquad [3.2]$$

The turbulence intensity is defined as the ratio of the standard deviation of the air velocity (σ_v) and the mean air velocity (v_m), expressed in percentage:

$$Tu = \sigma_v/v_m \ [\%] \qquad [3.3]$$

Humidity

Humidity is the amount of water vapour in air. Absolute humidity and relative humidity are different ways of expressing the water content in a parcel of air. Absolute humidity changes with air pressure.

Absolute humidity is the quantity of water (m_w) in a particular volume of air (V_a), expressed in grams per cubic metre:

$$AH = m_w/V_a \ [g/m^3] \qquad [3.4]$$

At 0°C the density of humid air is equal to 1.25kg/m³ and at 30°C it is equivalent to 1kg/m³.

The relative humidity is defined as the ratio of the partial pressure of water vapour in a gaseous mixture of air and water vapour ($p(H_2O)$) to the saturated vapour pressure of water ($p^* (H_2O)$) at a given temperature. Relative humidity is expressed as a percentage and is defined as:

$$RH = 100 x p(H_2O)/p^* (H_2O) \ [\%] \qquad [3.5]$$

For a mixture of water and air, Dalton's law is valid:

$$p_b = p_w + p_a \ [N/m^2] \qquad [3.6]$$

where:

- p_b = the pressure of the barometer (N/m^2);
- p_w = the partial water vapour pressure (N/m^2);
- p_a = the partial air pressure (N/m^2).

The ideal gas law is as follows:

$$c_w T_w = p_w/\rho_w \text{ and } c_a T_a = p_a/\rho_a \qquad [3.7]$$

where:

- c_w = specific heat for water (J/kgK);
- c_a = specific heat for air (J/kgK);
- T_w = temperature of water vapour (K);
- T_a = air temperature (K);
- ρ_w = mass density of water (kg/m^3);
- ρ_a = mass density of air (kg/m^3).

With the so-called Mollier diagram it is possible to characterize an air–water vapour mixture (see Figure 3.3). In this diagram, the water (vapour) is presented in g/kg, the temperature in °C, the relative humidity in percentage, the density of humid air in kg/m^3 and the heat contents or enthalpy in kJ/kg.

3.2.2 Mechanisms

When two systems are at the same temperature, no heat transfer occurs between them. When a temperature difference does exist, heat will tend to move from the *higher*-temperature system to the *lower*-temperature system until they are at thermal equilibrium (see also Box 3.1). This heat transfer may occur via conduction, convection or radiation, or combinations of them.

Heat transfer (Q) is directly proportional to temperature, the inverse of the heat resistance and surface area:

$$Q = A(T_1 - T_2)/R \ [W] \qquad [3.8]$$

where:

- A = surface area in m^2;
- R = heat resistance in K m^2/W or °C m^2/W;
- T = temperature in K or °C.

Conduction

The heat transfer coefficient of a material determines how fast heat (energy) can be transferred through the material. The heat transfer coefficient (U) for a particular material is defined as:

$$U = d/R \ [W/m°C] \qquad [3.9]$$

Box 3.1 Conservation of energy

In 1847, James Prescott Joule outlined the law of the conservation of energy in the form of heat as well as mechanical energy. However, the principle of conservation of energy had been suggested in various forms by perhaps a dozen German, French, British and other scientists during the first half of the 19th century. About the same time, entropy and the second law of thermodynamics were first clearly described in the work of Rudolf Clausius. In 1875, Ludwig Boltzmann made the important connection between the number of possible states that a system could occupy and its entropy, and Josiah Willard Gibbs developed much of the theoretical formalism for thermodynamics. In 1900, Max Planck published his explanation of blackbody radiation, and formed the base for quantum mechanics.

Thermodynamics is the study of states of matter at (or near) thermal equilibrium. The three laws of thermodynamics are:

1   Energy conservation principle: for all changes in an isolated system, energy remains constant.
2   Heat will not flow from a place of a higher temperature to one where it is lower without intervention of an external device.
3   The entropy at the absolute zero of temperature is zero, corresponding to the most ordered possible state.

Source: Encyclopaedia Britannica (1991c)

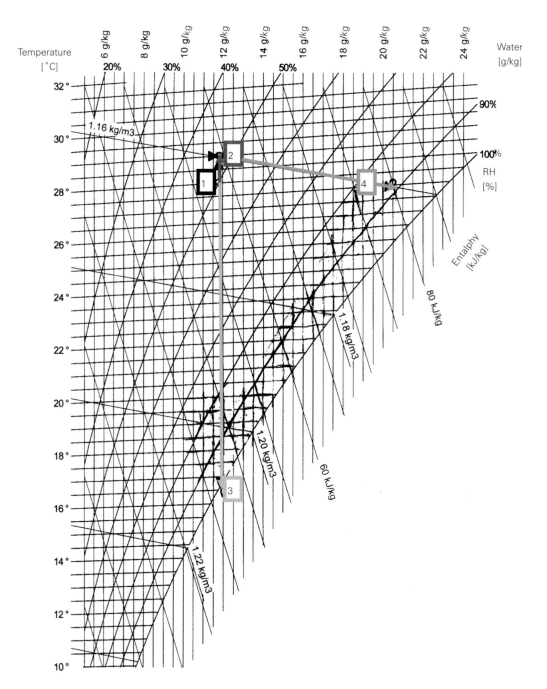

Notes: 1–2: temperature of air increases with the same amount of water vapour, resulting in a lower RH.

2–3: cooling down of air with constant absolute amount of water vapour until condensation takes place (100 per cent RH).

2–4: cooling down of air with constant density of humid air, thus adding water vapour (humidification) and increasing the RH.

Source: adapted from Lammers (1982)

Figure 3.3 *Mollier diagram for humid air with an atmospheric pressure of 1.013 bar*

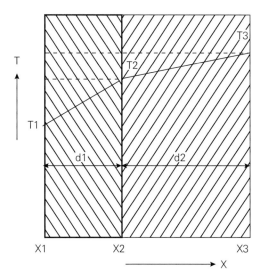

Source: Lammers (1982)

Figure 3.4 *Conduction through two layers*

Table 3.1 *Heat transfer coefficients for different materials with different temperatures*

Material	T (°C)	U (W/m °C)
Copper	20	415
	100	410
Aluminium	20	228
	100	228
Steel (different types)	20	17–59
	100	17–58
Water	0	0.57
	20	0.60
	100	0.68
Air	0	0.024
	20	0.026
	100	0.031
Glass	10	0.5–1.0
Concrete	10	0.7–1.3
Brick	10	0.7–5.0
Wood	10	0.1–0.3
Cork	10	0.5

Source: Lammers (1982)

where:

- d = thickness of material [m];
- R = heat resistance [°C m²/W].

Heat transfer is represented by:

$$q_t = AU(T_1 - T_2)/d \ [W]. \qquad [3.10]$$

For a number of layers (in serial order) with different transfer coefficients, heat transfer becomes (see Figure 3.4):

$$q_t = A(T_3 - T_1)/Rtot \ [W] \qquad [3.11]$$

where $Rtot = R_1 + R_2 = d_1/U_1 + d_2/U_2$.

Note that these equations are only valid when a stationary condition can be applied (i.e. the temperatures on both sides and in the material are constant). In practice, this hardly occurs due to changes in outdoor temperature and incoming solar radiation, amongst other factors. Table 3.1 presents heat conduction coefficients for different materials and temperatures.

Convection

Convection is the heat transfer of a solid medium to a flowing medium, and vice versa. In the indoor environment, this flowing medium is air. Again, heat transfer only occurs when there is a difference in temperature. When there is no imposed air movement and the warm air moves solely as a result of buoyancy, this is called natural or free convection. If the air is blown away, it is called forced convection. The area of the air where the temperature changes the most is called the thermal boundary layer (see Figure 3.5).

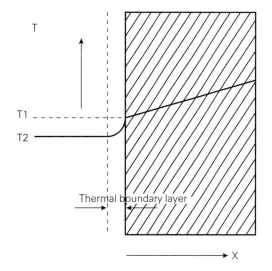

Source: adapted from Lammers (1982)

Figure 3.5 *Heat transfer by convection via a boundary layer*

The heat transfer by convection can be described by the following equation:

$$q_c = Ah_c(T_1 - T_2) \ [W] \qquad [3.12]$$

where:

- A = surface area in contact between solid and air (m^2);
- h_c = heat transfer coefficient for convection (W/m^2K).

The heat transfer coefficient for convection is influenced by several parameters:

- the flowing medium (air in the indoor environment);
- forced or natural convection (in the indoor environment, it is mostly a combination);
- the manner in which the flow is taking place: it is laminar (flow has the same direction at each location) or turbulent (spinning of air occurs); in general, with the same mean air velocity, h_c is smaller for a laminar flow than for a turbulent flow – the flow encountered in the indoor environment is mostly turbulent.

Because h_c is difficult to determine in practice, the heat transfer via convection is difficult to determine.

Radiation

All bodies above a temperature of absolute zero emit thermal radiation, which is produced by the vibration of the molecules of the emitting substance. Bodies that emit radiation also adsorb it. All physical bodies, with the exception of perfect reflectors, are therefore involved in an exchange of radiant energy with their surroundings. This results in a net flow from hotter to cooler bodies (McIntyre, 1980).

The Stefan Boltzmann equation states that the heat transfer is a function of temperature, and defines the radiant energy of a surface area as (see also Figure 3.6):

$$q_r = A\varepsilon\sigma T_s^4 \ [W] \qquad [3.13]$$

where:

- A = surface area (m^2);
- ε = emission coefficient;
- σ = the Stefan Boltzmann constant (= 5.67×10^{-8} W/m^2K^4);
- T_s = absolute surface temperature in Kelvin.

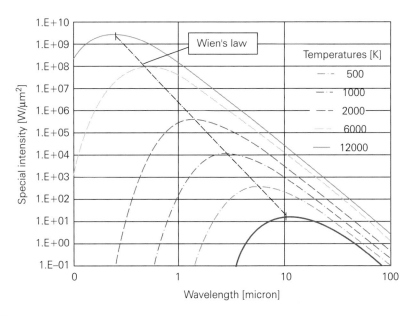

Source: C. A. Roulet (pers comm)

Figure 3.6 *Graphical presentation of the Stefan Bolzman equation: The Law of Wien, presented in Figure 3.7, is shown here as well*

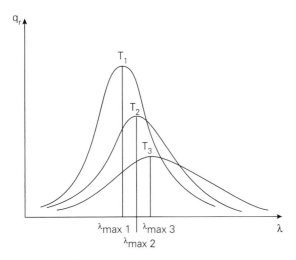

Source: adapted from Lammers (1982)

Figure 3.7 *Graphic presentation of the Law of Wien*

A black body is a perfect emitter of radiation, as well as a perfect absorber and therefore has an emission coefficient of 1. The emission coefficient of a material depends upon the wavelength. Most materials in the indoor environment behave as grey emitters, which have an emission coefficient of between 0.85 and 1. Polished metals such as polished aluminium and copper have an emission coefficient of around 0.1.

The radiation emitted changes in character (wavelength) and quantity with increasing temperature of the body; this is described by the Law of Wien:

$$\lambda_{max} \times T = 2.9 \times 10^{-3} \text{ [mK]} \qquad [3.14]$$

where:

- λ_{max} = wavelength at which maximum amount of energy is emitted (m);
- T = temperature of surface area (K).

The total amount of radiant energy emitted is the sum of all energy emitted per wavelength (see Figure 3.7).

Evaporation and condensation

With evaporation of water, the water molecules will escape from the water into the air as a result of a temperature increase. The water molecules increase their velocity; therefore, the adhesion powers between

the water molecules decrease. For evaporation of water, energy (heat) is therefore required, which is partly taken from the air passing along the surface at which the evaporation takes place. When the heat transfer coefficient for convection (h_c) increases, more heat can be transferred and, thus, more water can be evaporated. Evaporation of water from a surface area (via convection) can be described by:

$$\Phi_{water} = A\kappa(\rho_{w,w} - \rho_{w,o}) \text{ [kg/s]} \qquad [3.15]$$

where:

- Φ_{water} = amount of water evaporated (kg/s);
- $\rho_{w,w}$ = density of water vapour at the surface (kg/m³);
- $\rho_{w,o}$ = density of water vapour in the surrounding air (kg/m³);
- κ = transport coefficient = $1.1 h_c / \rho\, c_p$ (m/s);
- ρ = density of surrounding air (kg/m³);
- C_p = specific heat for air (J/kgK).

With condensation, there are more water molecules in the air than can be contained (saturated); therefore, they want to escape. This usually occurs when the temperature of the air is decreasing below the point at which air is saturated (100% relative humidity). Condensation of water on a surface area can be described by:

$$\Phi_{water} = A\beta(\rho_{w,o} - \rho_{w,w}) \text{ [kg/s]} \qquad [3.16]$$

where β = transfer coefficient (m/s).

3.2.3 Energy balance of a person

Fanger (1982) defined the total energy balance of a person as follows:

$$\begin{aligned} &\text{heat production = heat dissipation} \\ &M - W - q_d - q_{sw} - q_{re} - q_l = q_t \\ &\qquad\qquad = q_c + q_r \text{ [W]} \end{aligned} \qquad [3.17]$$

where:

- M = metabolic rate of human body (W);
- W = external mechanical power (W);
- q_t = heat transfer via conduction through clothing (W);

- q_c = heat transfer via convection from a clothed body (W);
- q_r = heat transfer via radiation from a clothed body (W);
- q_d = heat loss by water vapour diffusion through skin (W);
- q_{sw} = heat loss by sweat evaporation (W);
- q_{re} = heat loss by latent respiration (W);
- q_l = heat loss by dry respiration (W).

At normal indoor conditions, a person loses roughly equal quantities of heat by convection to the air and by radiation to the surrounding surfaces. The loss of heat by radiation becomes noticeable when sitting near a cold window, and is felt as a 'radiation draught'. But heat discomfort also depends upon the humidity of the skin (sweat production) and the evaporation of that water, which is related to the saturation rate of the surrounding air (the relative humidity). Air velocity is an important parameter in determining turbulence intensity: a measure of draught. Furthermore, a person also loses heat through breathing and diffusion through the skin.

For a person in the indoor environment, direct heat transfer from skin to the indoor environment plays a minor role, except when walking on bare feet. On the other hand, heat transfer from the skin to the outer surface of the clothed body (conduction through the clothing) forms the available heat that can be transferred to the environment via convection and radiation.

Heat conduction through clothing can be expressed by:

$$q_t = A(T_s - T_{cl})/0.155I_{clo} \text{ [W]} \qquad [3.18]$$

where:

T_s = temperature of skin (°C);
T_{clo} = temperature of clothing (°C);
I_{clo} = thermal resistance from the skin to the outer surface of the clothed body (clo).

The heat transfer of a person via convection (which is, for a normal dressed man in rest, at around 120W) can be described by:

$$q_c = A_c h_c(T_m - T_a) \text{ [W]} \qquad [3.19]$$

where:

- A_c = mean body surface area in standing position in m^2 (for a man this is $1.8m^2$ and for a women $1.65m^2$; for a sitting person, 75 per cent is taken);

- T_m = mean temperature of body surface (clothed and unclothed areas) (°C);
- T_a = air temperature in the space (°C);
- $h_c = 2.38(T_m - T_a)^{0.25}$ for $2.38(T_m - T_a)^{0.25} > 12.1\sqrt{v}$ and $12.1\sqrt{v}$ for $2.38(T_m - T_a)^{0.25} \leq 12.1\sqrt{v}$ (with v = air velocity in cm/s).

The exchange of radiant energy between surfaces in the indoor environment is of great significance to the thermal comfort of a person present. The heat transfer of an individual by radiation can be described by:

$$q_r = A_{eff} \varepsilon\sigma(T_m^{\ 4} - T_{mrt}^{\ 4}) \text{ [W]} \qquad [3.20]$$

where:

- A_{eff} = the effective body surface area = f x surface area of body (f depends upon position and on type of clothing) (m^2);
- T_m = mean temperature of body surface (clothed and unclothed areas) (°C);
- T_{mrt} = mean radiant temperature (°C).

The emission coefficient of skin is approximately 1 and of clothing 0.95 to 0.97, which makes 0.97 a good approximation.

Besides heat transfer via convection and radiation, the human body also loses energy via the skin and via breathing.

Heat loss via skin diffusion is not subject to thermoregulatory control. The magnitude is proportional to the difference between the saturated water vapour pressure at the skin temperature (p_s) and the partial pressure of water vapour in the ambient air (p_a):

$$q_d = C_{ev}kA(p_s - p_a) \text{ [W]} \qquad [3.21]$$

where:

- C_{ev} = heat of evaporation of water (J/kg);
- k = permeability of the skin (s/m);
- p_a = partial pressure of water vapour in the ambient air (kg/ms^2);
- p_s = saturated water vapour pressure at skin temperature (kg/ms^2).

Heat loss by evaporation of sweat can be described by:

$$q_{sw} = 0.42A(-58+(1 - \eta)(M/A)) \qquad [3.22]$$

where η = mechanical efficiency = W/M.

The breathing in and out of air is mainly related to the metabolic rate of the human body. Heat loss via breathing in and out can be divided into two parts: the latent respiration and the dry respiration heat loss. Latent respiration heat loss is a function of the amount of air breathed in and out and the difference in water content between expired and inspired air:

$$q_{re} = \Phi_{air}(H_{ex} - H_{in})c_{ev} \ [W] \qquad [3.23]$$

where:

- Φ_{air} = amount of air breathed in and out (kg/s);
- H_{ex} = humidity ratio of expired air (kg water/kg dry air);
- H_{in} = humidity ratio of breathed in air (kg water/kg dry air).

The dry respiration heat loss is:

$$q_l = \Phi_{air}c_p(T_{ex} - T_{in}) \ [W] \qquad [3.24]$$

where:

- c_p = specific heat of dry air at constant pressure (J/kg°C);
- T_{ez} = temperature of air breathed out (°C);
- T_{in} = temperature of air breathed in (°C).

3.2.4 Measurement

Methods and instruments for measuring the physical quantities of temperature (air, radiant, operative and surface), air velocity and absolute humidity are well described in the international standard ISO 7726 (ISO, 1998).

3.2.5 Control strategies

As mentioned in section 3.2.1, thermal comfort can be influenced by many factors: factors related to the indoor environment (air and radiant temperatures, relative humidity, air velocity and turbulence) and factors related to the individual of concern (clothing and activity). Heating, cooling and air conditioning (including mechanical but also natural and/or hybrid ventilation means; see section 3.4.4) of the indoor environment to which the individual is exposed is one

way of controlling thermal comfort; another way is the control of heat loss from the human body through clothing and activity intensity.

Heating, cooling and air conditioning

With respect to heating, cooling and air conditioning, there are several options available. Heating can be provided through convection, conduction, radiation and air systems (e.g. a central heating, ventilation and air-conditioning [HVAC] system in Figure 3.8). Regulation of relative humidity can be provided through (de)humidification systems via an air-conditioning system or locally.

In these systems, a medium (air or water) is transported from one place to another via ducts and pipes. For a moving medium, which is incompressible and moves without any resistance, the following equation can be applied (Law of Bernoulli):

$$p + 1/2\rho v^2 + \rho gz = \text{constant} \qquad [3.25]$$

where:

- p = static pressure (N/m²);
- ρ = density of moving medium (kg/m³);
- v = velocity of moving medium (m/s);
- g = gravitational acceleration (m/s²);
- z = height of gravity field (m).

Source: Bluyssen (2004b)

Figure 3.8 *An example of a heating, ventilating and air-conditioning (HVAC) system with an air filter in the inlet and outlet, a heating coil and a heat exchanger*

For horizontal moving media the formula, then, is:

$$p + 1/2\rho v^2 = \text{constant.} \qquad [3.26]$$

If this medium flows through a tube or duct, a pressure loss occurs as a result of:

- the resistance of the tube walls; but also
- the pressure loss caused by internal friction of the medium because of its movement.

The latter is characterized by the dynamic viscosity η. The larger this viscosity, the more difficult it is for the medium to move. Water has a viscosity of 1.01×10^{-3} and air 18.0×10^{-6}.

A laminar or Poiseuille flow is a flow in which all molecules are moving in the same direction, even though they have different velocities. In ducts or pipes, the flow is, however, never laminar: it is always turbulent. In a turbulent flow, molecules go, on average, in the same direction, but with different individual velocities and directions. Figure 3.9 provides velocity profiles for both types of flows.

For a flow through a tube or duct, the pressure loss can be defined as:

$$p_1 - p_2 = \gamma l/d(1/2\ \rho v^2)\ [\text{N/m}^2] \qquad [3.27]$$

where:

γ = resistance coefficient;
l = length of tube or duct (m);
d = diameter of tube or duct (m).

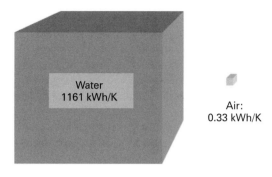

Source: Bluyssen (2004b)

Figure 3.10 *Comparison of heat transported by 1m³ of air and water*

The resistance coefficient depends upon the air velocity, temperature and the smoothness of the inner duct surface. For each narrowing, widening or corner of the duct, a pressure loss will occur due to internal spinning of the medium as a reaction to the changes in direction. These losses of pressure can all be expressed by the factor $1/2\ \rho v^2$, called the speed pressure, multiplied by some factor.

Comparing the media of air and water, water is a much more energy-efficient medium to transport heat. One cubic metre of air can only transport 0.33kWh/K, while 1 cubic metre of water can transport 1161kWh/K (see Figure 3.10). Furthermore, water can be hot when entering the radiator and cold when leaving it, while air cannot be hot when entering the room. Therefore, the temperature fall can be at least 50K for water and no more than 20K for air, and for heating, water can transport 60,000kWh/m³, while air only about 7kWh/m³. When cooling, the situation is a bit better for water since cold ceilings cannot be cooled down below the dew point. For this reason, the temperature rise cannot be more than 10K for both water and air. In this case, water is only 3500 times more efficient than air.

Energy use

The use of energy by a HVAC system depends upon:

- airflow rate;
- total resistance of the system;
- temperature and relative humidity (RH) settings;
- energy savings of a heat recovery system (if applied);

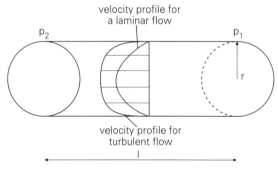

Source: adapted from Lammers (1982)

Figure 3.9 *Velocity profiles in a duct of both a laminar and a turbulent flow*

Box 3.2 Recirculation and heat recovery

At constant indoor air quality, recirculation just increases the required airflow rate, thus increasing the energy required for moving the air. Therefore, recirculation is not actually a good way to save energy: at normal hygienic airflow rate, recirculation does not save energy. It merely avoids wasting heat and pollutes the supply air with return air. Exfiltration and internal recirculation reduce the global efficiency of the system. External recirculation also reduces the global efficiency, but to a smaller degree. The real heat recovery efficiency of well-insulated systems in airtight buildings can be as high as 85 per cent of the efficiency of the heat recovery system itself. This is about 75 per cent in the best-case scenario. On the other hand, global efficiency may be zero if the system is not well designed and installed in a leaky building.

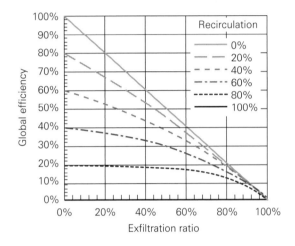

Source: Bluyssen (2004b)

Figure 3.11 *Reduction of heat recovery efficiency when exfiltration or recirculation is implemented: The exfiltration ratio is the percentage of the ventilated air that is removed via recirculation*

- recirculation (if applied; not recommended);
- operation strategy expressed in hours of running time;
- fan efficiency (total fan efficiency of fans, motors and frequency converters).

The energy performance of a building can be expressed as an energy index, defined as:

$$I_t = E/A_r = [MJ/m^2] \qquad [3.28]$$

where:

- I_t = total energy index, comprised of the energy indices of the different fuels used (MJ/m²);
- E = yearly energy use (MJ)
- A_r = gross heated floor areas, including walls (i.e. measured with the external dimensions of the building), but excluding unheated zones such as garages, cellars or unoccupied attics (m²).

3.3 Lighting parameters

3.3.1 Parameters and definitions

Light has two characteristics of particular interest: it is a form of energy that is always moving (if it stops moving, it is no longer light), and light transports information concerning the source of light and objects that it encounters on the way from one place to the other. So light is the means by which the interior is perceived. Light is an electromagnetic radiation that can be seen by the human eye, unlike other forms of radiation, and has a wavelength of between 380nm and 760nm (see Plate 1, centre pages).

Box 3.3 The origin of optics

Optics has its origin in Greece, especially in the works of Euclid (circa 300 BC), who stated many of the results in geometric optics that the Greeks discovered, including the Law of Reflection. During the 17th century, Kepler introduced the point-by-point analysis of optical problems; Descartes explained the phenomena of light entirely in terms of matter and ratio; Newton demonstrated that light consists of many colours; and Huygens regarded light as a pulse phenomenon. It was not until after 1924 that light was defined both in terms of waves and particles: an electromagnetic radiation with an oscillating electrical field and an oscillating magnetic field, perpendicular to the transport direction of light. The speed of light is in vacuum constant for all wavelengths: approximately 299,792 km/s.

Source: Encyclopaedia Britannica, 1991a

The perception of light is determined by the amount of the radiation energy that enters the eye (illuminance – amplitude) and the spectrum of this (frequencies – colours). Ultraviolet radiation (blue light) with shorter wavelengths and a higher frequency causes photochemical and bactericide reactions, and colours the human skin. Radiation with longer wavelengths, the infrared, is felt as heat.

The spectrum obtained by refracting light through a prism shows a number of characteristic regions of colour – red, orange, yellow, green, blue, indigo and violet (see Plate 1, centre pages). These regions represent large numbers of individual wavelengths; thus, the red extends roughly from 650nm to 780 nm; the orange

from 585nm to 650nm; the yellow from 575nm to 585nm; the green from 490nm to 575nm; the blue from 420nm to 490nm; and the violet from 380nm to 420nm.

The quality of light in an indoor space is determined by the sources of light present (natural and/or artificial), the distribution of the light in space and the way in which light is perceived (see Figure 3.12).

On the emitting side (the sources of light), we can distinguish the following parameters:

- *The light flux (Φ)*: the rate of the emission from a source expressed in lumen (or 1/680W, emitted with a wavelength of 555nm). A 100W light bulb

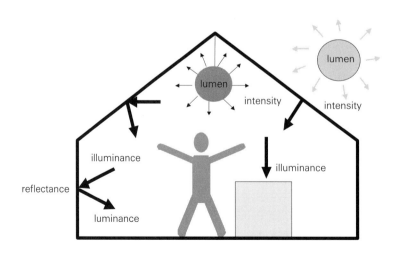

Source: Bluyssen

Figure 3.12 *Light parameters in an indoor space*

emits about 1200 lumens. This is valid only for light sources that emit in all directions homogeneously.

- *The intensity (I)*: the amount of light flux (lumens) being emitted by the source within a given cone (solid angle), expressed in lumen/steradian or candela (a wax candle has an intensity of approximately 1 candela). This unit is, in particular, defined for lamps not emitting homogeneously in all directions. In a sphere with a radius of 1m, a steradian (star) is the angle that is enclosed by a radius along a surface area of $1m^2$. Since the total surface area is equal to $4\pi r^2$, there are 4π steradians around a point (see Figure 3.13).
- *The frequencies of light (colour) emitted*: this is described by colour temperature and the colour index.

For the distribution of light in space, the following parameters apply:

- *The lighting level (E)*: the amount of light spread over the area receiving the light, also called illuminance, is expressed in lumen/m^2 or lux.
- *The reflectance (R)*: the reflection factor is the ability of a surface to reflect. A white surface has a reflectance of nearly 100 per cent, a black surface of about 2 per cent, and a medium grey surface of about 40 per cent.

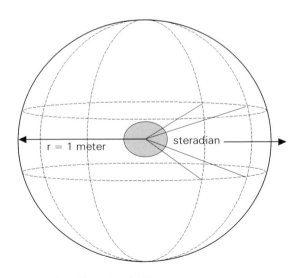

Source: adapted from Visser (1992)

Figure 3.13 *Intensity of the emitted light flux per unit of space angle (steradian)*

- *Luminance (L) distribution*: such as luminance ratios, the angle of the incidence of light, and the homogeneity of the illuminance and contrast (the ratio between luminance of the task and the luminance of the background) (NEN, 1997).

For the perception of light, besides the perceiver (see section 2.3 in Chapter 2), the parameters of importance are:

- the perceived light colour (colour impression) determined by the spectrum of the light falling on the object which is looked upon and the wavelength (frequency) dependency of the reflection factor of the object;
- view and daylight openings (see section 3.3.6 and section 5.1.2 in Chapter 5).

3.3.2 Mechanisms

For the impression of light, mechanisms with respect to level, colour and differences are important.

Level

The illuminance E at a point varies directly with the intensity I of the source and, inversely, as the square of the distance d between the source and the point (see Figure 3.14). If the surface at the point is normal to the direction of the incident light:

$$E = I/d^2 \text{ [lux]}. \qquad [3.29]$$

The required lighting level for a certain task depends upon the receiver performing the task, but also upon the visual task to be performed. The smallest noticeable subjective effect of a difference in lighting level is reached by changing the level with approximately a factor of 1.5. Under normal conditions, one need circa 20 lux to notice the features of the face; therefore this is chosen as the lowest on the recommended scale of lighting levels in lux (CEN, 2002): 20 – 30 – 50 – 75 – 100 – 150 – 200 – 300 – 500 – 750 – 1000 – 1500 – 2000 – 3000 – 5000.

In spaces where people are continuously present, a minimum level of 200 lux is recommended.

If the surface diffuses light equally in all directions, the brightness of the surface will be directly related to the illumination falling upon it:

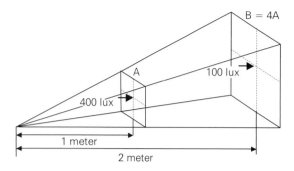

Source: adapted from *Encyclopaedia Britannica* (1991a)

Figure 3.14 *Illuminance E varies with intensity I: If we need an illuminance of 100 lux on a surface normal to the fixture that is at a distant of 2m, the intensity needs to be 400 lumens in the direction of the surface*

luminance L = illuminance E x reflectance. [3.30]

The proportion of light that is actually received on a surface (the coefficient of utilization) is equal to the ratio of light received to the flux emitted by the lamps present.

For completely indirect lighting, this coefficient is 0.15 (hits ceiling first and is then reflected downwards);

for general lighting (emitted in all directions), it is 0.3–0.4; and for direct lighting, it is about 0.6. The reflectance of a diffuse reflecting surface area is defined as:

$$r_d = L\pi/E \qquad [3.31]$$

where L = luminance (lux) and E = illuminance (lux)

Depending upon the direction in which the light falls onto a surface, this light can be completely or partly reflected, and depending upon the surface area reflectance (there may be different ones), light may be diffusely or completely reflected (like a mirror) (see Figure 3.15).

Colour sensation

The history of the specification of colour probably began with Albert H. Munsell, an American painter born in 1858. He was the first to identify three distinct qualities of colour – namely, hue, value and chroma. The equivalents to these words are now hue, lightness and saturation (Baker and Steemers, 2002):

- Hue: the nominal colour; the name that we give to a particular sensation (e.g. red, orange, yellow, green, etc.).

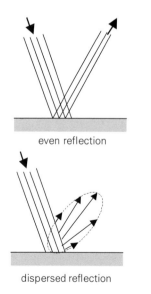

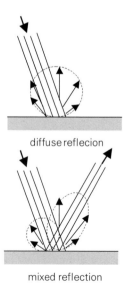

Source: adapted from Visser (1992)

Figure 3.15 *Different forms of reflection*

- Lightness or value: a description of the brightness of a colour on a scale of 0 to 10, from dark to light. This may vary within one colour.
- Saturation or chroma: the measure of the degree of vividness of a colour – from a pure hue, through varying tints of decreasing colour to grey.

A century after Newton had shown that white light contained all the spectral colours, the scientist Young proposed the tristimulus theory of colour perception. This states that any colour sensation can be generated by a combination of three primary light colours. A combination of any two of these results in a secondary colour sensation:

- red + green = yellow;
- green + blue = blue-green or cyan;
- blue + red = magenta.

The resultant colours are described as being complementary to the third colour (i.e. the primary colour not present in the combination):

- yellow is complementary to blue;
- cyan is complementary to red;
- magenta is complementary to green.

Complementary means that the two colours together provide the sensation of white light (see Plate 2, centre pages). Grassman's Laws go a step further (see Box 3.4).

It should be noted that the colours discussed are not the same colours used to paint; it is about the addition of coloured light, not pigments or dyes.

Colour impression

Colour impression can be characterized by colour temperature and the colour index. The *colour*

Box 3.4 Grassman's Laws of additive colour mixture

Any colour (source C) can be matched by a linear combination of three other colours – primaries (e.g. R (red), G (green), B (blue) – provided that none of these three can be matched by a combination of the other two. This is fundamental to colorimetry and is Grassman's first law of colour mixture. Therefore, a colour C can be matched by Rc units of red, Gc units of green and Bc units of blue. The units can be measured in any form that quantifies light power:

$$C = Rc(R) + Gc(G) + Bc(B).$$

A mixture of any two colours (sources C1 and C2) can be matched by linearly adding together the mixtures of any three other colours that individually match the two source colours. This is Grassman's second law of colour mixture. It can be extended to any number of source colours:

$$C3(C3) = C1(C1) + C2(C2) = [R1+R2](R)$$
$$+ [G1+G2](G) + [B1+B2](B).$$

Colour matching persists at all luminances. This is Grassman's third law. It fails at very low light levels where rod cell vision (scoptopic) takes over from cone cell vision (photopic):

$$kC3(C3) = kC1(C1) + kC2(C2).$$

The symbols in square brackets are the names of the colours, and not numerical values. The equality sign should not be used to signify an identity; in colorimetry it means a colour matching: the colour on one side of the equality looks the same as the colour on the other side.

These laws govern all aspects of additive colour work, but they apply only to signals in the 'linear-light' domain.

Source: Boer and Rutten (1974)

temperature is the absolute temperature of a black body (a reference light source), which emits light of which the spectrum depends upon the temperature (in Kelvin), with the same colour as the light source of concern. Only for temperature radiators, such as candles, incandescent lamps (light bulbs), halogen lamps and the sun, is a colour temperature relevant because these radiators have a continuous spectrum (just as a black body has). This means that all colours of the spectrum are presented and therefore it is possible for people to see all present colours in the indoor environment (Visser, 1992).

The spectrum of discharge lamps, such as fluorescent lamps, high-pressure mercury lamps and high- and low-pressure sodium lamps, is completely different. Because of the discharge, those lamps only show one or few colours of the visible spectrum: this is called a discontinuous or line spectrum. The added colour temperature is the temperature of the black body radiator that comes closest to the light colour of the non-temperature radiators such as fluorescent (discharge) lamps.

From 5000K to 7000K, the light colour is named cool white; from 3300K to 5000K, it is called white; and from 0K to 3300K it is called warm white. Paradoxically, colours that are often described as warm have, in fact, a lower colour temperature.

When two objects with the same colour seem to show a different colour under different light sources, metamism occurs. This is important, for example, when selecting objects during the day with daylight when the objects are to be used at night with artificial light. This is caused by the frequencies present in the light that is reflected (or not) by the object (selective reflectance). Good colour rendering may also help.

The *colour rendering index* R_a presents how much the colour impression of a series of test colours (normally 8, sometimes 14) emitted by the light source is similar to a temperature radiator with the same colour temperature. For each colour the difference is subtracted from 100 (100 means no deviation), resulting in R_i. The mean of the 8 or 14 R_is is the R_a. A colour index of 90 to 100 is good, between 80 and 90 is ok, between 50 and 80 is mediocre, and lower than 50 is bad. Using a lamp with an R_a lower than 80 is not advised.

Table 3.2 *Examples of colour temperatures and light sources*

Light source	Colour temperature
Candle	± 1700K
Light bulb	± 2750K
Halogen lamp	± 3000K
Fluorescent lamps	2750–7000K
Light from blue sky	Up to 26,000K

Source: (Visser, 1992; Boer and Rutten, 1974)

The structure of coloured objects also has an effect on colour impression. The colour of matt surfaces is almost always visible, but is less intensive due to the partial scattering of the light. A shiny smooth surface can increase the intensity of the colour, depending upon the direction of the light, or just mirror the light source. And when a matt surface is polished or varnished, the colour can achieve more 'body'.

Colour selection of a lamp depends upon many things: it is a matter of psychology, aesthetics, lighting level, and colours of the space, furniture, thermal climate, application, etc.

Differences

Significant differences include contrast and luminance ratios.

Contrast

There of two types of contrast: spatial contrast and temporal contrast (NEN, 1997). Temporal contrast is the change in luminance or colour over time of the same area. Sensitivity to temporal contrast depends upon the frequency (speed of change over time). Unintended temporal contrast (flickering) can be very annoying. Spatial contrast is the luminance or colour difference between areas that are simultaneously present in the vision field. Sensitivity to spatial contrast is determined by the speed of change with location: the spatial frequency. Maximum sensitivity lies between five and ten periods per degree (see Figure 3.16). With higher or lower spatial frequencies, a larger contrast is required.

The ability to distinguish between colours is related to the intensity of light: with small differences, a higher

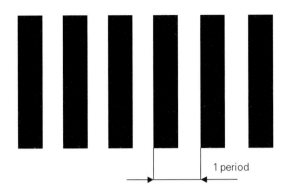

Figure 3.16 *Example of spatial contrast*

light level is required. The ability to see details (e.g. letters) can be increased by increasing the dimensions (bigger letter) or decreasing the distance to the object with the detail. Spatial contrast should have a ratio of approximately 1:5 to 1:10 (letters on background) for optimal reading.

Sharpness of sight is a measure of the ability to distinguish details (see Figure 3.17). It is expressed in the reciprocal of the number of minutes of arch:

$$\text{sharpness of sight} = 1/\text{minutes of arch.} \qquad [3.32]$$

A sharpness of sight of 1 means that a detail of 1mm on an object at a distance of 3400mm or more can be

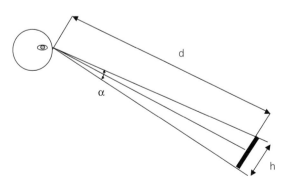

Figure 3.17 *Angle of view (α), distance (d) and letter height (h)*

distinguished. A sharpness of sight of 0.5 means that a detail of 1mm at a distance of circa 1700mm can be distinguished. Ninety-five per cent of the population are able to recognize a letter with a height of circa 1/350 of the view distance. This is equal to a sharpness of sight of 0.5. Seventy per cent have a sharpness of sight of 1 (able to recognize a letter with a height of circa 1/700 of the view distance).

Luminance ratios

Luminance ratios are necessary to perform a visual task, but can cause discomfort if they are too large. Recommended luminance ratios for a critical view and, frequently, changes of view are:

- for a visual task and the direct environment (a view angle of circa 20°), not higher than 3;
- for a visual task and the rest of the environment (periphery), not more than 10.

In general, ratios of 1:20 for direct and 1:30 for periphery are acceptable.

Blinding or visual discomfort can occur when the viewed object has a lower luminance in the centre compared to the background. For example, when a person stands with their back to a window, it is hard to see the face of the person. With very high luminances, absolute blinding can occur: the retina is on its border of adaptation capacity (see section 2.3.2 in Chapter 2).

Blinding caused by a lighting system can be calculated with the following equation (CEN, 2002):

$$\text{unified glare rating (UGR)} = 8\log_{10}(0.25/L_b \Sigma L^2 \omega/p^2) \qquad [3.33]$$

where:

- L_b = the luminance of the background in cd/m², calculated according to $L_b = E_{ind}\pi$, with E_{ind} equal to the indirect vertical lighting level at the eye of the receiver;
- L = the luminance of the lighting parts of each lighting system in the direction of the eye of the receiver in cd/m²;
- ω = angle (steradian) of the lighting parts of each light system, viewed from the eye of the receiver;

- p = the Guth position index for each individual lighting system, which is determined by the position of the lighting system towards the view direction.

3.3.3 Sources of light

A lighting source has two different effects: on the one side it lightens the objects that we want to see and, on the other side, it shines directly in our eyes. Lighting in spaces consists of two sources: daylight and artificial light.

Daylight

Daylight is a combination of direct sunlight and atmospheric light (dispersion of sun radiation by dust and water) with indirect and reflected components. Sunlight has a broad spectrum with a peak in the blue-green and a cut-off in the ultra-violet, with a wavelength of 290nm, caused by the atmosphere of the Earth, which works as a filter. Shorter wavelengths are intercepted by the atmosphere, the ozone layer playing an important role in this.

Daylight falling on a desk in a space comprises three components:

1 direct sunlight from the sky – the sky component (SC) normally refers to diffuse sky (i.e. it is not used to describe direct sunlight);
2 light that comes from external surfaces, such as buildings: the externally reflected component (ERC), particularly relevant in dense urban situations, tends to come from a low angle close to horizontal and will penetrate deeper into the space than the SC, although it is much weaker;
3 light that is reflected from internal surfaces: the internally reflected component (IRC) is normally fairly uniform all over the room.

Artificial light

Several sources of artificial light are available (see Table 3.3). They can be divided into temperature radiators, such as combustion-based and incandescent lamps, and non-temperature radiators. This last group can be divided into the arc or discharge lamps and electroluminescent (EL) lamps.

Incandescence is the release of thermal radiation from a body due to its temperature. It occurs in light bulbs because the filament resists the flow of electrons. This resistance heats the filament to a temperature where part of the black body radiation falls in the visible spectrum. The majority of radiation, however, is emitted in the invisible infrared and lower frequency spectrums, which is why incandescent light bulbs are very inefficient.

An arc lamp is the general term for a class of lamps that produce light by an electric arc (or voltaic arc). The lamp consists of two electrodes typically made of tungsten, which are separated by a gas, which is initially ionized by a voltage and is therefore electrically conductive. To start an arc lamp, usually a very high voltage is needed to 'ignite' or 'strike' the arc. The type

Table 3.3 *Different types of artificial light systems*

Group	Type	Mechanism
Temperature radiators		
Combustion based	Candles, fire, torches oil lamps, kerosene lamps, etc.	Burning of fuel
Incandescent lamps	Light bulbs, halogen light bulbs	Incandescence
Non-temperature radiators		
Arc or gas discharge lamps		Electric arc
• Low pressure	Fluorescent lamps, compact fluorescent lamps, neon and argon lamps, sodium lamps	Luminescence (e.g. fluorescence)
• High pressure	Sodium vapour lamps, mercury-vapour lamps	
Electroluminescent (EL) lamps	Light-emitting diodes (LEDS)/semiconductors	Electroluminescence

Source: (Visser, 1992; Boer and Rutten, 1974)

of lamp is often named by the gas contained in the bulb, including neon, argon, xenon, krypton, sodium, metal halide and mercury. The common fluorescent lamp is actually a low-pressure mercury arc lamp where the inside of the bulb is coated with a light-emitting phosphor. It relies on fluorescence (a form of luminescence, which occurs at low temperatures and is thus a form of cold body radiation). Inside the glass tube is a partial vacuum and a small amount of mercury. An electric discharge in the tube causes the mercury atoms to emit light. The emitted light is in the ultraviolet (UV) range and is invisible and harmful to living organisms, so the tube is lined with a coating of a fluorescent material, called the *phosphor*, which absorbs the ultraviolet and re-emits visible light.

The spectral distribution of a tube, or the distribution of the radiated (relative) energy over the wavelength of the electromagnetic spectrum, determines the lighting colour and colour performance, and depends upon the applied fluorescence powders. For different applications, different colour types are available: the colour caries from 'warm white' (more long-wave, yellow light), via 'fresh white' (neutral) to 'cool white' (more short-waved blue light). A tube contains more radiation in the near UV and the blue, and less red and infrared, than a light bulb. Compared to daylight, a tube contains less (near) UV as well as less (infra) red.

High-pressure discharge lamps operate at a higher current than the fluorescent lamp, and come in many varieties depending upon the fill material.

Electroluminescence (EL) is an optical and electrical phenomenon in which a material emits light in response to an electric current passed through it, or to a strong electric field. This is distinct from light emission resulting from heat (incandescence) or from the action of chemicals (chemo-luminescence). Electroluminescence is the result of radiative recombination of electrons and holes in a material (usually a semiconductor). Unlike neon and fluorescent lamps, EL lamps are not negative resistance devices, so no extra circuitry is needed to regulate the amount of current flowing through them. An EL layer can be very thin (around 1mm thick) and have low power consumption.

Blue-, red- and green-emitting thin-film electroluminescent materials have been developed that offer the potential for long-life and full-colour electroluminescent displays. The commonly used greenish colour closely matches the peak sensitivity of

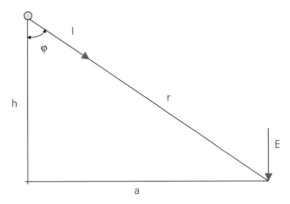

Source: adapted from Visser (1992)

Figure 3.18 *Direct luminance from a light source on a particular location at a distance r*

human vision, producing the greatest apparent light output for the least electrical power input.

Estimate of lighting level

To estimate the direct lighting level (illuminance) from a light source with an intensity I on a particular location at a distance r (see Figure 3.18), the following equation can be applied (Visser, 1992):

$$E = I \cos\varphi \; a/r^2 = I \; a/r^3 \; [\text{Lumen/m}^2] \qquad [3.34]$$

For a space with more light sources (equally distributed), the mean illuminance is estimated by:

$$E = n \; \Phi \; \eta/(l \times b) \; [\text{Lumen/m}^2] \qquad [3.35]$$

where:

- n = number of light sources;
- Φ = light flux of all light sources (lumen);
- η = output (efficiency) of light source;
- l = length of space (m);
- b = width of space (m).

3.3.4 Sources of non-visible electromagnetic radiation

Sources of non-visible electromagnetic radiation are sources that emit waves with either very low to extreme low frequencies, such as radio waves, microwaves and the electromagnetic field caused by electrical power transmission lines, or very high to extreme high frequencies, such as x-ray and gamma radiation. For the latter, the damage that it can cause is known; but for the first types of sources some doubt exists, and concern varies amongst the public. Non-visible electromagnetic radiation can be divided into electric magnetic fields at low frequencies and fields at extreme low frequencies (ELFs).

In the low frequency group, frequencies used are: in FM radio, around 100MHz; TV broadcasting, around 300 to 400MHz; and mobile telephones, from 900–1800MHz. To date, no health effects from radiofrequency fields produced by base stations or wireless networks have been shown to occur (WHO, 2006b).

The ELF group is concerned with two types of fields: wherever electric current flows, electric as well as magnetic fields exist (WHO, 2007):

- *ELF electric fields*: exposure to ELF fields in the frequency range from 0kHz to 100 kHz was investigated by a World Health Organization (WHO)-convened task group of scientific experts. They concluded that generally there are no substantive health issues related to ELF electric fields encountered.
- *ELF magnetic fields*: on the other hand, exposure to electrical ELF magnetic fields can have short-term (nerve and muscle stimulation and changes in nerve cell excitability in the central nervous system) and, possibly, long-term effects. ELF magnetic fields were therefore classified as 'possibly carcinogenic to humans' (limited evidence of carcinogenity in humans) (mainly based on childhood leukaemia) and there was less than sufficient evidence for carcinogenity in experimental animals by the International Agency for Research on Cancer (IARC).

3.3.5 Measurement

For the measurement of lighting parameters, the following instruments can be applied (CEN, 2002b):

- *Photometer*: for measuring photometric qualities such as illuminance or irradiance (light intensity). Most photometers are based on a photo-resistor or photodiode. They exhibit a change in electrical

properties when exposed to light, which can be detected with a suitable electronic circuit. A *spectrophotometer* is a photometer that can measure intensity as a function of the colour or, more specifically, the wavelength of light.
- *Colorimeter*: for measuring the absorbance of particular wavelengths of light by a specific solution. Changeable optics filters are used in the colorimeter to select the wavelength of light that the solute absorbs the most in order to maximize accuracy. Colorimeters can be used to provide colour profiles for equipment.
- *Reflectometer*: for measuring the reflectivity or reflectance of reflecting surfaces.

3.3.6 Control strategies

Comfortable light does not cause blinding (of lighting systems or direct sunlight) and glare (of computer screens), but does create a good colour impression and an equal distribution of light. Comfortable light also means controllability, and it is also important to provide healthy light (day–night rhythm). The latter can be provided by offering the right variation on light intensity and colour temperature at the right time (see section 5.1.2 in Chapter 5).

Luminance distribution

Luminance ratios influence visual comfort. Therefore, the following should be prevented:

- a too high luminance, which can cause blinding;
- too high luminance differences, which can cause tiredness because the eyes have to accommodate/ adjust all the time;
- too low luminance differences and too low luminance contrast, which can result in a non-stimulating environment.

The luminance of each surface area is important and is determined by the reflectance and lighting level on the surface. Useful reflectance of indoor surfaces comprises the following (CEN, 2002a):

- ceiling: 0.6 to 0.9;
- walls: 0.3 to 0.8;
- work surfaces: 0.2 to 0.6;
- floor: 0.1 to 0.5.

Reflections of high luminance in the visual task can influence the visibility of the task (see Plate 3, centre pages). This can be prevented by positioning lighting systems and workplaces; by surface area treatments (matt surface area); by limiting the intensity of lighting systems; by lighting systems with large openings for the light; and/or as a result of clear ceilings and clear walls.

The glare and blinding caused by daylight entry can be prevented by solar screens (self-controlled), solar reflecting glazing or division of spaces in such a way that no one looks into the direction of the window.

Light flickering distracts people and can lead to physical complaints such as headaches. Stroboscopic effects influence the perceived movement of circling or moving back and forwards machine parts,which can lead to dangerous situations. Light flickering and stroboscopic effects should be prevented by using direct current for light bulbs or by applying high frequencies (around 30kHz).

Integration of artificial and natural lighting

Although daylight is capable of supplying the lighting needed for a visual task, during the day its level and spectral assembly changes. Windows enable visual contact with the outside world and provide views. However, further away from the window, available daylight also diminishes. In order to guarantee a certain illuminance and to distribute light homogeneously throughout space, artificial lighting is required. Through automatic or manual dimming or intensification of light, it is possible to integrate artificial light with daylight. Clear light sources can cause blinding and therefore prevent the perception of objects. Blinding should be prevented through lighting systems and through solar window blinds (see Plate 4, centre pages).

The colour temperature is significant. Generally, the closer the match to daylight the better; but there are reservations. It is common that sources of high-colour temperature are extremely cold after daylight hours. The reason for this is not clear, but it could be related to our evolved response to the decrease in colour temperature of the setting sun, or our day–night rhythm (Baker and Steemers, 2002).

Daylight entrance admission

Transparent areas in an enclosure play a pivotal role in the human need for visual contact with the outdoors (visual comfort) and daylight, on the one hand, and thermal comfort, on the other. With regards to daylight, the daylight factor is the illuminance indoors, divided by the illuminance at a horizontal surface outdoors in free surroundings with a 'free' sky. The daylight factor is a geometric characteristic of the space and the window and, for a given sky illuminance distribution without direct sunlight, a constant in each point of the space:

$$daylight\ factor = E_i/E_0 \times 100\ [\%] \qquad [3.36]$$

where:

- E_i = illuminance indoors on the horizontal plane (lux);
- E_0 = horizontal illuminance outdoors in free surroundings on the horizontal plane (lux).

To determine the daylight entrance, a method of calculating 'the equivalent daylight surface area' has been developed (NEN, 2001). The total window surface is corrected for obstacles, such as projections outside or a pitch of the window, but also for daylight factor. Measurements have shown that typical daylight factors (DFs) are quite small, as low as 1 per cent. A room with an average DF of 5 per cent would be regarded as brightly lit (Baker and Steemers, 2002).

For thermal comfort, in particular, (one-sided) direct sun radiation may be uncomfortable, even though the air temperature may be pleasant. Furthermore, the issue of energy is inherently involved, particularly in relation to the influx of solar energy and the demand for cooling.

Generally, half of the energy influx through transparent glass surfaces appears as visible light and the other half is infrared radiation invisible to the eye. A comprehensive solution to the issues mentioned above does not exist; but besides traditional sunscreen, materials with selective transparency have been introduced, often known as 'solar-control' glass (Granqvist, 1991; Campagno, 1999). Essentially, their functionality rests on a spectrally selective transmittance of the visible light and increased reflectance of the rest. A step towards adjustable transparency is feasible due to new technology for new thin surface films or foils in multilayered systems, often using electro-chromic (i.e. vary transmittance upon electrical (dis)charging) (Monk et al, 1995) or alternative chromogenic (e.g. thermochromic) principles.

The availability and quality of daylight can be improved by increasing (Baker and Steemers, 2002):

- the size of apertures or making new ones or redistributing them;
- the transmittance of windows by reducing the obstruction due to framing or replacing the glazing material with one of a higher transmittance (typical values for 6mm glass are reflectance: 0.1; absorptance: 0.05; and transmittance: 0.85);
- the externally reflected component by treating nearby external surfaces with high-reflectance finishes;
- the internally reflected component by internal room surfaces with high-reflectance finishes;
- the penetration of light using special elements such as light shelves or prismatic glazing.

The use of daylight may be improved by (Baker and Steemers, 2002):

- enhancing daylight distribution in the room (i.e. reducing contrast);
- installing photosensitive control system.

Design for adaptation

Transient adaptation effects, such as those described in section 2.3.2 in Chapter 2, can be experienced when entering from daylight into a darkened room (i.e. a cinema) or the reverse. If these movements occur often, it is wise to design the adjacent spaces according to certain rules to prevent large adaptation-level changes. Baker and Steemers (2002) advise that average daylight factors do not differ by more than a factor of 3.

3.4 Indoor air parameters

3.4.1 Parameters and definitions

For indoor air quality, the exposure of an individual to pollutants present in a space is significant. This exposure can be defined as the concentration of the pollutants over time expressed in µg/m³. The concentration of pollutants depends upon several parameters (see Figure 3.19):

- the production of the pollutants in the space expressed by the emission rate of a pollutant (substance) in µg/s or µg/s per m² surface area of source;
- the ventilation rate of the space in which the pollutants are produced, expressed in m³/h or l/s;
- the concentration of the pollutants in the ventilation air, expressed in ppm or µg/m³.

The exposure to indoor air pollutants, emitted (primarily or secondarily) by construction and HVAC products is influenced by indoor environmental parameters such as ventilation rate, air velocity, temperature, relative humidity, the activities taking place in that indoor environment resulting in introduction or removal of the same or other pollutants, and the time (age of product) and duration of the exposure.

Small variations in indoor environmental parameters, activities or simply the introduction of another source make the prediction of emissions of products complicated. Figure 3.19 shows the relationship between the emission of pollutants and the processes of removal by ventilation and sorption to surfaces. The concentration (C_i) of pollutants in the room air and therefore the exposure of occupants depends upon these processes and upon the concentration of pollutant in the air entering from outside (C_o). This is therefore a dynamic situation as the rates of emission and the other parameters vary over time. It should be noted that actual indoor air quality does not depend upon a single product, but is a function of input from many sources and from ventilation.

The change in the amount of pollutant (mass) per volume of air over time can be expressed by:

$$V dC_i/dt = P_i - \text{removal (ventilation)} - \text{removal (exfiltration)} - \text{removal (sorption, decay, cleaning) } [\mu g/s] \qquad [3.37]$$

where:

- C_i = concentration of pollutant in indoor air ($\mu g/m^3$);
- P_i = production ($\mu g/s$);
- V = volume of space (m^3).

Ventilation efficiency (E_v) for a certain pollutant is here defined as the concentration difference of that pollutant between exhausted (C_e) and supplied

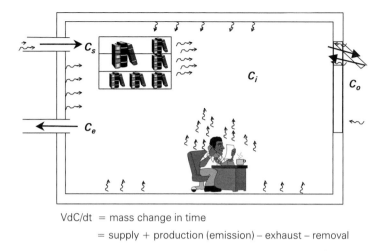

VdC/dt = mass change in time

= supply + production (emission) – exhaust – removal

Source: Bluyssen

Figure 3.19 *Factors determining the indoor concentration of an air pollutant: C = concentration of pollutant in supply air (s), exhaust air (e), indoor air (i) and outdoor air (o)*

air (C_s), divided by the concentration difference of that pollutant between room air (C_i) and supplied air:

$$E_v = (C_e - C_s)/(C_i - C_s) \qquad [3.38]$$

where:

- C_s = concentration of pollutant in the supplied air ($\mu g/m^3$);
- C_e = concentration of pollutant in the exhaust air ($\mu g/m^3$).

Ventilation or air exchange efficiency expresses how fresh air is distributed in a room. The air exchange efficiency, η_a is calculated by:

$$\eta_a = \frac{\tau_n}{2\langle\tau\rangle} \qquad [3.39]$$

where:

- τ_n. = the nominal time constant or the shortest time required to replace the air within the space at a given flow rate and space volume;
- $\langle\tau\rangle$ = the room's mean age of air, defined by the average of the ages of all the air particles in the room (s).

Air exchange efficiency is equal to 1 for piston-type ventilation (displacement), whereas for complete mixing it is equal to 0.5. While for situations in which the air supplied is almost immediately exhausted (i.e. short circuit), ventilation efficiency is much lower than 1, depending upon the location in the room (see Figure 3.20).

The time, τ_a, required on average to replace the air present in the space is given by the following expression (Sandberg and Sjöberg, 1984):

$$\tau_a = 2\langle\tau\rangle \; [s] \; . \qquad [3.40]$$

The *age of air* τ_r is called the residence time of the particle in the room, as if it were born when entering the room. Since there are numerous air compounds, we may define a probability density $f(\tau_r)$ that the age of compounds arriving at a given location is between τ and $\tau + d\tau$ and, with a probability $F(\tau_r)$ that this age is greater than τ. The following relationships always hold between these two functions:

$$f(\tau_r) = -\frac{dF(\tau_r)}{d\tau} \text{ and } F(\tau_r) = 1 - \int_0^\tau f(t_r)\,dt. \qquad [3.41]$$

The local mean age of air at a point r is then defined by the average age of all the air particles arriving at that point:

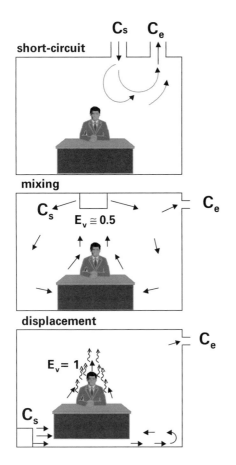

Figure 3.20 *Different ventilation situations*

$$\overline{\tau}_r = \int_0^\infty t\, f_r(t)dt = \int_0^\infty F_r(t)dt. \qquad [3.42]$$

The *nominal time constant* of a zone is the ratio of the volume, V, to the supplied fresh air flow rate $\dot{V}$ (including infiltration), or the ratio of the mass of air contained in the space m to the mass air flow rate $\dot{m}$:

$$\tau_n = \frac{V}{\dot{V}} = \frac{m}{\dot{m}}. \qquad [3.43]$$

Its inverse is the specific airflow rate or air change rate, n.

These parameters can be measured using a tracer gas, assuming a complete mixing of the tracer. However, even in the case of poor mixing, the nominal time constant is equal to the mean age of air at the exhaust:

$$\tau_n = \overline{\tau}_e. \qquad [3.44]$$

In a dilution system, incoming air is uniformly mixed with the interior air mass, whereas in a displacement system the interior air is displaced by incoming air with mixing kept to a minimum. In practice, combinations of the two approaches are common. While from an air quality aspect displacement approaches are generally preferred, very precise operating conditions are normally needed and their operation can be impaired by occupant activities, temperature fluctuations and door openings, etc. Where air is conditioned, or air heating is used, high recirculation rates and mixing ventilation systems may be necessary (see also section 3.2.5).

3.4.2 Pollutants and sources

Pollutants

The main groups of pollutants found in indoor air are chemical and biological pollutants (see Table 3.5). Among the chemical group one can distinguish gases and vapours (inorganic and organic) and particulate matter. The biological group consists of microbiological (dust) particles floating in the air that originate from viruses, bacteria, protozoa, moulds, mites, insects, birds, mammals and pollen.

Moulds (see Plate 5, centre pages) can form aerosols through their spores. Particles are understood to mean solid or liquid particles, or a mixture of the two. Typical

Table 3.4 *Nominal time constant and the room mean age*

Air exchange efficiency	η_a	35%	50%	75%	90%	99%
Mean age at exhaust or nominal time constant	$\tau_e = \tau_n$	1.00	1.00	1.00	1.00	1.00
Room mean age of the air	$<\tau>$	1.44	1.00	0.67	0.55	0.50

Table 3.5 *Main groups of indoor air pollutants*

Groups	Subgroups	
Chemical	Gases and vapours	Inorganic: CO, CO_2, NO_x, SO_x, O_3
		Organic: volatile organic compounds (VOCs), formaldehyde
	Particulate matter	Fibres: asbestos (natural fibres), mineral wool (synthetic), ceramic (vitreous and crystalline structures)
		Respirable suspended particles (RSPs), PM10
		Particulate organic matter (POM): biocides and polycyclic aromatic hydrocarbons (PAHs)
	Radioactive particles/gases (radon and its daughters)	
Biological	Micro-organisms, mould, fungi, mycotoxins, bioaerosols pollens, mites, spores, allergens, bacteria, airborne infections, droplet nuclei, house dust.	

Source: adapted from Bluyssen, 1996

examples are skin flakes, textile particles, smoke, dampness and fog. Particles are defined as aerosols (dust) when they are smaller than about 200µm and larger than 0.01µm. Smaller particles have the characteristics of gas, and larger particles are too heavy to stay suspended and will not be inhaled. Inhalable particles that can reach the pharynx have a maximum size of 200µm; particulate matter that is smaller than 10µm (PM10) can reach the larynx and the thorax; and respirable particles can go as far as the alveoli in the lungs (i.e. asbestos fibres) (Wal, 1990). Particles with a diameter of between 2µm and 5µm can precipitate in the alveoli; even smaller particles are exhaled again. Air sample analyses indicate that up to 99 per cent (by count) of particles present in the atmosphere are 1 micron or less in size (Beck, 1990).

Inorganic gases such as nitrogen dioxide (NO_2), sulphur dioxide (SO_2) and ozone (O_3) are present in all buildings. Ozone is a photochemical oxidant, formed at ground level when hydrocarbons and nitrogen oxides react with ultraviolet light. Ozone can also occur through discharge in laser printers and copying machines. Nitrogen dioxides and sulphur oxides are combustion products.

The important organic gases for indoor air are carbon monoxide (CO), an incomplete combustion product, carbon dioxide (CO_2), produced by human and animal breathing, and volatile organic compounds (VOCs).

The WHO classified volatile organic indoor pollutants according to four categories (WHO, 1989) (see Table 3.6):

1   very volatile organic compounds (VVOCs);
2   volatile organic compounds (VOCs);
3   semi-volatile organic compounds (SVOCs);
4   particulate organic matter (POM).

European Concerted Action (ECA) categorized chemical structures that are most often detected indoors (see Table 3.7) (ECA, 1994). In EN ISO 16000-6, total volatile organic compound (TVOC) is defined as the sum of VOCs sampled on Tenax TA®, between and including n-hexane and n-hexadecane, quantified by converting to toluene equivalents (CEN, 2004a).

Sources of pollution

Pollution sources, that emit substances in the indoor air directly or indirectly, can be divided into the following categories:

* outdoor sources (e.g. traffic and industry);
* occupant-related activities and products (e.g. tobacco smoke; equipment: laser printers and other office equipment; consumer products: cleaning, hygienic, personal care products);
* building materials and furnishings: insulation, plywood, paint, furniture (particle board), floor/wall covering, etc.;
* ventilation system components (e.g. filters, ducts, humidifiers; see Figure 3.21).

3.4.3 Emissions mechanisms

A product can emit substances (particles and/or gases) to the indoor air that originate from the product itself, that are caused by coming into contact with other

Table 3.6 *Classification of organic indoor pollutants*

	Boiling point range (°C)	Examples
VVOCs	<0 – 50 – 100	Formaldehyde and other carbonyl compounds (i.e. acetaldehyde, acetone, dichloromethane, tetrahydrofuran)
VOCs	50 – 100 – 240 – 260	Solvents and terpenes
SVOCs	240 – 260 – 380 – 400	Pesticides (e.g. chlorpyrifos, lindane and pentachlorophenol, which is a biocide) and plasticizers (e.g. phthalates) (biocides can originate from treated wood, impregnated textiles, etc.)
POM	>380	Biocides (e.g. pyrethroids) and polycyclic aromatic hydrocarbons (PAHs)

Source: WHO (1989)

products or that arise during the in-use phase of the product itself.

Emissions that originate from the product itself (primary emission)

- *Organic compounds*: VVOCs, VOCs, and SVOCs – for example, phthalates in polyvinyl chloride (PVC) products; pentachlorophenol (PCP) in impregnated floor coverings; formaldehyde in wood-based boards (a long-term continuous emission from a dry material); VOCs in non-water carrying paints (a short-term high emission from a wet material); and polycyclic aromatic hydrocarbons (PAHs) in coatings and bituminous materials.
- *Airborne particles*: for example, asbestos and mineral wool from insulation products.

Table 3.7 *Chemical structures of volatile organic compounds (VOCs) most frequently detected indoors, with examples*

Chemical structure	Examples
Alkanes	N-hexane, n-decane
Cycloalkanes and alkenes	Cyclohexane, methyl-cyclohexane
Aromatic hydrocarbons	Benzene, toluene, xylene
Halogenated hydrocarbons	Dichloromethane, trichloroethane
Terpenes	Limonene, alpha-pinene
Aldehydes	Formaldehyde,* acetaldehyde*, hexanal
Ketones	Acetone, methylethylethanol
Alcohols, alkoxyalcohols	Isobutanol, ethoxyrethanol
Esters	Ethylacetate, butylacetate

Note: * Not a VOC.
Source: ECA (1994)

Emissions caused as a result of the product environment

These consist of emissions resulting from the interaction of products (or primary emission compounds) with environmental elements such as ozone or water (see section 9.3.1 in Chapter 9).

Emissions that arise during the in-use phase of the product itself (secondary emission)

External substances may be adsorbed to the surface of the product and desorbed at a later time (e.g. certain cleaning compounds). A sink is defined as a source that shows adsorption and, after a while, emits those adsorbed pollutants again.

Microbial growth in or on the surface of the product can result in the emission of spores, mycotoxins, synergizers and VOCs. The material constituents and moisture retention characteristics of a product determine the risk for microbial growth; therefore, sensitivity to microbiological growth is a material characteristic just as adsorption and desorption ability are (see also section 9.3.2 in Chapter 9).

Emissions from HVAC systems

For HVAC system components that are not in the occupied space and where emissions are transported by air to the occupied space, the following major emission sources have been described (Bluyssen et al, 1993a; Bluyssen, 2004b) (see Figure 3.22):

- *Air filters*: both new and used filters pollute the air. Due to their constituent material, new filters emit VOCs.

Source: Bluyssen (2004b)

Figure 3.21 *Air ducts at a construction site (left) can cause considerable air pollution indoors after installation, caused by accumulated dust/debris; capping the ducts (right) is a good solution*

• *Air ducts:* oil residuals are the dominant source of pollution in new ducts. Depending upon the machinery used in the manufacturing process, new spiral wound ducts, flexible ducts and other components of the ductwork might contain small amounts of processing oil residuals. The oil layer is very thin and invisible. Growth of micro-organisms, dust/debris accumulated in the ducts during the construction at the work site (mostly inorganic substances) and organic dust accumulated during the operation period in the ducts can be sources of pollution as well.

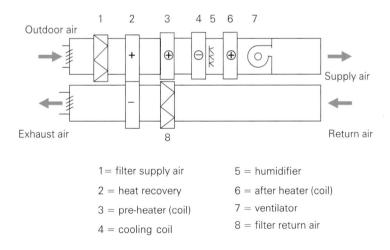

1 = filter supply air
2 = heat recovery
3 = pre-heater (coil)
4 = cooling coil
5 = humidifier
6 = after heater (coil)
7 = ventilator
8 = filter return air

Source: Bluyssen (2004b)

Figure 3.22 *The main components of an HVAC system*

Condensation in ducts passing through cold zones favours mould growth.

- *Air humidifiers*: micro-organisms are the main source of air pollution if the air humidifier is not used in the manufacturer-recommended way and/or if it is not properly maintained. Desalinization and demineralization devices/ agents can also contribute to pollution of the passing air.
- *Rotating heat exchangers (RHEs)*: in general, rotating heat changers are not pollutant sources in themselves, except when the wheels are dirty. RHEs may transport contaminants from the supply to the exhaust in three ways: through air caught by the wheel; by leakage between wheel and gasket; and by adsorption/desorption on the surface area of the wheel. Adsorption/desorption increases with the boiling point of VOCs; therefore, the recirculation rate of heavy compounds such as those found in bad odours may be rather high (more than 50 per cent).
- *Cooling and heating coils*: heating and cooling coils without condensed or stagnating water in the pans are components that make a small contribution to overall perceived air pollution. On the other hand, cooling coils with condensed water in the pans are microbiological reservoirs and amplification sites that may be a major source of pollution in the inlet air.

The emission of pollutants from materials or products, specifically volatile organic compounds, is determined by three fundamental mechanisms (Bluyssen, 1994):

1   diffusion in the product;
2   desorption of adsorbed or absorbed pollutants;
3   evaporation of the pollutants from the surface of the product to the air above the product.

Additionally, two other processes can take place that might result in emissions of products:

1   chemical reactions, followed by emission (diffusion and evaporation);
2   microbiological growth, followed by emission of products from micro-organisms.

Depending upon the substance emitted, a different pattern of emission over time can occur. In general, emission patterns are encountered as presented in Figure 3.23, although other patterns are also possible. The time axes in these curves can differ as well, depending upon the pollutant followed over time. Emission patterns from more pollutants emitted from a source can look quite complex.

Products, built up in different layers (e.g. with glue between the layers containing solvents), may start to emit substances with some delay due to slow diffusion processes. These kinds of processes are not shown in Figure 3.23, but they feature an emission curve like the SVOC curve. By understanding the mechanisms and the properties of the materials used in the product, predictions and explanations can be made on expected behaviour (level and time frame of release).

For a pollutant originally present in the material, this pollutant can diffuse through the material, reach the laminar layer and, depending upon the convection mass transfer coefficient, reach the buffer layer, in which – depending upon the turbulence (or Reynolds number) – it is transported by air to the turbulent region, where it is taken by the motions of ventilation in the space. Figure 3.24 presents this process. For each of the transfers an equation can be set up in the form of the following (see Spengler et al, 2001, Chapter 58):

$$\Phi_{ij} = h_{ij} A (C_j - C_i) \ [kg/s] \qquad [3.45]$$

where:

- Φ_{ij} = mass transport between i and j (kg/s);
- A = surface area (m²);
- C_i = concentration of pollutant in point i (kg/m³);
- C_j = concentration of pollutant in point j (kg/m³);
- h_{ij} = mass transfer coefficient in layer between i and j (m/s).

For the turbulent region (4 in Figure 3.24), the equation becomes:

$$\Phi_{ij} = Q (C_j - C_i) \ [kg/s] \qquad [3.46]$$

where Q = ventilation rate (m³/s).

For each of the mechanisms, the mass transfer coefficient is different. Important parameters include type of pollutant (polarity, volatility and vapour pressure), type of material/product (porosity, roughness and specific area) and the surrounding conditions (temperature, humidity and air velocity). Considering the number of pollutants in the air and the number of

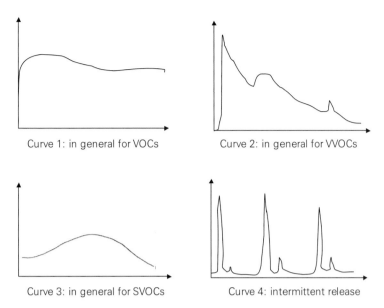

Curve 1: in general for VOCs

Curve 2: in general for VVOCs

Curve 3: in general for SVOCs

Curve 4: intermittent release

Note: Some VOCs show an intermittent release due to the conditions in the indoor space (temperature and humidity variations) influencing the emission rate or due to regular (maintenance and cleaning) activities related to the product. The latter are named secondary emissions.

Source: adapted from Wilke et al (2004); CEN-ISO (2007)

Figure 3.23 *Patterns of emission over time: Semi-volatile organic compounds (SVOCs) (the more involatile compounds) might have the opposite curve as very volatile organic compounds (VVOCs) and begin their emissions much later in time, but will, in general, eventually decrease again (e.g. some sealants)*

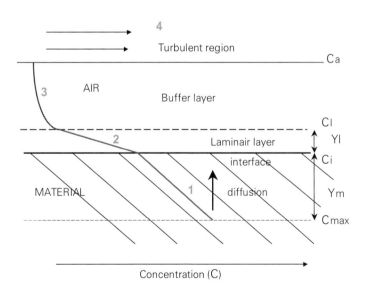

Source: Bluyssen

Figure 3.24 *Concentration level of a pollutant emitted via diffusion through a material: C is concentration in air (a), laminar layer (l), interface (i), and maximum in material (max); Y is distance (l) from interface to buffer layer (m), from maximum to interface*

different materials present in the indoor environment, it is difficult to determine the mass transfer coefficients for each combination of material and pollutant. Above all, it is not unlikely that slightly different conditions influence these transfer coefficients.

For a pollutant present at the surface of the product (secondary emissions or, for example, paints or varnishes), the emission mechanism will most likely comprise evaporation only.

The emission of substances is often controlled by diffusion; this implies that emission does not reach a plateau, but keeps on decreasing with time. If diffusion is assumed, an effective diffusion coefficient can be obtained from measurements, which allow for more accurate predictions of emissions.

Factors such as temperature (and, most likely, also humidity for some substances such as formaldehyde), loading and thickness of product may have a significant impact upon the emission. Figure 3.25 shows an example of the TVOC concentration ($\mu g/m^3$) measured in a dessicator as well as in a $15m^3$ chamber over time as a result of the emission of a piece of carpet, under different temperature conditions (Bluyssen et al, 1996). Here, it is clear that temperature may have a significant influence on the

emission rate, depending, however, upon the material or source tested.

Diffusion

The diffusion within a product to the surface is related to the diffusion coefficient of the pollutant of concern, which depends upon the characteristics of the pollutant (e.g. molar mass and dimensions), the temperature and the structure of the product. The diffusion coefficient of a pollutant is also influenced by the other pollutants present in the product and the homogeneity of the product.

Evaporation

The emission from evaporation is linear, related to the difference in vapour pressure between the surface and the air above. Because the vapour pressure is directly related to the concentration, the emission is proportional to the difference in concentration between the surface and the air above. The mass transfer coefficient is related to the diffusion coefficient in the air of the pollutant of concern, the turbulence in the border layer (laminar layer) and the thickness of that layer.

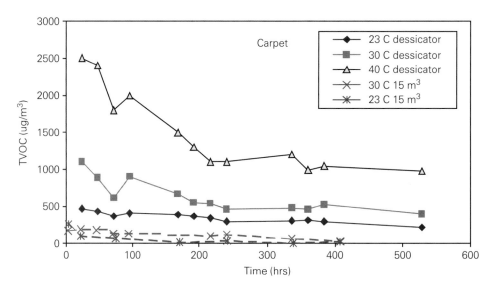

Source: Bluyssen et al (1996b)

Figure 3.25 *Influence of temperature on total volatile organic compound (TVOC) emission rate of a piece of carpet under different temperature conditions*

Sorption

Adsorption is defined as the presence of a higher concentration of a pollutant at the surface of a product than in the core of the product. It is, in fact, the almost completely homogeneous penetration of a pollutant in the product, although this is not common in the indoor environment, unless something is spilled.

Two types of adsorption can occur: Van der Waals, or physical, adsorption and activated adsorption, or chemosorption. Van der Waals adsorption occurs, in principal, with all pollutants, especially with low and medium low temperatures, characterized by a relatively low adsorption energy (5–10 kcal/mol), and is reversible. The force with which an adsorbed molecule adheres to the surface is similar to the cohesion force of liquid molecules. The amount of adsorption by a product is related to the ability of the adsorbed pollutant to condensate. Adsorption increases with increasing boiling point.

Chemosorption occurs in specific cases, requires higher temperatures, is irreversible and is characterized by a higher adsorption energy. An example is the adsorption of acid gases (e.g. SO_2 and NO_2) to a plastered wall.

For desorption, van der Waals adsorption is most interesting since chemically adsorbed pollutants are not desorbed. Chemically adsorbed pollutants create generally one layer with a thickness of one molecule, while van der Waals-adsorbed pollutants comprise more than one layer. Desorption can be described by diffusion and evaporation.

The sorption behaviour of volatile organic compounds, in particular, depends upon the sink material, the pollutant, the temperature, the water content of the material and the relative humidity of the air. Smooth materials, such as glass and stainless steel, hardly adsorb, while materials such as textile, wood and paper adsorb strongly.

3.4.4 Ventilation mechanisms

With ventilation, two elements are important:

1   The air change efficiency is as high as possible.
2   Clean air is supplied to the right places.

Thus, airflow patterns should, in principle, be organized so that new air reaches the heads of occupants as closely as possible, and so that vitiated air is evacuated as quickly as possible, before being mixed with the new air. Having the correct airflow rate to the appropriate locations is crucial in obtaining good indoor air quality. Leakage, where air is not channelled appropriately, should therefore be avoided. This requires an airtight building envelope and an airtight ductwork. Air tightness is measured by the air permeability of the envelope of the measured object. This type of measurement is standardized at an international level (ISO, 1998).

The driving force for ventilation may be either natural or mechanical. *Natural ventilation* is the passive way to exchange air with the outdoors and to evacuate indoor contaminants. Wind and air density differences, resulting mainly from temperature differences, create pressure differences that result airflow through ventilation openings or natural ventilation ducts. Other openings such as doors and windows are also used for natural ventilation when large airflows are needed. The advantages of natural ventilation are as follows:

- Its importance is generally well appreciated by a building's occupants, who understand and control it easily.
- Its cost is usually low.
- The energy for moving the air is negligible and free.
- It allows very large airflow rates (more than 10 volumes per hour), particularly in the case of passive cooling.
- It does not break down.

It has however some drawbacks, which are:

- It cannot be used in noisy or polluted areas.
- It is efficient only in rooms with a depth-to-height ratio smaller than 3 or having openings on both sides.
- Heat recovery is nearly impossible.
- The airflow rate varies with the meteorological conditions, and an adequate control is needed to ensure the ventilation requirements. An alternative solution is using self-regulated (pressure-controlled) ventilation grills.

Natural ventilation should be controlled by the use of ventilation openings, installed on purpose. Infiltration of air, which may occur through gaps such as small cracks in the structure and around poorly sealed components such as windows and pipe work, is not a proper way to ensure natural ventilation since the airflow rate through this leakage cannot be controlled.

Mechanical ventilation is often used where natural ventilation cannot fulfil the requirements, either because of poor outdoor conditions (noise, pollution and climate) or in locations that cannot be naturally ventilated. It has the following advantages:

• It allows ventilation of deep spaces with low ceilings and rooms that are not accessible to natural airflow.
• Where well designed and built in an airtight building, it ensures a total and continuous control of airflows and also permits better control of the indoor climate.
• It can protect from outdoor noise and pollution.
• Heat recovery from exhaust air is relatively easy.

Nevertheless, its drawbacks are as follows:

• Mechanical ventilation is often not well accepted by occupants, who lack control over it.
• The system, especially air ducts, uses a large part (up to 25 per cent) of the building volume.
• The installation and exploitation costs are high.
• It uses energy not only to condition the air, but also to move it.
• It can be noisy, especially at low frequencies.
• The quality of delivered air may be poor if special caution is not brought to it when building and maintaining the system.
• It may break down or function in an improper way.

Hybrid ventilation is a combination of natural (grids and opening windows) and mechanical ventilation facilities, both of which can be used, with natural ventilation being applied alone as much as possible. Combining natural and mechanical driving forces offers opportunities for improving the indoor environment and reducing energy demand.

3.4.5 Measurement

Measuring the emissions of certain sources can, in principle, be approached in three ways:

1   *The source:* identify the contents of the source (product characteristics) and predict what might be emitted, or subject the source to an extraction process that is indicative of emissions under intended use conditions.
2   *The air nearby the source:* identify the substances emitted under intended use conditions in a standard test chamber and predict the indoor air concentration for the intended use situation through modelling.
3   *Measurement of the air in the space with several sources:* identify the substances and try to deduct from which source it came (source identification).

The first approach requires a detailed knowledge of the composition of the source or product. A substance could be present in the product even though it has not intentionally been added, perhaps by being a trace component in feedstock material. Validation of extraction methods is required to show correlation with emissions under intended use conditions. This can be problematic when dealing with emissions consisting of many substances that may behave differently from each other, but can be applicable for specific substances and products. Therefore, up to now the second and the third approach have been the preferred methodologies. For the second approach, the translation into practice (the in-use situation) with modelling is complex: it provides information to compare products based on their emission patterns for specified groups of substances. The third approach is technically difficult as, in practice, it is often not easy to apportion all the measured substances in the air to a single or even a few sources and, as discussed previously, concentrations vary with time because of the dynamic nature of the determining factors.

In general, the measurement procedure requires two steps: sampling of the air to be tested on or in a medium, and the analysis (detection and characterization) of the pollutants in or on that medium. The substances emitted from materials/products have different characteristics and therefore also require different methods of sampling and of analysis. The available methods or instruments to measure indoor air compounds can be divided into two groups (Bluyssen, 1996). Those that:

• require an extractions step before making a physical or chemical analysis (i.e. chromatography; see Figure 3.26);
• make a direct physical measurement of some property of the sample (i.e. non-dispersive infrared spectrometry).

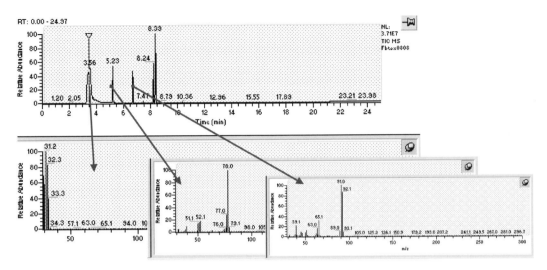

Source: Jan Boon, Forbo Krommenie BV 2006

Figure 3.26 *A gas chromatogram is shown above; the lower graphs show the identification of each by mass spectrometry*

Box 3.5 Methods to analyse indoor air pollutants

Chromatography is a separation technique in which an inert gas or liquid (mobile phase) flows at a constant rate in one direction through the stationary phase, a solid with a large surface-to-volume ratio or a high boiling liquid on a solid support. Gas chromatography is used for separation of volatile, relatively non-polar, materials or members of a homologous series; liquid chromatography for separation of, in particular, those materials with low volatility and labile or instable compounds; and thin layer and column chromatography for separation of inorganic or organic materials and low-molecular weight species up to high chain-length polymers.

Spectrometry or photometric methods make use of discrete energy levels of molecules and the emission or absorption of radiation that usually accompanies changes of a molecule from one energy level to another. They are generally based on the measurement of transmittance or absorbance of a solution of an absorbing salt, compound or reaction product of the substance to be determined. They include absorption spectroscopy, emission spectroscopy, laser spectroscopy, photo-acoustic techniques and X-ray analysis.

Mass spectrometry and flame ionization. In mass spectrometry a substance is analysed by forming ions and then sorting the ions by mass in electric or magnetic fields. The introduction of mere traces of organic matter into the flame of the flame ionization detector (FID) produces a substantial amount of ionization. The response of the detector is roughly proportional to the carbon content of the solute. The response to most organic compounds on a molar basis increases with molecular weight.

Chemical sensors for gas molecules may, in principle, monitor physisorption, chemisorption, surface defect, grain boundary or bulk defect reactions (Gardner and Bartlett, 1992). Several chemical sensors are available: mass-sensitive sensors, conducting polymers and semi-conductors. Mass-sensitive sensors include quartz resonators, piezoelectric sensors or surface acoustic wave (SAW) sensors (Elma et al, 1989; Nakamoto et al, 1990; Bruckman et al, 1994). The basis is a quartz resonator coated with a sensing membrane that works as a chemical sensor. With conducting polymers, the conductivity of the polymer film is altered on exposure to different gases (Gardner et al, 1990), and with semi-conductor sensors the electrical characteristics of the semi-conductor changes when the gas to be measured is absorbed (Gardner and Bartlett, 1992).

Sorbents are used to pre-concentrate volatile organic compounds (VOCs) from gaseous streams: organic polymer resins (e.g. Tenax and XAD), carbon-based sorbents (e.g. carbotrap and activated charcoal) and inorganic sorbents (e.g. silica gel, Florisil and inorganic molecular sieves) (NKB, 1995). It is advisable to use more than one sorbent or sampling method (ECA, 1994). Tenax is widely used because it has a low affinity for water, is easy to clean after sampling, has low background emissions and is thermally stable. Tenax can be used to determine VOCs (C_6-C_{18}), semi-volatile organic compounds (SVOCs) (if efficiently desorbed from the sampling tube) and some very volatile organic compounds (VVOCs) (C_3-C_5) by sampling at reduced temperatures (Tirkkonen et al, 1995).

Box 3.5 describes methods for analysing indoor air pollutants, while in Table 3.8 the possible detected compounds and detection limits of these different methods are presented. Recommended conditions for sampling asbestos fibres and suspended particulate matter, as well as radon in indoor air, are given by ECA (1989); for mycotoxins, by Schmidt-Etkin (1994); for bioaerosols, by Burge (1987); and for particles, in general, by Johnson (1989). Vacuum cleaning and extraction of dust samples have been widely used in the detection of house dust mites and allergens of animal origin.

3.4.6 Control strategies

The best way to control exposure to pollutants is to perform source control (i.e. minimize the emission of either primary or secondary pollutants to the air that we are exposed to). Besides source control, there are three other ways to control exposure: ventilation, air cleaning and activity control. An example of the latter is the designated smoking areas in a non-smoking building or the location of printers at places where no one is working. An additional control strategy is the addition of certain pollutants to the air to either mask or counteract other pollutants (odorous pollutants). This strategy, however, is not recommended. Air cleaning may require the removal of airborne particles, micro-organisms and gaseous pollutants. An example of a multistage filtering system is shown in Figure 3.27.

Particles

The characteristics of aerosols that most affect the performance of an air filter include particle size, mass, concentration and electrical properties (ASHRAE, 1992). Five main principles or mechanisms of particle collection can be distinguished (ASHRAE, 1992):

1   *Straining*: particles are strained through a membrane opening that is smaller than the particle being removed.
2   *Direct interception*: particles follow a fluid streamline close enough to a fibre so that the particle contacts the fibre and remains there. The process is nearly independent of velocity.
3   *Inertial deposition*: particles cannot follow fluid streamlines around fibre (they are too large); instead, they cross over streamlines and contact fibre and remain there (adhesion). At high velocities, a viscous coating stimulates adhesion.
4   *Diffusion*: very small particles have random motion about their basic streamlines (Brownian motion), which contributes to deposition on the fibre and creates a concentration gradient in the region of that fibre, further enhancing filtration by diffusion.
5   *Electrostatic effects*: particle or media charging can produce changes in the collection of dust.

Three operating characteristics distinguish the various types of air cleaners: efficiency, airflow resistance and dust-holding capacity (ASHRAE, 1992). Efficiency measures the ability of the air cleaner to remove particulate matter from an air stream. Airflow resistance is the static pressure drop across the filter at a given airflow rate. And dust-holding capacity defines the amount of a particular type of dust that an air cleaner can hold when it is operated at a specific airflow rate to some maximum resistance value or before its efficiency drops. In short (Beck, 1990):

*   *Arrestance* provides an indication of a filter's ability to remove the larger, heavier particles in the air (> 1 micron).
*   *Efficiency* is a measure of a filter's ability to remove the microscopic (submicron) stain-causing particles of carbon and other substances.
*   *Dust-holding-capacity* test determines how long a filter will last.

In general four types of tests, together with certain variations, determine air cleaner efficiency, according to ASHRAE (1992):

1   *Arrestance (synthetic dust arrestance)*: a standardized synthetic dust consisting of various particle sizes is fed into the air cleaner and the mass fraction of the dust removed is determined.
2   *Dust spot efficiency (atmospheric dust spot efficiency)*: atmospheric dust is passed into the air cleaner, and the discoloration of the cleaned air on

Table 3.8 *Measurement methods, detected compounds and detection limits for indoor air*

	Detected compounds	Detection limit	Additional detector/analysis
Chromatography			
Gas chromatography	SVOC	ppb range	XAD/FID/MS
	VOC	ppb range	FID/MS
	Volatile, relatively non-polar or members of homologous series		
High-performance liquid chromatography	Low volatile, labile or unstable formaldehyde	ppb range 0.5 ppb	Infrared; MS DNPH
Thin-layer chromatography	Inorganic and organic, low-molecular weight species up to high chain length; high VOCs difficult	Pictogram	Iodine vapour Fluorescent indicator
Column chromatography	Involatile		
Filtration			
Neocleopore, glass fibre membrane, polycarbonate pore granular beds; polystyrene fibre	Particles, mycotoxins, POMs	Depends on analysis	Gravimetric analysis Chemical/microscopy/light gravimetric/light/microscopy Chemical analysis Gravimetric analysis

	Detected compounds	Detection level	Remarks
Photometry			Speed, convenience, and relatively high precision and accuracy in the determination of micro- and semi-micro quantities of constituents. Spectral region should be known, and should be in the region of the absorption maximum
Absorption spectroscopy:			
• ultraviolet (200–780nm);	Aromatic; molecule containing a chromophoric group; many interferences	0.01–0.70µg/ml	
• infrared (780nm–0.5mm);	organic; water vapour	ppm range	
• non-dispersive infrared.	and carbon dioxide interference		
Emission spectroscopy:			
• fluorometry (300–800nm);	Selective	0.1–0.4 ppm	
• nuclear magnetic resonance.		0.04–0.70µg/ml	
Laser spectroscopy	Structures of proton-containing molecules; selective	ppb range	
Optical-pumped molecular lasers	Selective	ppb range	
Photo-acoustic techniques	Selective and non-selective	ppb range	
Photo-acoustic + lasers		<ppb range	
X-ray analysis	particles (even individual)	20µg	
Ionization			
Mass spectrometry		ppb range	
Flame ionization	Gaseous organics	ppb range	Reliable; highly sensitive; reasonably stable; moderately insensitive to flow and temperature changes; rugged Portable also available
Particle sensors			
Photometer/Tyndall meter			
Beta-particle monitor			
Piezo-balance			Includes quartz crystal
Portable gas chromatograph	VOC (also VVOC)		
Chemical sensors			
Mass sensitive: SAWS	TVOC	ppb range	Cheap, stable and reliable
Conducting polymers	TVOC	ppm range	Low selectivity, instable, not reproducible, often used only once, sensitive to pollution
Semi-conductors	TVOC	ppm range	Humidity dependent, not specific, unstable

Notes: XAD = styrene-divinylbenzene copolymer; DNPH = 2,4-Dinitrophenylhydrazine sampling medium; FID = flame ionization detector; MS = mass spectrometry.

Source: adapted from Bluyssen, 2006

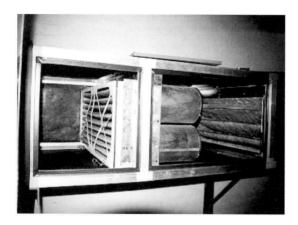

Source: Bluyssen

Figure 3.27 *A multi-stage filtering system that features an absolute active carbon and a filter bag*

filter paper targets is compared with that of the incoming air.

3 *Fractional efficiency or penetration*: uniform-size particles are fed into the air cleaner and the percentage removed by the cleaner is determined. The DOP (di-octyl phthalate or bis-phthalate (2-ethyl-exyl), an oily, high-boiling liquid) penetration test is used for high efficiency filters.

4 *Particle size efficiency*: atmospheric dust is fed to the air cleaner and air samples taken upstream and downstream are drawn through a particle counter to obtain efficiency versus particle size.

Box 3.6 describes several particle air cleaners.

Gases

For the removal of gaseous pollutants, the following parameters of the pollutant to be removed are significant: molecular mass, normal boiling point, heat of evaporation, polarity and chemical reactivity and chemosorption velocity (ASHRAE, 1991; ASHRAE, 1997). The physical/chemical principles available to remove gaseous pollutants are as follows:

- *Absorption*: a gaseous pollutant is dissolved in or reacts with the body of an absorbing medium, which can be either a porous solid or a liquid; this is called scrubbing.
- *Physical adsorption*: pollutant gas molecules strike a surface and remain bound to it for an appreciable time (Van der Waals's forces; reversible), such as activated carbons, molecular sieves, zeolites, porous clay minerals, silica gel and activated alumina.
- *Chemosorption*: pollutant gas molecules strike a surface and react chemically with the surface (in general, irreversible).
- *Catalysation*: chemical reactions occur at the surface of a catalyst, which assists but is not used up in the reaction. In addition to adsorption, activated carbons remove some gases/vapours by catalysing their conversion to other less objectionable forms. Most notable is the catalysis of ozone to oxygen.
- *Combustion*: temperature rises until substantial oxidation of the pollutant occurs.
- *Catalytic combustion*: the pollutant passes through a heated bed of catalysts and oxidizes.
- *Cryogenic condensation*: physical adsorption at a very low temperature (more effect than at ambient temperature).
- *Photo catalysis* (ASHRAE, 2007): uses light (usually UV) and a photo catalyst to perform reduction–oxidation (redox) chemistry on the catalyst's surface on the passing VOCs into water and carbon dioxide. This attractive technique still needs development; the production of reaction products such as formaldehyde and acetaldehyde are seen, for example, with an titanium dioxide (TiO_2)-coated honeycomb configured monolith reactor irradiated with fluorescent bulbs with peak irradiance near either 254nm or 365nm. These by-products are caused by incomplete mineralization of VOCs (Hodgson et al, 2007).
- *Biofiltration* (ASHRAE, 2007): uses uncharacterized mixtures of bacteria in the filter to clean the air.

Box 3.6 Particle air cleaners

Fibrous-media unit filters (most commonly applied in buildings): the accumulating dust load causes pressure drop to increase up to a maximum recommended value. These filters include the following:

- *Viscous impingement filters* are panel filters made up of coarse fibres with a high porosity, coated with a viscous substance (e.g. oil), which causes particles that impinge on the fibres to stick to them. Panel filters have a good efficiency for lint, but a low efficiency for normal atmospheric dust.
- *Dry-type extended surface filters* are random fibre mats or blankets of varying thicknesses, fibre sizes and densities. The media can be cellulose, bonded glass, wool felt and a variety of synthetics, and are frequently supported by a wire frame in the form of pockets, or V-shaped or radial pleats.

Renewable-media filters: here fresh media are introduced into the air stream, as needed, to maintain constant resistance and, consequently, constant efficiency. They include:

- *Moving-curtain viscous impingement filters*: fresh media are fed manually or automatically across the face of the filter, while the dirty media are rewound onto a roll at the bottom.
- *Moving-curtain, dry-media filters*.

Electronic air cleaners (ASHRAE, 1992) have, if maintained properly by regular cleaning, relatively constant pressure drop and efficiency. Three types can be distinguished:

- *Ionizing plate type*: uses electrostatic precipitation to remove and collect particulate contaminants such as dust, smoke and pollen. The filters consist of an ionization section (charging particles) and a collecting plate section. All high-voltage devices are capable of producing ozone; but electronic air cleaners with a negative potential (negative ions) produce more than electronic air cleaners with a positive potential (positive ions, which is more common).
- *Charged-media non-ionizing type*: consists of a dielectric filtering medium made of a mat of glass fibre, cellulose or similar material supported on a grid work of alternately charged or grounded members. Particles are polarized and drawn to the charged filter medium; they are not ionized.
- *Charged-media ionizing type*: particles are charged and then collected on a charged-media filter. A negative ionizer charges particles, but has no collection plate, which causes space charge and dirty walls.

Unfortunately, no standard procedure has been developed to test gaseous contaminant filters for general ventilation applications.

3.5 Sound parameters

3.5.1 Parameters and definitions

Sound is a wave motion from a sound-producing object. When a person opens his mouth and makes a sound, he moves the air in front of his mouth, but he does not push away all of the air in his vicinity. The motion compresses a small mass of air near his mouth into less than its normal volume. After removing the compressing influence, the air expands and the first mass of air moves some of the air adjacent to it, which is then compressed,

in turn, and expands and pushes against another bit of adjacent air. So the energy of the original compressing motion is passed on to the space surrounding the speaker. When a portion of it is intercepted by a receiver of sound, such as the human ear, it is perceived as a stimulus and the response of the ear is audition or hearing.

The velocity of particles in the air is represented by velocity (v); the velocity at which the air is being moved is represented by the speed of sound (c). When both are moving in the same direction, the wave is longitudinal. When they are perpendicular to each other, the wave is transversal. Condensed waves or flexible waves are combinations of both, seen in solid media. These waves are, in most cases, mechanical vibrations and not sound waves. Sound waves are, in general, longitudinal waves.

Box 3.7 Origin of the wave theory of sound

Although the wave theory of sound existed in a qualitative way for many centuries, the first attempt to apply it to a theoretical derivation of the velocity of sound was probably by Sir Isaac Newton during the 17th century. During the 18th and 19th centuries, many scientists tried to theorize and experiment on production and reception of sound in closed spaces. However, the real first acoustics date from the publication in 1877 by Lord Raleigh (John William Strutt) of the *Theory of Sound*, in which the basic theory of all aspects of production, propagation and reception of sound was presented.

Source: Encyclopaedia Britannica (1991b)

Each sound wave is characterized by its wavelength and the frequency of the disturbance. The wavelength is the distance between identical phases of the propagating disturbance (see Figure 3.28). Since the frequency is inversely proportional to the propagation time (T) of the disturbance, the propagation velocity of the disturbance or the wave velocity is given by:

$$v = \lambda f \qquad [3.47]$$

where:

- v = propagation velocity of the disturbance (m/s);
- λ = wavelength of the disturbance (m);
- f = frequency of the disturbance (s^{-1}).

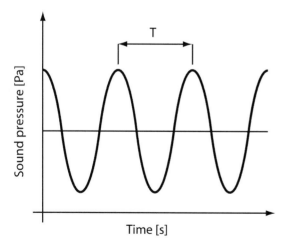

Source: adapted from Tol (1984)

Figure 3.28 *A harmonic wave – a pure tone*

This important relation holds for harmonic waves of all kinds (as well as light waves, water waves, etc.). Few sounds in daily experience are, however, pure tones (see Figure 3.28); most arise from more or less complicated combinations of harmonic waves, each with its own frequency.

A sound wave in air or any fluid is thus a compression wave. The velocity of sound in air is 344m/s at 20°C, substantially less than the velocity of light (3×10^8 m/s). It increases with temperature and is independent of density and pressure of the air over wide ranges.

The distinction between loud and soft sounds is caused by the differences in magnitude of the pressure changes involved in sound-wave propagation. One millionth of change in normal atmospheric pressure in front of the mouth is normal during conversation. The change in wave velocity corresponds, then, to only about 0.02cm/s. A sound wave represents the transmission of mechanical energy; an average rate of transfer of 10^{-16} per square centimetre is enough to produce hearing of an identifiable sound in a normal young person.

The loudness of the average power transmission in a sound wave per unit area of the medium perpendicular to the direction of the wave can be expressed by the *intensity level or the sound pressure level L_p*. The unit of this quantity is the bel; but in practice it is common to use a unit ten times smaller: the decibel (dB). Sound is equal to a number of decibels above the minimum audible and is given by:

$$L_p = 10\log(I/I_0) = 10\log(\rho/\rho_0)^2 \text{ [dB]} \qquad [3.48]$$

where:

- L_p = sound pressure level in decibels (dB);
- I = given intensity (W/m²);
- I_0 = 10^{-12} = minimum hearing intensity (W/m²);
- ρ = given sound pressure (Pa);
- $ρ_0$ = 2 × 10^{-5} = minimum hearing sound pressure (Pa).

From Equation 3.48, it can be seen that the minimum level of hearing is 0dB and the maximum level of hearing (pain limit) is 140dB (200Pa). An ordinary conversation at a distant of 1m of the mouth gives about 60dB; traffic at a busy street intersection, an average of 75dB; and a music band can reach about 110dB. One decibel is the smallest difference between two sound pressures, which can just be perceived under ideal conditions.

The *pitch of a sound*, as perceived by the human ear, is expressed with the *frequency* of the sound in Hertz (Hz), which is the number of times per second the disturbance at any point in the medium transmitting the wave is repeated (the number of pressure changes per second). The greater the number of repetitions, the higher is the perceived pitch. Frequency is therefore defined as:

$$f = 1/T \qquad [3.49]$$

where:

- f = frequency (Hz or s⁻¹);
- T = time between two disturbances of the same phase or between two maximum pressure changes (s) (see Figure 3.33 for a pure tone).

The range of frequencies that can be perceived by the human ear (20–20,000Hz) can be divided into

so-called isofones (an isofone presents the doubling of the frequency) (ISSO/SBR, 2006).

To take into account the sensitivity of the human ear in the evaluation of sound, the A-weighing is introduced. In the A-weighing, a correction is applied per frequency range, based on the 40dB isofone (see Table 3.9). These correction values are subtracted from the sound pressure levels in the specific isofone.

An isofone is a line at which the loudness level (often expressed in fones) is constant – in other words, each combination (see Figure 3.29) of frequency and related sound pressure level results in the same loudness. Because of this weighing, a low pitch of 40dB(A) can be perceived as loudly as a high pitch of 40dB(A).

The total sound pressure level is calculated by logarithmically adding the sound pressure levels of the different frequencies (after having subtracted the A-corrections):

$$L_{tot} = 10\log(10^{Lp1/10}+10^{Lp2/10}+..+10^{Lpn/10}). \qquad [3.50]$$

The quality of sound in an indoor space is determined by the sources of sound or noise (indoors and outdoors), the distribution of the sound in the space and the way the sound is perceived and interpreted.

On the *sound-producing side* (the sources of sound and noise), the frequency and the intensity of sound pressure are important parameters, as described above. For the *distribution of sound*, the space parameters used are reverberation time and sound insulation.

The time that it takes for the sound level to decrease after the source of sound in the space has been turned off is expressed in *reverberation time* (decrement of 60dB after the source of sound has been turned off) or the early decay time (EDT) (time in which the sound level decreases by 10dB after the source of sound has been turned off). The reverberation time can be calculated by the Sabine reverberation equation:

Table 3.9 *Isofones, frequencies and correction A-weighing*

Isofone	1	2	3	4	5	6	7	8	9	10
Middle frequency (Hz)	31.5	63	125	250	500	1000	2000	4000	8000	16000
Correction A-weighing (dB)	−39.4	−26.2	−16.1	−8.6	−3.2	0	+1.2	+1.0	−1.1	

Source: ISSO/SBR (2006)

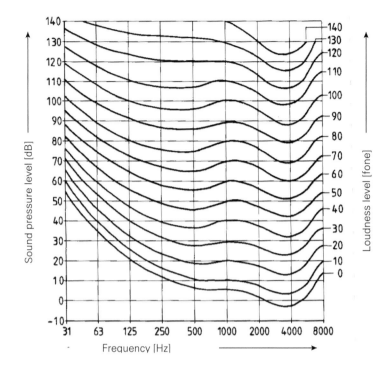

Source: adapted from Tol (1984)

Figure 3.29 *Isofones: Lines of the same loudness level*

$$T_r = V/6A_s \ [s] \hspace{3cm} [3.51]$$

where:

- T_r = reverberation time (s);
- V = volume of space (m³);
- A_s = total absorption surface area in space (m²).

Note that the constant factor 1/6 has a dimension of s/m because the velocity of sound c is part of it (Tol, 1984).

The total surface area that can absorb sound is calculated by:

$$A_s = \alpha_w A_w + \alpha_c A_c + \alpha_f A_f \ [m^2] \hspace{1cm} [3.52]$$

where:

- α_i = absorption coefficient of walls (i = w), ceiling (i = c) and floor (i = f);
- A_i = surface area of walls, ceiling and floor (m²).

Sound insulation of the surface areas of the space is a material characteristic and determines the sound transfer between spaces. The sound insulation for massive materials depends upon the mass of the material (a heavier product can resonate or vibrate less easily than a lighter product). The sound transfer through a wall can be defined as:

$$L_{receiver} = L_{send} - D \ [dB] \hspace{2cm} [3.53]$$

where:

- $L_{receiver}$ = the sound pressure level in the receiving space (dB);
- L_{send} = the sound pressure level in the sending space (dB);
- D = the damping or attenuation by the wall through which the sound is transferred (dB).

Attenuation depends upon the sound insulation of the wall (R) and the surface area of the wall (S) in relation to the adsorption surface area in the receiving space (A):

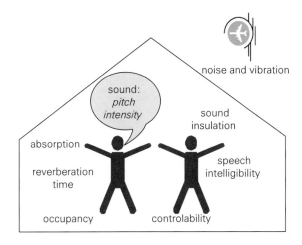

Source: Bluyssen

Figure 3.30 *Important sound parameters in the indoor environment*

$$D = R - 10\log(S/A) \text{ [dB]}. \qquad [3.54]$$

For the *perception of sound* – the parameters that affect well-being (annoyance and health) – concentration during an activity or speech intelligibility comprises (see Figure 3.30):

- the source – the sound level, the spectrum of the sound, the type of sound and the location of sound;
- the space – the reverberation time, construction, connections, sound insulation, absorption characteristics, and the occupancy of space;
- the receiver – the predictability and familiarity of sound, the controllability of sound, motivation, the attitude of employees with respect to sound, individual sensitivity to the disturbance of sound, information in the contents of sound, and the necessity of sound.

3.5.2 Mechanisms

Sound production

The sound pressure level in a *free space* (outdoors) depends upon the source and the distance to that source. Two types of sources can, in general, be distinguished: a point source and a line source.

A *point source* is in the view of the receiver a small object (the distance is 1.5 times larger than the diameter). If this source produces the same sound in all directions, the source can be considered a half globe. The sound pressure level perceived thus depends upon the sound pressure level produced, the distance and the reflecting surfaces present. The sound pressure level perceived is related to the quadratic distance to the source (Tol, 1984):

$$L_p \cong L_w + 10\log(1/4\pi r^2) \text{ [dB]} \qquad [3.55]$$

where:

- L_p = sound pressure level perceived at distance r (dB);
- L_w = sound pressure level in point (dB);
- r = distance (m).

A doubling of the distance results in a reduction of 6dB. With a *line source* – for example, a busy traffic street – the length is much longer. If the source produces the same sound in all directions (free space), the source can be considered by the receiver as a half sphere. The sound pressure level perceived is proportional to the distance of the source:

$$L_p \cong L_w + 10\log(1/4\pi r) \text{ [dB]}. \qquad [3.56]$$

A doubling of the distance results in a reduction of 3dB.

In *enclosed spaces*, the sound pressure level perceived also depends upon the characteristics of the space, such as volume and the finishing of the surfaces. The perceived sound pressure level is caused by the 'direct' perceived sound and the 'diffuse' sound, which has been reflecting a few times to the surface of the space. At *a small distance*, the source can be treated as if it was in free space. At *a certain distance*, the direct field is the same as the diffuse field. In a diffuse field, the sound level coming from all directions in a point is the same. In most enclosed spaces, it is fair to assume that a diffuse field is present:

$$L_p \cong L_w + 10\log(4/A) \text{ [dB]} \qquad [3.57]$$

where A = surface area of the enclosed space (m²).

However, when the enclosed space is large (such as a factory hall), this estimation is not correct. The sound pressure level is then merely determined by the repeated reflections of the sound against the surfaces:

$$L_p \cong L_w + 10\log(Q/4\pi r^2 + 4/A) \text{ [dB]} \qquad [3.58]$$

where: Q = direction of source factor (for homogeneous sound transmission, Q = 1).

At a certain distance, the direct sound is just as strong as the indirect reflected sound; this is called the reverberation radius (critical distance):

$$r_c = \sqrt{(QA/16\pi)} \text{ [m]} \qquad [3.59]$$

where: r_c = reverberation radius (m).

Sound absorption

When a sound wave falls onto a wall, part of the wave will be reflected (I_ρ), part will be absorbed in the wall (I_δ) and part will pass through the wall (I_τ). From the law of conservation of energy, it follows that (see Figure 3.31):

$$I_i = I_\rho + I_\delta + I_\tau; \text{ or} \qquad [3.60]$$

$$1 = I_\rho/I_i + I_\delta/I_i + I_\tau/I_i = \rho + \delta + \tau \qquad [3.61]$$

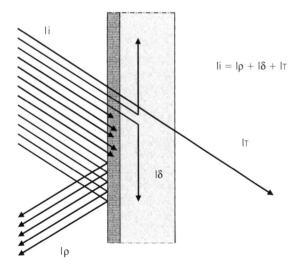

$$I_i = I_\rho + I_\delta + I_\tau$$

Source: adapted from Tol (1984)

Figure 3.31 *The distribution of sound falling on a wall*

where:

- ρ = reflection coefficient;
- δ = dissipation coefficient;
- τ = transmission coefficient, which is the reciprocal of the sound insulation measure.

These coefficients are all dependent upon the frequency and the angle of incidence. Often, the absorption coefficient is mentioned, while the sum of dissipation and transmission is meant. Therefore, in general, the absorption coefficient (α) is taken as:

$$\alpha = 1 - \rho. \qquad [3.62]$$

The sound insulation of a material is defined as:

$$R = 10\log 1/\tau \text{ [dB].} \qquad [3.63]$$

For a sound insulation of 20dB, 30dB or 40dB, this means that of the incoming intensity, 1, 0.1 or 0.01 per cent, respectively, is transmitted. R is independent of the surface area of the material as well as the absorption taking place in the sending and the receiving room. However, the received sound level depends upon these parameters (see Equation 3.53).

For a sound insulation of a wall comprising more than one type of material, the combined sound insulation is defined as:

$$R_{combined} = -10\log[(1/S_{surface})(S_1 10^{-R1/10} + S_2 10^{-R2/10} + ..)] \text{ [dB]} \qquad [3.64]$$

where:

- $R_{combined}$ = the combined sound insulation of surface areas i (dB);
- $S_{surface}$ = the total surface area of all surface areas i (m²);
- S_i = surface areas of surface i (with i = 1 to n) (m²);
- R_i = sound insulation for surface area i (dB).

The surface areas of all surfaces i determine the sound damping between two spaces.

Absorbing materials can be categorized on the base of their absorption mechanism:

- *Porous materials:* these are materials with an open structure. Larger pores (porosity) result in more of the wave remaining in the material. On the other hand, damping the sound in the material then depends upon whether the wave can flow easily through the material or not. Most damping occurs when the flow is restricted, while the thickness of the material also has an effect. A thicker material is required for low tones than for high tones. Examples of porous materials are glass fibre, polyurethane soft foam, or polyester- and polyether-based (open-structure) material. These materials absorb mainly high tones.

- *Resonating panels*: these are thin panels constructed on a layer of air (usually filled with mineral wool) before a hard wall. The panels absorb mainly low tones and can be compared to a mass spring system. The panel represents the mass and the air layer the spring. The system starts to resonate with its resonance frequency and the sound is transferred to heat (and is therefore being absorbed). The result is a high absorbance with the resonance frequency. The frequency band at which absorption takes place can be increased by introducing mineral wool.
- *Resonators and perforated panels*: these panels make use of one of the oldest forms of sound absorption, using the resonance principle of Helmholz (see Figures 3.32 and 3.33). An enclosed empty volume with air, connected via a small channel to the outside (comparable to the mass spring system), resonates with a certain frequency and energy will be absorbed through friction losses (damping) in or near the channel. This damping can be increased by introducing porous material behind the hole, which broadens the frequency area absorbed but lowers the absorption peak. An example is a perforated plate before an acoustical hard surface, with air volume in between.

Carpets, curtains and clothes behave as porous materials (absorbing high tones better than lower ones). If curtains are placed with a little space in between before an acoustical hard surface (glass), they will also absorb lower tones. Wooden floors on beams absorb low tones (but not much), and concrete, plastering, etc. hardly absorb. Examples of absorption coefficients for several materials are presented in Table 3.10.

Sound insulation

Sound insulation mitigates annoying sounds in a space, originating from another space, or reduces sound transmission from one space to another (Tol, 1984). Examples are:

- traffic noise in a bedroom (outdoor–indoor transmission);
- noise from neighbours (indoor–outdoor transmission);
- noise from music to the neighbourhood (indoor–outdoor–indoor transfer).

Transmission from inside to inside: in both spaces a diffuse field is assumed; in this case, Equation 3.53 can be applied.

Transmission from outside to inside: because a free field exists outside, the sending level differs at each location and the sound transmission can take place through more than one surface area (façade). Assuming

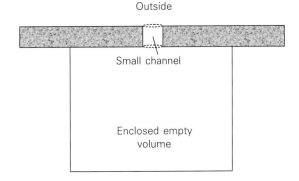

Source: adapted from Tol (1984)

Figure 3.32 *Principle of a Helmholtz resonator*

Source: Bluyssen

Figure 3.33 *Example of a perforated ceiling for acoustical purposes*

Table 3.10 *Absorption coefficients for several materials (percentage) – s is thickness in mm and d is distance between two panels in mm*

Material	d (mm)	s (mm)	Middle frequency (Hz)					
			125	250	500	1000	2000	4000
Walls:								
Plaster			2	2	3	4	5	6
Clean brickwork			2	3	3	4	5	7
Porous concrete			10	20	25	50	50	65
Wooden panels	6	50	30	20	20	10	10	10
Gypsum board	10	50	35	12	8	7	6	6
Floors:								
Smooth concrete			1	1	1	2	2	2
Carpet on concrete	5		2	3	5	11	30	60
linoleum			2	3	3	4	4	5
Ceilings:								
Mineral wool	50	400	90	95	99	99	99	99
perforated metal panels with mineral wool on top	40	400	30	45	50	60	70	70
Curtains:								
Cotton		50	15	45	96	91	100	100
Linen		50	8	53	85	94	100	100
Diverse:								
Single pane	6		10	4	3	2	2	2
Wooden non-furnished chair			2	3	4	4	5	5
Wooden furnished chair			11	18	28	35	45	42
One sitting person/m²			15	25	60	70	90	80

Source: adapted from Tol (1984)

that the sound falls only on one surface area, with an angle θ to the normal of this surface, the sound insulation is, then:

$$R_\theta = Lp_1 - Lp_2 + 10\log(S \cos\theta/A_2) + 6 \text{ [dB]} \quad [3.65]$$

where:

- Lp_1 = the sound pressure level on the outside surface area (dB);
- Lp_2 = the mean sound pressure level in the receiving space (dB);
- S = the surface area of the façade on which the sound falls (m²);
- A_2 = total sound absorption surface area in the receiving space (m²).

In general, noise produced by traffic, for example, does not fall onto the façade under one angle but under all angles between 0° to 90°. The sound insulation can then be estimated by the sound insulation occurring under an angle of 45°:

$$R_{0–90} = Lp_1 - Lp_2 + 10\log(S/A_2) + 3 \text{ [dB]}. \quad [3.66]$$

Because it is difficult to determine Lp_1, one can use the send level at 2m before the façade, at which the level is 3dB higher. The equation then becomes:

$$R_{0–90} = Lp_{2m} - Lp_2 + 10\log(S/A_2) - C_g \text{ [dB]} \quad [3.67]$$

where C_g = correction for type of façade (e.g. 0 for vertical flat façades; –2 for a balcony with closed balustrade).

Transmission from inside to outside: with this type of transmission the vibrating building façade influences the character of the sound transmitted. This is difficult to describe with theoretical formulas. However, assuming that the inside space is a completely diffuse field, the transmitted sound pressure level through a surface is estimated by (Tol, 1984):

$$L_{surface} = Lp_1 - R_{surface} + 10\log S_{surface} - 6 \text{ [dB]} \quad [3.68]$$

where:

- $L_{surface}$ = level of transmitted load per surface (dB);
- Lp_1 = sound pressure level in sending space (dB);
- $S_{surface}$ = surface area of surface (m^2);
- $R_{surface}$ = sound insulation of surface (dB).

Sound transmission

Two forms of sound transmission can be distinguished:

1   *Air sound transmission*: a sound source moves the air (vibration) and the air vibrates the separating wall; this wall vibrates the air on the other side.
2   *Contact sound transmission*: a source directly vibrates the wall or construction part (e.g. a hammer, footsteps or a door closing), after which this wall vibrates the air.

Some sources cause both forms of sound transmissions, such as a piano or the flushing of a toilet. The actual transmission depends upon the characteristics of the wall (or construction), but also upon the connections with other construction parts, transits for wires, ducts, pipes, etc., the so-called flank sound transmission and circulated sound transmission. The latter transmissions (flank and circulating) can be very important and can be the determining factor for the sound insulation of a wall between two spaces. However, the calculation for these transmissions is difficult and time consuming: acoustical models need to be applied.

3.5.3 Sources of noise

Sources of sound (or noise when it causes disturbances) produce different frequencies and/or combinations of different frequencies (tones), as well as different levels of loudness (see Figure 3.34). In general, low frequent sound (20–125Hz) (vibrations) is perceived as very annoying, while the ear is most sensitive to frequencies of between 3000–5000Hz.

Sounds produced by service equipment in buildings, such as elevators, sanitary and drinking water installations, and HVAC systems, are experienced by most people as noise. This is not strange because a large part of the experienced noise is caused by contact, circulated and flank transmission through the pipe systems into the building structure. The type of noise caused by an HVAC system is, in most cases,

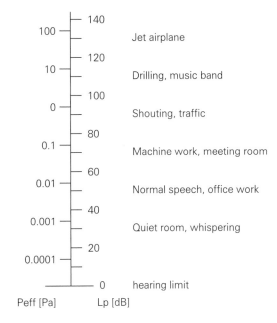

Source: Tol, 1984

Figure 3.34 *Examples of sound pressure levels and sound pressures*

continuous and results in constant background noise, while noise produced by a toilet only occurs at certain times (when flushing occurs). Sounds produced by traffic – in general, fluctuating noise – causes discomfort and can even result in sleepless nights. And last, but not least, wind-induced horizontal motion (tall buildings) can cause a whole range of complaints, from annoyance to even motion sickness (Esposito, 2005).

The loudness of the noise (the number of decibels) not only has an effect on speech intelligibility, but also on the health of the ear (see section 2.5.4 in Chapter 2).

For speech intelligibility, the background level (speech–background noise ratio) and the reverberation time are important to know. Three types of background sounds are distinguished:

1   human speech; buzzing;
2   pink background noise (trains);
3   white background noise (keyboard, circle saw, etc.);

3.5.4 Measurement

For *sound pressure level* measurement, several instruments are available, from very simple ones to highly sophisticated precise measurement equipment.

Guidelines and regulations are available with specifications for these instruments (CEN–IEC, 2003). Measurements are mostly taken to determine:

- the sound pressure level of a constant sound in order to calculate air and contact sound transmission between spaces: the *sound absorption and insulation* of a material or an element can be measured in a test chamber or estimated in the field (several standards are available; see below);
- the equivalent sound pressure level for fluctuating sound (e.g. to calculate the façade insulation in case of traffic noise);
- the reverberation time of a space, among others, to determine the audibility of a space (see also section 3.5.5).

In case the sound originates from outside, it is possible to use the following equation to determine the sound pressure difference caused by a façade:

$$D_{nT} = Lp_{2m} - Lp_2 + 10\log(T_2/T_n) \ [dB] \qquad [3.69]$$

where:

- D_{nT} = normalized difference in sound pressure level (dB);
- Lp_{2m} = sound pressure level at 2m for the façade with the highest sound load (dB);
- Lp_2 = the mean sound pressure level in a receiving space (dB);
- T_2 = reverberation time in a receiving space (s);
- T_n = the normalized reverberation time (for dwellings, 0.5 seconds) (s).

The sound pressure level at 2m for the façade needs to be measured, as well as the mean or equivalent sound pressure level in the receiving space. In addition, the reverberation time in the receiving space needs to be estimated or measured.

The *reverberation time* can be measured, calculated or estimated (NPR, 2007). Estimation is performed by taking the mean of reverberation multiplied by the middle frequencies in each of the isofones (see Table 3.9) between 250Hz and 4kHz. In order to determine speech intelligibility, the speech–background ratio needs to be determined. This ratio is determined by measuring the background noise level first and then the sound pressure level when speaking occurs. The speech-background noise ratio is equal to the difference between both measurements, and determines which type of background is present. With this information the so-called Speed Transmission Index (STI) (ISO, 2003) can be determined.

For vibrations (low frequencies) caused by internal or external sources, measurement procedures have been developed for both the very low horizontal motion frequencies (0.063– 1Hz) and the mechanical induced vibrations (1–80Hz) (see Box 3.8).

Box 3.8 Some standards for noise/sound and vibration determination

- EN 12354 Building Acoustics: estimation of acoustic performance of buildings from the performance of elements (comprises several parts) (Part 6; CEN, 2003);
- EN ISO 14257 Acoustics: measurements and parametric description of spatial sound distribution curves in workrooms for evaluating acoustical performance (CEN–ISO, 2001a);
- EN ISO 140 Acoustics: measurement of sound insulation in buildings and of building elements (comprises several parts);
- EN ISO 10052 Acoustics: field measurement of airborne and impact sound insulation and of service equipment noise; survey method (CEN–ISO, 2005);
- ISO 9921 Ergonomics: assessment of speech communication (ISO, 2003);
- EN ISO 18233 Acoustics: application of new measurement methods in building and room acoustics (CEN–ISO, 2006a);
- ISO 6897 guidelines for the evaluation of the response of occupants of fixed structures, especially buildings and offshore structures, to low-frequency horizontal motion (0.063–1Hz) (ISO, 1984);
- ISO 2631-1 Mechanical Vibration and Shock: evaluation of human exposure to whole-body vibration – Part 1: Vibration in buildings (1–80Hz) (ISO, 1997);
- ISO 2631-2 Mechanical Vibration and Shock: evaluation of human exposure to whole-body vibration – Part 2: Vibration in buildings (1–80Hz) (ISO, 2003b).

3.5.5 Control strategies

Control strategies can be performed to prevent noise from entering a space or approaching a person, or to make the space perform better acoustically.

Optimal speech intelligibility

Besides reverberation time and the speech–background noise ratio, speech audibility is influenced by the speaker, the communication channel and the listener. Speech intelligibility can therefore be improved by improving the speech–background noise ratio, by shortening the reverberation time, and by improving the clarity and loudness of speech. Normal speech at a distant of 1m has a volume of 60dB(A), while loud speech has a volume of 66dB(A).

A space with a long reverberation time is normally experienced as unacceptable. By introducing absorbing material and/or decreasing the volume, the reverberation time can be shortened. Introduction of absorption material also *decreases the sound pressure level*:

$$\Delta L_p = 10 \log A_{after} / A_{before} \qquad [3.70]$$

where:

- A_{after} = absorption of space after the introduction of more absorption material;
- A_{before} = absorption of space before the introduction of more absorption material.

This means twice as much absorption will result in a reduction of 6dB.

Introduction of absorption material also *suppresses echo*: echo is an annoying reflection that is derived from a hard surface or a hollow bowed surface (it bundles the sound waves). A flutter is an echo between two hard parallel surfaces. This can be prevented by introducing absorption material on the surfaces.

Improving concentration

Table 3.11 presents minimum concentration qualifications for different types of activities related to optimal and maximum acceptable equivalent sound pressure values. If the sound has a certain disturbing component, such as intermittent sound or a low or high frequency sound, this needs to be removed. If this is not possible, the levels presented should be reduced by 5dB or 10dB.

In open offices, a sound pressure level of 35db(A) or 45dB(A) can be too low: the background noise–speech ratio hinders audibility. For high-concentration activities, open offices do not seem to be suitable.

Sound leaks can occur as a result of:

- holes through a wall (e.g. for water pipes or electrical wires or from badly arranged stones, etc);
- connection details (e.g. of floors, façades or roofs);
- windows and doors.

The influence of such a leak can be estimated by taking a surface area S_{leak} with sound insulation zero ($R_{leak} = 0$)

Table 3.11 *Minimum concentration qualifications for different types of activities related to the optimal and maximum acceptable equivalent sound pressure values*

Type of activity	Qualification	Equivalent sound pressure level (dB(A))*	
		Optimal	Maximum acceptable
Factory	Very low	75	80
Cleaning	Low	65	75
Reception	Moderate	55	65
Laboratory	Reasonable	45	55
Teaching/study	High	35	45

Note:* Equivalent level means that a level equivalent to the average sound energy over the period is measured.
Source: NPR (2007)

in Equation 3.64. The influence of leaks is noticeable especially for high frequencies (>1000Hz). Sound leaks can be closed by increasing the damping in the leak via porous sound-absorbing material (mineral wool) or by increasing the insulation by closing the leak with an airtight material.

Prevention or reduction of *contact sound transmission*:

• Prevent construction from vibrating by introducing a resilient finishing layer (such as a carpet or rubber for mainly higher frequencies), a floating floor or vibration dampers (a real spring from rubber, synthetics or metal).

• Prevent sound from being radiated from construction to air by adding an extra construction (wall or ceiling) that is bendable (very high resonance frequency and therefore hardly any radiation in the frequency area of concern); but be careful about flanking sound transmission.

Active (anti-) noise control

Active noise control, the suppression of an undesired sound by the action of another sound, was invented by Paul Lueg in Germany in 1932 (Cunefare, 2004). Essentially, one or more microphones sense the noise and a noise-cancellation speaker emits a sound wave with the same amplitude and the opposite polarity (in anti-phase) from the original sound. The waves combine to form a new wave (interference) and effectively cancel each other out (phase cancellation). The resulting sound wave may be inaudible to human ears. Modern active noise control is achieved through the use of a computer, which analyses the waveform and then generates a reversed waveform to cancel it out through interference.

Active noise control has been used to control noise produced by industrial fans; to suppress noise in heating, ventilation and air-conditioning ducts; to reduce vehicle exhaust sounds; to create 'quiet zones' within vehicle interiors; and to reduce noise levels inside aircraft and spacecraft launch areas. Today, the most commonplace active noise control equipment are headsets in aviation and consumer use (Cunefare, 2004).

Active noise control works very well when the noise-cancellation speaker is co-located with the sound source to be attenuated or when the transducer emitting the cancellation signal may be located at the location where sound attenuation is wanted (e.g. the user's ear). Noise cancellation at other locations is more difficult. In small enclosed spaces (e.g. the passenger compartment of a car), such global cancellation can be achieved using multiple speakers and feedback microphones, and measurement of the modal responses of the enclosure.

Contrary to passive noise control methods (insulation, sound-absorbing ceiling tiles or muffler), active noise control uses a powered system. The advantages compared to passive ones are that they are generally more effective at low frequencies, less bulky and able to block noise selectively.

Part II

Health and Comfort in the Indoor Environment

4

Past, Present and Future of Health and Comfort in the Indoor Environment

In this chapter, an introduction to Part II is presented, as well as the link with Part III. The goal is to show an overview of how management of the indoor environment has developed over the years (Chapter 5) and which drivers of health and comfort in the indoor environment can be identified (Chapter 6).

During the last century, the scientific approach for managing the indoor environment merely focused on its single components (thermal comfort, light, air quality and noise) and, to some extent, on interrelations between these components in the bottom–up approach. The scientific approaches applied to cope with indoor environment quality are sketched and discussed in Chapter 5.

Drivers of health and comfort, which are described in Chapter 6, such as the wishes and demands of the end-user, are changing over time and are different than they were 100 years ago. With the increasing number of needs, the type of problems addressed appears to have undergone some kind of evolution. It is no longer the problem of heat supply or light fittings that we are concerned with, but questions such as how to improve the productivity of the worker? How to identify the changing needs of the end user? And how to cope with climate change effects in the indoor environment?

The main message of Part II is that, although the approaches developed are useful for specific situations, there seems to be a discrepancy between current practice and drivers for health and comfort in the indoor environment.

4.1 Introduction

The well-being of the population is largely affected by health, comfort and safety conditions during the main activities of living, working and transportation in an enclosed space in which people spend more than 90 per cent of their time (Jenkins et al, 1990). Recent research shows an obvious trend for time spent in the home to be increasing, especially with those who are younger and older (Bonnefoy et al, 2004). People spend most of their life indoors, at home – on average, nearly 16 hours per day during the week and 17 hours per day during the weekend. For children and the elderly, these figures are even higher – in the range of 19 to 20 hours a day.

During previous centuries, until the 1900s or so, the indoor environment was for most people merely a place for shelter, sleeping and eating, in fact, answering to the first four needs on Maslow's ladder (see section 6.2.1 in Chapter 6). This does not mean that health and comfort were not part of the design of buildings. In the renaissance architecture of the 16th century, several examples show the opposite to be true. Architects such as Andrea Palladio (1508–1580) tried, for example with the Villa Capra (1565–1566) near Vicenza, to achieve a balance of light and heat, during both summer and winter (Hawkes, 2008). Reyner Banham (1922–1988), who was a pioneer in arguing that technology, human needs and environmental

---

Box 4.1 Healthy buildings

In 1993, it was estimated that in more than 40 per cent of enclosed spaces, people suffer health-, comfort- and safety-related complaints and illnesses (Dorgan Associates, 1993). Fisk (2000) qualified only 20 per cent of the building stock as being healthy.

---

concerns must be considered an integral part of architecture, systematically explored the impact of health and comfort engineering on the design of buildings and the minds of architects (Banham, 1984). According to Banham, before and during the 18th century, technology was still a part of architecture. After the 18th century this changes, he noticed that mechanical services and even some non-mechanical devices, such as partial glass or acoustic surfaces, were passed on mainly to specialists and were therefore out of the control of architects. Together with the need to meet the demands of industrial production and urbanization, this might explain the alienation of health- and comfort-providing technologies from the practice of architecture, thus explaining some of the problems encountered today.

The 'new' findings in the science of physics and chemistry with respect to electricity, light, sound and substances in the air, also around 1900, made it possible to improve many indoor environmental aspects (e.g. artificial lighting and heating/cooling), but introduced additional health and comfort problems that had not been encountered before, such as Legionnaires' disease and, later, with the introduction of new materials, formaldehyde, and around the 1980s the so-called sick building syndrome (SBS) symptoms.

The development of indoor environmental aspects and parameters was influenced by so-called internal and external drivers (see Figure 4.1). External drivers can be inventoried via an external analysis (Kotler, 1997) and analysed according to what these mean to the stakeholders of this indoor environment and how to act on it (internal analysis). In an external analysis, one can distinguish four major drivers: regulatory, economic, social and technological developments; but it is, in general, very difficult to separate the four from each other, especially when focusing on the performance of indoor environments. Internal drivers can be inventoried via the stakeholders:

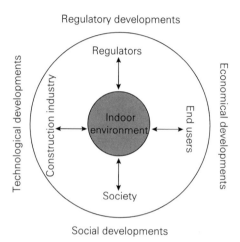

Source: adapted from Kotler (1997).

Figure 4.1 *External developments, stakeholders and the indoor environment*

- the real end user of the indoor environment: the person who uses the indoor environment for living, working or recreation;
- the construction industry, comprising all parties who have some relation with the creation and maintenance of the built indoor environment;
- the regulator: national, local, but also international, such as the European Commission;
- society: referring to all not included in the other three categories who can be of relevance to the indoor environment (e.g. the neighbour, the whole neighbourhood, the airplane that causes a noise problem, etc.).

The following drivers were found to be important to health and comfort in the indoor environment: climate change, the needs of the end user, the requirements of stakeholders, and regulatory developments.

4.2 Definition of health and comfort

During the early decades of the 20th century, the first relations between physical descriptors of environmental conditions within buildings – of heat, light and sound – and human needs were established. Building scientists such as Bedford, Dufton, Gagge, Houghten, Missenard, Vernon and Yaglou in the thermal field; Hartridge, Hecht, Luckeish and Walsh in lighting; and Sabine, Watson, Knudsen, Hope Bagenal and Wood in acoustics all carried out fundamental work (Hawkes, 2008). In many cases, these health and comfort theories still provide the basis of present-day indoor environmental design.

Research and practice merely focused on single components of the indoor environment: thermal comfort, light, air quality and noise. Considerable time was spent on identifying objective relations between indoor environmental parameters and human reactions (dose–response). The outcome can be seen in comfort models (e.g. thermal comfort) (Fanger, 1970), quantitative recommendations in the form of indices (Bluyssen, 2001) and/or criteria/limit values for temperature, light, noise, ventilation rates and certain substances in the air (e.g. CEN, 2002a, 2002b; WHO, 2003b, 2006; ASHRAE, 2004a, 2004b; EU, 2004; ISO, 2005). Only during the last decade of the 20th century was a first attempt made through epidemiological studies to approach the indoor environment in a holistic way (Burge et al, 1987, Skov et al, 1987; Preller et al, 1990; Bluyssen et al, 1996; Jantunen et al, 1998; Apte et al, 2000). The scientific approach towards the evaluation and creation of a healthy and comfortable indoor environment developed from a component-related to a bottom–up holistic approach (by trying to simply add the different components).

With regards to *thermal comfort*, since the beginning of the 20th century, a struggle has been going on between the heat exchange method and the adaptive approach. While followers of the heat exchange method strongly believed that comfort can be reached when the heat balance of the human body is neutral (Fanger, 1970), the adaptive approach focused on the reactions of people to restore their comfort when they are not (Bedford, 1936; Nicol and Humphreys, 1972; Auliciems, 1986). The latter reactions can be of a physiological, psychological,

social, technological, cultural or behavioural nature (Humphreys and Nicol, 1998). During the beginning of the 21st century, both theories came together in the adaptive comfort standard, which recommends comfort ranges for indoor operative temperature related to the mean outdoor air temperature (only applicable for naturally ventilated buildings) (ASHRAE, 2004a; CEN, 2005) based on field studies summarized by de Dear and Brager (1998) from 160 buildings all over the world.

Around the 1980s, the first computer simulation models (following up on thermal comfort models) made it possible to better understand phenomena such as air movement and temperature (e.g. in Lemaire, 1990). Predicting the integral building performance as experienced by the end user is, however, still too complex. The whole environment is more than the sum of its constituent stimuli and is therefore hard to predict (de Dear, 2004).

For *lighting*, research and practice was first focused on lighting comfort and task activities, and slowly shifted over the last 50 years or so to lighting and health. The need for lighting that does not cause health (and comfort) problems (see Wilkins et al, 1989), as well as the need for lighting to improve alertness and performance, became the focal point, together with daylight lighting in relation to energy (Baker et al, 1993; CEC, 1996; Fontoynont, 1999; Baker and Steemers, 2002). Artificial lighting can be used, but it should not cause negative effects; on the contrary, it should take care of the non-visual effects that we so desperately need (LHRF, 2002). A good balance in people's dark-light exposure is important to the rhythm of sleeping and being awake, as well as hormone regulation (Cajochen, et al, 2000; Brainard et al, 2001). Additionally, the psychological factor of (day)light, including not only colour and illuminance, but also a view of, or contact with, the outdoor environment, should not be underestimated (Meerdink et al, 1988; Hout, 1989; Vroon, 1990).

With regards to *indoor air quality*, for most of the 20th century, appropriate ventilation was considered to be enough. Good indoor air quality was always related to ventilation rates, and is, in fact, no more than an indicator. It was not until the 1990s that a different approach was considered: source control. It was finally acknowledged that occupants are not the only polluters in indoor environments (Bluyssen et al, 1996) and therefore a ventilation rate based on the carbon dioxide (CO_2) production of these occupants is no longer valid in buildings where they are not the dominant source of pollution. Furnishing and construction materials, ventilation system components and activities performed by people indoors can be major sources as well. The search for sources and the development of guidelines to control the sources is still taking place (EU, 2005). Besides ventilation rate, indoor air quality can be evaluated according to other aspects – for example, on its substances (WHO, 2000b, 2006) or on the direct judgement by panels of people (Yaglou, 1936; Cain et al, 1983; Fanger and Berg-Munch, 1983; Bluyssen, 1990). During the last decade, a transition can be observed from a focus on primary emissions towards secondary emission phenomena, such as products of ozone-initiated indoor chemistry (Bornehag et al, 2004; Weschler, 2004) and growth of micro-organisms (Adan, 1994; IUMS, 2005; Fisk et al, 2007), both found to be related to major health effects.

For *noise*, a shift in research and practice (regulation) is apparent, from noise being treated only as a disturbance, to the realization that noise can have major health effects. While, during the 1960s and earlier, few people recognized that citizens might be entitled to be protected from adverse sound-level exposure, setting maximum noise limits for road traffic and, especially, aircraft traffic noise during the late 20th century led to significant reductions of noise from individual sources (EU, 2004).

The relationship between health effects and noise became a major issue during the 1990s (EU, 1996), especially noise from traffic at night (Berglund et al, 1999). Since 2002, steps have been taken to protect the indoor environment. Dose–effect curves for road, aircraft and railway noise and multi-exposure, for example, have become available (WHO, 2003b). Currently, vibrations caused by mainly external sources, such as traffic, are under study (Defra, 2007). If significant vibration occurs, it can be a nuisance (or a disturbance) and/or a cause of poor health (e.g. sleep disturbance).

Environmental issues became more and more important towards the end of the 1980s, mainly due to the energy crises of the 1970s. In the first epidemiological studies of the 1980s, interrelations between different parameters, building components and health effects (categorized according to building-related illnesses, SBS and/or multiple chemical sensitivity;

Spengler et al, 2001) were outlined (Burge et al, 1987; Skov et al, 1987; Preller et al, 1990)). The research following these studies was still component related; but the relation with other components was better taken into account. During the 1990s, it was acknowledged that complaints and health effects related to the indoor environment are not caused by one single parameter (Bluyssen, 1992). Findings of studies performed with a larger population and a wider spread have shown a complex link between present-day housing conditions (thermal comfort, lighting, moisture, mould and noise) and human health and well-being – see the European Audit project (Bluyssen et al, 1996) and EXPOLIS (Jantunen et al, 1998) in Europe; the BASE study in the US (Apte et al, 2000); and the WHO study (Bonnefoy et al, 2004). SBS, for instance, has been shown to be a result of numerous problems with multifactor causes. Indeed, the mechanisms behind it are unknown. What is clear is that besides the physical factors, confounding factors (age, sex, working position, social status, etc.) and psychological factors are also involved (Bluyssen, 1992).

Besides analysing the causes of SBS, during the last decades multiple concepts and tools have been developed and used to evaluate the *performance* of the built environment, buildings, building parts or specific aspects of buildings (Bluyssen, 2001). Although many attempts have been made to include the user's demands, it is striking that many methods exist for 'trouble shooting' (occupancy phase) and few for 'prevention' (initiation and design phase).

4.3 Drivers of health and comfort

The needs of end users are not only context dependent, but are also influenced by so-called drivers (Kotler, 1997). Climate change and several social, economic and regulatory drivers are important for the health and comfort of people in the indoor environment. With regard to the regulatory drivers, it is seen that most national, European, nationwide and even worldwide organizations, for example, agree that indoor environments, including work and living spaces, can be a threat to one's health, and that indoor environmental parameters themselves can contribute to that threat. Directives and action programmes have been established and targets have been set to improve this situation. Since the middle of the 20th century, two interesting movements have contributed to the acknowledgement of health and comfort in the indoor environment from a regulatory point of view:

- from prescriptions of building components towards performance of buildings – for example, seen in the Essential Requirements for Building Products (EU, 1988) and the Energy Performance Directive for Buildings (EU, 2002b);
- towards health in all policies, of which the more recent European health strategy is a good example, where it is emphasized that 'Spending on health is not just a cost, it is an investment (health is the greatest wealth)' (EU, 2007a).

The cause of *climate change* and its possible consequences is called *radiative forcing*, which is defined as the change in average net radiation at the top of the troposphere (lower atmosphere) (Houghton, 2004). Why this problem is exactly occurring is still under discussion, but the fact remains that something is happening with our climate (IPCC, 2007; Svensmark, 2007). Although it is difficult to predict what will happen in the following centuries, some indications of consequences for health and comfort in the indoor environment can be given:

- The average rise in outdoor temperature will most likely lead to a higher number of air-conditioning systems used and a decrease in energy demand from heating systems.
- The increase in outdoor air pollution will also (most likely) lead to an increase in demand for air-conditioning systems cleaning the outdoor air before entering the (airtight) building. Design and maintenance of these systems is then more important than ever, ensuring that complaints related to noise or air pollution originating from air-conditioning systems are prevented.
- Increased wind speeds and the frequency of storms will most likely lead to increased perceived effects of noise and vibrations.
- The effect of storms and cloud forming, on the one hand, and the increased sun hours, on the other, will most likely influence the quality of daylight and, indirectly, affect the need for artificial forms of lighting that can rapidly adapt to changes.
- Psycho-social factors such as a fear of storms and flooding may cause people to stay inside even more than they already do, causing more stress and

probably an increase in mental disorders (extrapolation from findings of Bonnefoy et al, 2004).

In addition to the climate change driver, two social drivers of importance influence end users' needs: the *change from a family-oriented society to a multifunctional and diverse society* and the *increasing individualization caused by ageing and an increase in one- and two-person households* (WHO, 2002; EU, 2007a, 2007b). Both most likely lead to increasing and different needs for indoor spaces, such as a demand for higher quality, flexibility of buildings, and a focus on care for the elderly and social inclusion. At the same time, a change in the type of end users has been observed: cognitive needs (knowledge, meaning, etc.), aesthetic needs (appreciation and search for beauty, balance, form, etc.) and self-actualization (realizing personal potential, self-fulfilment, etc.) are no longer enough (Maslow, 1934). Transcendence needs – helping others to achieve self-actualization – will predominate: customer experience is a good example of this (Iacobuci, 2001).

Besides end users, direct *stakeholders of the indoor environment* (parties who initiate, create, build and maintain the indoor environments in which we all live, work and play) also have their stakes or needs in terms of taking part in the life-cycle of indoor environmental spaces. These are mainly economic related.

The drivers found to be important for health and comfort in the indoor environment can be translated for each of the different perspectives (social, technological, economical and regulatory) into stakes at different levels (society, city, neighbourhood and indoor space levels). Plate 7 (centre pages) identifies *stakes for the different levels and perspectives*. Note that these stakes are dynamic over time and highly volatile under the influence of future developments.

4.4 Link to Part III

Although science seems to be focused mainly on individual components of the indoor environment, some architects try to put the acquired knowledge into practice, moving beyond structure and external looks (Banham, 1984). The Larkin building by Frank Lloyd Wright (1905) is an example of a 'well-tempered environment' (Banham, 1984).

However, according to Hawkes (2008), there is a critical dimension: 'The complex sensory experience that we enjoy in buildings implies a wholly different dimension to the idea of the architectural environment from the pragmatic and mechanical process of climate modification and comfort engineering in quantitative terms such as degrees, noise levels, illuminance, etc.'. According to Hawkes, the architectural environment is much more than a matter of pragmatic prescription and technical realization. The merging of poetic sensibility with environmental technologies is important to the distinct and expressive character of buildings. This can, for example, be found in the work of 19th-century architects Henri Labrouste (in France: Bibliothèque Nationale) and Charles Rennie Mackintosh (Glasgow buildings), as well as in the works of many major 20th-century figures such as Le Corbusier, Mies van der Rohe, Alvar Aalto, Erik Gunnar Asplundm Sigurd Lwerentz, Louis Kahn and Carlo Scarpa. They all sought quite specific qualities in the conception and realization of the environmental character of their designs. And the same can be said for some contemporary architects: Sverre Fehn, Peter Zumthor, Rafael Moneo, Alvaro Siza, Caruso St John and Steven Holl.

However, the fact remains that not all workers and people are healthy and comfortable in the indoor environment of today. Improving the health, comfort and safety of populations in indoor environments has a huge potential for economic and societal benefits obtained as a result of increased productivity, reduced sick leave and medical costs, and fewer casualties from accidents (as well as the prevention of liabilities).

It should be emphasized that the context of people–environment interactions includes not only the environmental context, but also the cognitive and even the emotional context, affected by external and internal drivers. How to adapt the indoor environment to these different contexts and changing contexts over time is a major challenge.

In order to satisfy end users' wishes and demands (requirements and needs), a top–down approach that may be complementary to the traditional bottom–up approach could be part of the solution (see Part III). The individual human being forms the starting point for this approach, as the integrating 'sensor' of all indoor environmental parameters.

5

Defining Health and Comfort in the Indoor Environment

Twentieth-century approaches towards obtaining health and comfort in the indoor environment are presented. Research and practice merely focused on single components of the indoor environment: thermal comfort, light, air quality and noise. Much time was spent on identifying objective relations between indoor environmental parameters and human reactions (dose–response). The outcome is seen in comfort models – for example, for thermal comfort, quantitative recommendations in the form of indices and or criteria/limit values for temperature, light, noise, ventilation rates and certain substances in the air. During the last decades of the twentieth century, an attempt was made through epidemiological studies to manage the indoor environment in a holistic way. The scientific approach towards the evaluation and creation of a healthy and comfortable indoor environment developed from a component-related to a bottom–up holistic approach.

5.1 Component-related approach

5.1.1 From thermal comfort to simulation and adaptive comfort

Thermal comfort is:

> … that condition of mind which expresses satisfaction with the thermal environment. (ASHRAE, 2004a)

History

Research on thermal comfort essentially began with the establishment of the American Society of Heating and Ventilation Engineering (ASHVE) laboratories in Pittsburg (1919) (Janssen, 1999). The fast-growing air-conditioning industry needed thermal comfort criteria during the beginning of the 20th century. In the mid-1960s, the climate chamber of ASHVE was transferred to Kansas State University, US. The research performed there, called the heat-exchange approach, resulted in data that can still be considered as the basis for the current thermal comfort criteria, and led to several indices.

In tandem with these laboratory studies, field studies were performed that led to a number of empirical, statistically based indices for thermal comfort. The conditions for thermal comfort found in these studies (begun already by Bedford during the 1930s) varied from each other and were sometimes difficult to relate to the conditions calculated with heat exchange indices. A considerable difference exists between available physiological models and their more subjective interpretation (Auliciems, 1981). According to Auliciems (and others), the problem is related to the difficulty of separating direct responses to physical stimuli from subjective interpretations based on personal circumstances and experience. So, while the heat-exchange method, using laboratory data only, was the main approach followed in the US, doubts existed in Europe. Another approach, the adaptive approach, based on field studies of people in daily life, was developed that slowly took over the world. The outcome led to a different view than the heat-exchange method: the adaptive comfort model.

Heat-exchange method

In order to evaluate the general thermal state of a body, both in terms of comfort and heat or cold stress, it is important to analyse the heat balance of the human body (see section 2.2.2 in Chapter 2): a negative thermal storage indicates that the environment is too cool and vice versa. To provide comfort, the mean skin temperature also has to be within certain limits and evaporative heat loss must be low. Many thermal indices were developed during the last century based on this heat-exchange method, starting with total thermal body comfort and later including local thermal comfort aspects, such as draught, radiant asymmetry, vertical air temperature difference and floor surface temperatures. The data for these indices originated from laboratory studies focused on the heat exchange between a person and the thermal environment and the physiological conditions that are required for human comfort.

For total body thermal comfort, the most important indices are the following:

- *Operative temperature (t_o)*: the uniform temperature of a black environment (see Section 3.2.1) in which a person exchanges the same amount of heat via radiation and convection as in a real non-uniform environment. In most cases, if the difference between the mean radiant temperature and the air temperature is small (<4°C), the operative temperature is calculated as the mean of the air temperature and the mean radiant temperature.
- *Effective temperature (ET)*: the operative temperature with a relative humidity of 50 per cent, which causes the same heat loss as in the actual situation.
- *Predicted mean vote (PMV)*: an index that predicts the thermal sensation of a person for a certain combination of environmental parameters and a known clothing resistance and metabolism. The thermal resistance of clothing is expressed in clo. One clo is defined as the thermal insulation required to keep a sitting person comfortable, with a temperature of 21°C (ISO, 2005). The PMV index predicts the mean value of the thermal sensation votes of a large group of people on a seven-point scale (+3: hot; +2: warm; +1: slightly warm; 0: neutral; −1: slightly cool; −2: cool; −3: cold).

The PMV is deducted for stationary conditions, but can also be applied for small fluctuations of more than one variable if the mean of these variables during one hour earlier is applied. PMV values should only be used for values between −2 and +2, and only if the six main parameters lie in the following ranges:

- M = metabolism: 46–232W/m^2;
- I_d = thermal resistance of clothing: 0–0.310m^2 °C/W;
- t_a = air temperature: 10°–30°C;
- t_r = mean radiant temperature: 10°–40°C;
- V_a = air velocity: 0–1m/s;
- P_a = partial water vapour pressure: 0–2700Pa.

The metabolism can be estimated with ISO 8996 (ISO, 2004) and the thermal clothing resistance with ISO/DIS 9920 (ISO, 2006a), taking into account the type of work and the time of year. For varying metabolic rates, one should estimate a time-weighted average during the previous one-hour period. For sedentary people, the insulation of a chair must also be taken into account. Environmental parameters can be measured with the help of ISO 7726 (ISO, 1998); then the PMV can be calculated with the equation or determined with the use of tables. The PMV index can be used to determine whether a given thermal environment complies with the comfort criteria specified and to establish requirements for different levels of acceptability. With the PMV, ranges of *operative temperature* (t_o) in which the thermal climate can be found acceptable can be calculated.

When the PMV value has been determined, the predicted percentage of dissatisfied (PPD) can be calculated from Figure 2.9 in section 2.2.2 (see Chapter 2) or from the following equation:

$$PPD = 100 - 95\, e^{\left(-0.03353.PMV^4 - 0.2179.PMV^2\right)}\, [\%].\quad [5.1]$$

Local thermal comfort

The indices described above are valid for the whole human body. It is, however, possible that only a part of the body is heated or cooled, causing local thermal discomfort such as draught.

Draught is defined as a local cooling of the body caused by air movement. A draught risk model was

Box 5.1 Introduction of the weighing hour criterion in The Netherlands

During the 1990s, the weighing hour criterion was introduced in The Netherlands by the *Rijksgebouwendienst* to take into account aspects such as activities, type of climate system and construction of the building (Rgd, 1991). The number of hours that the predicted mean vote (PMV) >0.5 or <–0.5 is multiplied by a weighing factor. This weighing factor takes into account the extent to which the temperature (or PMV) is exceeded (see Table 5.1). The maximum number of weighted hours during which PMV is above 0.5 or below –0.5 is 150.

Table 5.1 *Weighing factors as a function of predicted mean vote (PMV) range*

PMV range	Weighing factor
0.5<PMV≤0.6 and –0.6≤PMV<–0.5	1.25
0.6<PMV≤0.7 and –0.7≤PMV<–0.6	1.50
PMV>0.7 and PMV<–0.7	1.85

Source: Rgd (1991)

developed to predict the rate of discomfort caused by draught (Melikov, 1989). This draught discomfort depends upon the mean air velocity, the frequency and amplitude of the mean air velocity, and the air temperature. The model can be used to determine the expected percentage of dissatisfied individuals in a certain situation for known values of turbulence intensity and air temperature. And the model can also be used to determine the allowed mean air velocity for an acceptable percentage of those dissatisfied.

The turbulence intensity is defined as the ratio of the standard deviation of the air velocity to the mean air velocity:

$$T_u = \sigma_{v_a} / v_a \; [\%] \qquad [5.2]$$

where:

- v_a = local mean air velocity (m/s);
- σ_{v_a} = standard deviation of local mean air velocity (3 minutes) (m/s).

The percentage of people predicted to be dissatisfied due to draught (draught rating: DR) may be estimated from the equation:

$$DR = (34 - t_a)(v_a - 0.05)^{0.62}(3.14 + 0.37T_u v_a) \; [\%] \quad [5.3]$$

where:

- t_a = the local air temperature $(19 < t_a < 27)$ (°C);
- for v_a < 0.05m/s, insert v_a = 0.05m/s, and for DR > 100%, use DR = 100%.

The model applies to people with a thermal sensation for the whole body close to neutral. The sensation of draught is lower at activities higher than sedentary and for people feeling warmer than neutral. The turbulence intensity may vary between 30 and 60 per cent in spaces with mixing flow air distribution. In spaces with displacement ventilation or without mechanical ventilation, the turbulence intensity may be lower.

Other local thermal comfort problems can be caused by:

- a large vertical temperature difference between head and ankles: between 0.1m and 1.1m above the floor;
- too low or too high floor temperatures: for people wearing light indoor shoes or even bare feet;
- too large radiant asymmetry: caused by a warm ceiling (vertical direction) or a cold window or another cold vertical surface area (horizontal direction);
- temperature fluctuations.

Adaptive approach

The adaptive approach is based on 'the biological insight that the human being is a comfort-seeking animal who will, given the opportunity, interact with the environment in ways that secure comfort' (Humphreys and Nicol, 1998). The starting point is the adaptive principle: 'If a change occurs such as to produce discomfort, people react in ways that tend to restore their comfort.' These reactions are referred to as adaptations and can include all physiological, psychological, social, technological, cultural or behavioural strategies that people might use to try to secure their comfort. A person is not a passive receiver of sense impressions, but is an active participant in dynamic equilibrium with the thermal environment. Time is an essential component in understanding comfort processes.

During the early 1970s, Nicol and Humphreys (1972) challenged steady-state comfort theories with the adaptive comfort theory: if occupants were allowed to adapt their environment either by adjusting clothing, controls or location, then they could tolerate environmental conditions outside those recommended by steady-state theories and, hence, the current thermal comfort standards. In 1978, Humphreys suggested that the optimum internal temperature for a building (i.e. the temperature at which most people will report comfort: the comfort temperature) could be related to the external temperature at that location over a considerable range (Humphreys, 1978):

* Weather and seasons exert a pervasive influence on our behavioural adaptations to the thermal environment. For example, we typically use information about expected maximum daily temperatures along with recent experiences when making decisions about what to wear on a particular day.
* Second, both the recent past and the predicted near future, along with long-term seasonal swings, determine our psychological adaptations in the form of thermal expectations.

In response to the criticism that the adaptive comfort theory is too complex, the adaptive control algorithm (ACA) was developed to provide building designers with a simple method of controlling internal temperatures utilizing the principles of adaptive comfort theory. Humphreys (1978) suggested that desired comfort temperature in a free-running building could be expressed by:

$$T_C = aT_{out} + b \qquad [5.4]$$

where:

* T_C = comfort temperature (°C);
* T_{out} = outside temperature index (°C);
* a, b = constants.

In the US, the equations were also determined for different buildings (free-running buildings, slow-acting buildings, with or without indoor climate control mechanisms, etc.), using a database with field studies on 21,000 sets of raw data compiled of field studies in 160 buildings located on four continents in varied climatic zones since the mid-1980s (de Dear and Brager, 2002). The data include a full range of thermal questionnaire responses, clothing and metabolic estimates, concurrent indoor climate measurements, a variety of calculated thermal indices, and concurrent outdoor meteorological observations. The buildings in the database were separated into those that had heating, ventilating and air-conditioning systems (HVAC) systems (with no or little control of occupants over their immediate thermal environment) and naturally ventilated buildings (with openable windows). The following was found:

* Occupants of HVAC buildings become more finely adapted to the narrow, constant conditions typically provided by mechanical conditioning, while occupants of naturally ventilated buildings prefer a wider range of conditions that more closely reflect outdoor climate patterns.
* In the HVAC buildings, the PMV was remarkably successful at predicting comfort temperatures, demonstrating that behavioural adjustments of clothing insulation and room air speeds fully explain the relationship between indoor comfort temperature and outdoor climate variation. However, in naturally ventilated buildings, the difference between these PMV-based predictions and the adaptive model (fitted to observed data) shows that such behavioural adjustments account for only half of the climatic dependence of comfort temperatures. The unexplained residual must come

from influences not accounted for by the PMV model, such as psychological adaptation (shifting thermal expectations).

The outdoor climatic environment for each naturally ventilated building was characterized in terms of mean outdoor dry bulb temperature $T_{a,out}$. Optimum comfort temperature can be calculated with:

$$T_{comf} = 0.31\ T_{a,out} + 17.8. \qquad [5.5]$$

A range of temperatures around T_{comf} corresponding to 90 and 80 per cent thermal acceptability was defined by using the PMV–PPD relationship. The resulting 90 and 80 per cent acceptability limits are shown in Figure 5.1.

The adaptive comfort standard can be used under the following circumstances:

- Naturally conditioned buildings, in which the thermal space conditions are regulated primarily by the occupants through opening and closing of windows.

- Spaces can have a heating system, but the method does not apply when it is in operation.
- Spaces cannot have a mechanical cooling system.
- Spaces can have mechanical ventilation with unconditioned air, but opening and closing of windows must be the primary means of regulating thermal conditions.
- Occupants of spaces must be engaged in near sedentary activity (1–1.3 met) and must be able to freely adapt their clothing to the indoor and/or outdoor thermal conditions.
- Outdoor temperature range of 10°–33°C. However, as soon as the mean outdoor air temperature rises above 33°C, the PMV is the only predictive tool to be used, which then leads to an unrealistic step change in allowable indoor temperatures.

In Europe, the European SCAT project conducted thermal comfort field studies across Europe between 1997 and 2000 (five buildings in each of the five countries of France, Greece, Portugal, Sweden and the UK) and developed the so-called adaptive comfort

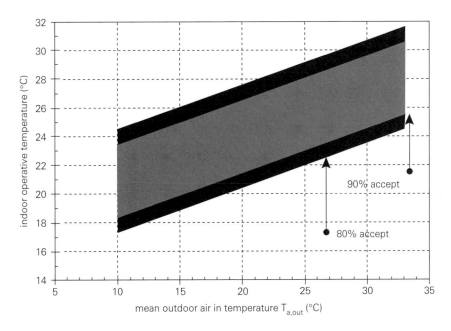

Note: Applying the ±0.5 and ±0.85 PMV criteria to each building's thermal sensation (assumed to represent dissatisfaction) as a function of indooroperative temperature produced a 90 and 80 per cent acceptable comfort zone, respectively, for each building.

Source: B. Oleson

Figure 5.1 *Proposed adaptive comfort standard for ASHRAE Standard 55, applicable for naturally ventilated buildings (de Dear and Brager, 2002)*

algorithm (ACA) (McCartney and Nicol, 2002). Using the ASHRAE database analysis of de Dear and Brager, comfort temperature was calculated. The results were similar to de Dear and Brager (2002), although some variation was seen within countries. Below 10°C, comfort temperature does not change with running mean temperature. Taking into account other environmental variables (light and noise) had little effect on the overall predictive power of the ACA.

It is clear that outdoor climate influences thermal perceptions beyond the clothing that we wear. Most likely, it has a psychological effect on expectations. Furthermore, it must be noted that the availability of personal control has positive effects far beyond just thermal comfort. Hawkes (1982) found that energy efficiency improved when people were given control of their environment. Wilson and Hedge (1987) found that fewer building-related ill health symptoms and greater productivity were achieved as the perceived level of individual control increased. And McIntyre (1980) suggested influencing thermal boredom by fluctuating interior temperatures to meet our inherent needs for sensory stimulation.

Building simulation models

Based on the thermal comfort models, computer simulation programmes were developed during the 1980s, when the first personal computers began to appear. They offered the possibility of predicting building performance during the design phase, taking historical data (such as temperature and humidity) into account. Building simulation programmes were also used to understand certain phenomena better, such as:

- energy analysis of buildings under different conditions and with different constructional elements;
- air movement and temperatures with, for example, a computational fluid dynamic model programme (Lemaire, 1990) (see Plate 9, centre pages);
- prediction of general heating and cooling demands;
- prediction of emissions over time from building products (Yang et al, 1998).

However, to predict integral building performance as experienced by the end user is still a bridge too far. Bluyssen and Lemaire (1992) tried to predict the

distribution of the perceived air quality in an office space with a mechanical air supply system, where several pollution sources were present, using a computational fluids dynamics model. The results were compared with the sensory evaluations of a trained panel. Computer simulations of the perceived air quality did not confirm these evaluations completely, which might have been caused by the assumed boundary conditions, the assumption that air (as it is perceived by a person) is transported in the same way as a neutral gas, and chemical and physical processes taking place, such as adsorption and desorption effects.

Standards

As described above, during the 1990s, several extensive field studies from 160 buildings all over the world summarized by de Dear and Brager (1998) showed that in buildings with HVAC systems, the PMV model seems to work well. However, the studies also showed that in naturally ventilated buildings (free running, no mechanical cooling), people seem to adapt (behaviourally and psychologically) and can accept higher indoor temperatures than those predicted by the PMV model. ASHRAE Standard 55, first based on the heat balance model of the human body, was revised to include the adaptive comfort algorithm (ASHRAE, 2004). In Europe, the EN15251 (2005) was also adapted. (see section C.1 in Annex C).

5.1.2 From daylight entry and visual comfort to lighting and health

Light plays a major role in architecture. Vision is the primary sense through which we experience architecture and light is the medium that reveals space, form, texture and colour to our eyes. But light is also strongly connected to thermal qualities. Light is energy, and whether diffuse or direct, will change to heat when it falls on a surface. Through the evolution of man and of society, light is associated with safety, warmth and community. Day lighting has always been a major consideration for designing a building. However, with the invention of artificial lighting (i.e. the fluorescent tube in 1938), building design could be totally independent of the outdoor provided light.

In 1904 the Commission International d'Eclairage (International Commission for Lighting) was founded and began to propose standards and develop the science of photometry. The art of lighting found in the architecture of the 19th century began to give way to the 20th-century science of lighting, focused in the beginning on lighting comfort and tasking activities and then slowly shifting towards lighting and health.

Daylight entry

Regulations on daylight entry date from the beginning of 1900. For example, the Dutch Safety Decision of 1913 stated that in a working space, daylight opening should be present with a total surface area of at least one tenth of the floor surface area. In the Dutch Workers' Decision of 1920, it was determined that a youthful person or a woman could only perform reading, writing or calculating work in an office where direct sun lighting could not be shut out.

In view of the development of office lighting, daylight as activity light came second. Daylight openings no longer seemed necessary; however, there was a growing recognition that daylight openings next to the entry of daylight could also provide contact with the outside world. In 1969, a Dutch policy thus emphasized the view demand. In 1978, this policy was stipulated in the daylight and view provisions of the safety decision for factories and workspaces. A workspace should be provided with openings for daylight entry and for views to the outdoor environment. The total surface area of daylight openings should be at least one twentieth of the floor surface area and the total width at least one tenth of the surface area of the workspace. Direct sunlight in workspaces should be prevented: applied artificial light should be sufficient and efficient.

At a European level, many manual design tools not requiring a computer for application were developed, such as daylight diagrams that determine the amount of daylight entering a specific window design and the amount falling on the work surface (TNO, 1979). So-called standard overcast skies, the CIE sky or the uniform sky, were used to determine daylight availability.

After the oil crisis, the energy dimension of light became a major issue. Obtaining energy for free through daylight and saving energy by not using electrical lighting became of great interest, and several European studies were conducted during the 1980s and 1990s to inventory the available daylight entering a space at a certain location and at a specific time – for example, the European Daylight project (Baker et al, 1993;

Fontoynont, 1999) and DAYLIGHT I and II (CEC, 1996) resulting, in respectively, a European reference book and European daylight atlas. It was found that local conditions at a building site may modify overall daylight climate due to obstructions (shading) or pollution (e.g. from nearby industries) and fog and haze (local variations in air temperature, wind and humidity).

During the 1990s, simulation programmes were developed as tools for daylight design to determine the level of illuminance of windows and other types of openings in the façade or roof, using average overcast skies or clear skies as standards (in southern Europe) and taking account of different surface reflectance. The latter is more complex due to the fact that a clear sky is much more changeable and dynamic with respect to the time of day and year. Direct sunlight can more easily introduce problems with glare and solar thermal gains. Examples of programmes are PASSPORT LIGHT, SUPERLIGHT, RADIANCE and ADDELINE (Baker and Steemers, 2002)). In the European Daylight project (Fontoynont, 1999), a daylight performance index (DPI) was developed because it was useful to have an objective method of evaluation to be used by both experts and non-experts. The DPI establishes a daylight factor contour of minimum daylight sufficiency, and a daylight factor contour of over illumination. Only the area of the building between these two contours counts positively towards the DPI.

Visual comfort

Visual comfort is largely influenced by the colours and luminances (brightness, glare, etc.) of our surroundings. With respect to the specification of colours, modern systems are still using the same principles as were applied by Munsell (i.e. the Munsell values and the way in which Munsell arranged these qualities of colours; see section 3.3.2 in Chapter 3). The Munsell system is still used to define paint colours, although only by colour matching. A modern approach is to define the colour of a surface, or light, in relation to the wavelength and the sensitivity of the colour receptors of the eye (Baker and Steemers, 2002). The tristimulus principle therefore forms the basis of modern colour specification systems.

The tristimulus values of a colour are the amounts of the three primary colours in a three-component additive colour model needed to match that test colour. Tristimulus values are most often given in the CIE

1931 colour space, in which they are denoted X, Y and Z (Hunt, 1998) (see Plate 10, centre pages). Any specific method for associating tristimulus values with each colour is called a colour space. CIE XYZ, one of many such spaces, is special because it is based on direct measurements of human visual perception, and serves as the basis from which many other colour spaces are defined.

Visual adaptation not only has implications for the time one needs to adapt (e.g. when moving from a bright location to a darker one), but also has implications for the apparent brightness. For example, the moon appears to be much brighter during night time (low adaptation level) than during daytime (high adaptation level), while the luminance of the moon remains the same in both cases. To be able to design for this concept of apparent brightness, since 1930, relationships between luminance, adaptation and subjective sensation of apparent brightness have been determined by several researchers. The exact relationship is still subject to debate; but it seems to be a power law just as any other physical stimuli that have been shown to relate to the human sensation estimation of the stimuli (Baker and Steemers, 2002):

$$\text{apparent brightness} = k(A).L^{b(A)} \quad [\text{lux}] \qquad [5.6]$$

where:

k(A) and b(A) are functions of the adaptation level A;
L = the absolute luminance (lux).

Additionally, the J index was developed to quantify visual comfort in terms of visual performance in the workplace (Baker and Steemers, 2002):

$$J = A_{max} - A/A_{max} \qquad [5.7]$$

where:

- A_{max} = maximum acuity (sharpness) that a person can reach in ideal lighting conditions;
- A = acuity obtained in a working place.

J varies according to the lighting conditions in the field of view between 0 (ideal situation) and 1 (worst lighting conditions due to either disability glare or excessively low luminance levels).

In order to qualify discomfort sensations, the unified glare rating (UGR) (see section 3.3.2 in Chapter 3) was introduced, which is now used to make comparisons between various lighting installations. Additionally, such values are used to estimate glare index values, which are defined by various national standards. However, when daylight becomes part of it, the evaluation is not as easy due to the dynamic nature of natural light.

View

Visual comfort is about more than providing a comfortable lighting environment for executing a task. A window has two functions: to make the entry of daylight possible and to provide a view, which occupants of (working) spaces need. A view that is completely or almost completely filled with building façades is evaluated negatively (Vroon, 1990). Occupants of offices show more appreciation for views that feature the following elements (see also Plate 11, centre pages):

- a visible skyline;
- visible objects and landscape located further away;
- 'greenery'.

Note that in offices located in an atrium there is no normal skyline in view, no (or only minimal) view of the sky, no visible objects and landscape located further; and the view is completely or almost completely filled with façades of its own building.

Views vary with height: views of the skyline, greenery and objects located further away look different from the fourth floor than from the 20th floor. In an investigation by Meerdink et al (1988) of four office buildings on the effect of daylight entry and views in relation to the comfort and satisfaction of 282 office workers, it was found that brightness in an office and the brightness of the surroundings influence the appreciation of daylight and outside views. Meerdink et al (1988) also found that the appreciation of view was influenced by the perception of weather, movements and greenery.

Office workers' activities as well as their personal characteristics (introvert or extrovert personalities) affect their perceptions and value judgements. In a study of three office buildings, in which 150 people received a questionnaire, a static view was preferred before a dynamic view (Hout, 1989). A neutral view was ranked last. Office work that requires a low concentration level necessitated a view with changing elements. On the other hand, office work with a high level of concentration required a view with few sources of distraction.

Lighting and health

During the 1980s, several studies were performed to investigate the influence of the spectral distribution and the flickering of light on people's health and comfort. Damage to the retina can occur when looking straight into a light tube for one hour and even more so for a light bulb (Padmos, 1988). The International Commission on Illuminance (CIE) concluded that with tube lighting of 500 lux the risk of skin cancer is 5 per cent of the risk associated with a yearly mean exposure to sunlight (CIE, 1988). And in a dermatological study performed by Harber (1985), a low dose of ultraviolet (UV)-A from tube lighting caused an increased risk of allergic skin reactions in oversensitive people.

Light flickers are also assumed to be a cause of ill health effects in connection to tube lighting, such as epileptic fits, physiological effects and effects on performance and tiredness. Padmos (1988) analysed these effects and concluded that 100Hz or 50Hz tremble tube lighting can increase the occurrence of eye tiredness and headache (Padmos, 1988). Epileptic fits have been reported in the case of flickering of defective lamps or starters. Wilkins et al (1989) showed that headaches and eye tiredness symptoms occurred twice as frequently when exposed to tube lighting with a tremble of 100Hz than an exposure to tube lighting with a high frequency (32kHz).

During the mid-1970s, Ott (1973) showed that light – in particular, spectral distribution – has a substantial influence on biological processes and the systems of plants and animals. Ott claimed that the energy of light, via chemical or hormonal control, has an effect on the growth of animals similar to the effect on the growth of plants via photosynthesis. The lack of certain wavelengths in the light spectrum (insufficient lighting), like malnutrition, causes biochemical or hormonal shortage in plant and animal cells.

Animals have certain sensors that are sensitive to electromagnetic radiation in the UV area: the Harderian gland and the Langerhans cells (MVROM, 1990). The Harderian gland plays an important role in the secretion of serotonin and melatonin by the pineal gland under the influence of light. The Langerhans cells, located in the epidermis, have been compared to chloroplasts in a plant cell, and may play a role in the

'conducting process' of UV radiation through the skin. Some investigators have claimed that something similar occurs with people. Behavioural studies with children have shown that full spectrum light (a simulation of natural light) has a positive effect and tube lighting a negative effect on the learning behaviour of children (Ott, 1974). Others researchers have claimed that all light information is perceived directly by the eye through the absorption of light by the receptors in the retina. From the receptor signal, no unambiguous information on spectral distribution can be determined – only the colour. Therefore, if the colour and light level are the same, tube light and bulb light cannot cause different effects via the eye. Components of near UV and infrared wavelengths cannot be absorbed by the receptors, are thus invisible to the eye, and are therefore not of importance to the vegetal, hormonal or psychological functions of light via the eye.

Nevertheless, besides the beneficial effect of UV light on the production of vitamin D through the skin (and the harmful effects such as skin cancer, skin burn, etc.), findings at the end of the 20th century showed that the amount of light entering the eye is also important to *non-visual* aspects (such as alertness and performance). This reopened lighting modelling, which is essentially based on the illuminance of the environment (LHRF, 2002). This new information indicates that brightness of the surroundings is the key element. In addition, another type of light-sensitive cells has been discovered (Brainard et al, 2001). These cells transmit the biological stimulating part of light to the brain; they are not used for visual function. Spectral sensitivity is highest at 460nm and therefore light with 460nm can be used to stimulate biological rhythms (the biological clock) at a much lower illumination than for other colours (Cajochen, et al, 2000).

The biological clock can be found in a small area of the brain, the suprachiasmatic nucleus (SCN), which is part of the hypothalamus, a large brain area regulating the secretion/production of hormones. The biological clock has an important role in several activities of the human being, such as the sleep–awake rhythm, the heart beat rhythm, and the functioning of organs and the brain. At night the epiphyses, which is controlled by the SCN, secrets the hormone melatonin, which makes us want to sleep (control of the sleep–awake rhythm). Melatonin was discovered in 1952 by Lerner (ISSO/SBR, 2007). Light, particularly short waves, suppresses the production of melatonin. Melatonin is also an antioxidant, like vitamin C, which stimulates the recovery of cell functions and of general resistance. Therefore, a good balance in the dark–light exposure of people is important to sleeping and waking rhythm and to hormone regulation.

Non-imaging forming (NIF) effects influence mood, concentration alertness, sleep and reaction time. Other NIF effects of light include colouring the skin, production of pro-vitamin D (UVA/B) and heating up (infrared). Psychological effects of light (colour and illuminance) can be different for different people. Change in colour and illuminance is quite normal for people (natural light changes all the time); therefore, dynamic lighting can have a positive influence on the well-being of a person.

Accidents at home and at work are often caused by poor lighting. Reflection, blinding, too little light and poor colouring of light can lead to tiredness of the eye or adaptation problems, decreased alertness and poor concentration.

Healthy and comfortable lighting depends upon eye task, the time of day, the weather and individual needs. The effect of lighting on performance and well-being depends upon illuminance, lighting period, timing and spectral distribution. Direct illuminance has an effect on alertness; a 24-hour light–dark pattern has an effect on the biological clock (e.g. with important night–day shifts).

Recent studies have shown that high vertical illuminances are associated with less tiredness and better sleep quality (Aries, 2005). However, high illuminances are often linked with less satisfaction. The best results are seen when illuminance is less than $1500cd/m^2$.

Standards

The current standards for indoor lighting conditions are as follows (for details, see section C.2 in Annex C):

- EN 12464-1 Lighting of Workplaces – Part 1: indoor workplaces (CEN, 2002a);
- EN 12665 Light and Lighting – Basic Terms and Criteria for Specifying Lighting Requirements (CEN, 2002b);
- EN 13032-2: Lighting Applications – Measurements and Presentation of Photometric Data of Lamps and Luminaries – Part 2: presentation of data for indoor and outdoor workplaces (CEN, 2004b);

- CIE 117 Discomfort Glare in Interior Lighting (CIE, 1995);
- NEN 2057 Daylight Openings of Buildings – Determination Method of the Equivalent Daylight Area of a Space (NEN, 2001).

These standards, nevertheless, do not take into account the most recent finding that the 24-hour light–dark pattern has an effect on an individual's biological clock and, thus, on health. Additionally, it is important to note that visual comfort is a combination of the actual ability to see fine detail and to avoid disabling glare together with the perception and enjoyment of the visual environment. It is difficult to separate the two.

Furthermore, attention must be given to the activities performed by the International Energy Agency (IEA) on daylight in buildings. The IEA was established in 1974 as an autonomous agency within the framework of the Organisation for Economic Co-operation and Development (OECD) to implement an international energy programme. IEA Taskgroup 21 produced a source book on day lighting systems and components, which gives a comprehensive overview of day lighting systems, the performance parameters and evaluation of their energy savings potential, and user acceptance (IEA, 2000).

5.1.3 From ventilation to source control

History

For most of the 20th century, appropriate ventilation was considered to be the only means to create acceptable indoor air quality. Recommendations for good indoor air quality were therefore always related to ventilation rate (see Figure 5.2).

Besides ventilation rate, indoor air quality can be evaluated according to different aspects, such as its substances or the direct judgement by panels of individuals.

In 1935, the first studies to measure air quality using the human nose as a sensor were performed by Lemberg, followed by Yaglou (1936) and, much later, by Cain et al (1983), Fanger and Berg-Munch (1983) and Bluyssen (1990). Panels of people, trained to evaluate perceived air quality, were used to measure the air quality in 56 office buildings in nine European countries, in the European Audit project (European Audit Project to Optimize Indoor Quality and Energy

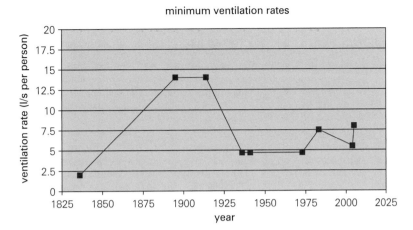

minimum ventilation rates

Note: The current recommended minimum ventilation rate by ASHRAE (2004) is 2.5l/s per person added to 0.3l/s per square metre for single-person cellular offices (10m²) and by CEN (2005) 4l/s per person added with 0.4l/s per m² for single-person cellular offices (10m²).

Source: Billings et al (1898); Cain et al (1983); Fanger and Berg-Munch (1983); CEN (2005)

Figure 5.2 *The recommended minimum ventilation rate changed over the years: From 2l/s per person by Tredgold in 1836, to 14l/s per person by Billings in 1895, back to 4.7l/s person in 1936 by Yaglou to 7.5l/s person in 1983*

Consumption in Office Buildings) during the heating season of 1993 to 1994 (Bluyssen et al, 1996a). In this audit, questionnaires and physical/ chemical analyses of air were also performed.

From this first European investigation of indoor air quality, it was shown that occupants are not the only major sources of pollution in indoor environments that have an effect on the comfort aspects of air quality. Furnishings and construction materials, ventilation system components and activities performed by people indoors can be just as polluting, or even more so (see Figure 5.3). The search for sources, emissions and effects became prevalent, and source control began to be the focus of attention.

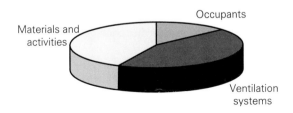

Source: Bluyssen et al (1996a)

Figure 5.3 *Sources of pollution in the indoor environment*

Sources and pollutants

The health and comfort effects of substances found in the indoor air are, in most cases, not clearly identifiable, and the sources of origin are also not always easy to determine (see Figure 5.4). Some substances may have adverse effects on their own, while others, seemingly harmless, become harmful when they interact with each other. In addition, people will react differently to the same exposure.

There are few examples where a direct correlation between a specific substance and health effects has been shown: one is formaldehyde, which is associated with allergies, hypersensitivity and cancer. However, in general, it is recognized that certain groups of substances can or might cause health effects, such as building-related illness (BRI), sick building syndrome (SBS) and multiple chemical sensitivity (Spengler et al, 2001).

After decades of research, it has been assumed that certain combinations of volatile organic compounds (VOCs), very volatile organic compounds (VVOCs) and semi-volatile organic compounds (SVOCs) can cause SBS symptoms, although a clear statistical relationship between concentrations and effect(s) has never been found. Available evidence on VOCs causing health effects is inconclusive (NRC, 2005). It has been

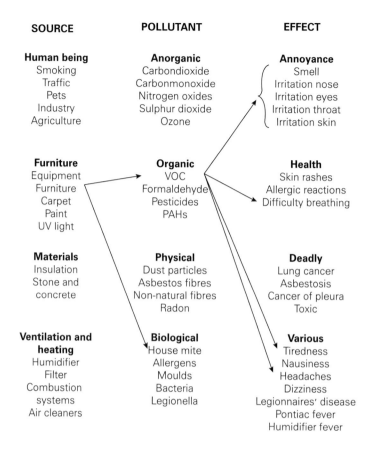

Source: Bluyssen

Figure 5.4 *Sources, pollutants and symptoms/complaints – furniture, for example, can emit several volatile organic compounds (VOCs), and can also foster the growth of house dust mites where people sit*

shown that a much broader analytical window of organic compounds than the classic window (as defined by the World Health Organization [WHO]) should be used to explain the effects (Wolkoff and Nielsen, 2001) (see Figure 5.5). For sensory irritation of the mucous membranes in eyes, which is probably one of the most important symptoms in SBS, no strong and reproducible association between exposure and response has been found in field studies.

However, in laboratory environments, it has been shown that several VOCs in combination will cause chemosensory irritation of the eyes and nasal passages, even when each individual compound is substantially below its threshold (Cometto-Muniz, cited in Spengler et al, 2001). This indicates the existence of agonism among chemicals. The degree of agonism increases with the number of compounds and with the lipophility of

such compounds (as a rule, larger homologs, with their long carbon chain length, are more lipophilic than smaller homologs, with their short carbon chain length). Studies of homolog chemical series have shown that the larger homologs (e.g. 2-heptanone), not usually considered particularly irritating compared to smaller homologs (e.g. acetone), have a stronger sensory potency because of their much lower odour and nasal pungency thresholds.

Thus, within families of organic compounds, more carbon atoms usually translate to an increased odour and irritation potential. Production products consisting of a compound with a high number of carbon atoms also have the ability to off-gas longer due to lower vapour pressure. Therefore, substituting with longer-chained hydrocarbons to reduce VOC emissions in the short term can have a contrary effect to that envisaged.

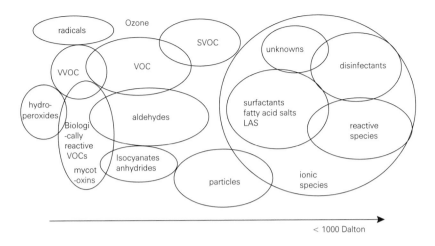

Source: adapted from Wolkoff and Nielsen (2001)

Figure 5.5 *Schematic presentation of the organic compounds in indoor air: Besides VVOCs and VOCs, intermediary species (e.g. radicals, hydro-peroxides and ionic compounds such as detergents), as well as species deposited onto particles, are included*

Although available evidence on VOCs causing health effects is assumed inconclusive for now (NRC, 2005), several recent studies indicate associations between health, asthma or allergy effects and phthalates (Bornehag et al, 2004, 2005; Mendell, 2007), dampness and mould (Hersoug, 2005; Fisk et al, 2007), and normal office dust (Spengler et al, 2001). Many compounds that are generated in the indoor environment are semi-volatiles, such as phthalates, flame retardants, polycyclic aromatic hydrocarbons (PAHs), chlorophenols, pesticides, organotins and metals, which may adsorb to particulate matter present in the indoor air and to house dust. These particles may be inhaled or ingested, depending upon their size. Particulate air pollutants have very diverse chemical compositions that are highly dependent upon their source, and they are also diverse in terms of particle size.

Table 5.2 presents the possible sources for the most prevalent VOCs identified in the European Audit project. The most important source of VOCs was materials, especially furnishings. The dominant volatile organic compounds detected in the majority of the buildings were solvents used in floor or wall coverings and pressed wood products (carpets, PVC flooring, floor adhesives, wallpaper, particle board, etc.). Table 5.3 lists other pollutants and their possible sources.

The substances emitted from construction products have different characteristics and therefore also require different methods of detection. The large group of volatile organic compounds are normally divided into subgroups depending upon their respective boiling points, each group requiring different methods of detection.

To be pragmatic, the total volatile organic compound (TVOC) concept was introduced a number of decades ago in order to cover a broad range of VOCs, (Mølhave, 1990), although in the meantime there has been wide consensus that TVOC is not a very good measurement for evaluating effects on health or comfort using a threshold (ECA, 1997).

Chemical analysis often does not relate to odour assessments: for most pollutants, the nose has a much lower detection limit than most chemical instruments and the interpretation capabilities of the human brain (giving an integrated evaluation of a mixture of pollutants) are superior. Therefore, sensory evaluation using human panels for labelling have been introduced – for example in Denmark and in Finland. Both trained and untrained panel methods have been developed (see Annex B). The Finnish M1 (Saarela and Tirkkonen, 2004) and the Danish Indoor Climate Labelling Scheme (DICL) (Wolkoff and Nielsen, 1996) both use human panels for odour testing of building products.

Table 5.2 *Possible sources of the most prevalent volatile organic compounds (VOCs) found in the audited buildings of the European Audit Project*

Number	Compound	O[1]	T[2]	E[3]	B[4]	F[5]	C[6]	Number	Compound	O	T	E	B	F	C
				Materials								Materials			
1	$(CF_2)_n$						x	31	Benzene	x	x			x	x
2	1,1,1-trichloroethane					x	x	32	C_3-alkylbenzenes	x	x		x	x	x
3	$C_2Cl_3F_3$						x	33	M-xylene	x	x		x	x	x
4	Tetrachloroethylene						x	34	O-xylene	x	x		x	x	x
5	Dichloromethane				x		x	35	P-xylene	x	x		x	x	x
6	Dichlorobenzene						x	36	Toluene	x	x		x	x	x
7	Butane	x						37	Naphthalene						x
8	N-hexane	x	x	x			x	38	Phthalate comp.					x	
9	Aliphatic C_7H_{16}	x					x	39	1-butanol				x	x	x
10	N-heptane	x					x	40	1-ethoxy-2-propanol					x	
11	Octane	x	x	x				41	2-butoxy-ethanol					x	x
12	Aliph. C_9H_{20}				x	x	x	42	2-phenoxy-ethanol					x	x
13	Nonane				x	x	x	43	C_5-alcohol					x	x
14	Decane $C_{10}H_{22}$				x	x	x	44	Ethanol				x		x
14	Undecane				x	x	x	45	Ethoxy-ethoxy-ethanol					x	x
16	Dodecane						x	46	4-methyl-2-pentanone		x			x	
17	Tetradecane						x	47	Acetone					x	
18	Pentadecane						x	48	Cyclohexanone						x
19	2-methylbutane	x						49	Benzaldehyde				x	x	x
20	2-methylpentane	x						50	Nonanal	x	x			x	
21	3-methylpentane	x						51	Decanal	x				x	x
22	2,4-dimethylhexane	x				x		52	Acetic acid butyl ester					x	
23	2-methylhexane	x				x		53	Acetic acid ethyl ester					x	
24	Nonane/o-xylene					x		54	Butoxy-ethoxy-Ethylacetate					x	
25	Nonane/styrene					x		55	Acetic acid				x	x	
26	Dimethylcyclopentane					x	x	56	Benzoic acid						x
27	Methylcyclopentane					x	x	57	Dodecanoic acid					x	x
28	Methylcyclohexane	x				x	x	58	A-pinene					x	x
29	cyclohexane					x	x	59	L-limolene						x
30	2-methyl-1,3-butadiene					x		60	Terpene comp.						x

Notes: 1 = outdoor air (O); 2 = tobacco smoke (T); 3 = office equipment (E); 4 = building materials (B); 5 = furnishings (F); 6 = consumer products (C).

Source: Bluyssen et al (1996)

Both procedures are value judgements of indoor air quality and both make use of the so-called continuous acceptability scale (Gunnarsen and Fanger, 1992).

Standards and regulations

Of the following remedial actions – dilution by ventilation, reduction by air cleaning and prevention of emissions by product amelioration – the latter should always be given preference. Source control reflects the general philosophy of environmental protection: preventing rather than curing. At European as well as national levels, several initiatives have been undertaken to apply one or more of these strategies.

Source control

At a European level, several activities are concerned directly or indirectly with source control.

DG Enterprise in cooperation with the European Committee for Standardization (CEN) is closely working with national standardization bodies (e.g. NEN in The Netherlands) to implement mandates for

Table 5.3 *Pollutants and their possible sources and causes*

Pollutant	Possible sources and causes
Organic gases	
Formaldehyde (CH_2O)	Building materials: chipboard, urea-formaldehyde insulation
Benzene (C_6H_6)	Anthropogenic sources: fuel, tobacco smoke
Naphthalene ($C_{10}H_8$)	Moth balls
Acetaldehyde (C_2H_4O)	Human breath; cooking hamburgers, coffee roasting; and from some building materials such as rigid polyurethane foams and some consumer products such as adhesives, coatings, lubricants, inks and nail polish remover
	As a flavour and in perfumes; synthetic rubber, paraldehyde, paper, dyes, plastics
	Vehicle exhaust
Toluene (C_7H_8)	Paints, household aerosols, thinners, cleaning agents, coatings, rubber, nail polish and other cosmetics, adhesives, resin and printing products
Xylenes (C_8H_{10}) meta (m-), para (p-) and ortho (o-)	Paints, inks, dyes, adhesives, pharmaceuticals and detergents
Styrene (C_8H_8)	Polystyrene, acrylonitrile-butadiene-styrene resins, styrene-butadiene rubbers and latexes, and in reinforced plastics
	Natural styrene sources such as cinnamic acid-containing plants (e.g. balsamic trees) and a by-product of fungal and microbial metabolism
Limonene ($C_{10}H_{16}$)	Pine gum, paper and pulp mills, plastic materials, synthetic resins, perfumes, cosmetics and other toilet preparations, organic solvents and lubricating oils and greases, furniture polishes and room fresheners
α-pinene ($C_{10}H_{16}$)	Paint, cleaning and sanitation products, paints and varnish removers, wooden furniture and waxes
Carbon dioxide (CO_2)	Cooking in inadequate conditions (presence of local exhaust equipment), combustion appliances (gas, kerosene, wood-fuelled appliances), tobacco smoking, the breath of occupants, exhaust from vehicles on nearby roads or in parking lots or garages
Carbon monoxide (CO)	Cooking in inadequate conditions (presence of local exhaust equipment)
	Combustion appliances (fireplace, gas cooking stoves)
	Tobacco smoking
	Exhaust from vehicles on nearby roads or in parking lots or garages
	Presence of nearby industrial furnaces
Inorganic gases	
Nitrogen dioxide (NO_2)	Cooking in inadequate conditions (presence of local exhaust equipment)
	Combustion appliances
	Exhaust from vehicles on nearby roads or in parking lots or garages
Ozone (O_3)	Laser printers, photocopiers, any equipment which uses high voltage or ultraviolet light, electronic air filters, equipment that uses ozone to purify air or water, exhaust from vehicles on nearby roads
Ammonia (NH_3)	Natural breakdown of manure and dead plants and animals
	Burning of coal, wood and other natural products, and volcanic activity
	Synthetic fibres, plastics, explosives and many cleaning products; used as a refrigerant
Radon	Soil and stone-like materials
Particulate matter	Cooking in inadequate conditions (presence of local exhaust equipment)
	Combustion appliances
PM10	Tobacco smoking, dust from indoor demolition, airborne dust or dirt (e.g. circulated by sweeping and vacuuming), paper in open shelves, exhaust from vehicles on nearby roads
PM2.5	Dust from outdoor demolition and outdoor industrial emissions
Asbestos	Has been used in construction because of its properties (chemical and thermal stability and thermal insulation); is no longer allowed
Trace metals	Via filtration of outdoor air transported indoors, such as lead and mercury
	Lead is a metallic element used in the construction and printing industry sectors
Biological pollutants	
Endotoxins	Endotoxins are potentially toxic; natural compounds are found inside pathogens such as bacteria, which are released mainly when bacteria are lysed
	Prototypical examples of endotoxins are lipo-polysaccharide (LPS) or lipo-oligo-saccharide (LOS) found in the outer membrane of various gram-negative bacteria
Mycotoxins	Chemicals manufactured by fungi, some of which are extremely toxic to humans and animals

Source: Bluyssen

the Construction Product Directive (CPD) (EU, 2005) and the Energy Performance Building Directive (EPBD) (EU, 2002b).

In December 2005, a proposal for regulation was made in the European Parliament and the Council of Europe on Registration, Evaluation, Authorization and Restriction of Chemicals (REACH), establishing a European Chemical Agency and amending Directive 1999/45/EC (EU, 2006). It provides provisions for substances and preparations that do not adversely affect human health or the environment.

The programme of work within CEN/TC 350 will provide a standardized voluntary approach for the delivery of environmental information on construction products, assessing the environmental performance of buildings. The objective is to cover all kinds of building products and all kinds of buildings, both new and existing, as well as other construction works, if appropriate.

The second generation of harmonized product standards under the Construction Product Directive requires harmonized test methods for the release or emission of dangerous substances to satisfy the requirements of Essential Requirement 3 (ER 3) of the CPD. The European Commission issued Mandate M/366 to CEN: 'Development of horizontal standardized assessment methods for harmonized approaches relating to dangerous substances under the Construction Product Directive (CPD) – emission to indoor air, soil, surface water and ground water' on 16 March 2005 (EU, 2005).

The most widely applied standard series for testing construction products at the moment is the EN ISO-16000 series (CEN-ISO, 2001b, 2004, 2006b–d) (see Box 5.2). The DIBT regulation on floor coverings (DIBT, 2005) and a number of voluntary labelling schemes in Europe use these series as a base, although some differences can be identified (see section C.4 in Annex C). The standard series comprises standards for sampling products, for simulating emissions in either a small-scale emission test cell or a larger emission test chamber, and several different ways of sampling and analysing the emitted substances.

For the measurement of aldehydes of wood-based panels, a slightly different standard has been developed: the EN 717-1, 2 and 3 (CEN, 2004b).

Substances under ban, such as asbestos, polychlorinated biphenyl (PCB), certain metals and flame retardants, should not be put in new products at all. However, it is becoming more and more common to recycle old materials and to mix virgin materials with recycled material in the process of making new

---

Box 5.2 EN ISO 16000

The international standard EN ISO 16000 consists of several parts. Some have been elaborated upon by CEN/TC264 and others by ISO/TC146, and they have been mutually accepted under the Vienna Agreement. In practice, the tester starts with sample handling (Part 11), then selects a test chamber (Part 9 or 10) and finally performs the analysis of sampled air from a test chamber (Part 6 for volatile organic compounds (VOCs) and total volatile compounds (TVOCs) and Part 3 for aldehydes). The full procedure is illustrated in Box 5.3 for a flooring material:

- Part 3: Determination of formaldehyde and other carbonyl compounds – Active sampling method;
- Part 6: Determination of volatile organic compounds in indoor and test chamber air by active sampling on Tenax TA sorbent, thermal desorption and gas chromatography using mass spectrometry (MS)/flame ionization detector (FID);
- Part 9: Determination of the emission of volatile organic compounds from building products and furnishing – Emission test chamber (earlier: EN 13419-1);
- Part 10: Determination of the emission of volatile organic compounds from building products and furnishing – Emission test cell method (earlier: EN 13419-2);
- Part 11: Determination of the emission of volatile organic compounds from building products and furnishing – Sampling, storage of samples and preparation of test specimens (earlier: EN 13419-3).

Box 5.3 Testing procedure of a flooring material

1 Taking a sample

2 Wrap the sample in aluminium foil

3 Wrap the sample in polyethylene foil

4 Send the airtight package to the testing laboratory

5 Cut the test specimen out of the sample roll

6 Mount the specimen on an inert support; seal the edges with aluminium tape

7 Place the test specimen in the chamber

8 The conditions are accurately controlled and monitored

9 Or, alternatively: use the Field and Laboratory Emission Cell (FLEC) cell method

10 The analytical equipment: thermal desorption-gas chromatography-mass spectrometer

11 The separation process of the complex mixture takes place in the (brown) gas chromatography column

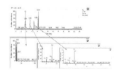

12 Each peak in the gas chromatogram is identified by mass spectrometry

Source: Jan Boon, Forbo Krommenie BV

products. This may cause unintentional contamination of new products by substances now under ban, and an unspecified dilution of dangerous substances throughout. The solution could be to verify that the material to be recycled is 'clean' when it comes to banned substances; or to verify that the performance of the finished product is below any limit values.

For asbestos, regulations are based on two parallel approaches: the ban of asbestos and the control and management of the materials containing asbestos that have been used before the ban (WHO, 2006a). The last change to Directive 76/769/EED, adopted on 26 July 1999, added together the different partial bans of asbestos taken from 1976 and made the ban compulsory, at the latest on 1 January 2005, for all types of asbestos and all types of products, with temporary exception for particular products and existing products.

For fibres, some standards are available; but they are mainly concerned with an analytical procedure for fibres in air, not with the emission of fibres from products. It is not likely that fibres will suddenly be released into the air if no mechanical motions of the product itself are involved. However, when maintenance work is involved (e.g. even cleaning of ceiling panels), fibres could be released.

Recommendations for several pollutants are presented in section C.3 of Annex C.

Ventilation (energy use)

The European Directive 2002/91/EC on Energy Performance of Buildings (EU, 2002b) came into force on 16 December 2002 in order to be implemented in the legislation of the member states in 2006. Four main elements define the requirements that needed to be integrated within national legislation:

1 establishment of a methodology for an integrated calculation of the overall energy performance of buildings;
2 definition of minimum energy efficiency requirements per member state based on this methodology;
3 energy efficiency certification of new and existing buildings;
4 regular inspection of heating and air-conditioning systems.

On the basis of the EC standardization mandate M/330, CEN is developing methodologies for calculating the energy uses and losses of heating and cooling, ventilation, domestic hot water, lighting, natural lighting, passive solar systems, passive cooling, position and orientation, automation and controls of buildings, and auxiliary installations necessary for maintaining a comfortable indoor environment. With respect to ventilation, recommendations can be found in ASHRAE Standard 62.1 (ASHRAE, 2004b) and EN15251 (CEN, 2005) (see section C.3 in Annex C).

Clean air

The proposal for the Ambient Air Quality and Cleaner Air for Europe Directive adopted by the European Commission in September 2005 will merge into a single legislative act setting the legally binding standards and targets for ambient air quality and defining provisions for the assessment and management of air pollution – namely, the 1996 Framework Directive on Air Quality and its so-called daughter directives of 1999, 2000 and 2002.

The European Commission proposal, as it stands, maintains existing standards for all major pollutants such as ozone, nitrogen and sulphur dioxide, including those for particles smaller than 10 micrometres, known as PM_{10}. In addition, it introduces an annual limit on airborne concentrations of fine dust particles smaller than 2.5 micrometres, and a target to reduce population exposure to these particles by 20 per cent between 2010 and 2020. $PM_{2.5}$ causes serious heart and respiratory disease and is responsible for nine out of ten of all the deaths that can be attributed to air pollution in Europe.

Activity control

With respect to activity control strategies, laws implementing bans on indoor smoking have been introduced by many countries in various forms over the years.

Prevention measures

Prevention measures are, of course, very effective and many guidelines and recommendations are available (see Figure 5.6), comprising:

• maintenance measures such as measures to prevent house dust mite from growing by regularly turning mattresses and letting the sun (daylight) into the bedroom;
• design measures that, for example, prevent the growth of Legionella by ensuring that water in cold

Source: Bluyssen (2004b)

Figure 5.6 *Cleaning and maintenance of an HVAC system is also a preventive measure*

water pipes is not located near warm water pipes (Legionnella grows between 20° and 50°C); or
- fixed procedures, such as flushing frequently, especially before using water out of a drink water system or a shower to prevent Legionella from growing.

What is striking is that it is not until a disaster happens or authorities start to intervene that recommended prevention measures are followed.

5.1.4 From noise disturbance to noise, health and vibrations

Noise disturbance

During the 1960s and earlier, few people recognized that citizens might be entitled to be protected from adverse sound-level exposure. Most concerted actions consisted of citizens' groups organized to oppose a specific highway or airport, and occasionally a nuisance lawsuit would arise. However, around the 1970s and 1980s, regulations in several countries began to emerge, starting with the national Noise Control Act in Japan, addressing mainly workplace and construction noise (Government of Japan, 2000), and followed by the US

Noise Pollution and Abatement Act (more commonly called the Noise Control Act, or NCA, of 1972) (NCA, 1988). This was followed somewhat later in Europe by the 1979, 1985, 1993 and 1994 Noise Abatement Acts in The Netherlands, France, Spain and Denmark, respectively. At first these acts were largely concerned with workplace and construction noise; but slowly environmental noise pollution was included as well. Setting maximum noise limits for road traffic and, especially, aircraft traffic noise is still an important issue.

In The Netherlands, the 1979 Noise Abatement Act came into force at various stages. By the end of 1987, all sections of this act had become mandatory. The act covers all sources of environmental noise. In particular, the following relevant sections of the act became mandatory on the dates indicated:

- zoning around airports and zoning close to new roads and industrial areas (1982);
- insulation of homes (1983);
- treatment of noise around existing railways (1986);
- zoning around railway lines (1987).

Legislation on road traffic noise became mandatory in 1982, and the Railways Decree of 1987 underwent minor changes in 1989, with more substantial changes taking place in 1993. Whereas the Noise Abatement Act regulates all sources of noise, the Environmental Protection Act (revised during the 1980s) is particularly relevant to smaller enterprises; and, under the Aviation Act of 1978, the first zoning came into force in 1992, with the latest zoning taking place at Amsterdam airport in 1996.

At a European level, the Green Paper on *Future Noise Policy* (EU, 1996a), adopted and, published by the European Commission in November 1996, was the first step in the development of a noise policy, with the aim that no individual should be exposed to noise levels that endanger health and quality of life (Fifth Environmental Action Programme). For more than 20 years, European Community environmental noise policy has essentially consisted of legislation fixing maximum sound levels for vehicles, airplanes and machines with a single market aim, or implementing international agreements in the case of aircraft, linked to certification procedures to ensure that, at the time of manufacture, new vehicles and equipment comply with the noise limits laid down in the directives (see Box 5.4).

Thanks to this legislation and technological progress, significant reductions of noise from

---

Box 5.4 Directives for outdoor noise pollution

For *road traffic* the distinction is made between noise from four-wheel motor vehicles, noise from two- and three-wheel motor vehicles and rolling noise between tyres and road surfaces.

Noise from four-wheel motor vehicles. Directive 70/157/EEC8 (EU, 1970) was the first European harmonized noise requirements for road vehicles relating to the permissible sound level and the exhaust system of four-wheel motor vehicles. This directive has since been amended several times. Due largely to a significant increase in road traffic, no improvement has been made regarding overall exposure to noise generated by road vehicles.

Noise from two- and three-wheel motor vehicles. Directive 97/24/EC (EU, 1997) sets permissible sound levels for two- and three-wheel vehicles and their exhaust systems, including replacement parts, and provides measures to counter tampering.

Rolling noise between tyres and road surfaces. Complementing legislation on vehicles themselves, Directive 2001/43/EC (EU, 2001) provides for the testing and limiting of tyre-rolling noise levels, and for their phased reduction.

For *railway noise*, the European Commission has set up a railway noise working group in order to elaborate upon the technical and economic aspects of reducing noise emissions from rail transport systems. The most important railway noise source identified is rail freight.

For *aircraft noise*, the directives introduced started with banning certain type of airplanes (the noisiest ones were no longer allowed to operate in the European Union after April 2002), followed by limiting the operation of aircraft fitted with 'hush kits' (muffler devices fitted to engines to make them less noisy) in 1998, to rules and procedures with regard to the introduction of noise-related operating restrictions at community airports in 2002 (Directive 2002/30/EC) (EU, 2002c).

Industrial noise. Noise is one of the environmental issues that member states' authorities must consider when issuing permits to operators of the large industrial and agricultural installations covered by the Integrated Pollution Prevention and Control (IPPC) Directive 96/61/EC (EU, 1996b). This directive is fully applicable to new installations and to existing installations that are to undergo a substantial change. All existing installations covered by the directive have to comply with permit conditions based on the use of best available technology (BAT) by October 2007.

Equipment for use outdoors and tractors. Directive 2000/14/EC (EU, 2000) lays down noise provisions on noise from 57 types of outdoor equipment. It sets out four types of action to achieve this: harmonization of noise emission limits and standards; harmonization of conformity assessment procedures; harmonization of noise level marking; and compilation of data on noise emissions.

Recreational craft. Directive 2003/44/EC (EU, 2003a) extends its scope to include personal watercraft and complements its design and construction requirements with environmental standards regarding exhaust and noise emission limit values for recreational craft.

Source: EU (2004)

---

individual sources have been achieved. For example, the noise from individual cars has been reduced by 85 per cent since 1970 and the noise from lorries by 90 per cent. Likewise, aircraft footprints around an airport made by modern jets have been reduced by a factor of 9 compared to aircraft with 1970s technology. However data covering the past 15 years do not show significant improvements in exposure to environmental noise, especially road traffic noise. The growth and spread of traffic in space and time and the development of leisure activities and tourism have partly offset

technological improvements. Forecast road and air traffic growth and the expansion of high-speed rail risk exacerbating the noise problem. In the case of motor vehicles, other factors are also important, such as the dominance of tyre noise above quite low speeds (50km/h) and the absence of regular noise inspection and maintenance procedures.

During the 1990s, the relation between health effects and noise became a major issue. One of the first outcomes of this focus were the guidelines for community noise published in 1999 by WHO (Berglund et al, 1999) – the result of an expert meeting held during the same year. In this document, community noise is defined as noise emitted from all sources except noise at the industrial workplace (main outdoor sources: road, rail and air traffic, industries, construction and public work, and the neighbourhood; main indoor sources: ventilation systems, office machines, home appliances and neighbours). The health effects of noise are discussed and several guidelines are presented. A distinction is made between continuous noise and distinct noise events. For more-or-less continuous noises, the LAeq,T (the energy average equivalent level of the A-weighted sound over a period T) should be used, while for distinct noise events, as with aircraft or railway noise, obtaining additional measures of individual events, such as the maximum noise level (LAmax) or the weighted sound exposure level (SEL), is recommended.

SEL is defined as the constant sound level over a period of 1 second that would have the same energy as the complete noise event:

$$SEL = LAeq,T + 10log(T/T_0) \text{ with } T_0 = 0 \text{ seconds}$$
$$LAeq,T = 10log\{(1/T)\int(L_p(T)/10)dt\} \text{ [dB(A)]}. \quad [5.8]$$

Health risks

Noise seriously harms human health and interferes with people's daily activities at school, at work, at home and during leisure time. Traffic noise alone affects the health of almost every third European today. According to a recent European Union publication (Berglund et al, 1999), about 40 per cent of the population in EU countries are exposed to road traffic noise at levels exceeding 55dB(A), and 20 per cent are exposed to levels exceeding 65dB(A) during the daytime. More than 30 per cent are exposed to levels exceeding 55dB(A) during night time. Detailed information on the different forms of health risks are presented in Box 5.5.

The main health risks caused by noise and identified by WHO are as follows (Berglund et al, 1999; WHO, 2003b):

- pain and hearing fatigue;
- hearing impairment, including tinnitus;
- annoyance;
- interferences with social behaviour (aggressiveness, protest and helplessness);
- interference with speech communication;

- sleep disturbance and all its long- and short-term impacts;
- cardiovascular effects;
- hormonal responses (stress hormones) and their possible consequences for human metabolism (nutrition) and the immune system.

Noise and health

The European Union Directive on the assessment and management of environmental noise (Directive 2002/49/EC 2002) (EU, 2002d) requires EU member states to establish action plans to control and reduce the harmful effects of noise exposure. The WHO Children's Environment and Health Action Plan for Europe (2004) states, in its Regional Priority Goal IV, that children should be protected from exposure to harmful noise at home and at school. And with the European Directive 2002/44/EC on the minimum health and safety requirements regarding the exposure of workers to the risks arising from physical agents (vibrations) (EU, 2002e) and the European Directive 2003/10/EC on the minimum health and safety requirements regarding the exposure of workers to the risks arising from physical agents (noise) (EU, 2003b), the step towards protecting the indoor environment is taken as well. The latter two directives are individual directives within Article 6 of Council Directive 89/391/EEC of 12 June 1989 on the introduction of measures to encourage improvements in the safety and health of workers at work (EC, 1989).

Aircraft noise and its daytime and night-time effects on human beings were studied in 2001. Relationships between noise exposure and annoyance, sleep disturbance in adults and children, hearing impairment in adults and children, productivity reduction in adults and interference with cognitive effects on children were studied in 2002. From these studies it can be concluded that there is sufficient and reliable data to derive exposure–response relationships between noise and annoyance. Dose–effect curves already exist for road, aircraft, and railway noise and multi-exposure (WHO, 2003b).

In order to provide guidance in estimating the level of disease related to environmental noise, with preliminary estimates for the European region, WHO/Europe has carried out an assessment study

Box 5.5 Health risks

Hearing impairment is defined as an increase in the threshold of hearing, which may be accompanied by tinnitus (ringing in the ears) and occurs predominantly in the higher frequencies (3000–6000Hz), with the largest effect at 4000Hz. It is not expected to occur below LAeq,8h levels of 75dB(A) and for long-term exposure to Laeq,24h noise levels of up to 70dB(A) (ISO, 1990). In order to avoid hearing loss from impulse noise exposure, peak sound pressures should never exceed 140dB for adults and 120dB for children. It is estimated that 120 million people worldwide have disabling hearing difficulties (Berglund et al, 1999). How much is related to noise-induced hearing impairment is not known. Studies and data are insufficient to derive relationships between community/social noise-specific exposure and hearing impairment in adults and children.

Speech intelligibility is affected by noise. Speech interference can result in a large number of personal handicaps and behavioural changes. When listening to complicated messages, the signal-to-noise-ratio should be at least 15dB with a voice level of 50dB(A) (indicating a background level of less than 35dB(A) for clear speech perception). In small rooms, a reverberation time below 1 second is necessary for good speech intelligibility, and for sensitive groups (e.g. the elderly), even below 0.6 seconds.

Sleep disturbance is largely caused by environmental noise and results in primary effects during sleep and secondary effects assessed after night-time noise exposure. Primary effects are difficulty in falling asleep, awakenings and alterations of sleep stages or depth, increased blood pressure, heart rate and finger pulse amplitude, vasoconstriction, changes in respiration, cardiac arrhythmia, and increased body movements. The secondary or after effects during the following morning or day(s) include reduced perceived sleep quality, increased fatigue, depressed mood or well-being, and decreased performance. For a good night's sleep, the equivalent sound level should not exceed 30dB(A) for continuous background noise and individual noise events exceeding 45dB(A) should be avoided. Furthermore, attention should be paid to the character of the noise (e.g. number of noise events, combinations of noise and vibrations, and low-frequency noise components). Exposure-response curves exist for awakenings, based on laboratories and self-assessment questionnaires. Nevertheless, many questions remain on how poor sleep relates to or causes poor health. The long-term effects of poor sleep for children exposed to noisy sleep environments (e.g. insomnia later in adult life) are still very uncertain and require evaluation.

Physiological functions may be affected due to prolonged exposure, such as hypertension, increased blood pressure, cardiovascular effects and ischemic heart disease associated with exposure to high sound levels. Increased stress hormone levels and elevated resting blood pressure have been recorded in children from noisier areas.

Mental illness is not caused by noise directly, but it is assumed that it can be accelerated and intensified. Findings on environmental noise and mental health effects are inconclusive so far.

Performance at work and at school of cognitive tasks can be adversely affected by noise, resulting in productivity loss. Although noise-induced arousal may produce better performance in simple tasks in the short term, cognitive performance deteriorates for more complex tasks (memory recall, reading, attention, problem-solving), causing errors and accidents.

Annoyance and social and behavioural effects can also be caused by noise. During the daytime, few people are highly annoyed at Laeq levels below 55dB(A) and few are moderately annoyed at Laeq levels below 50dB(A). The correlation between noise exposure and general annoyance is much higher at group level than at individual level. Noise above 80dB(A) may also reduce cooperative behaviour and increase aggression. If noise is accompanied by vibrations and contains low-frequency components, or when noise contains impulses, such as a shooting noise, stronger reactions have been observed. At night and in the evening, sound levels should be 5–10dB lower than during the day.

Source: WHO (2003b)

(Niemann and Maschke, 2004), concluding that in Western countries, sleep problems are an increasing problem due to lifestyle and environmental factors. Sleep disturbance is one of the most serious effects of environmental noise. Children are more vulnerable to environmental risks than adults because they have often less control over their environment and behave differently than adults.

Noise from service equipment

Sanitary appliances (i.e. flushing toilets), elevators, ventilation systems and their pipes and drinking water systems can cause noise annoyance problems, created by pipe noise (mostly frequencies between 125–2000Hz). Prediction models for estimating sound levels due to certain equipment, such as toilets and washing machines, whirlpools, valves and pipe systems, have been and still are being investigated (Bron-van der Jagt, 2007).

Vibrations

While noise from night-time traffic was already acknowledged as causing serious health effects, the realization that vibrations are also a nuisance came much later. Research on vibrations and its effects are still ongoing (see section 9.3.5 in Chapter 9).

Standards and regulations

Noise control can be pursued through standards and/or regulations from several points of views:

- to minimize the noise produced (the sources);
- to minimize the noise received (obstructions in the form of insulation and absorption);
- human health and comfort requirements with respect to sound and/or noise.

If relations between sound parameters and health effects are not clear, the latter are difficult to define. On the other hand, enough information is currently available to give indicative requirements. At a European level, guideline values in specific environments are recommended by Berglund et al (1999) (see section C.5 in Annex C). In The Netherlands, the Noise Annoyance Law prescribes limit values for sound levels at the façade of dwellings (newly constructed) (see section C.5). From the production side, several European directives have established limit values for noise produced from road traffic, railway, aircraft, industry and other sources (EU, 2004).

And from the reception point of view, limit values of sound insulation characteristics for separation walls indoors and outdoors, and sound absorption characteristics of materials in spaces, also exist. For example, in The Netherlands, measures are taken at

different levels (see section C.5 in Annex C for details):

- Regulatory level: in the building decree, minimum requirements for certain building elements are regulatory.
- Voluntary level: several classification systems exist to classify buildings and/or building elements according to their noise management capabilities.

With respect to vibrations caused largely by external sources such as traffic, measurement protocols are available (ISO, 1997, 2003b). However, the dose–response relations are not yet clear.

5.2 Bottom–up holistic approach

5.2.1 More than one parameter

The technologies available during the 1960s, economic expansion and the increase in income have stimulated the development of new building constructions, new heating systems and new ventilation systems. In the past, due to low energy prices, high ventilation rates were not a concern. The high increase in energy prices due to the energy crises of the 1970s significantly changed this situation. Research activities during the second half of the 1970s and the beginning of the 1980s were primarily focused on strategies to reduce energy consumption. Environmental issues became more and more important towards the end of the 1980s. Health issues and increased concern related to the quality of the indoor environment were of considerable interest to the public and the media. Thus, the energy crisis had a major effect on scientific approaches: not only was the effect of indoor energy use on the outdoor environment studied, but also, later, the effect of energy reduction measures on indoor environment quality.

Some time during the 1990s, there was a realization that complaints and health effects related to the indoor environment were probably not caused by a single parameter; however, criteria and indices were still only defined per parameter.

The first epidemiological studies focused on indoor environmental quality and energy use provided results with which interrelations between different parameters, building components and health effects could be made. These health effects are evident in BRI, SBS and/or multiple chemical sensitivity (see Box 5.6). Current research is still component related; but the relation with other components has begun to be more rigorously taken into account.

The sick building is commonly characterized by a higher prevalence of the same symptoms that are reported in the non-sick building, but at a lower frequency. It is seldom possible to explain symptoms as the result of a single factor such as formaldehyde or dust. It is also possible that more than one factor results in the same symptom (e.g. heat radiation and formaldehyde can cause dryness of the eyes).

It seems reasonable, then, to apply the hypothesis that several factors together (though not alone) cause symptoms – this is known as the synergistic effect. In other words, multifactor cause–effect problems are related to occupancy in buildings. A more profound knowledge of the mechanisms behind these effects is still required. Many of the so-called causes may only be indicators of others.

What has been found?

All studies so far have shown that naturally ventilated buildings have less symptomatic workers than air-conditioned buildings. Women are more susceptible than men, and public-sector workforces have more problems then those in the private sector. The mechanisms for the symptoms are, however, not yet defined (Bluyssen, 1992).

Investigations show that besides the difference between the frequency of symptoms of men and women, working conditions can also have an influence. For example, people in leading positions, in general, complain three times less then people in other groups. Psychological conditions are also important factors and are associated with the named symptoms either directly (tiredness) or by increasing the sensitivity towards physical and chemical exposure. In some cases it is still a question of which of the two groups of factors, psychological or physical, is the determining element or whether they all interfere.

As a basis for solving indoor climate problems, occupants should be questioned about their problems and the frequency with which these problems occur. This can, in part, point to the main factors affecting occupants (heat, cold, etc.), and can also establish whether these exposures may be associated with sickness symptoms.

Symptoms related to buildings are supposed primarily to depend upon the quality of the air and thermal climate and, to a lesser degree, on sound and lighting conditions. Draught and high and low temperatures frequently appear in connection to

---

Box 5.6 Health effects of the indoor environment

- Building-related illnesses (BRIs): caused by biological, physical or chemical agents in indoor environments, consisting of:
  - airborne infectious diseases (e.g. Pontiac fever and Legionnaires' disease);
  - hypersensitive diseases: resulting from an abnormal or maladaptive response of the immune system to a substance recognized as foreign to the body, such as allergic asthma, allergic rhinitis and hypersensitivity pneumonitis (mostly associated with fungi and bio-aerosols);
  - toxic reactions: exposures to contaminants, such as pesticides, that may lead to acute disruption of a variety of organ functions and/or increased risk of chronic diseases such as cancer.
- Sick building syndrome (SBS): a constellation of symptoms that have no clear etiology and are attributable to exposure to a particular building environment. Symptoms include eye, nose and throat irritation, and the sensation of dry mucous membranes; dry, itching and red skin; headaches and mental fatigue; high frequency of airway infections and coughing; hoarseness and wheezing; nausea and dizziness; and unspecific hypersensitivity.
- Multiple chemical sensitivity: decreased tolerance that leads many individuals to report symptoms upon exposure to products and sources common in indoor environments; however, this term is still contentious.

Source: Spengler et al (2001)

unspecified complaints. A high temperature level causes higher emission rates and higher microbiological activity. A low temperature level reduces the frequency of symptoms but increases draught sensation. Microbiological growth (e.g. in connection with water damage, humidity absorbed by dirty carpets from water used during cleaning processes or growth in humidifiers) is probably an essential cause of the increase in symptom occurrence.

Hypersensitivity is an umbrella term used to describe conditions in which the sensitivity of organs in the body to different substances is pathologically increased. This increased sensitivity is due to either immunological (allergy) or non-immunological (non-allergic hypersensitivity) mechanisms. The relation between hypersensitivity and air quality is one of the major contemporary problems encountered in buildings.

Since such a wide range of problems are associated with unhealthy buildings, it is unlikely that a single common cause exists. And as the Gestalt school of psychologists already promoted during the 1970s, the whole environment is more than just the sum of its constituent stimuli: people–environment interactions include not just the environmental context, but also the cognitive and even the emotional context (de Dear, 2004). The notion of a 'one size fits all' thermal environmental prescription implied in deterministic engineering comfort standards does not fit well with environmental psychologists.

5.2.2 Epidemiological studies

During the 1980s, the first epidemiological studies were performed on a national basis:

*   In the UK, 4373 office workers of 42 office buildings were studied to estimate the seriousness of SBS (Burge et al, 1987). Naturally ventilated buildings scored the best and the highest scored symptoms were lethargy (57 per cent), nose/throat complaints (47 per cent) and headache (43 per cent).
*   In a Danish investigation of 14 town halls, 4369 employees were asked to fill in a questionnaire (Skov et al, 1987). The results are presented in Table 5.4. Forty-five per cent of the respondents found the air too dry and 33 per cent complained about the temperature. Irritation or concentration difficulties scored the highest (90 per cent).
*   In The Netherlands, more than 7000 people responded to a questionnaire (Preller et al, 1990). Fifty-three per cent of those respondents reported complaints on temperature, 45 per cent on air quality and 42 per cent perceived the air as too dry (see Table 5.5).

Table 5.4 *Reported complaints in 14 Danish town halls*

Complaint	Mean percentage (%)	Complaint	Mean percentage (%)
Eyes, nose and throat	28.4	Air quality	35.2
Skin	7.0	Temperature change	33.2
Headache, tiredness, discomfort	36.1	Irritation or concentration difficulties	89.8
Dry air	45.1	Lighting	13.9
Static shocks	14.2	Noise in offices (in winter)	21.8

Source: Skov et al (1987)

Table 5.5 *Reported complaints in 61 Dutch buildings*

Complaint	Mean percentage (%)	Complaint	Mean percentage (%)
Skin	6.4	Air quality	44.7
Eye	18.4	Lighting	29.9
Nose/throat	19.4	Dry air	42.0
Neurological	22.3	Noise	24.7
Fever	8.5	Static shocks	10.6
Temperature	52.5	Dirty taste in mouth	7.0

Source: Preller et al (1990)

In Europe, the first study focusing on the indoor environment (more specifically, indoor air quality) was the European Audit project (Bluyssen et al, 1996a). Questionnaires, checklists and physical and chemical measurements were performed in 56 office buildings in nine European countries during the heating season of 1993 to 1994. The audits were performed according to a standard procedure (see Box 5.7) within the framework of the European Audit Project to Optimize Indoor Air Quality and Energy Consumption in Office Buildings, sponsored by the European Community through the Joule II programme.

The main aim of this EC audit was to develop assessment procedures and guidance on ventilation and source control, which help to ensure good indoor air quality and optimize energy use in office buildings. Fifteen institutes from 11 countries (The Netherlands, Denmark, France, Belgium, the UK, Greece, Switzerland, Finland, Norway, Germany and Portugal) participated. A common Europe-wide agreed-upon method to investigate mainly indoor air quality in office buildings, including a common agreed-upon questionnaire and walk-through survey checklist, was developed (Clausen et al, 1993).

A total of 6537 occupants representing more than 30,000 occupants in the audited buildings participated in the questionnaire survey (Groes, et al, 1995). The response rate averaged 79 per cent. The occupants of the office buildings comprised, on average, 47 per cent males and 53 per cent females; however, in Dutch buildings the average was 72 per cent males and only 28 per cent females. The mean number of smokers was 31 per cent, with the highest percentage of smokers in Greek buildings (48 per cent). Although the average TVOC in µg/m³ toluene equivalents, the mean particulate matter, and CO_2 and CO concentrations generally met the requirements of existing national standards and European guidelines, and the ventilation rates were quite high (with an average of 1.9l/sm² or 25l/sperson, which is well above existing ventilation standards), nearly 30 per cent of the occupants and 50 per cent of the visitors found the air unacceptable. Tables 5.6 and 5.7 show the mean reported symptoms and complaints.

In all of the buildings, the air was perceived by occupants as being dry. In general, the buildings were perceived as being between neutral and slightly warm. A substantial variation was found between the European buildings, however, where no systematic regional differences regarding occupants' responses were observed.

In the US in 1994, the US Environmental Protection Agency initiated a major cross-sector study – the Building Assessment Survey and Evaluation Study (BASE) – to characterize key characteristics of indoor air quality (IAQ), occupant health symptoms and perceptions of IAQ in public and commercial office buildings (Apte, et al, 2000). Between the summer of 1995 and the winter of 1997 to 1998, data and samples were collected in 100 public and private office buildings across the continental US using a standardized protocol over a one-week period during either the summer or winter season. These buildings were randomly selected without regard to indoor air quality concern, except that buildings with highly publicized indoor air quality problems were excluded. Data and samples were collected on VOCs (including aldehydes); particulate matter; radon; microbiological contaminants; carbon monoxide and carbon dioxide; temperature and relative humidity; building characteristics; and occupant symptoms and perceptions of IAQ. Data were also collected regarding characteristics (including ventilation rates), operation and maintenance of HVAC systems.

And in the European EXPOLIS study (Air Pollution Exposure Distributions of Adult Urban Populations in Europe) population exposure to key air pollutants in six European cities was measured between 1996 and 1997 (Jantunen et al, 1998). The pollutants studied in EXPOLIS were fine particulates ($PM_{2.5}$), CO, 30 VOCs, and nitrogen dioxide (NO_2). The populations studied were working-age urban populations from six European cities. The metropolitan area of Helsinki was the smallest of participating cities (1 million). The largest was Athens (4 million). Information on the exposure of population samples and micro-environmental concentrations in the homes and workplaces of the same subjects, together with long questionnaires and two-day time-activity diaries were gathered.

At the beginning of the 21st century, worldwide, several field studies were performed, focused either on a large sample to define statistically relevant relations or on a smaller sample to provide indications of relations – for example, studies on household exposure to indoor air pollutants on a national level in France (Kirchner et al, 2002) and in the UK (Raw et al, 2002); indoor

Box 5.7 Procedures for the European Audit Project to Optimize Indoor Air Quality and Energy Consumption in Office Buildings

In nine of the eleven countries, six buildings represented the building stock in terms of age and type of construction. Public- or private-sector buildings were equally acceptable. In order to avoid high and unstable emissions in new buildings, the buildings were at least two years old. There was no restriction on the type of ventilation used in the buildings. The buildings were located in areas where the outdoor air quality was reasonably fresh.

The study population comprised at least 125 employees in each building, occupying offices representative of the building. It was preferable, but not a requirement, that the population in each building was a homogeneous group of white-collar/clerical workers (e.g. in a bank, an insurance company or other administration offices). Furthermore, gender was also an important factor, since men typically report fewer symptoms than women. Buildings with an equal distribution of men and women were preferred.

In each building physical and sensory measurements were performed at five selected locations. The locations were all in one or more large open-plan offices or in cellular offices. Both smoking and non-smoking workplaces were included. The selected offices should have been representative of the building. The main activity of the offices was general office work. Computer terminal rooms and photocopying rooms were avoided.

A location near the office spaces being studied was required in order to refresh the panel's senses. The location was a nearby office where it was possible to open the windows or an area outside the building.

A technical survey of the building and its installations was made based on a walk-through survey with the use of a check-list and on ground plans and information from the building maintenance staff. The walk-through survey was performed before the main investigation.

In order to achieve similar conditions with regard to building temperature in the different countries, the experiments in all nine countries were conducted during the heating season. Considering the one-month recall period of the questionnaire, the experiments were conducted in November/December or February/March.

The buildings were studied while normally occupied and ventilated to quantify the total pollution load caused by the occupants and their activities, the ventilation systems, and the sources in the spaces themselves. The investigation included physical and chemical measurements, assessment of perceived air quality in the spaces by a trained sensory panel, and measurement of the outdoor air supply to the spaces. The physical and chemical measurements in the spaces included measurements of noise, concentrations of carbon dioxide (CO_2), carbon monoxide (CO) and total volatile organic compounds (TVOCs), and the thermal parameters: operative temperature, air temperature, relative humidity and air velocity. Airflows between the selected spaces and adjacent spaces were measured, when necessary. Additional measurements in the adjacent spaces included measurements of CO, CO_2 and TVOCs, and assessments of the perceived air quality. In mechanically ventilated buildings, perceived air quality of the supply air in the five selected spaces was assessed by the panel. At one of the five selected locations of each building, measurements were also taken of individual volatile organic compounds (VOCs) and of airborne particulate matter. All chemical and particulate measurements were also performed outdoors. A questionnaire for evaluating retrospective and immediate symptoms and perceptions was given to the occupants of the buildings. The building characteristics were described through the use of a checklist. The annual energy consumption of the buildings and the weather conditions were registered.

Time schedule for measurements in the building

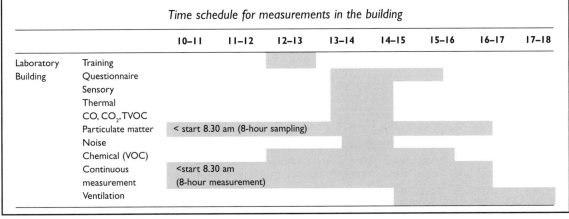

		10–11	11–12	12–13	13–14	14–15	15–16	16–17	17–18
Laboratory Building	Training								
	Questionnaire								
	Sensory								
	Thermal								
	CO, CO_2, TVOC								
	Particulate matter	< start 8.30 am (8-hour sampling)							
	Noise								
	Chemical (VOC)								
	Continuous	<start 8.30 am							
	measurement	(8-hour measurement)							
	Ventilation								

Table 5.6 *European Audit project: Reported symptoms*

Symptoms	Mean past month (%)	Symptoms	Mean past month (%)
Dry eyes	39	Flu-like symptoms	25
Watering eyes	17	Dry skin	25
Stuffy nose	33	Irritated skin	11
Runny nose	18	Headache	42
Dry throat	36	Lethargy	52
Chest tightness	15	Flu-like symptoms	25

Source: Bluyssen et al (1996a)

Table 5.7 *European Audit project: Reported complaints*

Complaints	Mean past month	Scale
Indoor air quality	0.9	−5 (clearly not acceptable) to +5 (clearly acceptable)
Air dryness	2.5	1 (dry) to 7 (humid)
Air stuffiness	4.3	1 (fresh) to 7 (stuffy)
Air odour	3.0	1 (odourless) to 7 (smelly)
Thermal comfort	0.2	−3 (too cold) to +3 (too warm)
Light quality	2.6	1 (satisfactory) to 7 (unsatisfactory)
Noise	3.2	1 (satisfactory) to 7 (unsatisfactory)
Control ventilation	2.4	1 (none) to 7 (full control)
Cleanliness of office	4.4	1 (unsatisfactory) to 7 (satisfactory)

Source: Bluyssen et al (1996a)

environmental quality (IEQ) and student performance in 30 classrooms of 674 pupils in Brasil (Jurado, 2006); and IAQ in 57 sick houses in Japan (Yoshino et al, 2006). In addition, worldwide, a study is being performed among 20,103 children in Sweden, Bulgaria and Singapore (Zuraimi, et al, 2006) to investigate the relation between dampness and allergies and asthma.

The findings of a pan-European housing survey by WHO clearly indicate a link between present-day housing conditions, including the immediate environment, and human health and well-being (see Table 5.8) (Bonnefoy et al, 2004).

These data confirm that the indoor dwelling characteristics that most affect human health are connected to thermal comfort, lighting, moisture, mould and noise. But their interrelation is also clearly complicated.

International standards for the indoor environment are written by the International Organization for Standardization (ISO), the European Committee for Standardization (CEN) and the American Society of Heating, Refrigerating and Air Conditioning Engineers (ASHRAE). Until the 1990s, these standards were separated into standards for ventilation (air quality), thermal comfort, lighting and noise. In 1998, for the

first time, a new concept was introduced in a European Technical Report, CR1752 (CEN, 1998), where criteria for indoor air quality, ventilation, thermal comfort and noise were included; for the first time, recommendations for an acceptable indoor environment were specified in classes. This technical report finally became a CEN standard in 2005 (CEN, 2005).

5.2.3 Psycho-social effects

As mentioned earlier, the context of people–environment interactions does not only include the environmental context, but also the cognitive and even the emotional context. Some thoughts and theories on this subject follow below.

The psyche and symbols

The human mind or the psyche comprises a conscious and an unconscious part. Gustav Carl Jung believed that the psyche can be divided more accurately into the following (Jung, 1966–1976):

- *Conscious*: thoughts and actions that relate to the will.

Box 5.8 Utopia

In 1516, Sir Thomas More described an imaginary island called Utopia that enjoyed perfection in politics, law and family relations. Utopia comes from the Greek *Ou* (not) and *topos* (place) to emphasize that Utopia did not and probably could not exist, although it was an ideal towards which men could strive.

We are dealing with hierarchies of needs and interdependencies, with ecosystems rather than isolated individuals and groups. There is no situation that is ideal for everyone all of the time. This is the true meaning of Utopia as a non-place.

Source: Sommer (1969)

Table 5.8 *Established relations between physical parameters and health and comfort problems*

Physical parameter	Comfort	Human health: Determined links
Temperature	50% (highly) dissatisfied with thermal comfort	Respiratory diseases, cold and throat illness, multiple allergies
Light	25% people (highly) dissatisfied (daylight)	(Trends of) depression, chronic anxiety, household accidents
Noise	25% people annoyed (e.g. traffic, neighbours)	Hypertension, (trends of) depression, fatigue, accidents
Moisture and mould	25% of dwellings: mould growth in >1 room	Respiratory diseases, asthma, allergies
	8% of dwellings: smells, dampness	
Indoor air quality (general)	10% dissatisfied	Fatigue, (trends of) depression, anxiety, respiratory diseases

Source: Bonnefoy et al (2004)

- *Pre-conscious*: mental capacities and memories that can be easily called into consciousness.
- *Personal unconscious*: a reservoir of personal memories (perceptions, experiences and suppressed desires).
- *Collective unconscious* or objective psyche: instinctive thoughts and behavioural patterns or emotions and values that cannot be called into consciousness and can only be managed via symbols. Jung named those symbols archetypes – the common legacy of all people. An archetype is a generic, idealized model of a person, object or concept from which similar instances are derived, copied, patterned or emulated. In psychology, an archetype is a model of a person, personality or behaviour.

According to Jung, people are healthy when a dynamic balance exists between the conscious and unconscious parts of the mind. An internal conflict emerges when the flows of energy between the two parts to satisfy each other's needs are interrupted.

Psychoanalysis is a search for the meaning of behaviours, symptoms and events. The *analysis of dreams* is the most common channel to reach this greater self-knowledge; others may include expressing feelings through works of art, poetry or other expressions of creativity. Thus, symbols from dreams are clues for psychological problems and indicators for recovery (self-knowledge and self-actualization). These dreams can take place at the:

- Non-symbolic level: can be taken literally; usually about the experiences and activities of the last days, coming from the pre-conscious.
- Global symbolic level: makes use of symbols to present contents; related to essential bodily functions such as food, comfort and health, emotions and care of one's own person (in short: survival).
- Higher symbolic level: comes close to our desire for the meaning of life, which goes beyond the physical, emotional and sexual; comes from the collective unconscious. These dreams are symbolic and pre-linguistic because they relate to parts of the unconscious that developed before human beings learned to use language; but it seems that the meaning of the symbols is recognized by our psyche and translated into words at a certain level.

In addition, Jung introduced different psychological types or temperaments: the extravert and the introvert (Jung, 1966–1976). Extraverts desire breadth and are action oriented, while introverts seek depth and are self-oriented. According to Jung, the conscious psyche is an apparatus for adaptation and orientation, and consists of a number of different psychic functions. Among these he distinguishes four basic functions:

1 *Sensing*: perception by means of the sense organs.
2 *Intuition*: perceiving in an unconscious way or perception of unconscious contents.
3 *Thinking*: function of intellectual cognition; the forming of logical conclusions.
4 *Feeling*: the function of subjective estimation.

Thinking and feeling functions are *rational*, while sensing and intuition are *irrational*. According to Jung, rationality consists of figurative thoughts, feelings or actions with reason (a point of view based on objective value), which is set by practical experience. Irrationality is not based on reason. Jung notes that elementary facts are also irrational, not because they are illogical but because, as thoughts, they are not judgements. In any person, the degree of introversion/extraversion of one function can be quite different from that of another function (Fontana, 2007).

Emotional and behavioural responses

Emotional and behavioural responses are related to the individual's psycho-physiological state of mind and are part of a cognitive process and largely influence how people perceive and behave in certain environments. According to Farshchi and Fischer (2000), emotional or behavioural responses to environmental situations can be expressed in:

*   *Emotional episodes*: emotional reaction to something, with the reaction typically involving coordinated and distinctive physiological, behavioural and mental changes (i.e. someone suffering grief at death or getting angry at someone).
*   *Moods*: the feelings of a person's subjective state at a certain moment in time.
*   *Affective appraisal*: judgement of things as pleasant, attractive, valuable, likeable, preferable, repulsive, etc.

*   *Emotional dispositions*: relate to long-term emotions, a tendency to do or think or feel particular things when the right circumstances occur.

Geometric shapes and colours can affect our emotions and result in subtle mood changes. They can make us agitated, calm, stimulated or depressed (Fontana, 2007) (see Box 5.9).

In general, one has emotions to probe the nervous system to cope with threatening or stressful situations. Emotions are a crucial mechanism for survival and, in fact, an adaptive response of the organism to environmental stimuli.

The indoor environment can cause physical stress, such as being too warm or too cold, and can limit a person in coping with this stress – for example, not being able to control the temperature in their office or to open a window to get outdoor (fresh) air, or not having a view. In addition, psycho-social factors such as working stress, mental well-being, relationships with the boss and colleagues, etc. can influence (mainly negatively) the perception of these physical and coping stressors.

Stress is, in fact, the divergence between people's needs and goals and the opportunities or possibilities that the environment offers. Coping is a strategy to deal with this divergence. With external coping, the environment is adjusted to the needs and goals; with internal coping, the needs and goals are adjusted to the limitations of the environment, or the mental effort is increased. Internal coping can, however, lead to negative effects, such as a lower tolerance for a certain stimulant (e.g. noise of an air-conditioning system) or an increase in blood pressure due to more strenuous mental effort. External coping leads to fewer negative effects. A form of external coping is to increase the controllability of a person's own environment (i.e. to be able to set our own room temperature, to open a window, to dim a light, etc.). This directly relates to the second of the four behavioural laws that, according to Vroon (1990), exist and which perhaps explain some of the occurring sick building symptoms (see Box 5.10).

With respect to the first behavioural law, the need for change in our environment, we know that the most primitive learning process is habituation. After a while, we do not notice a continuous monotone stimulation anymore – as, for example, certain background noises (air conditioning). This has its origin in the survival mechanism of people and animals: noticing changes is important. But if we do not notice them anymore,

---

Box 5.9 Examples of environmental symbols

Geometric shapes:

- angular shape with irregular pointing edges: symbolizes anger;
- symmetric round shape: relaxation, inner piece;
- circle: infinity, perfection and eternity;
- square: firmness, unmoving, earthly and tangible perfection;
- triangle: pointing up – rise to heaven, fire and active male; pointing down: heavenly favours, water and passive female;
- half moon: newborn, magical power that can change shapes;
- star: dignity and sovereignty.

Colours:

- red: power of life, energy through our body, colour of war;
- yellow: gold, unfaithful, treason, illness;
- blue: colour of peace, water and coolness, air and eternity;
- purple: mystic colour;
- black: symbol of death, sorrow and the underworld;
- white: purity and virginity;
- gold: truth;
- green: sensorial perception, nature, growth and decline, associated with jealousy.

Source: Fontana (2007)

---

there are no changes in our environment and then, according to Vroon (1990), the opposite might occur: we want to create changes to become stimulated. These changes can be related to hearing and sight, but also to skin sensations (no draught, constant temperature). Changes in the indoor environment are considered to be a form of stimulation.

An unknown odour is one example of the third law: stimulation needs explanation. Another example is being exposed to a noise that is unpredictable in strength and duration, or new and unusual noises. Controllability, predictability and/or the need for stimulation are thus very important.

With respect to the last law – people protect and expand their territory – Sommer (1969) describes four types of territories in human societies: public, home (public areas taken over by groups or individuals), interaction (areas where social gatherings may occur)

Box 5.10 Basic behavioural laws

- People and animals need change in their environment (fresh air, ventilation, temperature, humidity). A too homogenous environment will lead to discomfort.
- People want to interfere with their environment (e.g. changing the furniture, noise levels and ventilation within one's office).
- Stimulation needs explanation. An odour that is present and which cannot be recognized will lead to a chronic alarm status.
- People protect and expand their territory. In open-plan offices, this is difficult. For centuries, people have lived in closed constructions that do not have contact with nature. Views of the outdoors are important in this context.

Source: Vroon (1990)

and body territories (personal space). Personal space refers to an area with invisible boundaries surrounding a person's body into which intruders may not come. There is considerable similarity between personal space and individual distance, which may be outside the area of personal space. Spatial arrangements in small groups are functions of personality, task and environment.

The relationship between single environmental elements and complex human behaviour is not simple (Berglund and Cain, 1989). The effects of environmental changes are mediated by individual needs and group processes. In an atmosphere of trust and understanding, an office worker will accept environmental changes as indications that his boss is interested in his welfare. In an atmosphere of distrust and hostility, the office worker will, perhaps, wonder how his boss hopes to exploit him by changing his working conditions; he looks upon environmental programming as manipulation.

Any building must meet the diverse needs of occupants whose interests frequently conflict. In a changing world, it seems reasonable to establish variety and flexibility as important goals in a building programme. Variety infers a multiplicity of settings and spaces that people can select to suit their individual needs. Flexibility is expressed in such terms as multipurpose, multi-use and convertible spaces. It is closely tied with personalization since it permits a man to adapt a setting to his unique needs.

Happiness levels and indices

Striving for happiness is a step further than meeting the needs of end users. Four levels of happiness can be observed (see www.lifeprinciples.net), following Maslow's hierarchy of needs (see section 6.1 in Chapter 6):

1   *Happiness level 1*: happiness in a thing. Happiness comes from phenomena outside ourselves and involves one or more of the five senses. The pleasure that these senses give is immediate and direct, such as eating ice cream, and is short lived and intermittent. It must be replaced by another ice cream to feel happy again.
2   *Happiness level 2*: the happiness of comparative advantage. This involves the ego (which is Latin for I), and occurs whenever 'I' am in control, the focus of attention and the object of admiration, and whenever I see myself as superior to others. It

results from competition with another person and is rather unstable; if one fails, it can lead to unhappiness and a sense of worthlessness.
3   *Happiness Level 3*: blessedness. This happiness comes from seeing the good in others and doing good for others. Humans also desire love, truth, goodness/justice, beauty and being. These desires are often expressed in acts of charity – seeking cures, being concerned with one's neighbour, making sacrifices, forgiving personal injuries. The common good is an integral part of our personal happiness.
4   *Happiness level 4*: sublime, which means to lift up or elevate. It encompasses a desire for fullness and the perfection of happiness – the fullness, therefore, of goodness, beauty, truth and love, something beyond our imagination, beyond our complete understanding.

Happiness has been related to neurobiological systems via functional magnetic resonance imaging (fMRI) and electro-encephalography (EEG) tests (Klein, 2006). Several happiness indices have also been or are being developed, using the average self-reported happiness (subjective life satisfaction) from surveys asking people how happy they are. For example:

*   Happy life years: a concept that combines self-reported happiness with life expectancy (Veenhoven, 2007).
*   The Happy Planet Index combines happiness with life expectancy and ecological footprint (The New Economics Foundation, 2006).
*   Gross national happiness is a concept introduced by the King of Bhutan (Revkin, 2005).

5.3 Performance concepts and indicators

5.3.1 Performance evaluations

Performance is a concept that has gained increasing attention over the last few decades. In 1982, the International Council for Research and Innovation in Building and Construction (CIB, 1982) presented statements that define performance for the building industry:

*   The performance approach is thinking and working in terms of ends rather than means.

- Performance is concerned with what a building or building product is required to do and not with prescribing how it is to be constructed.
- A design solution, traditional or novel, will always need a quantitative base for testing and evaluating its performance.

During the last decades, multiple concepts and tools have been developed and used to evaluate the performance of the built environment, buildings, building parts or specific aspects of buildings. The focus of these concepts and/or tools varies (technical, functional, etc.) as well as the target group for whom they are meant.

For the different phases of a building's life, different methods or concepts can be used and have been presented. However, most concepts and methods are focused on the occupancy phase of a building and only a few on the building's initiation phase. It seems that, in general, many methods exist for 'trouble shooting' and few for 'prevention'.

No method or concept is available to evaluate the performance of a building during its whole life – that is, from initiation to breakdown – except perhaps for the aspect sustainability for which several life-cycle analysis (LCA) methods exist and a framework for the development of indicators for buildings presented in the ISO/TS 21929-1 (ISO, 2006b). But no concept or method is available that is focused on requirements (demands) for all parties involved from start to finish.

Many attempts are being made to include the user's demands, whatever they may be, in these performance concepts by defining user profiles of some kind or by defining the aspects that should be considered. Most concepts and methods comprise numerous categories of aspects and sub-aspects. However, the criteria related to these aspects and sub-aspects are not always known or complete – for example, with respect to indoor environmental quality. The aspects that are mostly incomplete or missing are related either to the occupants themselves (e.g. their productivity), indoor environment quality (e.g. odour and irritation) or financial output.

Finance or profit is the main focus of most parties involved. Nevertheless, financial performance is still largely focused on the cost aspects of the building only, comprising the costs for land, construction material, building and in some cases costs for maintenance. In general, the revenue of certain actions (e.g. higher productivity, less sick leave) is not taken into account. The potential for a better indoor environment, for example, has been demonstrated by several authors; but this hasn't yet been translated into performance criteria for the buildings itself or in methods to measure this quantitatively. Neither has there been easy access to data on the performance of alternative solutions in order to support decision-making.

Several categories of performance evaluations or methods can be outlined (Bluyssen, 2001):

- Evaluations that determine the desired performance or quality of a building in the design phase, such as the Dutch Building Decree (Scholten, 2001), the RgD (*Rijksgebouwendienst*) performance contract (Ang et al, 1995), and the SBR (Stichting Bouw Research) methodology (Wijk and Spekking, 1998) in The Netherlands.
- Techniques that respond to user needs, changing organizational requirements, and the continuing demand for higher productivity, such as organizational workplace analysis (OWA) (Baird, 1996), ORBIT (project and rating process on organization, buildings and information technology) (Vijverbereg, 1999), BOSTI (Buffalo Organization for Social and Technological Innovation) (Wagenberg and Wilmes, 1989), building use studies (Leaman, 1996) and the building-in-use method. In the latter, in which the perception and evaluation of the workplace is central (Vischer, 1989), the evaluation is expressed in complaints of users (employees) with respect to seven parameters: air quality; thermal comfort; difference in noise level between workplaces; the available space; privacy; quality of light; and noise at the workplace.
- Methods that explicitly explore occupants' requirements (demands) as well as the capabilities of buildings to meet these requirements (supply), such as building quality assessment (BQA) (Bruhns and Isaacs, 1996) and serviceability tools and methods (STM) (Vijverberg, 1999; ASTM, 2000). In The Netherlands, the foundation Real Estate Norm Nederland (REN) introduced a method to compare the quality of office locations and buildings (REN, 1991, 1992).
- Techniques that are focused on the occupancy phase of a building, such as BREEAM (Baldwin et al, 1998), TOBUS (see Annex A and section 8.4.4 in Chapter 8) and post-occupancy evaluation (POE) (Cohen et al, 2000).

- Evaluations that are focused on particular aspects of building performance, such as finances, productivity, health and comfort of occupants, sustainability, strategic decisions and indoor environmental quality.

Dutch Building Decree

In October 1992, the Dutch Building Decree came into force. Later, further deregulations were implemented by amending this decree. The regulations were developed more or less in line with an international perspective, taking the newest views on the structure and contents of building regulations (Scholten, 2001). The building decree distinguishes three categories of buildings:

1 buildings meant for occupancy;
2 buildings not meant for occupancy (e.g. an office building);
3 building structures that are not buildings.

The starting points of the building decree are as follows:

- A building or construction should not be unsafe or unhealthy under normal use.
- A new and existing building should be usable.
- A new building should not be a large energy user.
- A new building should be environmentally friendly.

For each of these starting points, the building decree provides regulations for each type of construction, defined in so-called performance criteria and based on functional descriptions. A performance criterion is a quantifiable limit value that can be measured by an objective measurement method. The functional description comprises the motive of the defined performance criterion. However, performance criteria have not been defined for all items.

Building use studies

Building use studies, a category 2 method, uses a standard questionnaire for different purposes, ranging from diagnostic investigations of humidity problems to post-occupancy evaluations (Leaman, 1996). In this way, building use studies have been able to build up a database that allows comparisons to be made among building types, sectors and occupant groups. Standard

questions fall into eight groups: environmental comfort (36 questions); health symptoms (10); satisfaction with amenities (5 to 15); time spent in the building (1); time spent at the task (1); productivity (1 to 3); perceived control (5); and background data (3 to 10). Extra questions are added or some questions are removed in individual studies at the clients' request.

Building quality assessment (BQA)

Both building quality assessment (BQA) and serviceability tools and methods (STM) are methods that can be placed under category 3. BQA is a tool for scoring the performance of a building-relating performance to requirements for user groups in that type of building (Bruhns and Isaacs, 1996). Users of buildings are divided into two main groups: providers of buildings, including the owner and/or investor, and the occupants of buildings, including tenants, visitors and other people, such as maintenance and cleaning personnel. Building users have different requirements, some of which may conflict. In developing BQAs, the approach taken was to identify requirements that are common to most or all users of a building and those of specific groups. BQAs provide a common basis for measurement by different people in different places at any time.

Common user requirements of buildings have been identified and organized into a number of groups. These groups reflect how users perceive their requirements, based on what a building actually does. The use of building evaluation for briefing purposes led to the development of a checklist structure with six major attribute headings: corporate; site; construction; space; internal environment; and building services. BQA is based on nine categories that link the physical functions of buildings and the concepts used to describe them: presentation; space; access and circulation; business services; personnel amenities; working environment; health and safety; structural considerations; and manageability. The first seven are concerned with what the building does for its users and the last two are concerned with retaining that level of service. The nine categories are divided into sections that represent the effects of the building that a user will be aware of (what the user feels, sees, hears, etc.). Each section comprises a number of measurable factors for use in the assessment process. Plateaus provide a scoring scale for measuring each factor, ranging from 10 down to 0. The plateaus cover the range of practice for each factor, with the highest score set at the level of best practice. In addition to the numerical score, the assessor provides a written commentary on issues affecting each factor.

Neither the categories nor the factors are all of equal importance; therefore, a weighing system is incorporated.

The overall BQA is a weighted combination of the category and factor scores. Each individual factor is scored from 0 to 10, multiplied by a factor weight (from 0 to 100), and the weighted factor scores are then summed for each category and normalized by the sum of the weights for that category. The category score (out of 10) is multiplied by the category weight and summed across the nine categories to give the overall BQA. Profiles on the different levels (factors and categories) can be used, for example, to compare buildings.

Serviceability tools and methods (STM)

STM was developed by the International Centre for facilities in Canada (Vijverberg, 1999; ASTM, 2000), and was designed to bridge the gap between facility programmes written in user language, on the one hand (demand–occupant requirements), and outline specifications and evaluations written in performance language, on the other (supply – serviceability of buildings) (Davis and Szigeti, 1996). The method starts with determining the organization profile that is desired (demand), followed by the evaluation of the building (supply). The building and organization profile is than matched. At the heart of STM is a pair of multiple choice questionnaires. On the demand side, a set of scales for setting functional requirements using non-technical words is applied. On the supply side, a set of scales for rating the serviceability of buildings and building-related facilities using technical and performance terms to describe indicators of capability for combinations of features is applied. These scales cover over 100 topics of serviceability and assess more than 340 building features. Each has a scale from 1 to 9, with 9 representing more and 1 representing less, rather than good to bad. Each question concerns a topic (sub-aspect) related to 'serviceability'. These sub-aspects are categorized into 19 aspects, which are divided into three groups (working places and spaces, real estate and management, and regulation). A relation is determined with a total of 340 building characteristics. A profile of

points is the result, not one number. The information is presented in understandable, not technical, language and the questionnaires are supposed to be completed by a user (occupant). Costing is not included.

The STM method is the major subject of standardization by ISO and ASTM (ISO, 2006b; ASTM, 2000). The ASTM standards on whole building functionality and serviceability comprise an evaluation procedure that captures the quality (i.e. the performance) of a building by comparing present-day requirements set by the occupant with a rating of the facility. This is one of the several examples of serviceability rating, as a part of the post-occupancy evaluation, that are available and applied in practice.

Annex D provides a summary of the attributes and factors of the BQA checklist, as well as the topics of serviceability scales of the STM method, because they give a good overview of all the attributes and factors that one can possibly encounter.

BREEAM

In category 4, BREEAM is given as an example. BREEAM is a method introduced by the Building Research Establishment (BRE) in the UK that determines building quality and performance in terms of energy, environmental impacts and health indicators. BREEAM is a tool that allows the owners, users and designers of buildings to review and improve environmental performance throughout the life of a building. It is independent and authoritative, and is based on many years of construction and environmental research carried out at BRE, together with the input and experience of the construction and property industries, government and building regulators (Baldwin et al, 1998).

A BREEAM office assessment comprises three parts: a core assessment of the building fabric and services, which is always carried out, and two optional parts that deal with the quality of the design, procurement and management, and operating procedures, and can be included as appropriate. In addition, preassessment design support can be provided by the licensed assessors.

Key performance indicator (KPI)

An example for category 5 is the key performance indicator (KPI), used by managerial staff and owners to make strategic decisions. A KPI is usually a quantitative entity, not necessarily the physically measured one, representing the performance topic in terms that are convenient for managers (e.g. a grade on the scale of 0 to 10 related, for example, to the number of injuries per year, the number of complaints, etc.). In the area of business administration, benchmarking of KPIs is used to enable comparative investigation of a given situation to the commonly existing cases. Databases of business-oriented KPIs are now available for various topics, including those relevant to the construction sector. KPIs have also been adopted by the manufacturing industry for monitoring and upgrading production, as well as for monitoring and maintenance and operation of the machines and production lines (Scharpf, 1999; Millen, 2002).

5.3.2 Financial evaluation

The investors and project developers of this world, in general, evaluate a project or building on its financial performance, today and/or in the future. Several simple indices are used for this – for example, the internal rate of return (IRR) and the gross starting yield (BAR) (Rust et al, 1995). More complex and/or adjusted indicators using one of these as a base are used, taking into account the taxes, depreciation, debit and credit interests, etc. (see Box 5.11) In principle, however, the performance is evaluated on the cash flows that are expected in the future, whether these are in the near future (BAR and total rate of return, or TRR) or a little later (IRR).

Essentially, the following equation should hold, in which PV = present value:

$$\text{investment} \leq \text{PV}_{\text{all income}} - \text{PV}_{\text{all costs}}. \qquad [5.9]$$

Positive cash flows (gross rent, rest value of ground, rest value of building) and negative cash flows (exploitation costs, maintenance costs, replacements, renovations, etc.) can be taken into account. The investment comprises value of the land, value of the building in a renovated state, costs, etc.

What is not included in these indices or performance indicators are the costs or profits related to the employees who occupy the building. Annual costs for running a modern office building consist of the following (Flatheim, 1998):

- building and equipment depreciation on invested capital costs: circa 6 per cent;

- operational costs: energy, cleaning and maintenance: circa 2.7 per cent.
- employees: circa 91.3 per cent.

5.3.3 Savings and productivity gains

Productivity, the highest potential gain of a healthy, comfortable, safe and secure space, has received a lot of attention in the past years (see Box 5.12).

Productivity depends upon many aspects: well-being, mental drive, job satisfaction, technical competence, career achievements, home-work interface, relationships with others, personal circumstances, organizational matters, etc., and last, but not least, environmental factors (indoor and outdoor environment) (Clements-Croome, 2000). Productivity can be measured:

- *Objectively*: for example, by measuring the speed of working and the accuracy of outputs through designing very controlled experiments with well-focused tests (e.g. productivity effects as related to thermal comfort (Wyon, 1993) and air quality (Wargocki, et al, 2000)).
- *Subjectively*: by using self-estimated scales and questionnaires to assess the individual opinions of people concerning their work and environment (Raw, 1990).
- By *combined measures*: for example, by using physiological measures such as brain rhythms to see whether variations in the patterns of the brain responses correlate with the responses assessed by questionnaires (e.g. alertness and light; LHRF, 2002).

Besides productivity (the quantitative and/or qualitative work output of people – the products or services they deliver), sick leave (number of days sick, away from the workplace, per year) and estimates of life expectation, health-related financial indicators exist as well. Milton et al (2000) investigated the sick leave for 3720 employees in 40 buildings with 115 independently ventilated work areas, and found a consistent association of increased sick leave with lower levels of outdoor air supply. Humidifier use and indoor environmental quality complaints were also associated with increased sick leave. However, complaint areas were not associated with lower ventilation. Costs for sick leave comprise more than only the number of hours of sick leave multiplied by salary costs – for example, a reduction in turnover because another employee is doing the work with a lower productivity or the work is not done at all.

Box 5.11 Some financial performance indicators

The *yield (y)* or *interest of a project* can be expressed by:

$$y_{[t-1,t]} = P_t/C_{t-1} \ [\$] \tag{5.10}$$

where:

- $t-1$ to t is the time period of which the yield is evaluated;
- P_t = Profit = $INC_t - OUT_t + C_t - C_{t-1}$ ($);
- $INC_t - OUT_t$ = cash flow ($);
- $C_t - C_{t-1}$ = capital or value development during time period $t-1$ to t ($);
- INC_t = income during time period $t-1$ to t ($);
- OUT_t = payment during time period $t-1$ to t ($);
- C_{t-1} = capital/value at beginning of period ($);
- C_t = capital/value at end of period ($).

This results in:

$$C_t = C_{t-1}(1+y) + OUT_t - INC_t. \ [\$] \tag{5.11}$$

The *IRR is the internal rate of return*, and it concerns the whole investment period. It is a profitability indicator and can be calculated with the following equation:

$$NPV = -CFL_0 + CFL_1/(1 + IRR) + CFL_2/(1 + IRR)^2 + \ldots + CFL_{n-1}/(1 + IRR)^{n-1} + CFL_n/(1 + IRR)^n \ [\$] \tag{5.12}$$

where:

- $CFL_{0, 1, 2, \ldots n-1, n}$ = cash flow at time 0, year 1, year 2 ... year $n-1$ and at the end of the investment period ($);
- NPV = net present value ($).

TRR is the total rate of return over a certain interval (one year) of the investment period and can be defined as:

$$TRR_{[t,t-1]} = C_t - C_{t-1} + INC_t - OUT_t / C_{t-1}. \tag{5.13}$$

BAR is the gross starting yield and is defined as:

$$BAR = \text{rent conform market}_{\text{year 1 with complete letting out}} / \text{total investment.} \tag{5.14}$$

Estimates of life expectation include the following (Carrothers et al, 1999):

- *Value of statistical life (VSL)*: approach to value reductions in premature deaths attributed to short-term pollution episodes. VSL measures how much wealth people are willing to forego for small reductions in mortality risk. For example, a worker might be paid a wage premium of US$480 per year to accept an added fatality risk on the job of 1 in 10,000. Use of this VSL in the air pollution context assumes that the deaths attributed to air pollution are comparable to occupational deaths, which is not the case. Therefore, the US Environmental Protection Agency (EPA) presented an alternate method based strictly on life expectancy. By assuming that each air pollution death was premature by 4.5 years and using a value

---

Box 5.12 Savings and productivity gains

Fisk (2000) estimated the potential annual savings and productivity gains for the US through indoor air quality (IAQ) improvements with the 1996 US$ comprising:

- *Reduced respiratory disease*: US$6 to $14 billion (four common respiratory illnesses cause about 176 million days of lost work and 121 million days of restricted activity: a 100 and 25 per cent decrease in productivity respectively). Assuming a US$39,200 annual compensation, the annual value of lost work is US$34 billion. Healthcare costs are about US$36 billion. This results in an annual cost for respiratory infections of about US$70 billion. Better IAQ could reduce this by 9 to 20 per cent (or 16 to 37 million avoided cases of common cold or influenza).
- *Reduced allergies and asthma*: US$2 to $4 billion (costs for allergies and asthma are approximately US$15 billion (53 million allergy sufferers and 16 million asthma sufferer). A reduction of 8 to 25 per cent is feasible).
- *Reduced SBS symptoms*: US$10 to $30 billion (the number of workers with at least two symptoms is 15 million). Assuming a 2 per cent productivity decrease, the annual cost of SBS symptoms is in the order of US$60 billion. Evidence suggests reductions of symptoms in the order of 20 to 50 per cent.
- *Direct improvements in worker performance that are unrelated to health*: US$20 to $160 billion (to estimate potential productivity gains, only changes in performance that are related to overall productivity in a straightforward manner are considered – for example, reading speeds and time to complete assignments are considered, not error rates). Literature reports performance changes of 2 to 20 per cent; Fisk (2000) estimates 0.5 to 5 per cent. Considering only US office workers, responsible for an annual gross national product (GNP) of approximately US$32 trillion, this performance gain increase is roughly US$20 billion to $160 billion.

---

of US$120,000 per life year saved, the EPA estimated the value of preventing an air pollution death at US$540,000.

- *Quality-adjusted life year (QALY)*: the QALY approach deals with changes in expected survival (i.e. years of lost life), and it weighs the years lived by a measure of their health-based quality. It estimates the longevity and quality-of-life changes attributable to each health effect, converted into economic figures. Valuation derived from QALY approaches may give substantially different results to VSL methods.

5.3.4 Health and comfort

While comfort is a general feeling, health can be expressed in more objective terms. Comfort should be viewed in the context of well-being, while well-being is not concerned only with personal health. Several performance indicators and concepts have been developed:

- *Building Symptom Index (BSI)*: the BSI is the number of symptoms from a questionnaire related to a building. For the calculation of BSI (mean number of symptoms reported by occupants) a procedure similar to the one used in the European Indoor Air Quality Audit project (Bluyssen et al, 1996a) can be used (see Box 5.13).
- *Building Comfort Index*: IEQ can be divided into separate elements (thermal comfort, acoustics, light and air quality), each addressed in a questionnaire. Therefore, for each of these issues it is possible to define a number or qualitative expression to describe the situation before the refurbishment/retrofit, according to the occupants. For each aspect, respondents can answer whether they feel annoyed or experience symptoms often, regularly, sometimes or never. When a correspondent answers a question with 'often or regularly', this is considered a complaint or a symptom. The total number of complaints or symptoms per question is divided by the total number of respondents. This results in the percentage of respondents who have complaints or symptoms per question (see Box 5.14).
- *Weighted descriptor profiles*: Berglund et al (2000) proposed a method to measure sick building syndrome because, in their opinion, SBS-sensitive

Box 5.13 Building Symptom Index

For the calculation of the Building Symptom Index (BSI) (mean number of symptoms reported by occupants), first the Personal Symptom Index (PSI) is calculated from the answers on the following questions of the occupant questionnaire.

If you are at the office for more than four hours, do you experience any of the following symptoms (tick one box)?

	Often	Regularly	Sometimes	Never
27. Dry/watering eyes	☐	☐	☐	☐
28. Blocked/runny nose	☐	☐	☐	☐
29. Dry/irritated throat	☐	☐	☐	☐
30. Chest tightness	☐	☐	☐	☐
31. Dry/irritated skin	☐	☐	☐	☐
32. Headaches	☐	☐	☐	☐
33. Lethargy/tiredness	☐	☐	☐	☐
34. Pain in neck, shoulders or back	☐	☐	☐	☐

When a symptom is experienced often or regularly, it is counted as a symptom. The PSI is calculated by summing the total number of symptoms per person. If a question for an individual symptom has not been answered, then it is treated as a 0 (zero) when summing up all symptoms. However, if all answers for questions 27 to 34, are missing then the PSI is treated as missing data.

The PSI is mainly affected by job type (manager, specialist, clerical or other) and sex (male, female). Normally, male managers, who tend to have the least symptoms, are taken as a reference. When comparing buildings, a correction factor should be applied to PSI. However, in previous investigations the response rate of male managers was often quite low. Using their answers as a reference then has no meaning. Therefore, calculations will be made using the category of female clerical as a second reference.

The calculations should be performed as follows:

Step 1: for each building calculate the mean PSI for each gender and job type (2 x 4 = 8 combinations).
Step 2: take male managers as the baseline (correction = 1); divide the mean PSI of the other sex and job type combination by the mean PSI for male managers to create correction ratios per building.
Step 3: take female clerical as the baseline (correction = 1); divide the mean PSI of the other sex and job type combination by the mean PSI for female clerical to create correction ratios per building.
Step 4: calculate the mean correction ratios for each gender and job type across the set of evaluated buildings; this results in seven overall correction factors for each reference (male managers and female clerical).
Step 5: divide the PSI for each job type/gender combination per building by the overall correction factors for each reference.

Steps 4 and 5 can be carried out after evaluating all buildings. The BSI is the corrected mean PSI score for each building.

occupants, who are generally affected by the building, should be diagnosed and used for identifying building-related causes of SBS. SBS assessment is based on every occupant's qualitative perceptions separately analysed for the eyes, upper airways and facial skin. For each body site, occupants scale how often each descriptor was experienced when staying in their apartments ('during the last three weeks' using a five-category response scale from 'never' to 'always'). The method comprises three steps:

1   Step 1: structural equation modelling (SEM) is applied to hypothetical descriptor models, resulting in three models for eyes, upper airways and facial skin.
2   Step 2: creation of weighted descriptor profiles for each occupant.

Box 5.14 Comfort Index

For thermal comfort, indoor air quality (IAQ), light and noise, a comfort index is calculated by averaging the percentages of complaints for the different questions/aspects related to each issue (see Annex A for questionnaire):

- thermal comfort: questions 12, 13, 14, 15, 16, 17;
- IAQ: questions 9, 10, 11;
- light: questions 18, 19, 20, 21;
- noise: question 23.

The equation is as follows:

$$\text{Comfort Index}_{issue} = \sum \text{percentage complaints}_{aspect} / \text{total number of aspects per issue} \qquad [5.15]$$

In this (pragmatic) approach, there is no weighing of different aspects when calculating a percentage of complaints for an issue. The results can be presented graphically (e.g. in a radar diagram, see Figure 5.7).

3   Step 3: clustering of occupants based on weighted profiles results in a way of identifying sensitive occupants.

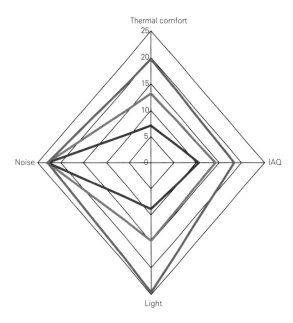

Source: Bluyssen (2001)

Figure 5.7 *Example of radar diagram with average, minimum and maximum percentages of complaints for thermal comfort, IAQ, light and noise reported*

- *Health-adjusted life years (e.g.* disability-adjusted life years, *DALY):* public health focus has gradually changed from life expectancy to health expectancy, which does not include mortality but, rather, aspects of quality of life (Hollander and Melse, 2006) such as:
- aggravation of pre-existing disease symptoms (e.g. asthma, chronic bronchitis, cardiovascular or psychological disorders);
- severe annoyance, sleep disturbance or reduced ability to concentrate, communicate or perform normal daily tasks;
- feelings of insecurity or alienation, unfavourable health perception and stress in relation to the poor quality of the local environment, and perceived danger of large fatal accidents.

During recent years, therefore, indices have been developed that transform any type of mortality into an equivalent number of life years, such as the health impact measure DALY, based largely on the 'burden of disease' developed by Murray and Lopez (1996). It combines years of life lost and years lived with disability, which are standardized by means of severity weights. According to Hollander and Melse (2006), who studied the pros and cons of DALY, it seems a good health metric to help in environmental health policy 'as long it is not considered the ultimate health coin'.

6

Drivers of Health and Comfort in the Indoor Environment

Drivers of health and comfort in the indoor environment are presented mainly for the developed Western world, including climate change, the needs of the end user, the requirements of stakeholders and some major regulatory developments. These drivers are different than 100 years ago and are important to take into account when designing healthy and comfortable buildings. Although society seems to be aware of the need for performance- and health-focused indoor environments, end users' needs and the communication process between all stakeholders involved need attention.

6.1 External drivers

6.1.1 Economic drivers

Economic transitions went hand in hand with technology developments and political and social demands. The economy went from *an agrarian, to an industrial, to a knowledge economy*, and is now in the middle of the *creative economy* (see Figure 6.1). Considering the importance of climate change, one could easily imagine that a transition from the creative economy to a *climate-change oriented* economy is taking place.

An economy is a system for the production, exchange and consumption of goods and services. The three traditional production factors of an economy are labour, nature and capital. Originally, in the *agrarian economy*, these three were in balance. In the *industrial economy*, the emphasis was on the combination of capital, machines and blue collar workers (internal oriented); while in the *knowledge economy*, it was important to combine knowledge and technique in such a way that the value for customer and market enlarged the value of the company (external oriented). The production factor knowledge became very important. In the knowledge economy, it was important to react quickly on unexpected and unusual

questions and, at the same time, to take into account the different stakes of the increasing number of parties. This demanded 'value-based knowledge management' (Tissen et al, 1998).

In the industrial economy, information technology was used to provide information, while people were required to interpret this. In the knowledge economy, people are still fed with information, but this information is transferred to knowledge. People do not need to understand this information; it is being done

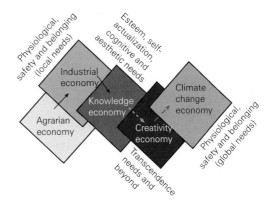

Source: inspired by Tissen et al, 1998

Figure 6.1 *Economic transitions*

for them through information technology (simulation of the brain). A shift is taking place from routine work to intellectual work, which fits in the shift from agricultural labour to industry and services.

By applying knowledge, innovation is possible, which leads to new products and services and economic growth. In the Lisbon strategy of 2000 (European Parliament, 2000), one of the targets for Europe was to become the most knowledge-intensive economy in 2010.

The *creative economy* is based on ideas generated by human capital (Howkins, 2001). It produces goods and services that create, teach and generate technical innovation, and drive, design and cultivate change.

There has been a rapid spread of patents, copyright and trademarks. People with ideas, people who own ideas, have become more powerful than people who work with machines and, in many cases, more powerful than the people who own machines. Creativity is the ability to generate something new. Creativity is not necessarily an economic activity, but may become so when it produces an idea with economic implications or a tradable product. As a consequence, the number of patents has continued to grow. And consumer expenditure on pleasure has focused on more than housing or food. Creative people and organizations are becoming more businesslike and business is becoming more dependent upon creativity.

Applying Maslow's hierarchy of needs, the first three basic needs were the focus of the agrarian and industrial economy (biological and physiological needs, safety needs and belonging and love). Esteem was on the way and, in the knowledge economy, self-actualization and aesthetic and cognitive needs were added. Today, during the beginning of the 21st century in the Western world, people's material needs have been largely satisfied, and matters of the mind have become more and more important, implying the need for fulfilling 'transcendence' needs.

In the *climate change economy*, climate change and the scarcity of fossil-fuel energy will be the dominant factors; therefore, we are back to basic needs, but now on a global instead of a local level in the agrarian economy. There will be a definitive need for another way of living, in which energy use and health are intertwined.

6.1.2 Social drivers

Besides the climate change driver and the driver for human basic needs, there are two important social drivers that have increasingly influenced indoor environments: the *change from a family-oriented society to a multifunctional and diverse society* over the last decades and the *increasing individualization caused by ageing and the increase in one- and two-person households*. The consequences are more and different needs for indoor spaces. The growing number of senior people will live independently longer and will be active at a high age. The increasing group of one-person households and the growing group of two-income couples will demand higher quality and will need a different type of indoor environment than the multi-person households and the one-income families.

Increasing individualization will also lead to a need for flexibility within buildings, which indicates that buildings need to be able to change faster in order to comply with the needs of the 'new' user. Consequently, buildings require a shorter economic lifetime or an increased redundancy to accommodate change, and the construction industry needs to adapt to this. Life expectancy has risen from 50 to 80 years in less than a century, while the housing stock has only been renewed

---

Box 6.1 China's effect on the world

Globally, the People's Republic of China must be mentioned in an economic context. Since 1978, the Chinese government has been reforming its economy from a Soviet-style centrally planned economy to a more market-oriented economy, while remaining within the political framework provided by the Communist Party of China. The economy of China is the third largest in the world after the US and Japan with a gross domestic product (GDP) of US$4.3 trillion (2008) (www.wikipedia.org). China underwent the economic transitions presented in Figure 6.1 in a relatively short time. The consequences are not clear yet but undoubtedly China will have its share of climate change problems and social driven matters, which in turn will have to be taken seriously on a global level.

by 60 per cent over the same period (Doll and Haffner, 2001).

By 2050 it is expected that the percentage of people aged 65 and over will have increased by 70 per cent, and the percentage of people aged 80 and over by 170 per cent for the EU-25 (EU, 2007a). This ageing population causes a corresponding increase in high-risk groups from the point of view of health, safety and well-being. Care for the elderly and social inclusion will become significant house-related issues.

The growth rate of the older population in the Americas (South and North America) has been higher than that of the total population for many decades (US Department of Commerce, 2000). There was a decline in the 60-and-over growth rate during the 1970s and especially during the 1980s, reflecting the low numbers of births in some countries during and after World War I. This decline is being mirrored by the 75-and-over growth rate as we move into the 21st century. As a whole, however, the older (60+) population will grow rapidly in the coming years. By the year 2010, the growth rate of the older population will be 3.5 times as high as that of the total population, and the growth of the 75-and-over segment will be accelerating. Although the 60-and-over growth rate will decline somewhat after 2010, it is expected to remain well above that of the total population into the foreseeable future.

Worldwide, the World Health Organization (WHO) reports that while in 2000 there were 600 million people aged 60 and over, there will be 1.2 billion by 2025 and 2 billion by 2050 (WHO, 2002). Today, about two-thirds of all older people are living in the developing world; by 2025, it will be 75 per cent. In the developed world, the very old (aged 80+) are the fastest growing population group. Women outlive men in virtually all societies; consequently, in very old age, the ratio of women to men is 2:1. The old-age dependency ratio (i.e. the total population aged 60 and over divided by the population age of 15 to 60; see Table 6.1) is primarily used by economists and actuaries who forecast the financial implications of pension policies. However, it is also useful for those concerned with the management and planning of caring services.

It is worthwhile mentioning that most of the older people in all countries continue to be a vital resource to their families and communities. Many continue to work in both the formal and informal labour sectors. Thus, as an indicator for forecasting population needs, the dependency ratio is of limited use.

Table 6.1 *Old-age dependency ratios for selected regions*

2002		2025	
Japan	0.39	Japan	0.66
North America	0.26	North America	0.44
European Union	0.36	European Union	0.56

Source: WHO (2002)

In Europe, new and large forces of immigrants are expected to come towards Europe (EU, 2007b). The US population is also becoming increasingly diverse: the labour force is constantly evolving and being affected by new technology, services, and types of work and work organization (NIOSH, 2004).

In 2002, almost 400 million people aged 60 and over lived in the developing world. By 2025, this will have increased to approximately 840 million representing 70 per cent of all older people worldwide. In terms of regions, over half of the world's older people live in Asia. Asia's share of the world's oldest people will continue to increase the most, while Europe's share as a proportion of the global older population will decrease the most over the next two decades. This rapid ageing in developing countries is accompanied by dramatic changes in family structures and roles, as well as in labour patterns and migration. Urbanization, the migration of young people to cities in search of jobs, smaller families and more women entering the formal workforce mean that fewer people are available to care for older people when they need assistance (WHO, 2002).

6.1.3 Policies, directives and regulations

Towards the performance of buildings

During the 1970s, it was recognized that regulations should not excessively restrict technological developments, so many of these provisions were exchanged with prescriptions of building components' performance properties (thermal resistance, fire resistance, acoustic separation, etc.), thus enabling various solutions with the same purpose.

However, during the 1990s, most Western countries acknowledged the fact that ensuring whole building performance requires more than prescribing the performance properties of building components. They thus started to produce more basic performance-based documents, focusing on performance requirements and associated criteria. The previous descriptive as well as prescriptive specifications were given a non-mandatory status in the form of possible solutions. Australia and The Netherlands were the first to officially publish and implement performance-based regulations (Jasuja, 2005).

The European Council Directive of 21 December 1988, 89/106/EEC on the approximation of laws, regulations and administrative provisions of the member states related to construction products (EU, 1988) included in its Annex I the following statements of the essential requirements for building products:

> The products must be suitable for construction works which (as a whole and in their separate parts) are fit for their intended use, account being taken of economy, and in this connection satisfy the following essential requirements where the works are subject to regulations containing such requirements. Such requirements must, subject to normal maintenance, be satisfied for an economically reasonable working life. The requirements generally concern actions, which are foreseeable.

This was the first step at a European level towards the performance requirements of buildings. A similar situation exists in the US, Canada, Australia, New Zealand and Israel (Jasuja, 2005).

For the quality of the indoor environment as perceived by occupants, essential requirements 3, 5 and 6 are particularly important (see Box 6.2).

Essential Requirement 3 is the underlying requirement for Mandate 366 of the Construction Product Directive (EU, 2005), which requires harmonized methods to test the emissions of dangerous substances from construction products to indoor air and groundwater and soil. Harmonized performance criteria for construction products with regards to emissions are perhaps the next step.

Essential Requirement 6 is one of the underlying requirement for the Energy Performance Building Directive (EU, 2002b), which promotes the improvement of energy performance of buildings, taking into account outdoor climate and local conditions, as well as indoor climate requirements and cost effectiveness. Comfortable indoor climate conditions should be safeguarded, and possible negative effects of energy saving measures such as inadequate ventilation should be avoided.

With respect to noise, several directives have been produced, although they are merely focused on the reduction of noise emissions by controlling outdoor sources (railway, road traffic and aircraft). Lately, more attention is paid to the protection of workers at their workplace, as well as to measures to reduce

---

Box 6.2 Essential Requirements 3, 5 and 6

Essential Requirement 3: Hygiene, health and the environment: The construction work must be designed and built in such a way that it will not be a threat to the hygiene or health of the occupants or neighbours, particularly as a result of the following:

- the giving-off of toxic gas;
- the presence of dangerous particles or gases in the air;
- the emission of dangerous radiation;
- pollution or poisoning of the water or soil;
- faulty elimination of wastewater, smoke, or solid or liquid wastes;
- the presence of damp in parts of the works or on surfaces within the works.

Essential Requirement 5: Protection against noise: The construction works must be designed and built in such a way that noise perceived by the occupants or people nearby is kept down to a level that will not threaten their health and will allow them to sleep, rest and work in satisfactory conditions.

Essential Requirement 6: Energy economy and heat retention: The construction works and its heating, cooling and ventilation installations must be designed and built in such a way that the amount of energy required in use shall be low, having regard to the climatic conditions of the location and the occupants.

exposure in homes and at schools (see section 5.1.4 in Chapter 5).

Health in all policies

Society has experienced a shift from prosperity to well-being during the last century, expressed in environmental policies, work and living policies, but also in the increasing awareness of consumer and producers. Health is a major driver and this becomes more and more obvious.

With regard to health, most national, European, nationwide and even worldwide organizations agree that indoor environments, including work and living spaces, can be a threat to one's health and that indoor environmental parameters themselves can contribute to that threat. Directives, action programmes and targets have been set to improve this situation (see Box 6.3).

The policy of the regulators and policy-makers has begun to focus more and more on performance criteria. End-user focus, sustainability and energy reductions are the themes, as well as maintenance of existing buildings in such a way that they are acceptable for users. However, even though the European directives

on safety and health of workers (EU, 1989) were taken almost 20 years ago, we still cannot say that all workers and people are healthy and comfortable in the environment (indoors or outdoors). In a study performed by Fisk, only 20 per cent of the building stock was qualified as being healthy (Fisk, 2000). For the US (270 million inhabitants), annual savings and productivity gains from reduced allergies and asthma reduced sick building syndrome (SBS) symptoms, and direct improvements in worker performance that are related to comfort were estimated (see Table 6.2).

The more recent European health strategy (EU, 2007a) emphasizes that 'Spending on health is not just a cost, it is an investment (health is the greatest wealth).' In this strategy for 2008–2013, the following objectives are presented:

- *Fostering good health in an ageing Europe*: improving the health of children at home and in schools, and of adults of working age and older people will help to create a healthy, productive population and support healthy ageing now and in the future. Healthy life years (HLY) is a key factor for economic growth.

Box 6.3 Examples of health actions and targets

Article 152 of the EC Treaty
    A high level of human health protection shall be ensured in the definition and implementation of all community policies and activities

Safety and health at work

- Directive 89/391/EEC, Safety and Health of Workers at Work (EU, 1989);
- Directive 91/322/EEC, Protection of Workers from the Risks Related to Exposure to Chemical, Physical and Biological Agents at Work (EU, 1991).

Health targets specified by WHO Europe (WHO, 2000)

- By the year 2015, people in the region should live in a safer physical environment, with exposure to contaminants hazardous to health at levels not exceeding internationally agreed standards (European Health 21, Target 10).
- By the year 2015, people in the region should have greater opportunities to live in healthy physical and social environments at home, at school, at the workplace and in the local community (European Health 31, Target 13).

6th Environment and Health Action Plan (2004–2008) (EU, 2002a)

- Achieve a quality of the environment where the levels of man-made contaminants, including different types of radiation, do not give rise to significant impacts on or risks to human health.

Table 6.2 *Estimated savings in the US as a result of a more comfortable and healthy indoor environment*

Buildings	Savings (US$ billion/year)
Reduced allergies and asthma (based on a 10–30% decrease in symptoms)	US$2–4 billion
Reduced sick building syndrome symptoms (based on 20–50% reduction and 2% productivity improvement)	US$10–30 billion
Increased productivity through comfort related improvements (based on 0.5–5% increase in worker performance)	US$20–160 billion

Source: Fisk (2000)

- *Protecting citizens from health threats*: this includes workers' safety, accidents at home, as well as emerging health threats such as those linked to climate change (floods, severe colds, heat waves, etc.).
- *Supporting dynamic health systems and new technologies.*

Box 6.4 shows a limited overview of facts and figures on (un)healthy buildings (based on a literature review).

In *Improving Quality and Productivity at Work: Community Strategy 2007–2012 on Health and Safety at Work* (EU, 2007b), it is apparent that the focus of attention at the workplace is shifting from physical complaints towards mental illness (depression). The previous strategy (2002–2006) has seen a significant fall in the rate of accidents at work. Over the period of 2000–2004, the rate of fatal accidents at work in the EU-15 has fallen by 17 per cent, while the rate of workplace accidents leading to absences of more than three days has fallen by 20 per cent. The 2007–2012 strategy states that new risk factors are emerging (e.g. violence at work, including sexual and psychological harassment and addictions), as well as work pattern transformations (working life is becoming more fragmented).

In the US, the National Institute for Occupational Safety and Health (NIOSH) has published the yearly *Worker Health Chartbook* since 2000. It is a descriptive epidemiologic reference on occupational morbidity and mortality in the US. In the 2004 edition (NIOSH, 2004), similar trends were reported by the EU (EU, 2007a). The rates of fatal occupational injuries and

---

Box 6.4 Some facts and figures on (un)healthy buildings

- Approximately 20 per cent of the European population is allergic to mites and fungi, and the prevalence of asthma and allergies in domestic buildings is increasing (Institute of Medicine, 2000). A meta-analysis of the health effects of dampness suggests that building dampness and moulds are associated with increases of 30 to 50 per cent in a variety of asthma-related health outcomes (Fisk et al, 2007).
- Most countries suffer from 5 to 25 per cent winter mortality. In the UK, this involves an estimated 20,000 to 40,000 death (Clinch and Healy, 2000). There are clear indications that excess winter mortality is connected to poor thermal insulation and to fuel 'poverty'. The same accounts for an increase in respiratory and cardiovascular ailments. Similar effects of cold stress have been pointed out in a Harvard study (Levy et al, 2003).
- Sleep disturbance, linked to a multitude of indoor physical parameters, increases the risk of household accidents by at least 46 per cent. Some 350 million Europeans complain regularly about sleeping problems (Bonnefoy et al, 2004).
- In 1998, more than 10 million accidental injuries in and around the house occurred in the EU-15 countries. This resulted in more than 1 million hospital admissions and more than 42,000 deaths. The most common interior causes appear to be inadequate lighting, insufficient working space in kitchens and staircases (Bonnefoy et al, 2004).
- It is estimated that, in general, 25 per cent of families have at least one member suffering from a mental disorder, which is the leading cause of disability worldwide. Depression affects 19 per cent of adults and increases strongly with age. Antidepressant prescriptions have more than tripled during the ten years (Bonnefoy et al, 2004). A rise in obesity is leading to increases in diabetes and the risk of cardiovascular disease. Obesity reduces life expectancy (EU, 2007a). Both obesity and mental disorder appear to be linked to the conditions of homes and neighbourhood, as well as to the amount of time that people are now spending indoors (Bonnefoy et al, 2004).
- In 2000, approximately 350,000 people died in the EU prematurely due to outdoor air pollution caused by fine particulate matter ($PM_{2.5}$) alone. 11.5 per cent of children suffer from asthmatic symptoms in Europe (EU, 2007a).

non-fatal occupational injuries and illnesses have declined significantly, and Americans are living longer, healthier lives. The overall fatal occupational injury count for 2002 (5524) was 6.4 per cent lower than the count for 2001. The fatal occupational injury rate for 2002 was 4 per 100,000 employed workers. The trend in rates reflects a decline beginning in 1993. On the other hand, rates of anxiety, stress and neurotic disorders decreased between 1992 and 2001, indicating that the trend observed in Europe, from physical complaints towards mental illness, has not yet been observed in the US.

Box 6.5 describes a number of health-related institutions and organizations in the US.

The WHO is the directing and coordinating authority for health within the United Nations (UN) system. It is responsible for providing leadership on global health matters, shaping the health research agenda, setting norms and standards, articulating evidence-based policy options, providing technical support to countries, and monitoring and assessing health trends. The WHO's constitution came into force on 7 April 1948, defining health as 'A state of complete physical, mental, spiritual [added in 1999] and social well-being and not merely the absence of disease or infirmity.'

In the yearly updates of the Global Burden of Disease database (existing since 1996), the WHO reports on some 200 causes of death and illness (including injury) by age and sex, separately, for 14 regions of the world. Managed by the WHO, the largest comparative risk assessment (CRA) exercise ever attempted was initiated in 2000, in which two questions were asked (Smith, 2003):

Box 6.5 Health-related institutions and organizations in the US

In the US, the Environmental Protection Agency (EPA) has been working for a cleaner, healthier environment for the American people since 1970. The mission of the EPA is to protect human health and the environment. The EPA works to develop and enforce regulations that implement environmental laws enacted by the US Congress. The EPA is responsible for researching and setting national standards for a variety of environmental programmes, and delegates to states and tribes the responsibility for issuing permits and for monitoring and enforcing compliance. Where national standards are not met, the EPA can issue sanctions and take other steps to assist the states and tribes in reaching the desired levels of environmental quality.

In 1970, the US Congress passed the Occupational and Safety Health Act to ensure worker and workplace safety. The goal was to ensure that employers provide their workers with a place of employment free from recognized hazards to safety and health, such as exposure to toxic chemicals, excessive noise levels, mechanical dangers, heat or cold stress, or unsanitary conditions. In order to establish standards for workplace health and safety, the act also created the National Institute for Occupational Safety and Health (NIOSH) as the research institution of the Occupational Safety and Health Administration (OSHA). OSHA is a division of the US Department of Labor that oversees the administration of the act and enforces standards in all 50 states.

Since 1975, the Consumer Product Safety Commission is the office that deals with the safety of more than 15,000 types of products used in daily life. The commission has information on formaldehyde in mobile homes, fibreglass in insulation and other building materials, the safety of all terrain vehicles, and equipment used for children's safety.

The National Research Council (NRC) functions under the auspices of the National Academy of Sciences (NAS), the National Academy of Engineering (NAE) and the Institute of Medicine (IOM). The NAS, NAE, IOM and NRC are part of a private non-profit institution that provides science, technology and health policy advice under a congressional charter signed by President Abraham Lincoln that was originally granted to the NAS in 1863. Under this charter, the NRC was established in 1916, the NAE in 1964 and the IOM in 1970. The four organizations are collectively referred to as the National Academies.

The mission of the NRC is to improve government decision-making and public policy, to increase public education and understanding, and to promote the acquisition and dissemination of knowledge in matters involving science, engineering, technology and health. The institution takes this charge seriously and works to inform policies and actions that have the power to improve the lives of people in the US and around the world.

As in Europe, these organizations represent regulations and standards at the US level; for local regulations, local (city or county) or state environmental/health agencies are in charge.

1   How much ill health would not exist today if exposure to the risk factor was as low as feasible in the past (attributable risk)?

2   How much ill health in the future could be eliminated if the risk factor were brought under control today (avoidable risk)?

Results are published yearly in the WHO's annual reports.

Unfortunately, unhealthy buildings are not treated as a separate risk factor in the assessment. Therefore, Smith (2003) tried to estimate the burden of disease of unhealthy buildings by using risk factors that were assessed in the WHO CRA, such as indoor air pollution (2.9 per cent of total global burden); outdoor air pollution (0.6 per cent of total global burden); airborne carcinogens and particles (0.3 per cent of total global burden); and injuries, noise and ergonomics (1.3 per cent of total global burden). Without including risk factors such as climate change and physical inactivity, the estimated burden from unhealthy buildings was about 11 per cent of the global burden of ill health, which is quite high (tobacco, alcohol and drugs make 9 per cent; sexual/reproductive risks come to 7 per cent; and malnutrition, 15 per cent). However, most impacts of unhealthy buildings occur in the poorest countries (76 per cent) and most fall on young children (65 per cent). The current programme is therefore focused largely on the health of children.

6.1.4 Climate change

A very important driver, perhaps the most important, of how our indoor environments should perform in the future is climate change. Since the first measurements of carbon dioxide (CO_2) in 1958 by Revelle (Gore, 2006), scientists have warned us about climate change and possible consequences.

The problem is known as *radiative forcing*, which is defined as the change in average net radiation at the top of the troposphere (lower atmosphere). Positive radiative forcing warms up the surface of the Earth to keep the heat balance. Negative radiative forcing cools down the Earth's surface (Houghton, 2004). Controversy exists in the scientific literature on what actually caused radiative forcing – particularly the relative importance of anthropogenic- or human-induced sources versus natural influences, such as the variability of solar activity and radiation (Svensmark, 2007).

Natural climate change

Natural forcings arise due to solar activity, explosive volcanic eruptions and changes in cloud cover. Solar output has increased gradually in the industrial area, causing a few tenths of W/m^2 in addition to the cyclic changes in solar radiation following an 11-year cycle (IPCC, 2007). Observations of the direct solar radiation by satellites since 1978 show only a cyclic variability of radiative forcing of about $0.3W/m^2$ between solar maxima and minima, with no significant long-term trend. However, some scientists claim that the indirect effects of the solar magnetic field on the generation of cloud cover by cosmic rays also have an effect on radiative forcing at least as large as the human-induced advanced greenhouse effect of $1.6W/m^2$ since 1750 (Svensmark, 2007). They argue that the Earth's temperature increase is linked to the increase in cloud formation below 3km in altitude. According to such scientists, cloud formation is influenced by cosmic radiation consisting of electrically charged atomic particles (muons). The formation of cloud condensation nuclei is assisted by the ionization of air through these cosmic rays. Magnetic fields arising from coronal mass emissions of the sun shield the Earth partly from the incoming cosmic radiation. Coronal mass emissions are explosions in which a substantial amount of gas is launched into space with a mass of more than 10 billion kilograms and velocities of between 500km/s and 2500km/s. Depending upon the activity of the sun, the magnetic field shielding the incoming cosmic radiation is more or less effective, and therefore cloud formation and cloud coverage will change. More cloud coverage will cause a higher reflection of incoming solar radiation and, as a consequence, a lower surface temperature. In turn, less cloud coverage will cause a higher surface temperature.

It is been possible to observe cloud properties at different altitudes from the global dataset of the International Satellite Cloud Climate project (ISCCP-D2) (Rossow et al, 1996). Results show that the total global cloud fraction decreased from 1987 to 2001 by 4 per cent with respect to the total fraction of 63.3 per cent cloud coverage. With a current climatic estimate for the net forcing of the global cloud cover of $27.7W/m^2$ cooling in the atmosphere, this corresponds to a change in radiative forcing of $1.74W/m^2$ warming (Hartmann, 1993). This amount of radiative forcing is equal to the total net anthropogenic radiative forcing since 1750. However, for the period of 2001 to 2006, an increase in the mean annual surface temperature was observed.

From this, it is clear that the change in the cloud coverage fraction during the period of 1983 to 2006 has an important effect on climate. In addition to the possible influence of solar activity on cloud coverage, there are a number of other natural events occurring during this time period, such as the El Niños and volcanic eruptions, which may have caused cloud changes. Therefore, the cause of these cloud variations is not yet completely understood. Moreover, the predicted changes by human activities since 1750 are similar in magnitude to those shown here. It is clear that more data with records of cloud coverage over a much longer time are necessary to explain the difference between natural and human-induced climate change.

Finally, it has been shown (ICCP, 2007) that only a combination of the natural variability of climate and changes produced by human activities can explain observed climate changes completely (see Box 6.6).

Human-induced climate change

Many scientists claim that, in addition to natural causes, an important part of radiative forcing is due to changes in the atmospheric abundance of greenhouse gases and to changes in land use. According to findings, naturally occurring concentrations of water vapour, carbon dioxide and some minor gases present in the atmosphere have caused the so-called *greenhouse effect*. By absorbing thermal radiation leaving the Earth's surface, they act as a partial blanket (just as glass does in a greenhouse), ensuring that the Earth's surface has an average temperature of 15°C instead of –6°C (in the event that these gases are not present). In very simple terms, it comes down to the following: if the concentrations of these gases increase, the amount of absorbed thermal radiation will also rise, including the temperature of the Earth's surface as well. This is called the *advanced greenhouse effect*. In reality, the processes are much more complex due to convective heat transfer taking place as well as the so-called carbon cycles between the reservoirs in the oceans, soil and all living things.

The *greenhouse gases* of concern are (Houghton, 2004):

- carbon dioxide (CO_2) produced by men and animals when exhaling, but mainly produced by the burning of fossil fuels;
- methane (CH_4) or natural gas produced by burning fossil-fuel sources; per molecule, methane has an approximately eight times greater greenhouse effect than CO_2;
- nitrous oxide (N_2O) produced by biomass burning, fertilizer use and the chemical industry;
- chlorofluorocarbons (CFCs) used in refrigerators and banned since 1996 in developed countries and since 2006 in the developing countries; CFCs destroy ozone (O_3), causing ozone holes and, per molecule, they have a 5000 to 10,000 times

---

Box 6.6 The physical science basis for climate change

Radiative forcing (RF) is a concept used for quantitative comparisons of the strength of different human and natural agents in causing climate change. The combined anthropogenic RF is estimated to be +1.6W/m², indicating that, since 1750, it is extremely likely (more than 95 per cent confidence level) that humans have exerted a substantial warming influence on climate. The RF estimate is likely to be at least five times greater than that due to solar irradiance changes. For the period of 1950 to 2005, it is exceptionally unlikely that the combined natural RF (solar irradiance plus volcanic aerosol) has had a warming influence comparable to that of the combined anthropogenic RF. Increasing concentrations of long-lived greenhouse gases (CO_2, CH_4, N_2O, halocarbons and SF_6) have led to a combined RF of 2.6 ± 0.26W/m². The global concentration of CO_2 in 2005 was 379ppm (280ppm in 1750), leading to an RF of 1.66 ± 0.17 W/m². Past emissions of fossil fuels and cement production have likely contributed about three-quarters of the current RF, with the remainder caused by land-use changes.

Source: IPCC (2007)

greater greenhouse effect than CO_2 – substitutes (hydrochlorofluorocarbons and hydrofluorocarbons) contribute as well.

Regulations forbidding the use of CFC to prevent ozone layer depletion are beginning to show effect. The assessment panel of the Montreal Protocol on substances that deplete the ozone layer predicts that ozone layer depletion will ameliorate over the following decades (WMO/UNEP, 2006).

Gases with an indirect greenhouse effect are carbon monoxide (CO) and nitrogen oxides (NO and NO_2) emitted, for example, by motor vehicles. CO reacts and forms CO_2 and OH (hydroxyl radical), which affects the concentration of methane.

Aerosols in the atmosphere also play an important role: they absorb radiation from the sun and scatter it back to space. These small particles (between 0.0001mm and 0.01mm in diameter) arise from natural causes (blown off from land, forest fires, etc.) and human activities (burning of fossil fuels, biomass burning, etc.). Sulphate particles, in particular, caused by sulphur dioxide emissions (so-called acid rain pollution), are of concern, leading to degradation of forests and fish stocks. The negative radiative forcing caused by aerosols is, however, very small compared to the positive radiative forcing caused by greenhouse gases, of which the increase in CO_2 concentration is the main concern.

Changes in the concentration of the Earth's atmospheric gases over the last millennium are presented in Table 6.3.

After the first measurements of CO_2 in 1958, it took 30 years before the climate change issue was taken seriously on a global level. In 1988, the Intergovernmental Panel on Climate Change (IPCC), a scientific intergovernmental body, was set up by the

World Meteorological Organization (WMO) and by the United Nations Environment Programme (UNEP).

The IPCC published its first report in 1990. This report played a decisive role in establishing the United Nations Framework Convention on Climate Change (UNFCCC), which was opened for signature at the Rio de Janeiro Summit in 1992 and entered into force in 1994. It provides the overall policy framework for addressing the climate change issue. The IPCC *Second Assessment Report* of 1995 provided key input for the negotiations of the Kyoto Protocol in 1997; the *Third Assessment Report* of 2001, as well as special and methodology reports, provided further information relevant for the development of the UNFCCC and the Kyoto Protocol. The IPCC continues to be a major source of information for the negotiations under the UNFCCC.

Climate change and its consequences

In 2007, the IPCC presented its *Fourth Assessment Report* on climate change and its consequences (IPCC, 2007) and concluded:

> Warming of the climate system is unequivocal, as is now evident from observations of increases in global average air and ocean temperatures, widespread melting of snow and ice, and rising global mean sea level.

Observational evidence from all continents and most oceans shows that many natural systems are being affected by regional climate changes, particularly temperature increases. Human influences have:

*   *very likely* contributed to sea level rise during the latter half of the 20th century;
*   *likely* contributed to changes in wind patterns, affecting extra-tropical storm tracks and temperature patterns;
*   *likely* increased temperatures of extreme hot nights, cold nights and cold days;
*   *more likely than not* increased risk of heat waves, area affected by drought since the 1970s and frequency of heavy precipitation events.

Continued greenhouse gas (GHG) emissions at or above current rates would cause further warming and induce many changes in the global climate system during the 21st century that would *very likely* be larger than those observed during the 20th century.

Table 6.3 *Changes in the concentration of the Earth's atmospheric gases*

Gas	Period 1000–1750	Year 2000	Increase (%)	No action* 2050
CO_2	280ppm	368ppm	31 ± 4	±600ppm
CH_4	700ppb	1750ppb	151 ± 25	±3000ppb
NO_2	270ppb	316ppb	17 ± 5	±375ppb
O_3	Varies with region		35 ± 15	–

Note: * Estimated from graphs in Houghton (2004).
Source: adapted from Houghton, 2004

The IPPC projects for the next two decades a warming of about 0.2°C per decade. If the concentrations of all greenhouse gases and aerosols had been kept constant at year 2000 levels, the IPCC predicts a further warming of about 0.1°C per decade.

Altered frequencies and intensities of extreme weather, together with sea-level rise, are expected to have mostly adverse effects on natural and human systems. Examples for selected extremes and sectors are shown in Table 6.4. Plate 13 (centre pages) shows a street view shortly after a hailstorm in The Netherlands.

The National Research Council (NRC, 2001) concluded that climate change has the potential to influence the frequency and transmission of infectious disease, to alter heat- and cold-related mortality and morbidity, and to influence air and water quality. Depending upon the scenarios occurring from now on, the NRC identified some aspects of the indoor environment that will change or have to change in order to be able to cope with the impacts of climate change:

- *Direct temperature effects*: particular segments of the population such as those with heart problems, asthma, the elderly, the very young and the homeless can be especially vulnerable to extreme heat.
- *Extreme events*: extreme weather events can be destructive to human health and well-being. An increase in the frequency of extreme events may result in more event-related deaths, injuries, infectious diseases and stress-related disorders.
- *Climate-sensitive diseases*: climate change may increase the risk of some infectious diseases, particularly those diseases that appear in warm areas and are spread by mosquitoes and other insects. Although average global temperatures are expected to continue to rise, the potential for an increase in the spread of diseases will depend not only upon climatic but also upon non-climatic factors, primarily the effectiveness of the public health system (WHO, 2003a).
- *Air quality*: respiratory disorders may be exacerbated by warming-induced increases in the frequency of smog (ground-level ozone) events and particulate air pollution. Ground-level ozone can damage lung tissue and is especially harmful for those with asthma and other chronic lung diseases.

Table 6.4 *Examples of the possible impacts of climate change due to changes in extreme weather and climate events, based on projections to the mid to late 21st century*

Phenomenon	Examples of major projected impacts by sector	
	Human health	Industry, settlement and society
Over most land areas, warmer and fewer cold days and nights; warmer and more frequent hot days and nights	Reduced human mortality from decreased cold exposure	Reduced energy demand for heating; increased demand for cooling; declining air quality in cities; reduced disruption to transport due to snow and ice; effects on winter tourism
Warm spells/heat waves Frequency increased over most land areas	Increased risk of heat-related mortality, especially for the elderly, chronically sick, very young and socially isolated	Reduction in quality of life for people in warm areas without appropriate housing; impacts upon the elderly, very young and the poor
Heavy precipitation events Frequency increases over most areas	Increased risk of deaths, injuries and infectious respiratory and skin diseases	Disruption of settlements, commerce, transport and societies due to flooding; pressures on urban and rural infrastructures; loss of property
Area affected by drought increases	Increased risk of food and water shortage; increased risk of malnutrition; increased risk of waterborne and food-borne diseases	Water shortage for settlements, industry and societies; reduced hydropower generation potential; potential for population migration
Intense tropical cyclone activity increases	Increased risk of deaths, injuries, water and food-borne diseases; post-traumatic stress disorders	Disruption from flood and high winds; withdrawal of risk coverage in vulnerable areas by private insurers; potential for population migrations and loss of property
Increased incidence of extreme high sea level (includes tsunamis)	Increased risk of deaths and injuries by drowning in floods; migration-related health effects	Costs of coastal protection versus costs of land-use relocation; potential for movement of populations and infrastructure; see also tropical cyclones above

Source: IPCC (2007)

Sunlight and high temperatures, combined with other pollutants such as nitrogen oxides and volatile organic compounds, can cause ground-level ozone to increase. Climate change may increase the concentration of ground-level ozone; but the magnitude of the effect is uncertain. Climate change may indirectly affect the concentration of particulate matter pollution in the air by affecting natural or 'biogenic' sources of PM, such as wildfires and dust from dry soils.

Climate change and the indoor environment

The major effects of climate change that are directly relevant for the indoor environment are the average rise in outdoor temperature and the increase in change of weather conditions: more heat spells, shorter periods of precipitation, and sudden higher wind speeds and storms. For each of the indoor environmental parameters, some consequences in relation to health and comfort may be mentioned:

- *Thermal comfort*: the average rise in outdoor temperature will lead to a rise in demand for air-conditioning systems, on the one hand, and a decrease in energy demand for heating systems, on the other. The increased change of temperature and humidity conditions caused by increased precipitation (rainfalls), causing changes of humidity conditions indoors, will most likely also lead to an increase in the need for highly adaptable buildings (including air-conditioning systems). This means that control systems as well as the building materials used need to be able to anticipate changes very rapidly. The fact that winter temperatures will rise (in the Northern Hemisphere) will most likely decrease energy consumption during milder outdoor temperatures in winter. However, the situation in summer in combination with well-insulated and reasonably air-tight buildings will lead to uncomfortable thermal comfort indoors due to the 'warming up' (heat remains trapped in the construction). Therefore, use of air conditioning will most likely increase.
- *Air quality*: as a result of the increased storms and wind speed, air pollution comprising dust particles (from fine to heavy) are most likely to be transported more easily from one area to the other. For example, the orange dust coming from the Sahara (covering cars after a rainfall) could become a more frequent

sight in European countries. This increase in outdoor air pollution (fine particles) may lead to a more frequent need to keep buildings airtight (see also section 9.3.4 in Chapter 9), relying again more on air-conditioning systems that clean the air before it enters the building. Attention should be paid, then, to the cleaning and maintenance of air-conditioning systems since they have proven to be a major source of health and comfort problems indoors (Bluyssen et al, 2003a). Ozone is another pollutant of concern because elevated outdoor ozone concentrations can lead to an increase in secondary pollution indoors (see section 9.3.1 in Chapter 9). High temperatures and ultraviolet (UV) radiation stimulate the production of photochemical smog as well as ozone precursor biogenic VOCs (Wilby, 2007). The primary pollution of building products indoors can be influenced by an increase in indoor air temperature, but this effect (with increases of a few degrees) is most likely not very important. On the other hand, higher precipitation, both in summer and winter, could result in higher relative humidity, producing more conducive environments for the propagation of moulds and bacteria (see section 9.3.2 in Chapter 9).

- *Lighting quality*: as pointed out earlier, the day–night rhythm (biological clock) of a person is influenced by the daylight pattern that one is exposed to (see section 9.3.3 in Chapter 9). One of the consequences of climate change may be that people will stay inside even more than they already do. Additionally, in an attempt to shut the sun out, blinds and curtains will be used. As a result, exposure to daylight will diminish and alternatives will have to be introduced to mitigate this effect. The effect of storms and clouds forming may also influence the quality of daylight and indirectly affect the need for artificial forms of lighting that can rapidly adapt to changes.
- *Acoustical quality*: increased wind speeds and frequency of storms influence indoor acoustical quality through perceived noise and vibrations. Vibrations can be a nuisance and a reason for poor health (see section 9.3.5 in Chapter 9). Additionally, the increase in the use of air-conditioning systems may cause more people to complain about their noise.

The indoor environment can cause physical stress – for example, when it is too warm or too cold – and can limit a person in coping with this stress (e.g. not being able to control the temperature in an office and open the window to gain access to outdoor (fresh) air, or having to work without a view). In addition, psycho-social factors, such as a fear of storms or flooding and mental well-being, etc. can influence (mostly negatively) the perception of these physical and coping stressors (see section 5.2.3 in Chapter 5 and section 9.2.2 in Chapter 9). And since the amount of time spent indoors might well increase as a result of climate change, more stress and probably a rise in mental disorders are likely to occur (see Bonnefoy et al, 2004).

Although it seems clear that something is happening with our climate (or, has happened), the cause of the change is not so clear and even more so: what will happen in the next centuries is even more difficult to predict. As Al Gore (2006) states in his book *An Inconvenient Truth*: 'The truth about the climate crisis is an inconvenient one that means we are going to have to change the way we live our lives.'

This conclusion should be taken seriously, no matter what the causes are behind it. The consequences of climate change, apparent during the last decades (flooding, hurricanes, temperature changes, etc.), are really happening. Global temperature rise is a fact (see Figure 6.2). Our built environment has to take this into account. It is better to prevent illness than to cure the unhealthy.

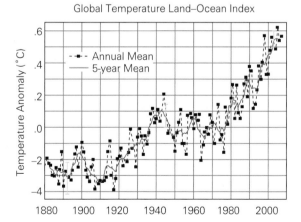

Global Temperature Land–Ocean Index

Source: http://data.giss.nasa.gov/gistemp/2007

Figure 6.2 *Annual surface temperature anomalies relative to 1951–1980 mean, based on surface air measurements at meteorological stations and ship and satellite measurements of sea surface temperatures*

6.2 Internal drivers

The real end users of a building are many and varied: occupants of dwellings, employees in an office building, employers, labour workers, personnel in a shop, etc. What they have in common is that they all like to be in a state of well-being that they can accept. This state of well-being can influence their productivity in the tasks that they are performing and their state of mind and body.

Besides end users, direct stakeholders of the indoor environment are the parties who initiate, create, build and maintain the indoor environments in which we all live, work and play. These parties all have their own stakes or needs for taking part in the life cycle of indoor environmental spaces. The parties involved are:

- the party who pays: the investor;
- the party who initiates: the project initiator or developer (often also the investor);
- the party who designs: the design team including an architect and several consultants (systems, construction, etc.);
- the party who builds: the contractor and sub-contractors;
- the party who owns/buys the building: the building owner (can be different from the end user);
- the party who produces building products: construction, furnishing and heating ventilation and air conditioning (HVAC) system components producers;
- the party who maintains: the facility manager;
- the party who regulates: the regulator provides regulations and rules to keep;
- the end user who has his basic needs and personal wishes.

The parties mentioned can have double functions – for example, the project developer can also be the investor and the builder, and even the facilitator. The party who owns the building can be the end user.

For the sake of understanding the terms used in this chapter, Box 6.7 provides some definitions.

6.2.1 Basic needs of end users

As Abraham Maslow realized, people are motivated by needs. We are born with basic needs, evolved over tens of thousands of years, such as our need for protection

Box 6.7 Some definitions of terms used in this chapter

End user: the party who occupies the built environment.

Key performance indicator (KPI): one of the general performance indicators required to evaluate the built environment. Examples are sustainability, health and safety. To determine the value of these KPIs, several values of performance indicators or performance parameters might be required.

Performance: competence or ability of a certain activity or functionality.

Performance criterion: a criterion with which one can evaluate the performance. For example, the performance criterion of a heating system is a certain capacity (production of kWh).

Performance indicator: used to estimate or indicate a certain performance, if the correct performance parameter is unknown or unavailable. For example, a widely used performance indicator for air quality is CO_2 concentration.

Performance parameter: the parameter with which the performance can be evaluated. For this parameter a criterion can be given. For example, for the performance of a surface with a certain reflection, a reflection factor is the parameter.

Stake: the interest of a stakeholder; the most important item or parameter to this stakeholder. For example, an investor has a financial interest. The value given to that stake is expressed in Euros.

Stakeholder: a party who initiates, creates, builds, occupies and/or maintains the built environment in which we all live, work and play.

Value: a way of expressing the (expected) performance of something. This can be a numerical value or a non-numerical value (good, bad).

against the outdoor environment, and the need for food, sleep, etc. With this knowledge, during the 1940s to 1950s, Maslow developed the hierarchy of needs model of five basic needs (Maslow, 1943) (see Figure 6.3). This model was later adjusted by other people, adding and altering a few steps in the hierarchy. The hierarchy of needs helps to explain how these needs motivate us all. It is important that the first basic need (physiological) is satisfied; only then can we continue with satisfying the following need. On the other hand, if one of the lower needs in the hierarchy is swept away, we need to go back and first mend this need. We are no longer concerned with the higher order need at that moment.

Source: adapted from www.wikipedia.org

Figure 6.3 *Maslow's hierarchy of needs*

The first four layers of the pyramid are what Maslow called 'deficiency needs' or 'D-needs': the individual does not feel anything if they are met, but feels anxious if they are not met. The deficiency needs are:

- *Biological and physiological needs*: air, food, drink, shelter, warmth, sex, sleep, etc. The physiological needs, those enabling homeostasis, controlling our thoughts and behaviours, are of utmost importance. If these needs are not fulfilled, people can feel sickness, pain and discomfort. This is, for example, what can happen when the basic indoor environmental physiological parameters are not in balance. Health and comfort problems can then result in a decrease in productivity and sickness.
- *Safety needs*: protection from elements, security, order, law, limits, stability, etc. When physiological needs are met, the need for safety and security will emerge. In the indoor environment, this means protection from rain, wind, noise from the outdoors and cold/heat, as well as security of personal property against crime (feeling of safety) and privacy (e.g. noise from neighbours will be a burden on privacy).
- *Belonging and love needs*: work group, family, affection, relationships, etc. After physiological

and safety needs are fulfilled, the third human need is social – the psychological aspect of Maslow's hierarchy. This involves emotionally based relationships, in general, such as friendship, sexual intimacy, and having a supportive and communicative family. Humans need to feel a sense of belonging and acceptance, whether it comes from a large social group or small social connections. They need to love and be loved (sexually and non-sexually) by others. In the absence of these elements, many people become susceptible to loneliness, social anxiety and depression. This need for belonging can often overcome physiological and security needs, depending upon the strength of the pressure. For example, an anorexic ignores the need to eat and the impending health effects.

- *Esteem needs*: self-esteem, achievement, mastery, independence, status, dominance, prestige, managerial responsibility, etc. People need to be respected, to have self-respect and to respect others. Therefore, people need to engage themselves and act, whether in a job or other activity, to gain recognition to feel accepted and self-valued. If this need is not in balance, low self-esteem, inferiority complexes, or snobbishness can result. There are two levels of esteem needs: the lower of the levels relates to elements such as fame, respect and glory; the higher level represents confidence, competence and achievement. People with low esteem need respect from others and may therefore seek fame or glory, which again are dependent upon others. However, confidence, competence and achievement only need one person and everyone else is inconsequential to one's own success. Acceptance of oneself is, however, required before receiving fame, respect and glory. Psychological imbalances such as depression can prevent one from obtaining self-esteem on both levels.

With respect to the fifth basic need, self-actualization, this was adapted in 1970 and transformed into three needs, adding cognitive and aesthetic needs.

- *Cognitive needs*: knowledge, meaning, etc. Humans have the need to increase their intelligence and therefore search for knowledge. Cognitive needs are the expression of the natural human need to learn, explore, discover and create in order to gain a better understanding of the world around them. Examples are change in the indoor environment and the opportunity to learn something new by creating a place to watch television, work, read, etc.
- *Aesthetic needs*: appreciation and search for beauty, balance, form, etc. People need beautiful images or something new and aesthetically pleasing in order to approach self-actualization. Humans need to refresh themselves in the presence of beauty. The selection of colours, shapes and furniture in the indoor environment are important to these needs, as well as the view out of a window and the surroundings of the indoor environment.
- *Self-actualization needs*: realizing personal potential, self-fulfilment, seeking personal growth and peak experiences. Self-transcendence is also sometimes referred to as spiritual needs. Self-actualization is the intrinsic growth of what is already in the organism or, more accurately, what the organism is. It is the instinctual need of humans to make the most of their abilities and to strive to be the best they can. Through so-called peak experiences, people find a route to achieve personal growth, integration and fulfilment. Peak experiences are unifying and ego-transcending, bringing a sense of purpose to the individual and a sense of integration. Although the deficiency needs may be seen as 'basic' and can be met and neutralized (i.e. they stop being motivators in one's life), self-actualization and transcendence are 'being' or 'growth needs' (also termed 'B-needs') – that is, they are enduring motivations or drivers of behaviour. During 1990, the transcendence needs were added to the hierarchy of needs.
- *Transcendence needs*: helping others to achieve self-actualization. Total customer experience is a good example of this (i.e. applying the demands and wishes of targeted consumers in such a way that they do not only receive and use separate products of the indoor environment, but perceive it as a total experience). Consumer targeting – determining who your consumer is – is the first step, as well as establishing the actual product or service you are going to address. This consumer insight is the basis for developing a product or service that addresses unmet goals. For example, companies who applied the consumer insight very well are (Iacobuci, 2001):

- Starbucks: targets people seeking an indulging experience rather than simply coffee consumption;
- Body Shop: targets people who embrace a particular set of values (natural origin, no animal testing and investment in developing economies) rather than ones who are merely striving to make themselves more attractive;
- Burggraaff (www.burggraaffbouw.nl): targets people who have their own vision on living rather then people who just want a building to live in.

It is thus very important to know the needs of occupants of certain indoor environments in order to be able to set the performance criteria of such an environment. The indoor environment no longer only provides us with shelter; it might also need to provide an environment in which we can achieve self-actualization. Additional needs that have recently been defined include the ten emerging needs of consumers (www.6minutes.net).

6.2.2 Stakes of direct stakeholders

The stakes of direct stakeholders as discussed here are largely based on a small investigation performed in The Netherlands (interviews of several stakeholders: Bluyssen et al, 2001) and may show some discrepancy with the opinions of stakeholders in other countries or other stakeholders in The Netherlands. It is based on the traditional process in which the project developer initiates a new project. From the acquisition of a construction location until completion, the regulator, the contractor, the design team (normally only the architect) and the owner are involved. After the first phases, the investor is also involved, normally approached by the developer.

The most important criterion for all parties is a positive or healthy financial result. In general, only measurable criteria are used for a financial evaluation. Other types are normally not used, with the exception of the regulator who also evaluates the energy burden. All other criteria are evaluated on gut feeling.

The investor

Investors are interested first and foremost in the profits made by their investment (in the short or long term).

The project developer, banks, insurance companies, pension funds and owners can all be investors.

The success of a building project in meeting its targets and fulfilling its performance requirements is a prerequisite for ensuring the sales, rent and satisfactory operation of the facility. Meeting user requirements can also promote user satisfaction and positively affect workers' productivity. The proper performance of a facility thus becomes an asset to the entrepreneurs, owners and renters, as well as to the investors, whose risk for reduced profits due to unpaid debts diminishes. However, despite their role, investors are not familiar with the building's professional tools and frameworks, and are usually silent stakeholders who may be affected by the entire process but who provide little input.

Besides the role of investor, insurance companies provide the financial backup to what may be erroneous decisions taken by the design team, as well as to possible poor workmanship by the contractors. Building owners may insure their property against natural disasters such as earthquakes, storms and floods, as well as against fire. Insurance companies base the premium rates on the existing local regulatory framework, design standards, quality of workmanship, and location, type and age of the building.

The investor evaluates whether he should invest or not by comparing the return on investment with the mean return on investment of the type of projects (it should be higher) or comparing the return on investment with other types of investment such as investment in stocks. Additionally, the investor evaluates the quality of the project on the basis of the construction (technical location, division, etc.) and the planning of the project. For the latter, a sort of performance description or project progress report is used, in which time, quality and money are followed over time.

Initiator

The project initiator is involved with all parties. In some cases, at the initiation of a project, a team is formed, including an architect, regulator, city planner, etc. But in most cases, the first contact is with the regulator (to obtain a location), then the architect and, again, the regulator, followed by the contractor, the end user and, finally, the investor.

The initiator is the main stakeholder of a project. His interests are expressed through a variety of targets that motivate the process and affect all of the project stages. The performance of the building in its use phase is not always an essential part of these targets and occurs generally when the initiator does not intend to remain the building's owner or its main user. On the other hand, the initiator will always prefer a reliable building process that ensures value/money without risking excessive delays in the delivery of the finished building and/or excessive litigations upon its occupation.

A distinction can be made between a public and a private initiator. When a governmental agency or any other public entity initiates a building project, it is mostly for its own people to use. A similar situation exists when a private initiator builds a facility for its own use. In that case, adequate performance of the building in the use phase is part of the main targets.

When a private entrepreneur initiates a building project that he does not intend to use, the specific function of the building is not necessarily his main target. Long-term financial investment or short-term quick profits may be dominant factors, each leading to a different approach towards the building's performance in use. The shorter the period that the entrepreneur would remain attached to the facility, the less is his natural devotion to ensuring its adequate long-term performance. Consequently, unless improved performance can promote sales, the entrepreneur will in this case prefer to provide the minimal performance levels stipulated by the regulatory framework and build the 'best-selling' building. When the private entrepreneur remains the owner, he is concerned with the long-term performance of the facility, depending upon if he uses it or rents it out. These different scenarios may affect his preferences and lead to setting elevated performance levels for some aspects, mainly for the durability of the building's infrastructure and façades. Independent of the long-term relations between the entrepreneur and the built facility, the project's scope and main targets need to be defined and transferred to the design team together with the design brief.

Besides the financial result (construction costs against turnover by sale), the initiator's criteria for evaluating whether the project is of interest, are:

- aura – location, grand entrée, and the aesthetics of building and surroundings (will the built environment still be attractive in 20 years?);

- quality – mostly determined by the user afterwards through user complaints or user satisfaction, and by testing against regulations.

Both are influenced by the possibilities of regulation (planning of municipalities; minimum quality requirements). Location is an important factor: it determines the price for the ground and also for a major part of the rent (which determines attractiveness to the investor and/or the end user). Sometimes, the long-term relation (based on trust) is seen as an important factor by the developer and the contractors. If a long-term relation is jeopardized, a possible loss is taken for granted. Other developers may find this relation the least important of all (they have no 'regular client' concept).

At the time of the interviews, the initiator was, in general, sceptical with respect to (alternative and sustainable) systems and materials for a better environment: 'Everyone is interested until it costs money.' According to the initiator, more knowledge is required in order to give guarantees and the turnover for the involved parties has to be clarified. The impression is that it always leads to a higher investment and the aftercare is complicated (for the contractor). Furthermore, the policy of the regulator is unclear on this point.

Other performance criteria are:

- accessibility;
- parking: enough parking spaces against a reasonable price;
- view;
- identity;
- added value of total project (e.g. if an office building is part of a larger complex, which results in a loss);
- risk: profit margin is larger if the risk is higher (in case a project is sold before it is built, the investor takes the risk and wants to pay less);
- quality of the systems;
- time;
- personal aspects (such as travelling times and social security);
- architecture and furnishings;
- service and guarantees;
- usability in the long run;
- total life-cycle cost.

For the initiator, it is important to deliver what has been agreed upon with the parties involved even if this is in conflict with the stakes of other parties. Regulation is not always consistent and applicable, specifically when it concerns innovative technologies. This makes communication with the regulator difficult and it can take forever before the project has been approved.

The regulator

The regulator issues laws, regulations and/or guidelines, to which a building (and an indoor environment) should comply with. In general, the regulator is also responsible for inspection of compliance with these rules. The objective of the regulator is to create safe and healthy buildings that are sustainable and make economic growth from the point of view of environment and society possible.

The regulator can also have a major role as an inspector and as a supplier of land, and therefore largely has contact with the initiator (project developer). Depending upon the municipality, the local regulator interferes with the design (contact with architect and city planner) and inspects during the actual construction works (and therefore also has contact with the contractor).

Two levels of regulators can be distinguished – the national and local authorities:

1   *National authorities* are concerned first and foremost with ensuring the basic needs (health, safety, security, hygiene, comfort, habitability and durability) of the direct and indirect end users and small owners who do not participate in the design and construction stages of the building facility, but are the main group affected by its performance. Their main concern is the duty of care (i.e. addressing true needs, which market forces may neglect to take care of properly or to an adequate extent). For some industrial occupancies, where building performance may affect the products manufactured in the building that may subsequently have an impact upon the health of people using them (such as public kitchens, food production industry, pharmaceutical industries, etc.), national authorities are also concerned with special minimal cleanliness and hygiene needs. In addition, national authorities are concerned with the long-term protection of the environment as a result of the building's direct and indirect impacts during its entire life cycle, from cradle to grave

(including effects stemming from depletion of resources, emissions, energy consumption, etc.).

Besides protecting the needy, national authorities are interested in maintaining a vital and economically stable building market, in promoting export, and in preventing raised building costs due to unjustified barriers on imports, excessive mandatory demands or complex regulatory procedures. In addition, they can be called upon when natural or man-made disasters occur. They bear the financial burden for rescue and immediate help, as well as for compensation when insurance does not cover the event.

Consequently, the national authorities are usually involved in the stages of setting concepts for and writing/adoption of regulations, codes, standards and any other formal documents that dictate the overall mandatory procedures and the levels of overall mandatory requirements.

2   *Local authorities* are usually concerned with overall aspects of the built environment, with the direct effects of the building on the public infrastructure and service systems (water and gas supply, sewage, transportation and parking, etc.), and on other buildings and public areas in its vicinity, and with the effect of the built environment on the general public. In addition, concepts embedded in the zoning ordinance and urban planning documents issued by the municipality may affect the performance of individual buildings (e.g. the orientation and size of land lots, as well as aesthetic requirements for building façades may prevent the employment of solar systems; the proximity of building façades to traffic-carrying roads affects acoustic criteria for the building envelope; the distance between buildings affects the fire resistance required for the exterior walls and the maximal dimensions of windows).

Local authorities evaluate a project through:

*   national strategies (e.g. for health and the environment);
*   the municipality's mission, if it is available (e.g. knowledge intense, sustainable, intensive space use, energy use);
*   quality requirements for a zoning plan;
*   financial resources;
*   experience with a project developer/initiator;

- delivery made on time;
- regulations and laws;
- usability (checklist with aspects such as accessibility, division, image, air quality);
- benefits for the area (employment, tourists and quietness).

The building owner

Building owners are concerned with the long-term everyday performance of the building when they are also its main users. When owners rent out their property to others, they are usually concerned with those performance aspects that affect renting rates, as well as with durability and maintenance of all those parts for which they remain responsible. However, when potential owners are not the developers who initiated and constructed the facility, they cannot be involved in the design process and have no ability to affect the building's performance level. When looking for a building, a set of performance requirements (together with objective but simple assessment tools) may help to make the proper choice.

In a given project, when the entrepreneur intends to remain the building owner as well as its main user, he may be interested in ensuring improved performance levels regarding safety, security, comfort and serviceability conditions. His motives for improving performance may stem from various targets, including increased prestige and image of the facility, increased employee motivation, increased efficiency and productivity, preparing for future upgrading of requirements, prevention of accelerated deterioration, and increased flexibility of space utilization, etc. In each of these cases, he may have different preferences for the various parts of the facility, with different priorities for the various performance attributes. Moreover, according to his main target, the entrepreneur's personal priorities would not necessarily coincide with those of the actual end users. Improving performance levels above the minimal ones stipulated by the regulatory framework is thus a per-project task.

The facility manager

Facility management (including maintenance and, in some cases, renovation or refurbishment) of buildings is performed by a facility manager. This manager can be hired by the owner or renter. In general, the target of the facility manager is an optimal operating building at lowest possible cost.

During the service life of the facility, the owner manages, maintains and operates it with the assistance of a facility manager. The latter is the most direct person responsible for the building's actual performance in use. However, facility managers are hired for their task at a very late stage along the building process and usually have no influence on its design. At later stages of the building life cycle, and mainly when repair, refurbishment and internal changes are considered, the facility manager most likely assesses the existing performance levels, determining the needs for actions and establishing the new performance criteria for their outcomes.

The facility manager, in general, uses exploitation costs of energy and work inspection audits as performance evaluation tools.

The builder

The builder or contractor contributes to construction, maintenance and renovation normally assigned by the initiator and/or owner of the building. They strive to a maximum profit (and, therefore, as low as possible costs) and to a minimal risk during construction. The contractor has contact with the initiator and with its subcontractors and suppliers.

The contractor evaluates a project on:

- return on investment;
- acquisition – aura;
- flexibility;
- location: spacious, good;
- complaint aspect (in The Netherlands a contractor is responsible for ten years for the state of construction): material choices and guarantees play an important role; some contractors estimate costs based on complaint registration per project;
- reciprocity: future permanent client/contact.

Taking too much time to build is the main concern of builders: time is money.

The designer

The role of designers is usually fulfilled by a design team, which is composed of numerous professionals, including architects and engineers. In the traditional framework, the architects are considered as the building's designers, while the rest of the team is regarded as 'consultants'. Depending upon the process, the architect is usually assigned by the initiator (the person who handles the assignment and is, in general, not the end user of the building). Although there are good exceptions (see section 8.1.2 in Chapter 8), many architects just apply the design brief as provided by the initiator and focus mainly on aesthetic quality – with functionality coming second.

In interviews, the architect pointed out that it is difficult to discuss the quality of a building and the end result when the end user is not present. An architect is often a designer, whose job it is to conceive of and construct buildings. In a more global way, the architect works on and creates:

- surfaces (façades, grounds and zones);
- volumes (spaces of connection);
- atmospheres (light games, echo, sound enfeeblement, colour games, textures).

In general, the architect focuses on the following artistic and functional values:

- aesthetic matters;
- building tradition and culture;
- space arrangements;
- environment and sustainability matters;
- innovations.

The 'consultants' generally consist of:

- Structural engineers: engineers and technicians who lead all the theoretical calculations necessary for the stability of the constructed building, but also during the time of its erection. Structural engineers necessarily have to respect regulations in force.
- Building services engineers: these engineers design the building services, such as heating, ventilation and air-conditioning systems, security systems, fire safety, etc.

The product producer

Product producers draw upon different sectors, depending upon the type of product or material that is being delivered:

- structural materials;
- complementary materials for structures;
- installations;
- fittings and equipment;
- consumption articles (e.g. paint, glue, plaster, etc.).

The product and material industry is responsible for a considerable part of the development of their products. This industry dominates the international standardization work concerning these products and the processes of manufacturing. Practically no other group of stakeholders is so involved. Occasionally contractors are engaged in standardization and product development.

Product development does not only mean adjustments and research concerning specific material, but also the development of new systems where the products can be used either in a new way or can meet new requirements. These requirements and qualities are often set by the material industry stakeholders themselves. In doing so, they strongly influence the requirements asked for by other stakeholders. This means that the requirements and standards of a separate project can seldom be seen as separate from the general supply of developed materials and systems in the material market. As a result, there is a reciprocal relationship between supply and demand in these matters.

It is certainly the case that development efforts from the material industry are a forceful driver for the design of new projects. A clear example is the production of material for glass architecture: better heat insulation, sun protection, systems for glass assembly, etc. Façade systems in concrete or plaster have been developed. Another example is the furnishing of modern kitchens; innumerable systems and brands exist on the market. Other fields deal with HVAC installation systems, such as entire duct systems for ventilation with various techniques for air treatment, or electrical power systems and equipments integrated, for instance, within suspended ceilings.

It is obvious that the material industry puts more effort into research and development than any other stakeholder. Construction product producers of building materials, products, components and entire building systems produce the same series of products by means of the established process and materials, and by testing product samples regularly through means of simple quality-control tests. The European

Construction Product Directive (CPD) utilizes the *Conformité Européenne* (CE) marking as a means of communicating the 'fitness for use' information implied by the standard procedures (see section 6.1.4).

Additional roles

Some additional roles exist that may include one or more of the above roles or that behave differently:

- *Developer*: a project developer is, in general, the initiator of the project, the investor and sometimes also the designer (in this case, the idea is developed first and a location is searched for afterwards).
- *Construction client*: the construction client is not just the person who pays for the construction, but is the bridge between the 'stakeholders' (all of the people who have an interest in the final output from the project, such as users, owners, financiers,

'the public', etc.) and the people who will design and construct it (the architects, engineers, contractors, suppliers, etc.). The construction client is responsible to all stakeholders for the success of the project. The construction client role continues throughout the whole project life cycle. It includes:

- helping all the various 'stakeholder' interests to express their requirements;
- communicating these to designers and other members of the supply chain;
- setting up procurement and contractual arrangements that best suit the project;
- maintaining communications throughout the project;
- taking delivery of the final project output;
- overseeing initial use;
- arranging for the performance of the final output to be monitored in order to inform future projects.

10^-18	10^-16	10^-14	10^-12	10^-10	10^-8	10^-6	10^-4	10^-2	1	102	104	metres

Cosmic   gamma   röntgen   UV   infrared microwaves radio

Visible light

nanometers

400   450   500   550   600   650   700   750

Source: adapted from Visser (1992)

Plate 1 *Spectrum of electromagnetic radiation*

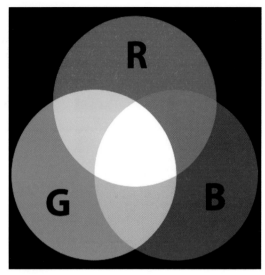

Source: www.wikipedia.org

Plate 2 *The superimposition of two of the three primary colour lights (red, green and blue) produces the secondary colours yellow, blue-green (or cyan) and magenta; the addition of the third primary colour produces white*

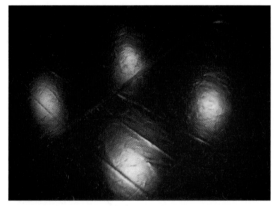

Source: Bluyssen

Plate 3 *Reflections of ceiling lights on a shiny smooth floor: This situation can cause enormous eyestrain*

Source: Bluyssen

Plate 4 *Integration of daylight and artificial light: In this situation the solar blinding placed on the inside of the glazing is not efficient at remedying overheating caused by solar radiation*

Source: Bluyssen

Plate 5 *Mould growth in shower cabins almost always occurs on the water-resistant sealant*

Source: Bluyssen

Plate 6 *Protecting ears from noise*

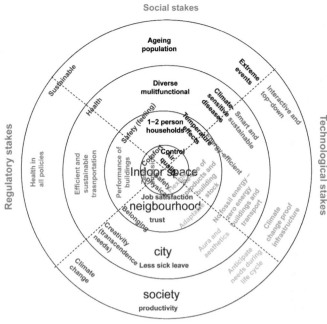

Source: Bluyssen (2008)

Plate 7 *An example of stakes at different levels*

Source: painting by eight-year-old Anthony Meertins

Plate 8 *Humans in their indoor environments should feel as much at home as a fish in water*

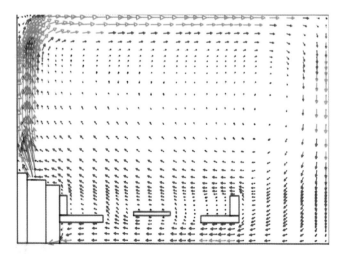

Source: Bluyssen and Lemaire (1992)

Plate 9 *Air movement with a computational fluids dynamic model program*

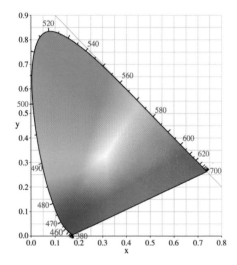

The outer curved boundary is the spectral (or monochromatic) locus, with wavelengths shown in nanometres. Since the human eye has three types of colour sensors that respond to different ranges of wavelengths, a full plot of all visible colours is a three-dimensional figure. The Y parameter is a measure of the brightness or luminance of a colour.
Source: www.wikipedia.org

Plate 10 *The CIE 1931 colour space chromaticity diagram*

Plate 11 *View from office window: A visible skyline, greenery and objects located further away*

Plate 12 *Trained panel in the European Audit project evaluating outdoor air quality*

Plate 13 *Street view shortly after a hailstorm with 20mm hailstones – the leaves were ripped off the trees and mixed with hail on the street*

Plate 14 *Involving the end user in the life-cycle of a 'building'*

Plate 15 *Challenges for the future: Still component-related, but from a holistic point of view*

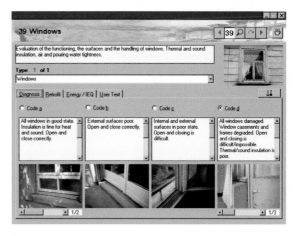

Plate 16 *Example of a diagnosis page in the TOBUS tool for element windows*

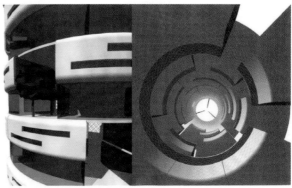

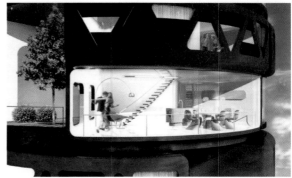

Plate 17 *The OMNIUM concept, focused on energy and quality of life*

Plate 18 *An example of a light-emitting diode (LED)*

Plate 19 *Solar collectors on the roof of an apartment building*

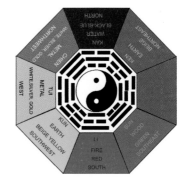

Plate 20 *A* pa kua *with various attributes of different systems used*

Part III

Management of the Indoor Environment

7

An Interactive and Sustainable Approach

An introduction to Part III is presented. In addition to the more traditional bottom–up approach, a new approach towards managing health and comfort in the indoor environment is introduced (see Chapter 8), with a focus on individual interactions (see Chapter 9) during the whole building life cycle. There appears to be a discrepancy between current standards and end users' needs. Combined with new 'drivers', new insights and changing end-user requirements, the need for a different approach towards managing the indoor environment is justified.

In Chapter 8, the top–down approach is presented as analogous to the system engineering methodology used in other disciplines. This top–down approach only works well if the interactions taking place at several levels and places are well understood. Therefore, in Chapter 9, the interactions occurring in, with and between the indoor environment and human beings are described. It becomes clear that no single parameter of the indoor environment can be evaluated on its own. Different environmental parameters interact and influence the perceptions of people.

7.1 Introduction

Taking a holistic approach allows the quality and integrity of a dwelling to be displayed through each component, and the significance of each component to be clearly understood. In considering the wider issues, greater flexibility is achieved, which improves the ability for customization, improving the suitability of a design to an increased range of situations. (Engström et al, 2007)

As presented in Chapter 6, the drivers of the indoor environment, today and in the near future, are not different from the drivers of the overall economy and society: climate change and changes in demography, leading to different and varying needs, and requirements for outdoor and indoor environments with respect to health, comfort, safety and, more than ever, energy use.

The scientific approach, with regard to health and comfort of people in the indoor environment, has merely focused on its single components (see section 5.1 in Chapter 5) and, to some extent, on some interrelations between these components (see section 5.2). The scientific community, as well as the construction industry and the regulators, are becoming more and more aware that this approach is not satisfactory. Some attempts have been made to involve the end users' wishes and demands in a holistic way.

Climate change, as described in Chapter 6, will cause the outdoor environment to have a greater influence on the indoor environment. Indoor environments need to be able to anticipate these changes, as well as the changing wishes and demands of end users. A holistic design approach is required in which all stakeholders (not only the end user and the architect), during the whole building life cycle, are involved in order to be able to design, build, maintain and renovate or demolish the indoor environment in a way that is satisfying to all stakeholders.

In 2001, the Ecospace® concept was introduced as an answer to this integrated approach. According to the concept, in order to create healthy, comfortable, safe, smart and sustainable spaces, so-called Ecospaces®, several steps need to be taken (see Figure 7.2). The first

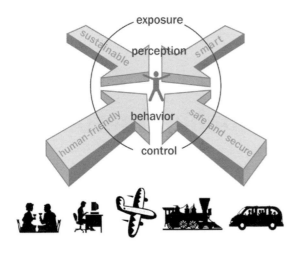

Source: Bluyssen and Adan (2006)

Figure 7.1 *Stakeholder values in the built environment*

and last step require an integrated approach focused mainly on people and communication processes, while the second and third steps require individual innovative breakthroughs with respect to products, materials or production processes, depending upon techniques and materials available.

Essentially, it comes down to the following two questions:

1   How to define the starting point (the end users' requirements and other stakeholder requirements in relation to health and comfort); and

2   How to translate these requirements to requirements of the different phases (initiation, design, construction, maintenance and breakdown), the different stakeholders, and the different environmental parameters and parts (materials, products and systems) of the indoor environment.

Performance and human perception: To determine and test measurable performance indicators and criteria for healthy, comfortable and safe spaces. *The human requirements with respect to health, comfort and safety need to be clearly identified. A comprehensive and coherent knowledge basis for human health, comfort and safety in enclosed spaces under living, working and transportation conditions is therefore required.*

Interaction enclosure space (passive): To create 'added-value' materials and products contributing to a high basic level of health, comfort and safety in enclosed spaces.
Based on human performance criteria, the system and material requirements (enclosure of space) can be identified and innovative techniques and systems can be applied to comply with human requirements. An enhanced high-performance enclosure that guarantees a high basic level of health, comfort and safety in enclosed spaces can then be created.

Interaction human space (active): To create optimal opportunities for human beings to control environmental performance of their (local) space individually. *The demand from the occupant's point of view should be regulated through the supply side (possible enclosure-environmental configuration) with the use of sensors, interfaces and actuators. An adaptive space, allowing individual control of the environmental conditions in the personal space, should thus be created.*

A holistic approach of Ecospaces®: To realize healthy, comfortable and safe spaces integrating existing and new products and services for materials, systems and control (the other clusters). *And last but not least, all of the above should be integrated in a holistic design (concept) of the 'space' considered. Healthy, comfortable and safe spaces can then be realized and maintained in a smart and sustainable way.*

Source: Bluyssen and Adan (2006)

Figure 7.2 *Ecospace® concept*

7.2 Some facts

There is a discrepancy between *current standards and end users' needs* (Bluyssen and Adan, 2006): indoor environmental quality as experienced by occupants is often not acceptable and may even be unhealthy, even if standards and guidelines for individual environmental parameters are met. Current standards and guidelines have been and are still being developed with the traditional 'bottom–up' approach. Focusing on defining threshold values for indoor environmental parameters, different subsequent steps are taken:

- Step 1: identify sources and other influencing factors.
- Step 2: define dose–effect relationships.
- Step 3: establish threshold values for recognized dangerous substances.
- Step 4: assimilate or integrate all factors into end-user satisfaction.

Except for health-threatening substances, the complexity and number of indoor environmental parameters, as well as a lack of knowledge, make a performance assessment using only threshold levels for single parameters difficult and even meaningless.

Environmental *stimuli*, the input for our bodily sensations, result in behavioural or evaluative reactions (Taylor, 2006). Via the three major regulation and control systems of the human body (the nervous system, immune system and endocrine system), both mental (e.g. memories, anxiety, etc.) and physical effects (escape, fight, protect, symptoms, etc.) are created. These stimuli can cause unconscious changes in our psychological state, and can at the same time be harmful to our physical state of well-being (e.g. invisible light, gases, chemical compounds, radiation, etc.).

In terms of food, we are taught how to make our preferences clear; but for a house or for the function of living, we are often not articulate about our needs. Most people cannot indicate their own physical and mental needs. In fact, they often tell us something completely different than what they really need. The way in which information is processed – consciously (cognitive) and unconsciously (emotional) – is a probable cause. Understanding this processing at physiological and psychological levels is important.

Evaluating (perception) and responding (behaviour) to our environment are two different processes (Vroon, 1990).

Over the years several approaches have been presented to explain how our mind works. In these approaches *consciousness* is applied and/or defined differently. The following generalizations regarding these approaches, which are, in fact, compatible, can be made: from '*inside to outside*' (e.g. in TRI, 2007) and from '*outside to inside*' (Lehar, 2003), the main difference being that consciousness is considered to encompass contents and data (consciousness of) versus consciousness that is treated as part of the inner self.

The attributes or factors influencing behaviour are a combination of emotional and cognitive factors, which differ per situation (*context*), per individual, and which can have different scores that change over time. Attributes can, for example, be (Lupton, 1999; Loewenstein et al, 2001):

- social-cultural – social control, personal hygiene, individualism, norms and values, etc.;
- economical – efficiency, net present value, return on investment, etc.;
- technological – intelligent, bearing capacity, sustainable, etc.;
- personal – such as sex, gender, experience, anticipatory emotions, etc.;
- metaphysical or indoor related – water, wind, fire, material characteristics, etc.;
- dynamic (flexibility) or static (remain as they have been selected/chosen/fixed).

Current performance indicators or risk measures for health and comfort, attempting to normalize behaviour by capturing a number for these attributes, in general miss the individual 'emotions' part and the time parameter (dynamic versus static). This can at least partly explain the deviations encountered in practice between what the 'norm' says the end user wants and what the end user is 'wishing' for. One universal measure for health and comfort seems to be unrealistic.

The relationship between indoor environmental factors and complex human behaviour is thus not simple. Nevertheless, this indoor environment must meet the diverse needs of occupants whose interests frequently conflict.

7.3 The interactive top–down approach

Managing the indoor environment is an issue for many stakeholders at different scales. It is a dynamic issue that has to take into account changes in time at these scales and changing stakeholders. Therefore, besides defining end-user requirements at the start of a project, the *communication between the stakeholders* involved is just as important in order to translate the end users' requirements in an appropriate way. During the traditional process, the most dominant stakeholders determine the result, which may result in dissatisfied end users. Because they often use the so-called over-the-bench methodology, a real team is not formed. Parties do not understand each others' stakes or products and end users' wishes and demands are only incorporated on an individual basis. Next to the communication process, understanding the needs and requirements of the end users, before thinking about the solutions, is crucial.

Both for the establishment of end users' wishes and demands (requirements and needs), and the communication process required to facilitate the design, construction, maintenance and occupation of an indoor environment, an *interactive top–down approach* is required. This 'top–down' approach may act in a complementary fashion to the traditional bottom–up approach used to determine end users' needs. A number of points must be taken into account if this top–down approach is to function properly:

- understanding the end users' wishes and needs, both now and in the future;
- understanding the context (social, economic, political-legal and technological), whether at global or local levels, and associated attributes (factors of influence on health and comfort and on boundary conditions);
- understanding the stakeholders responsible and involved in creating an indoor environment, and the required communication processes;
- understanding the full spectrum of human–indoor environment–building–outdoor environment interactions.

After evaluating some of the available innovative design approaches – such as the performance-based building (CIB, 1982), the open-building approach (Habraken.com) and the value-domain model (Rutten and Trum, 1998) – the system engineering approach appeared to be the most promising (Blanchard, 2004) as the underlying model for the *top–down approach*. With the engineering approach, it is possible to define and translate the end users' requirements in the appropriate way. This approach suggests a form of cooperation between demand and supply, including all of the stakeholders and possibly also the involvement of other stakeholders. In this approach, a system consists of interrelated components, which are studied, along with their interrelationships, and then put back together. A system has inputs (identification of consumer requirement(s) – i.e. need), outputs (a system that will respond to a consumer need in an effective and efficient manner), imposed external constraints (technological, economic, social, legal and environmental), and required mechanisms to realize the desired results (human, equipment/software, facilities/data, materials, maintenance support). Within the system there are products and processes. The system's life cycle, or the indoor environment to be designed, built and maintained, includes the identification of need, design and development; production and/or construction; operational use and maintenance support; retirement and material disposal.

The top–down approach comprises the following steps:

- *step 1: demands and wishes* (system requirements);
- *step 2: from demands and wishes to technical requirements* (conceptual design);
- *step 3: from technical requirements to experimenting* (preliminary system design);
- *step 4: prototyping* (detail system design and development);
- *step 5: demonstration and marketing* (production and/or construction phase);
- *step 6: occupation and change* (operational use and system support phase);
- *step 7: breakdown and recycling* (system retirement and material recycling/disposal).

Throughout the system design and development, there are many different alternatives (or trade-offs) requiring some form of evaluation. It is essential that good communications between the stakeholders are established from the beginning since they start with setting the system requirements. The 'team' required varies from phase to phase because required expertise changes as system development progresses. After setting the system requirements, the designs for the different disciplines are made and system analysis can be performed. All choices are made based on trade-offs of options with respect to materials, dimensions, installations, structure, shape, etc., but always referring to the system criteria set. The design is reviewed, tested and evaluated and the design(s) are revised, changed and updated for another round until the results are satisfactory and the next step in the process can be taken. Most importantly, it should be emphasized that all through the phases of the process, the 'team' is doing it and not just one individual.

Several techniques are available to determine *end users' wishes and demands*: modelling (e.g. Berglund and Cain, 1989; Farshchi and Fisher, 2000; Roulet et al, 2006b); observation of behaviour (e.g. Sommer, 1969; Perner, 2007); questionnaires or surveys (e.g. Caccavelli et al, 2000; Grimwood et al, 2002; Schultz and Schultz, 2006); evaluation of prototypes (e.g. von Hippel, 1986); and end users involved in the design team (e.g. Adan and Bluyssen, 2004). It is difficult to pinpoint one single method as the best. Depending upon the end goal, one chooses methods to suit the problem. But no matter which method or methods are chosen, it is important to realize that the way in which we evaluate our environment (perception) and the way in which we respond to our environment (behaviour) are two different processes – we process information consciously (cognitively) and unconsciously (with our emotions). Understanding this process at physiological and psychological levels is thus important for modelling or predicting human behaviour under different environmental conditions.

In a first attempt to apply the system engineering approach for an integrated design of social housing, a team was collected for the OMNIUM project (Bluyssen and Adan, 2006). Together with the European Space Agency (ESA), an innovative housing corporation in The Netherlands, an architect and several experts on materials, construction, services, financial matters and sustainability from different companies, the goal was to design and create a social housing template for the year 2030. After the first two steps of the approach, it was concluded that there is still a long way to go. It is very difficult for some team members to keep their minds open to more than one option. Some team members had a difficult time in letting go of the traditional roles

they are used to playing. And fulfilment of some system requirements involves combined design efforts, which might lead to conflicting requirements. Separating the responsibility for the technical design from that for the functional and architectural design is not the solution, but an easy pitfall.

In a current running European project InPro (www.inpro-project.eu), in which the final objective is to develop an open information environment (OIE) supporting the early design phase for the construction life cycle of a building, stakeholder wishes and demands (including those of the end user) are captured applying the same top–down approach. In this project one of the first targets is to define a list of possible wishes and demands of all stakeholders, which are then related to possible requirements for:

- products of a building to be constructed; and
- processes to be executed in order to build and maintain the building.

Another attempt is the conceptual performance-based framework, developed to inventory and relate performance criteria of different objects as desired by the different stakeholders in the varying phases of a building (Bluyssen and Loomans, 2003). The framework was developed from the assumption that the number of performance definitions and the different contexts in which they can be applied make it difficult to keep track of all the building performance information that is available. This also accounts for the translation rules that are required to translate subjective performance information at one stage (e.g. the design phase) into the next stage (e.g. specific quantitative information for the construction phase). Therefore, a system was developed that allows for a logical ordering of all the information available.

For the translation of end users' wishes and demands to the requirements or performance criteria of the indoor environment (and its products or components), as well as the processes taking place, understanding the various interactions that occur is necessary for the creation and maintenance of a healthy and comfortable indoor environment. This is one of the reasons why the approach described in this book is given the name 'interactive' top–down approach. The second reason is the interactive nature of the approach between all stakeholders involved, setting the requirements together in an interactive way.

Essentially, the following interactions determine how well you feel, how healthy you are and how comfortable you are at a certain moment in time, and determine *your interaction with your environment* over time:

- *Interactions at the human level*: receiving information (sensations) can be perceived from the viewpoint of the human body's physiology and/or from a psychological point of view. Interactions occur on both levels. Interactions between people should also not be forgotten; these interactions can also have a significant effect on the physical and psychological state of a human being in the indoor environment.
- *Interactions at the indoor environmental parameter level*: important interactions include, for example, chemical reactions between pollutants in the air and microbiological growth at indoor surfaces, as well as interactions between chemicals and (fine) dust and interactions between natural and artificial lighting.
- *Interactions at the building level*: interactions between elements of the building and between the building and the environment, such as interactions of the building with the ground upon which it is built (the foundation); interactions between the outdoor environment and the building (protection and transmission characteristics of the façade); and interactions between the building and the indoor environment (such as maintenance and emissions of indoor surfaces and the lighting, heating, cooling and ventilation systems that may be integrated within the façade).

7.4 Some challenges for the future

New 'drivers', new insights and changing end-user requirements, as well as the observed discrepancy between current standards with end users' needs, result in the necessity for a different approach towards managing health and comfort in the indoor environment. This chapter outlined such an approach, taking into account end users' needs through an engineering system approach. It is clear that end users need to be involved in the design process in order to make their wishes and demands more clear. But how these wishes and demands should be put into practice is another story.

When designing and constructing a new building, it is necessary to establish a risk assessment procedure for the health and comfort of people in the indoor environment in which the traditional bottom–up approach is used next to the top–down approach. Such a procedure could, for example, comprise the following steps (inspired by Hollander and Hanemaaijer, 2007):

1   Identify the end users' wishes and demands, as well as their profile (if possible, the mental and physical status of the end users of concern, including the context and attributes discussed above), and try to translate these to boundary conditions and criteria for the indoor environmental (step 1 of the top–down approach).

2   Identify the possible risks involved, with the assistance of all stakeholders involved (including the end users), related to the defined environmental criteria and the end users' profile(s).

3   For simple or known risk problems with few uncertainties, the classical bottom–up approach can be applied using quantitative statistics (e.g. using existing standards on formaldehyde, particulate matter, etc.).

4   For comfort-related risks (with the possibility of becoming a health risk), the end user needs to be directly involved. A prototype of the object of concern or a reconstruction of the intended activity could be applied. If necessary, (scientific) experts need to be consulted. Do not assume that there is a standard response that applies to all people.

5   For health-related risks associated with more than one factor and for which no acceptable standards or guidelines are available, the balance between efficiency and fairness needs to be discussed. For example, the risks of getting sick from the growth of a micro-organism on a certain material are unclear, even if one knows that it can happen. Discuss whether it is right to use this material in places conducive to growth, such as in bathrooms. Another example is the use of heating ventilation and air-conditioning (HVAC) systems in relation to issues of energy conservation versus health.

6   If controversy exists regarding risk (other than the probability and extent of health damage), or a risk is identified to be unknown and new, stakeholders should be involved in the

discussion. For example, in terms of the risks of high-voltage wires and mobile phone masts, or risks associated with new design concepts using new materials and configurations, it is perhaps necessary to perform behavioural observations, interviews, etc.

7 If uncertainties increase together with the seriousness and extent of associated implications (e.g. climate change effects or [fine] dust from the outdoors), a scientific analysis or even a political societal debate is required. This will result in a definition of the risk, a strategy to measure and/or monitor the problem, and, eventually, a decision framework.

In order to translate indoor environmental requirements to the technical performance requirements of the built environment, the interactions presented are of the utmost importance, but so is the applied communication process in the top–down approach, as well as the realization that performance requirements, wishes and demands can change over time and are context related. Eventually, the wishes and demands of end users have to be translated into real building products (building and elements) and processes (maintenance, energy use, security, environmental services) by the stakeholders involved in the whole life cycle of the indoor environment in a component-related and holistic manner (see Plate 15, centre pages).

8

The Top–Down Approach

This chapter argues that current standards, determined using a bottom–up approach, are in general not in line with end users' needs. Together with a far from optimal communication process between the stakeholders involved in the life cycle of an indoor environment, it is not strange that health and comfort problems occur. A new approach, called the top–down approach, is therefore presented as analogous to the system engineering methodology used in other disciplines, taking account of end users' needs throughout the life cycle of an indoor environment.

8.1 A top–down approach complementary to the bottom–up approach

8.1.1 Discrepancy of current standards with end users' needs

Currently, in several standards and guidelines, human indoor environmental requirements for spaces are expressed by physical and chemical indicators (e.g. temperature, noise, illuminance, CO concentration, etc.) (see section C.3 in Annex C). Although these standards and guidelines may be met, it is evident from several studies that indoor environmental quality as experienced by occupants is often unacceptable and even unhealthy, causing health and comfort problems.

This mismatch can be caused by several reasons:

- The relationship between objective measurement and human assessment is not known for all physical/chemical parameters. No consensus model is available for air quality. For light, recent findings show that brightness of the surroundings is the key element, not only illuminance (LHRF, 2002).
- Even if mature models for separate subjective issues exist – for example, thermal comfort (Fanger, 1982) and noise – the holistic effects of all separate physical/chemical factors are still largely unknown.

Besides physical/chemical indicators, other indicators are also being used, such as the percentage of dissatisfied occupants, productivity numbers (Clements-Croome, 2002), sick leave, estimated life expectations (Carrothers et al, 1999) and even the number of deaths associated with a building-related illness.

A quantitative assessment of an individual parameter of the indoor environment is only possible if:

- The parameter concerned shows a clear relation with a symptom/complaint of the occupant (dose effect).
- The influence of other factors on this relation is known and quantified as well.

In the traditional 'bottom–up' approach, focusing on defining threshold values for indoor environmental parameters, a number of steps are required:

- step 1: identification of sources (e.g. physical and chemical) and other influencing factors (e.g. psycho-social);
- step 2: definition of dose–effect relationships;
- step 3: establishing threshold values for recognized dangerous substances to human health;
- step 4: assimilating or integrating all factors into end user satisfaction.

Current standards and guidelines have been and are still being developed in the context of such an approach. Except for the self-evident need to set threshold levels for health-threatening substances, it is questionable whether this approach may reach the final objective of a healthy, comfortable and safe indoor environment in the not too distant future. Most standards are based on averaged data, overlooking the fact that buildings, individuals and their activities may differ widely. Furthermore, considering both the numerous indoor contaminants and the lack of a solid scientific basis, making the final and complex integrating step appears improbable.

Indoor air quality is a good example of the complexity of standardization. For indoor air quality, in general, minimum ventilation rates (in l/s per person and/or l/s per m^2 floor area) and threshold levels for some specific compounds (e.g. CO_2, CO, NO_2, O_3, PM_{10} and $PM_{2.5}$) are applied. Emissions from building materials and people, mainly volatile organic compounds (VOCs), that could have an effect on comfort (e.g. odour and irritation) and/or health (e.g. cancer, asthma, etc.) are meant to be covered by these recommendations. But are they really?

According to Persily (2005), clear gaps exist in the science upon which ventilation rates are based – for example, the health and comfort effects of contaminants and differences in these impacts among individuals. Indoor air comprises a complex mixture of compounds whose sources and effects are largely unknown; as a result, threshold levels seem unrealistic given the numerous compounds.

The indoor air session of the European Geosciences Union (Carslaw and Wolkoff, 2006) concluded that observed health effects (except for odour perception) are also caused by the presence of analytically unstable products as a result of oxidation, and that odour thresholds for many VOCs are probably considerably lower than previously reported. These findings indicate that very low concentrations of organic compounds are responsible for the odour caused by pollution emissions, although the major emitted compounds may not be responsible. Newly formed or decreased emissions caused by reactions with ozone, and influenced by light, make the process even more complex.

The question, thus, is do we use the correct parameters in our standards to describe indoor air quality? Are minimum ventilation rates, mainly based on human bioeffluents (with CO_2 as an indicator) and, to an extent, on primary emissions of some building materials, enough? Or do we need something else?

Complexity and the number of indoor environmental parameters, as well as a lack of knowledge, make a performance assessment using only threshold levels for the single parameters difficult and even meaningless.

It is clear that, although the guidelines are met, complaints and symptoms still seem to occur. What is the reason for this? Can it be that psycho-social effects are of more importance than we thought (see section 5.2 in Chapter 5)? Or is it the complexity of the whole? Several attempts have been made to define performance criteria based on human requirements (see section 5.3).

From the first studies on work-related complaints in office buildings, it appears that complaints related to thermal comfort occur frequently in spite of the extensive comfort criteria for thermal comfort (Skov et al, 1987; Preller et al, 1990). Besides the influence of the design of the building and its ventilation and heating system, and the limited knowledge on non-stationary conditions, psycho-social factors can also influence thermal comfort and thus can partly explain the complaints related to thermal comfort. To be *able to control* the temperature is one of those psycho-social factors.

8.1.2 Communication stakeholders

Besides the end users or occupants in the indoor environment, there are numerous other stakeholders who are directly or indirectly involved in creating and maintaining the indoor environments in which we live, work and relax (see section 6.2.2 in Chapter 6). Each of these parties has different stakes in indoor environmental quality or performance, and, thus, different perspectives (see Figure 8.1).

It is obvious that all stakeholders have their own demands or views. They all play a different role in the various stages of establishing a space. This complex process inherently includes many conflicts of interest. Eventually, the most dominant stakeholders determine the result, which may result in dissatisfied end users. During negotiations between different stakeholders, user-oriented and long-term aspects are often underestimated. Individual needs become more and more important.

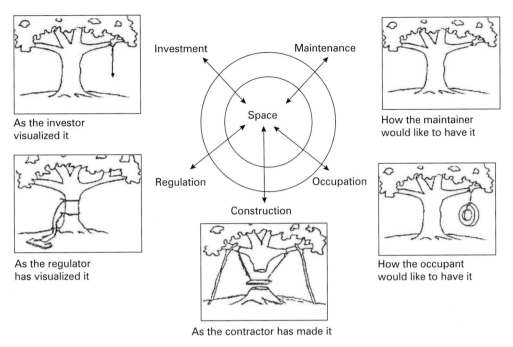

As the investor visualized it

As the regulator has visualized it

As the contractor has made it

How the maintainer would like to have it

How the occupant would like to have it

Investment

Maintenance

Space

Regulation

Occupation

Construction

Source: adapted from BSRIA (1994)

Figure 8.1 *Miscommunication in the building process*

In qualitative terms, from the occupants' viewpoint, a building performs well along its entire life cycle when (Jasuja, 2005), among others:

- The functional spaces can be furnished and equipped to suit the activities taking place in them at first occupancy, as well as during refurbishment.
- Thermal, visual and acoustic conditions needed for all these activities are adequate.
- Indoor air quality is pleasant and causes no sickness.
- Energy costs are not excessive.
- There are no building-related disturbances that interfere with any activity.
- Under regular use and climatic conditions the building fabric does not deteriorate excessively, no visible cracks develop and there is no build-up of dampness or moisture stains.
- Operation and maintenance are efficient and not too costly.
- Fire safety is ensured so that evacuation can occur within a short period.
- Fire does not spread easily beyond the room of origin.

- In case of flashover, the building structure does not collapse.
- Structural serviceability is ensured so that under regular service conditions structural deformations and displacements are not noticeable, and structural vibrations are not observed.
- Structural safety is ensured so that at the strongest winds or earthquake, no severe structural damage is caused.

The owner may want additional features that are not directly relevant to the occupants' needs, such as a readjustment facility for the internal division of spaces; building features do not prohibit rehabilitation or change of occupancy; the building's visual features are impressive and attractive to renters; etc. The authorities may also have additional expectations from a well-performing building that are of no concern to the occupants or owner, including minimizing building-related environmental impacts; the life of emergency and rescue personnel should not be excessively threatened in case of fire; under extremely severe winds or earthquakes, which have a return period more frequent than buildings' life expectancies, structures would not collapse, and so on.

In order to deliver 'good performance' it is crucial for the stakeholders in the building process to have a common understanding of the needs and requirements of the end users – both sides need to have a shared understanding of the desired outcomes. In other words, industry professionals must capture, understand and define user and stakeholder needs before they start thinking about the solutions. The main problem is that one side knows only 'user language' related to the users'/clients' own perceptions and vocabulary. The supply-side building partners tend to think in terms of 'solution concepts', using 'technical language'. The performance concept as presented in the international state of the art report of the European PeBBu project could bring about considerable improvement, as this concept offers an 'intermediate language' that makes it possible to match demand and supply (see Figure 8.2) (Jasuja, 2005).

Nevertheless, there should still be explicit efforts to develop and explain methods of bridging this language gap, and to improve existing briefing tools and/or develop new tools to better match demand and supply. As user and stakeholder needs may vary in time, tools for managing user and stakeholder requirements are needed in all stages of a facility's life cycle.

The road towards implementation and realization of a healthy, comfortable, safe, smart and sustainable space inherently requires communication between supply and demand, knowledge and/or technology transfer between sectors and stakeholders, tuning of separate products and services, and an integrated and holistic approach.

Successfully creating and realizing a space that is healthy, comfortable and safe depends strongly on integrating existing and new (added-value) products and services. Optimizing as well as integrating their functionalities for various applications in different user sectors should encourage fine-tuning products and services from the design to the production stage. This may also lead to new production technology. In sum, this refers to early communication between involved producing industries.

Normally, before a building is designed, the 'imagined' requirements and wishes of end users are listed without the actual end users being present. The design brief is usually considered as a collection of applied performance criteria. The regulator and the end user have a lot of influence on this list, even though the end user is hardly aware of this and does not always know how to present his or her requirements. In addition, the end user normally has no knowledge of cost-quality ratios or cost-turnover ratios, so requirements might be found ridiculous by the investor, who has to pay for it all. In turn, the investor is unaware of operational costs if a certain investment is not made – for example, sickness costs due to a sub-optimally designed lighting system or a noisy heating, ventilating and air-conditioning (HVAC) system.

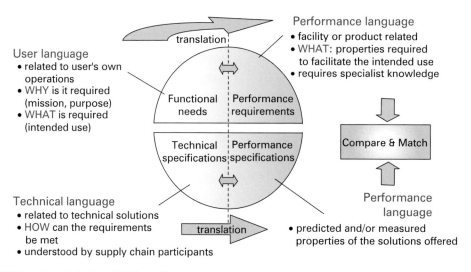

Source: Jasuja (2005), with permission from W. Bakens, CIB

Figure 8.2 *Performance language as an intermediate between user language and technical language*

It is also clear that there is a whole gamut of values and needs that will determine the desired functions of a space and that there is not a direct corresponding one-to-one relationship between a specific function and the accomplishment of a particular value, or vice versa. In the building industry, this approach can also be referred to as the performance-based building concept: 'thinking and working in terms of ends rather than means' (CIB, 1982; Foliente et al, 1998) (see also section 5.3 in Chapter 5).

Communication (i.e. interaction between supply and demand, and knowledge and/or technology transfer between sectors and stakeholders) is of utmost importance. Several communication, design and even cooperation forms have been developed to make this interaction possible and clearer. Examples are the open building approach (Kendall and Jonathan, 2000), the value-domain model (Rutten and Trum, 1998), and public–private cooperation (PPC) (Bergsma, 2007). Each of these examples make use of an underlying structure (organizational structure, model or even a contract) to accommodate the communication process, making it more effective and efficient while reducing the risks that overall project goals are not achieved.

Innovative cooperation

Besides the traditional form of cooperation between the contractor and the client (the assigner), several new forms of cooperation have emerged during the last decade, varying for the different phases of the building life cycle: construction team, design and build, turnkey, and PPC.

In a *construction team*, a design is made for a project required by a client. The cooperation is valid during the period of the contract (i.e. the design phase). The participants (often the client, the contractor and the architect) are considered equal in all phases of the project and the activities are fine-tuned through the processes of coordination, control and advice given to each other. The client puts the team together and a construction team contract is set up in which preparations for the execution as well as cooperation is determined. Even though it is not determined beforehand who is going to build the project, the contractor and architect involved have the first right to make an open offer to the client. If the client finds this offer acceptable, the project proceeds. If the offer is not acceptable, the client has the right to ask other parties to make an offer.

While, in the construction team, the contractor is involved in the design process, in the *design and build*

model the contractor has an even bigger role. The contractor creates the design based on a design brief from the client, often accompanied by a preliminary design. During the design and build phases, the client checks progression at certain predefined moments. Risks can be shared in this form of cooperation.

In a *turnkey* contract, the contractor is responsible for the design, construction and whatever more is agreed upon against a fixed price (lump sum). The client is only involved at the start when the design brief is handed over. In principle, the contractor takes all the risks, but in practice this is more complex. The client often wants to have some involvement through checks now and then, and therefore also takes part in the risks responsibility.

In the *public–private cooperation* (PPC), one private party receives the assignment from the public party to design, build, finance, maintain and operate (DBFMO) the building. How this private party is carries out all of these tasks is the responsibility of the private party. This assignment is fixed in the so-called DBFMO contract (Bergsma, 2007), usually running for 20 to 30 years (the life cycle of the building). The risks are divided among the private and public party, but depend strongly on the agreements made in the contract. The starting point is that the risks should be taken by the party who is able to manage those risks. With respect to financial matters, the private party has to take care of the investment; the public party pays for the services he receives once the building is available, as agreed upon in the contract.

When a project developer designs a project without having a location and sells the concept first, this could be considered an innovative cooperation as well as an innovative design approach (see below). Examples are presented in section 8.1.4.

Design approaches

In general, the focus of architecture is almost always on the aesthetic aspects, occasionally in combination with a certain structural solution or style. Even though the building is built for the people in it, design approaches that focus on other issues than aesthetics are not very common. These are issues that will come later when the first design is ready. Fortunately, there are some design approaches that do include the wishes and demands of the end user from the start, such as the open building approach – the approach based on the value-domain model and innovative briefing.

Table 8.1 *Value frames and performance indicators*

Value frame	Performance indicators
Human being: basic value	Protection, safety, health, comfort, spatial perception
Organization: users' value	Production support, controllability, reliability
Society: perception value	Emanation
Environment: ecological value	Energy- and water use, material use, emissions, waste
Time: strategic value	Changeability
Owner: economical value	Foundations costs, market value, operational costs

Source: Rutten and Trum (1998)

Different parties evaluate the performance of a building on different aspects. It is therefore important to inventory these aspects. For this purpose, the *value-domain approach* was developed in which different value domains are distinguished; for each domain, performance indicators can be appointed (Rutten and Trum, 1998). This is done by a team set up by the client (see Table 8.1). Value domains can play an important role in defining demands (design brief) and the choice of alternatives in the design process. Time is an important factor for all parties because the demands and wishes of these parties can change over time.

In the *open building approach* theories are formulated about the built environment as seen in a dynamic way and in order to develop complementary methods of design and building construction. In The Netherlands, a not-for-profit Open Building Society was instituted during the 1980s to pursue the 'support/infill' approach (Kendall and Jonathan, 2000). This society was active until the year 2000, when it was decided that its goals were sufficiently accepted by the government and industry.

Open building is the term used to indicate a number of different, but related, ideas about the making of the environment – for example, the idea of/that:

- distinct levels of intervention in the built environment, such as those represented by 'support' and 'infill', or by urban design and architecture;
- users/inhabitants may make design decisions as well – more generally, designing is a process with multiple participants, including different kinds of professionals;
- the interface between technical systems allows for the replacement of one system with another performing the same function;
- the built environment is in constant flux and change must be recognized and understood; it is the

product of an ongoing, never ending design process in which the environment is transformed, bit by bit.

Despite its importance, briefing remains a chronic problem in everyday practice. This is particularly true of large and complex projects, in which clients tend to have difficulty in identifying and communicating their specifications, while designers have difficulty capturing and interpreting clients' needs. Implicit and inconsistent specifications as well as limited accessibility and out-dated information are common briefing problems.

According to Ree et al (2007), a serious breakthrough in overcoming these problems can come from the application of modelling techniques. Information modelling techniques can help to define and capture client specifications in a more systematic and manageable way. In an information model, specifications are no longer presented in implicit text, but in an explicit model. This means that all information is captured in what are called 'objects', 'properties' and 'relations'. This technique he named *innovative briefing*.

Ree et al (2007) developed the BriefBuilder tool, which makes use of advanced product knowledge modelling techniques. These techniques enable clients to identify, communicate and test their specifications in a highly systematic and transparent way. Their wishes, ideas and needs are no longer captured in a voluminous 'paper' report or document, but in an intelligent semantic computer model. Fragmented knowledge about end users, building performance and technical solutions is incorporated within one single system.

In addition, it becomes possible to systematically assess tenders, design proposals, construction solutions and building performance against client specifications. Instant access to up-to-date information and notification of any changes in the brief is ensured through a project website. From here, the brief can also be linked to existing computer-aided design (CAD) and costing systems so that physical and financial consequences can be assessed.

According to Ree et al (2007), the BriefBuilder ensures a more effective and efficient construction process through:

- a high-quality and more manageable brief;
- better communication between clients and the construction industry;
- instant access to accurate information and the possibility of tracking and tracing modifications;
- systematic assessment of tenders, design proposals and construction solutions;

• reduced failure costs and prevention of even more expensive misfits.

In fact, this innovative briefing method is not that different from the methodology used in the system engineering approach described in section 8.2.

8.1.3 Performance-based framework

Performance according to the *Merriam-Webster Dictionary* is defined as: 'The fulfilment of a claim, promise, or request (implementation), the manner in which a mechanism performs (efficiency) and a manner of reacting to stimuli (behaviour)'. This definition of performance is valid under all circumstances; however, the performance of something is always context based. The stakeholder, the building phase or a building object are examples of a context: the user will have different performance requirements (stakeholder values) than the contractor. The user wants to live comfortably in the building, whereas the contractor is interested in the performance of individual building objects to obey to the design plan.

As Cain (2002) described, health and comfort are complicated performance parameters as they include a large number of variables that affect health and comfort. But this is only one part of the puzzle. Besides a qualification/quantification of health and comfort, there is also a need to include these parameters in the design, construction and user process. To facilitate the latter, a conceptual framework was developed (Bluyssen and Loomans, 2003).

The framework has been developed from the assumption that the number of performance definitions and the different contexts in which they can be applied make it difficult to keep track of all the building performance information that is available. This also accounts for all the translation rules that are required to translate subjective performance information at one stage (e.g. the design phase) into, for instance, specific quantitative information for the construction phase. Therefore, a system is required that allows for a logical ordering of all the information available.

Stakeholders, building phases and building objects are regarded as important components of the approach. Interrelations between the building phase and the type of stakeholder are obvious, as is the case for building objects and building phases. Each specific performance criterion can therefore be related to the individual contexts. By presenting these contexts on axes in a three-dimensional format, a matrix is developed that facilitates the performance-based framework (see Figure 8.3).

In the framework, all information that defines the required performance for the given combination of

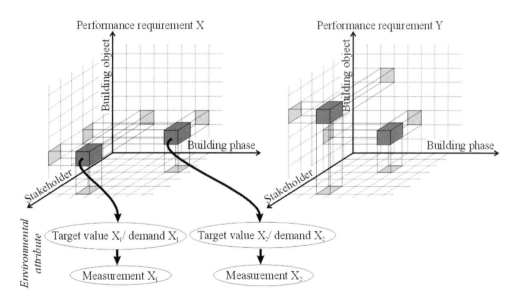

Source: adapted from the work of Hill (1997) and Foliente et al (1998)

Figure 8.3 *Performance-based framework, filtered for attribute X: For attribute Y, other/different positions in the matrix may be important*

stakeholder, building phase and building object can be gathered. The framework contains the specific performance/target values and gives a method for evaluating the performance, all in an unambiguous way. Obviously, one point in the matrix may contain many performance criteria and subsequent evaluation methods, or one performance criterion may overlap several stakeholders, building phases and/or building objects.

If the required information is put in the matrix, it can be seen that a certain environmental attribute X may be dealt with at different positions in the matrix and that the specific target values and evaluation procedures may differ. Considering another attribute, other positions in the matrix may be dealt with.

The matrix approach presents a database that makes it possible to identify specific performance requirements for a specific building phase or stakeholder. It may also relate to a specific environmental attribute X or Y, addressed differently at several points in the building process. The translation of a certain subjective performance requirement to environmental attributes and target values and evaluation methods is, currently, the most important issue. The 3D matrix presents a logical structure to cope with the enormous amount of information.

The following definitions have been applied in the framework introduced above:

* *Stakeholder*: the person/entity who is responsible and/or has the means to influence or adjust/set the conditions for a certain performance criterion – for example, the investor who sets requirements for the building; the user who should be able to indicate the performance desires; the architect and HVAC consultant who are responsible for ensuring that these criteria are met in the design; the building contractor who is responsible for constructing the actual building; and the regulator who may put forward additional criteria that should be met on a legal base.
* *Building phase*: the phase of the building in which a certain performance criterion can be set or influenced. In principle, performance criteria can be set or influenced throughout the whole building life cycle. The main difference in performance criteria between the different phases is found in the way in which the performance criteria are dealt with, more subjectively or more objectively.

Between phases, therefore, translation rules will usually be required to interpret the performance criteria from one building phase to another.

* *Building object*: the part/component of the building through which a certain performance criterion is set or influenced. Building objects can be broken down in different component levels, starting from a material up to a building system level. Performance criteria can, therefore, be defined for the material level, but also at system level. Inherently, the specified criteria and level of criteria specification will be linked to the building phase. Examples of building objects are the structure, the envelope, the material used, installations, etc.
* *Environmental attribute*: a physical, chemical and biological parameter that is related to a certain performance criterion, such as temperature and volatile organic compound (VOC) concentration.
* *Target value and/or demand*: a quantitative target value or a qualitative demand that is related to the environmental attribute that influences a certain performance criterion. A target value will often not be one value. Normally, this will be represented by a value with a bandwidth, as, on the one hand, performance requirements cannot always be determined with great precision and, on the other hand, the data for a target value will often be based on, for example, statistical information so that also reliability, safety and risk are included.
* *Evaluation procedure*: the method or procedure that is applied to check the target value/demand.

To get a better idea of the framework and its possibilities, an indicative example is given in Table 8.2 for the performance criterion 'it should not smell in the building'. What is needed to fulfil this criterion and how one should quantify it is generally not known for all contexts. If a performance-based framework were available, filtering for this criterion would be possible and information on, for example, target values and evaluation procedures for air quality, ventilation rate and material use could be identified. This information would become available at different positions in the matrix, depending upon the stakeholder, the building phase and building object. In Table 8.2 reference to VOCs with regards to the performance criterion is made, showing that in the brief, an air handling unit (AHU) could be incorporated in the design in order to

Table 8.2 *Example of a performance-based framework result for the criterion 'It should not smell in the building'*

Environmental attribute	Building object	Building phase	Stakeholder	Target value/demand	Evaluation procedure
Air quality: VOC	AHU	Brief	Architect	Include an HVAC system	Brief
	AHU filter	Final design	HVAC consultant	Select a filter that ... TVOC <300μg/m^3	Checklist TVOC measurements
	AHU filter	User/maintenance	Facility manager	Change filter at least once per year, etc.	Checklist
	Air distribution network Etc.	Final design	HVAC consultant	Select ductwork that ...	
Ventilation: individual control Etc.	Control system for mechanical ventilation Etc.	Brief	HVAC consultant	Include possibility of individual control	Brief

Source: Bluyssen and Loomans (2003)

adhere to the criterion, although alternatives can also be found (e.g. natural ventilation). The requirements for this building object, related to the performance criterion, thus need to be checked in the different phases of the building's life.

For the initiator, performance is not necessarily related to indoor air temperature or insulation thickness. The identification of a comfortable environment, under given specific conditions, should be sufficient. Energy efficiency and health are similar, rather high-level, (abstract) requirements. However, translation rules are required in the design process to convert these integral requirements into objective design rules and to define evaluation procedures. Translation and evaluation procedures are found in, for example, legislation, rules of thumb and more sophisticated tools such as modelling and case/knowledge-based reasoning.

Considering these points, two important issues should be outlined:

1   How to define the starting point: (the end users' requirements and other stakeholder requirements, if relevant for health and comfort)?
2   How can one translate these requirements to requirements of all the different phases, stakeholders and objects in the framework?

With respect to health and comfort, we can find several initiatives on defining performance criteria and translating them into design solutions: the European

Union Fifth Health Optimization Protocol for Energy-Efficient Buildings (HOPE) project (Bluyssen et al, 2003b) and the ISIAQ–CIB TG42 *Performance Criteria of Buildings for Health and Comfort* (ISIAQ–CIB, 2004). In the latter publication, performance criteria and design information have been collected into guidelines for designing healthy buildings. The guideline has been developed from the information that has become available from, amongst others, the HOPE project and from the FiSIAQ approach, as described below.

Recommendations currently available for indoor environmental and building quality are largely focused on the user phase of a building. For example, the Finnish Society of Indoor Air Quality and Climate (FiSIAQ) has combined specific performance criteria in order to come up with a classification of the indoor climate (FiSIAQ, 2001). The classification deals with target and design values, amongst others, for thermal conditions and indoor air quality, with criteria for construction cleanliness and moisture control, and criteria for material emissions and clean HVAC components. For these topics a categorization is proposed from which target values and material use are derived, including general verification procedures. The classification affects the design as well as the construction phase (e.g. specific categories rank construction cleanliness). For building materials, classification labels have been developed that objectively qualify a building product. In general, the highest classification for construction and building materials is required to obtain the highest classification for the indoor climate. This classification has been in existence in Finland since 1995 and has been developed further since then. The FiSIAQ classification is voluntary, but currently it is a code of practice to apply this classification of the indoor climate, especially when it is used for marketing purposes. Developments in the building industry (e.g. labelling of materials and cleanliness of HVAC systems) are adapted to this procedure. So far, a significant reduction in material emissions has been achieved.

8.1.4 A top–down approach

Because it is so difficult to directly relate single measurable physical and/or chemical parameters with health and comfort effects in the indoor environment, methods using some sort of a risk assessment have been developed – for example, the European Union HOPE project (Cox, 2005). A healthy housing index has also been developed in the UK, the Housing Health and Safety Rating System (HHRS) (Office of the Deputy Prime Minister, 2004), to rate the severity of hazards in relation to health and safety of a dwelling (see section

D.3 in Annex D). In New Zealand, this concept is used for the Healthy Housing Index (Bierre et al, 2004), a tool to measure how likely it is that a house will affect the health of people who live in it. And in The Netherlands several attempts have been made in the same direction (Hasselaar, 2004). These methods inventory the risk that a certain source or action poses to health, safety or comfort in an *existing* situation with the goal of labelling the dwelling of concern. In addition, the risk assessment is, in most cases, based on available knowledge and does not include the occupants' instantaneous wishes and demands.

Recent research shows that occupants have become more and more involved in choosing what is right for them. The outcome, as studied by Clausen and Wyon (2005), is that each occupant makes his own selection of which environmental conditions should be improved upon – indicating that 'performance on demand' might be the way to go.

Clearly identifiable connections have been found between certain building characteristics/user patterns and self-reported (health) complaints. The association between 'to fulfil recommendations for design, operation and maintenance of HVAC systems' (see Box 8.1) from

---

Box 8.1 Recommendations of the AIRLESS project

A number of recommendations were taken from the AIRLESS project, largely related to indoor air quality, in order to realize an optimum balance between indoor air quality (IAQ) and energy consumption (Bluyssen, 2004b). A good way to reduce airflow rate (and energy use) while increasing indoor air quality is to reduce the pollutant source strength indoors in combination with a reduction of the ventilation rate. Related actions are:

- Avoid smoking indoors.
- Use building and furnishing materials that do not emit pollutants.
- Evacuate contaminants close to sources with local exhaust (hoods) (e.g. printers and copy machines).
- For efficient and controlled ventilation, the building envelope should be airtight so that all the air passes through the (natural or mechanical) ventilation system: to reduce energy use while maintaining adequate ventilation, the airflow rate should be controlled and should therefore pass through control devices. Computer simulations indicate that the tightness of the building envelope can have effect on energy demand up to a factor of 2.

A number of recommendations were also formulated for the HVAC system and its components:

- *Commissioning and regular servicing of the air handling system*: keep heat exchangers, ducts, etc. clean and change filters on time.
- *Recirculation*: do not use recirculation; supply only fresh air. Pollution is also re-circulated in this way. Tune system settings with operation strategies, but make sure that the system is restarted early enough before air is required in order to purge the building of contaminants accumulated during off time before occupants arrive.

- *Heat recovery*: use heat recovery, but only if the envelope is airtight, there is no parasitic (external) recirculation and no leakage in the ventilation unit (internal recirculation). Rotating heat exchangers should only be installed if some recirculation of odours is acceptable. If you do use them, select a wheel equipped with a purging sector and install it with the purging sector on the hot side of the wheel. Avoid using hygroscopic wheels. In office buildings audited within the HOPE project, the perceived air quality in winter in the 14 buildings equipped with rotating heat exchangers was, on average, significantly worse than in the 36 buildings without heat recovery or with other airtight heat recovery systems.
- *Humidification*: the basic strategy of not humidifying the air should be mentioned. In most European climates, humidification is not necessary. Furthermore, a lower relative humidity generally results in a better perceived air quality (lower odour intensity). However, an excessively low relative humidity (RH <30 per cent) can cause complaints such as dry air, eye irritation, dry/irritated throat, dry/irritated skin and nose. And excessive humidity favours mould growth. Therefore, an RH between 40 and 60 per cent is considered to be optimal.
- *Air filtering*: with common filter techniques (bag filters), filtering leads to an increasing film of dust collected on the filter. If fresh outdoor air is transported through dirt accumulated on the filter, this is asking for problems. Therefore, filters should be changed or cleaned often enough to prevent the filter from becoming a pollution source:
  - Change the filter, depending upon the situation, traffic and other loads, once every 3 to 12 months, but, in general, every 6 months for highly polluted areas (urban) and once a year for low-polluting areas (countryside). Change the filters only when the system is off.
  - Inspect the filter regularly for penetration, deposit at the bottom of the system below the filter, leakage of the connections of the filter to the system, wetness and possible mould growth. Check whether the filter emits any odours with one's own nose (in off condition) once a month.
- *Air ducts*: start with clean, oil-free ducts, and then prevent dirt from entering the system through efficient filtering. Quality management on the construction site should be a principal focus. Oil residuals are the dominating sources in new ducts. Growth of micro-organisms, dust/debris accumulated in the ducts during construction at the work site, and organic dust accumulated during the operation period can also be sources of pollution.
- *Heating and cooling coils*: without condensed or stagnating water in pans make a small contribution to overall perceived air pollution. On the other hand, cooling coils with condensed water in the pans are microbiological reservoirs and amplification sites that may be major sources of odour in the inlet air:
  - Use a droplets catcher downstream of cooling coil. Cooling coils may also release water droplets from condensation. These droplets wet the devices located downstream, such as filters or acoustic dampers, which then are a good place for mould growth.
  - Increase/decrease set-point for cooling/heating as much as possible (with respect to comfort for occupants). Air quality is perceived as being better when the air is cooler.

the European AIRLESS project and the number of self-reported complaints in the HOPE project, are examples of this (Roulet et al, 2006a) (see Table 8.3). When relations between certain building characteristics/activity patterns and (health) complaints are known, it is possible to set new/different guidelines (performance indicators and performance criteria) and evaluation methods based on which new building concepts can be realized.

Traditionally, the initiation phase of a building starts with defining the brief (statement of requirements). The following phases (design and construction) take this brief and in general do not look back. The technical requirements are defined in the design phase and the customer/end user is no longer involved until the building is ready for occupation. Requirements set in the brief are translated into technical requirements for individual components or objects focused on optimization of that particular component only. Integration of these separate issues is often not taken into account. The risk that the end user is not content with the end result is consequently very high.

Table 8.3 *Comparison of buildings that have adopted the AIRLESS recommendations*

		Residential buildings				Office buildings			
Ventilation		Yes	Partly	No	Probability	Yes	Partly	No	Probability
	Number	3	10	4		12	10	7	
	BSI	0.55	1.85	1.2	0.5%	1.6	1.9	2.6	1%
	IAQ	2.34	3.12	2.73	0.4%	3.3	3.9	4.4	0.01%
	Comfort	2.3	2.8	2.6	2%	3	3.4	3.6	0.1%
	kWh/m²	109	202	238	NS	275	190	211	NS
Heating and cooling	Number	3	8	3		9	10	8	
	BSI	0.54	1.88	1.33	2%	1.7	1.7	2.7	0.2%
	IAQ	2.29	3.11	2.86	2%	3.4	3.8	4.3	0.6%
	Comfort	2.3	2.8	2.7	9%	3	3.3	3.6	4%
	kWh/m²	109	205	292	2%	276	198	207	NS

Source: Roulet et al (2006a)

Bødker and Grønbaek (1991) suggest that designers need to know the context and users' needs and personalities, while users need to understand what is possible to achieve. Mitchell (1995) stresses that in order to make an environmental design truly responsive, end users must be intimately involved in the design process. Sins (1999) also believes that understanding projects and end user needs is crucial; therefore, some form of cooperation between the user and the designer is desirable.

This book recommends a top–down approach that may act in a complementary manner to the traditional bottom–up approach. People form the starting point for this approach as the integrating 'sensor' of all indoor environmental parameters. The *top–down approach* suggests an approach with six steps:

1   step 1: demands and wishes (integration of the end user in the building process);
2   step 2: from demands and wishes to technical requirements;
3   step 3: experimenting;
4   step 4: prototyping;
5   step 5: demonstration and marketing;
6   step 6: occupation and change.

The metaphor of dining in a restaurant, presented in Box 8.2, illustrates the basic principle of involving the end user from the beginning of (and throughout the whole of) the building life cycle.

The metaphor presented in Box 8.2 is nice, but misses one aspect: the assumption that the client really 'knows' what he wants and can also communicate this. With respect to food, we have been brought up to communicate what we like and we can, within limits, inform the cook of our preferences in terms of salty, sweet, bitter and sour. We are much less educated and capable in expressing our expectations for our living environment. In most cases, we are confronted with an existing house or design and have to fulfil our needs within specific boundaries. Most people cannot indicate or pinpoint which needs (physical and mental) they have, and this makes performance on demand difficult.

Some attempts have been made to include the end user in the initial phase. For example, in The Netherlands the *Wenswonen* concept was developed in which real end users (buyers) can make choices via a three-dimensional choice menu adapted to the selected project (www.wenswonen.nl). Each choice shows immediately the end product for the price. Possible choices are predefined per project, but, in general, comprise choices such as dimensions, number of rooms, design (appearance) of the façade and garden architecture.

Another example is the *Sekisuihouse* in Japan (www.sekisuihouse.com). Sekisui developed different house types, interior styles and garden designs for end users (buyers). Additionally, several options are offered, such as facilities for pets, adjustments for different age

---

Box 8.2 Dining in a restaurant

Just imagine that your have decided to go to a restaurant and have a meal. You are the client. You enter a restaurant that – instead of offering a fixed menu – shows the possibility of a full choice of a meal. This is irrespective of your preference for Chinese, Spanish or Italian food and allows a maximum freedom of choice. This is the first restaurant where, indeed, the customer is always right!

The waiter approaches and asks: 'What do you want on the menu?' (*step 1: end user demands and wishes*).

In addition, the chef introduces himself, making suggestions and presenting specials. Together with you, different alternatives are discussed and finally you make a choice. You are still relaxed, but you do not have all the time in the world. You may order something that you expect to enjoy, but that you have never tasted before (*step 2: from wishes and demands to technical requirements*).

The chef returns to the kitchen and starts to create amazing new recipes according to his client's ideas and wishes (*step 3: experimenting*). You are invited for a pre-tasting (*step 4: prototyping*), so ingredients and recipes can be tuned to your preferences before a full meal is cooked.

Finally, you are satisfied and the taste is even better than you hoped for. The new recipes are added to your personal menu. The chef orders his assistant cooks in the kitchen to carry out full cooking and the meal is finally served on breathtaking plates, with candles and excellent wine (*step 5: demonstration and marketing*). When you leave, you know that you will return (new partnership) and that you will recommend the restaurant to your friends.

You return (*step 6: occupation and change*). This time you want something completely different and present a list of criteria to the chef (you have learned from the first time). The chef returns to the kitchen to check whether this is possible. And the cycle starts again. The kitchen is flexible enough to accommodate your wishes and demands; will your home or office workplace do the same for you?

Source: Bluyssen and Adan (2006)

---

groups, home entertainment systems, etc. Included is a ten-year guarantee, while a customer service centre checks maintenance requirements and remodelling requests. A model house can be tested in reality and an architect helps buyers to make the necessary decisions.

The *top–down approach* suggests a new form of cooperation between demand and supply, with all stakeholders involved. In a traditional design and construction process, the players are diverse and numerous, as is shown in Figure 8.4. It is therefore not strange to notice that briefing – the identification and communication of end users' needs – can pose difficulties. Briefing is the most important activity of the whole life cycle of a building. If this is already a problem, the translation of end users' needs into technical requirements will most likely not result in the necessary requirements.

The parties involved often use the so-called *over-the-bench methodology*: when one has finished his work it is given to the next without looking back (no longer my responsibility). A real team is not formed. Parties do not understand each others' stakes or products. Besides the need for end users' involvement in the process, a drastic change is required in the communication process between the stakeholders. Currently, end users' wishes and demands are only incorporated on an individual basis (i.e. the supply industry on a component level, and the architect in the aesthetic design or via the contractor on innovative ways to build faster, cheaper or more labour friendly). However, neither of these incorporations is initiated by or on behalf of end users.

A drastic change is required to promote integration on all levels, as well as to incorporate the end users' demands and wishes (from a product-based to a service-oriented approach). Communication (i.e. interaction between supply and demand, and knowledge and/or technology transfer between sectors and stakeholders) is of utmost importance (see also section 8.1.2).

Boschi and Pagliughi (2002) brought us back to the times of Vitruvius (100 BC) and Palladio (1570) with,

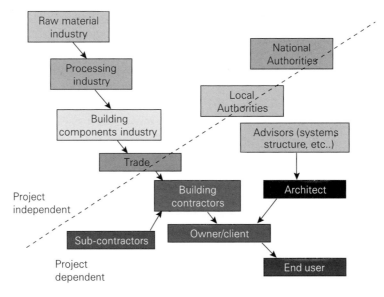

Source: adapted from Lichtenberg (2002)

Figure 8.4 *Traditional building-sector stakeholders and relations*

respectively, their ten and four books of architecture, in which they both established a clear link between architecture, occupants' health, comfort and social needs, and beauty within a specific (cultural) context. Already in those days, effective communication between the different disciplines involved was seen as a necessity. In fact, nothing has changed, although the number of disciplines and experts involved in the design and construction process have increased, making the communication process more complex.

8.2 System engineering management

8.2.1 System engineering

As was pointed out in section 8.1, besides the definition of the end users' requirements at the initiation of a project, the whole life-cycle process with the stakeholders involved is just as important in order to translate the end users' requirements in the appropriate way. The process requires a holistic approach and a more balanced team, which the fragmented nature of the building profession, including the design team structure, does not support.

In fact, many of the problems encountered are the direct result of the following:

- A disciplined system approach in order to meet the desired objectives is not applied.
- The overall requirements are not well defined from the beginning.
- The perspective in terms of responding to consumer (user) needs is, in most cases, short term.
- In many cases, the approach that is followed is: design now and fix later.

Since the 1950s and early 1960s, *system engineering* has been a subject of interest, mainly coming from the military, to overcome the problems sketched above (Blanchard, 2004). Other related concepts are:

- *Concurrent or simultaneous engineering* (originating from the mid-1980s), in which the various parts of a building's life cycle are viewed on a concurrent basis and, in fact, should be included in the system engineering process.
- *Total quality management (TQM)*: the principles of TQM are inherent to system engineering. The emphasis is on total customer satisfaction, the

iterative practice of continuous improvement, and an integrated organizational approach.

- *Life-cycle cost (LCC)*: includes all costs associated with the system life cycle and therefore also of interest to system engineering (research and development costs, production and construction costs, operation and maintenance costs, and system retirement and phase-out costs).

A system consists of interrelated components, such as in a building (see Figure 8.5). Because of the interactions among components, it is impossible to produce an effective design by considering each component separately. One must view the system as a whole, break down the system into components, study the components and their interrelationships, and then put the system back together.

A system has inputs (identification of consumer requirement(s) – i.e. need), outputs (a system that will respond to consumer needs in an effective and efficient manner), imposed external constraints (technological, economic, social, political and environmental), and required mechanisms to realize the desired results (human, equipment/software, facilities/data, materials, maintenance support).

Within the system there are products and processes. The system's life cycle includes identification of need,

design and development; production and/or construction; operational use and maintenance support; retirement and material disposal.

Blanchard (2004) defines system engineering as the application of scientific and engineering efforts to:

- transform an operational need into a description of system performance parameters and a system configuration through the use of an interactive process of definition, synthesis, analysis, design, test and evaluation, and validation;
- integrate related technical parameters and ensure the compatibility of all physical, functional, and programme interfaces in such a way that design is optimized;
- integrate reliability, maintainability, usability (human factors), safety, production, supportability (serviceability), disposability and other such factors into a total engineering effort to meet cost, schedule and technical performance objectives.

As a result, system engineering requires (see also Box 8.3):

- a top–down approach, viewing the system as a whole;

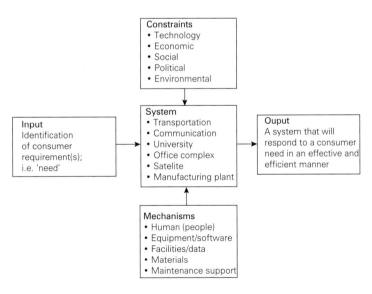

Source: adapted from Blanchard (2004)

Figure 8.5 *System engineering*

Box 8.3 Definitions of a system

- Comprises a set of interrelated components working together with the common objective of fulfilling some designated need.
- Constitutes a complex combination of resources in the form of human beings, materials, equipment, software, facilities, data, money, etc.
- Is contained within some form of hierarchy – for example, an airplane may be included within an airline, which is part of an overall transportation capability that is operated in a geographic environment, which is part of the world, and so on.
- Is therefore highly influenced by the performance of the higher-level system, and these external factors must be evaluated.
- May be broken down into subsystems and related components, the extent of which depends upon complexity and the function(s) being performed. They interact with each other, and these interactions must be understood.
- Must have a purpose. It must be functional, be able to respond to some identified need, and be able to achieve its overall objective in a cost-effective manner. There may be a conflict of objectives, influenced by the higher-level system in the hierarchy, and the system must be capable of meeting its stated purpose in the best way possible.
- Must respond to an identified functional need. It should include items that directly relate to the accomplishment of a given scenario or mission profile, as well as items of logistics and maintenance and support infrastructure that must be available and in place should a failure of a prime element(s) occur.

Source: Blanchard (2004)

- a life-cycle orientation;
- a better and more complete effort to relate the initial identification of system requirements to specific design goals, the development of appropriate design criteria, and the follow-on analysis effort to ensure the effectiveness of early decision-making in the design process;
- an interdisciplinary effort (or team approach) throughout the system design and development process to ensure that all design objectives are met in an effective manner.

When taking the building as a system and applying the system engineering approach to the building engineering process and, more specifically, to the engineering of the indoor environment, there seems to be great possibilities in improving the current approach. In fact, the recommended top–down approach in section 8.1 is similar:

- *Step 1: system requirements* (demands and wishes): results in the description of the problem and a plan.
- *Step 2: conceptual design* (from demands and wishes to technical requirements): results in a conceptual

design and system design requirements (system specification).
- *Step 3: preliminary system design* (from technical requirements to experimenting): results in system design reviews and the development of process, product and material specifications.
- *Step 4: detail system design and development* (prototyping): results in a critical design review, as well as process, product and material specifications.
- *Step 5: production and/or construction phase* (demonstration and marketing): the system is produced and constructed.
- *Step 6: operational use and system support phase* (occupation and change): the system operates, is modified, is maintained, etc.
- *Step 7: system retirement and material recycling/disposal:* feedback and corrective action is given.

Throughout the system design and development, there are many different alternatives (or trade-offs) requiring some form of evaluation. For example, there are alternative system operational scenarios, alternative maintenance and support concepts, and so on. The process of investigating these alternatives, and the evaluation of each in terms of certain criteria, is an ongoing effort.

It is essential that good communications between the stakeholders are established from the beginning. Defining the true need, conducting feasibility analysis, developing operational qualitative requirements and the maintenance concept, and identifying specific quantitative and qualitative requirements at the system level are critical.

In order to ensure that the specified requirements are being met prior to entering into a subsequent phase of effort, and to ensure that the necessary communications exist across organizational lines, there is a need for formal design reviews (i.e. conceptual, system, equipment/software and critical design reviews). In fact, there is a need to provide ongoing assessment and validation of the system. The objective is to ensure that consumer requirements are being met and to establish a baseline for the purposes of benchmarking and for the initiation of continuous improvement.

8.2.2 The system engineering team and process

The 'team' required varies from phase to phase because required expertise changes as system development progresses. In the advance planning and conceptual design phase, individuals with more broadly oriented backgrounds are needed, rather than detailed design specialists, whereas the reverse may be true during the detailed design and development phase. But what is valid in all phases is that the need for good communications is essential, as well as a good understanding of the numerous interfaces that exist.

One of the causes of problems with current system designs lies in the fact that certain disciplines have not been adequately addressed or reflected, perhaps because of a lack of understanding and appreciation for these areas or, indeed, just ignorance. It is therefore important to consider all possible disciplines needed in all phases of the process, specifically for the team required to set the system boundaries and requirements, where it all begins. Box 8.4 outlines the possible members of such a team.

With the starting team, the system requirements are set and the designs for the different disciplines are made. System analysis is performed, trade-offs are made, the design is reviewed, tested and evaluated, and the design(s) are revised, changed and updated for another round until the results are satisfactory and the next step in the process can be taken.

When considering the indoor environment or a building as a system, the same can be said. All choices are made based on trade-offs of options with respect to materials, dimensions, installations, structure, shape, etc., but always referring to the system criteria set.

In a first attempt to apply the system engineering approach for an integrated design of social housing, a team was collected for the OMNIUM project (Adan and Bluyssen, 2004). Instead of the full system engineering approach, the following two phases were focused on: *definition of the system boundaries (the need) and the conceptual design phase. The concurrent design approach* (see Box 8.5) is a method created, tested and successfully used by the European Space Agency (ESA) (www.esa.int/cdf) was applied. This methodology enabled ESA to reduce the duration of conceptual design and/or feasibility studies by a factor of 4 and the cost of these activities by a factor of 2. Depending upon the desired results and system requirements, the necessary expertises were identified and experts representing these expertises were invited by the customer to join the team.

The following roles were part of the team:

- customer;
- team leader, who orchestrates the team as a process manager, ensuring that the methodology is followed;
- system engineer – the project manager; the expert who has a system view (the complete technical picture);
- system assistant, who is the assistant to the system engineer, supporting him with the methodology;
- expert team members, comprising an architect, materials expert, cost expert, comfort expert, installation (water, electricity, heating) experts, energy systems experts, sustainability expert, building connector expert (combining data in 3D models and checks regulation), and a construction expert.

Box 8.4 Possible members of the system engineering team

- *Software engineering*: deals with the process of bringing software into being.
- *Reliability engineering*: reliability can be defined as the probability that a system or product will perform in a satisfactory manner for a given period of time when used under specified conditions.
- *Maintainability engineering*: corrective maintenance and/or preventive maintenance. Ease, accuracy, safety and economy determine the performance of maintenance actions. It can be measured in terms of a combination of maintenance times, personnel labour hours, maintenance frequency factors, maintenance costs, and related logistic support factors.
- *Human factors engineering*: deals with anthropometric (measurement of the dimensions and the physical characteristics of the human body, structural (body is a fixed, static state) and functional (body is engaged in physical activity, a dynamic state), female and male, human sensory, physiological and psychological factors, and people's ability to deal with and process information, and subsequent human response.
- *Safety engineering*: deals with both personal safety and equipment safety through a safety programme, starting with planning, management and control tasks, followed by design and analysis tasks (fault-tree analysis, hazard analysis and risk analysis) and ending with test and evaluation tasks.
- *Security engineering*: to prevent intentionally inducing faults that will destroy the system, cause harm to personnel and/or have an impact that will endanger society and the associated environment.
- *Manufacturing and production engineering*: deals with operations of a manufacturing/ production capability, including the life-cycle issues associated with maintenance and support.
- *Logistics and supportability engineering*: deals with logistics and maintenance and support infrastructure, designed for supportability and for effective and efficient support through the system's planned life cycle.
- *Disposability engineering*: deals with waste and its impact on the environment; objectives are to eliminate waste, minimize cost and preclude negative impacts on the environment.
- *Quality engineering*: deals with meeting or exceeding the requirements, expectations and needs of the consumer (customer).
- *Environmental engineering*: deals with external factors, such as technical, economic, ecological, political and social factors. The system being developed should be socially acceptable, compatible with political structure, technically and economically feasible, and should not cause any degradation to the overall environment. Ecology, air pollution, water pollution, noise pollution, radiation and solid waste are of particular concern.
- *Value/cost engineering (life-cycle costing)*: deals with all costs (R&D, production/ construction, operation and maintenance, retirement and disposal) and revenues (benefits) throughout the system's life cycle.

Source: Blanchard (2004)

Eight concurrent design sessions were held at ESA to create an integrated design according to the concurrent design methodology. The sessions, lasting four hours each, were a combination of presentations and *ad hoc* calculations, discussions, checking the status of the design with respect to the system requirements, launching new values and new parameters in the team, and constantly steering the whole design so that it would converge with the system requirements:

- Session 1 was used to present the current baseline design and to redefine the system boundaries, system requirements and activity requirements. The system requirements were used to define the design drivers and performance parameters.
- Sessions 2 and 3 were used to get the parameter exchange up and running (which implies that each team member has to ask for parameters from others, if necessary).

Box 8.5 Concurrent design approach

The concurrent design approach is a multidisciplinary design tool that specifically targets the very early phases of product/ system design. It combines the viewpoints, the knowledge and the creativity of many expertises in one integrated design model from day one.

(a)

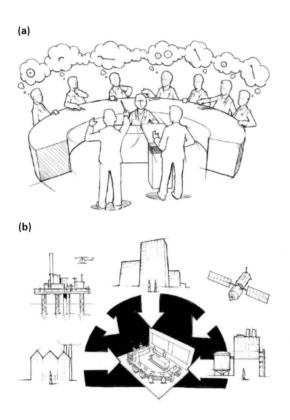

(b)

Source: J-CDS BV (www.j-cds.nl)

Figure 8.6 *Combining multidisciplinary points of view*

Implementing the concurrent design (CD) approach can be seen as a service implementing both a specific methodology and software tools to support the methodology. Concurrent design structures, standardizes, enhances quality, enables decision tracing and permits real-time multidisciplinary work from day one during the first design phase (idea via feasibility/conceptual study to first specifications).

Source: J-CDS BV (www.j-cds.nl)

- Sessions 4 to 7 were used for the real concurrent design, presenting/discussing the different discipline designs and linking this with the performance parameters to create an integrated design. These sessions allowed one to check the compliance matrix and to steer the design towards the system requirements. This iterative process was performed until no further changes affected the approximation of the design with the requirements (it converged).

• Session 8 was used for an internal presentation of the design.

In between the sessions, each team member can/must continue working on the solution for his expertise/subsystem. The system engineer, system assistant and team leader prepare the next sessions and continue steering the team, using the distributed capabilities of the CDF.

Although the OMNIUM integrated design provided the necessary information to make an assessment of the total required investment, the cost and the income over the building's life cycle, as well as the technological feasibility, and although it provided a first iteration of the actual design solution, there are some critical points to be made with respect to the process and the team selected:

• It was very difficult for some team members to keep their minds open to more than one option; thinking directly in technical or architectural solutions is a major bottleneck for the 'setting the boundary conditions and the system requirements' phase. Not everyone is capable of doing this; therefore, the first team members need to be selected on this capability.

• A major player in the building design process is the architect. Generally, the architect still plays a traditional role, with an idea/dream that may have nothing to do with energy use/savings, sustainability, comfort, maintenance, flexibility, and all other criteria. When form precedes function in the design phase, artistic and cultural aspects of the facility's design may be in conflict with solutions needed to satisfy the more prosaic performance requirements.

• Architecture may be beautiful, but it should be more than that; it must enclose space in which certain activities can take place, comfortably and efficiently. Not only must form follow function, but it must assist it in every way. The visual thinking of an architect contrasts substantially with the abstract analytical thinking of the social scientist, philosopher and most laymen, and

represents a serious impediment to fruitful dialogue between them.

• The consultants hired, such as the installation and energy consultant, the material expert and even the structural engineer, also kept treating themselves as consultants who solve a problem: 'We will make this design energy neutral.' They did not see the challenge in producing their own design: what is the optimal shape/design of the building from the constructor's point of view? What structure does this building need in order to be able to cope with climate change? Questions like these were not answered. So, in addition to this expertise, further participation from outside the building industry could help. A structural engineer used to designing boats, planes or even bridges might be more eager to think outside of the box.

• Delegation of power to entrepreneurs, owners and users: some designers do not like the extent of control and influence that other stakeholders have in specifying a building's performance, and vice versa.

• Conflicting requirements and difficulties in separating responsibilities: fulfilment of some performance requirements involves combined design efforts, which might lead to conflicting requirements. Separating the responsibility for the technical design from that of the functional and architectural design is not the solution.

8.3 End users' wishes and demands

In the European HOPE project (Bluyssen, et al, 2003b):

A building is defined healthy, comfortable and energy efficient if the building does not cause or aggravate illnesses in the building's occupants; it ensures a high level of comfort for the building's occupants; it minimizes the use of energy to achieve desired internal conditions.

This is a very general statement; but in most cases it is all that an end user can tell you. In order to ensure a healthy and comfortable environment, a distinction should be made between essential needs, which are in most cases stipulated by the regulatory framework of the authorities, and optional needs. These optional needs can vary over time and per occupant and should therefore be addressed per project and selected carefully by all the relevant stakeholders (Jasuja, 2005).

Several models or procedures are available to achieve these optional needs – for example, the International Organization for Standardization (ISO) Standard 6242 (ISO, 1992a) and the building performance code of the International Code Council (ICC, 2003). In the ISO Standard 6242, for each of the thermal comfort, indoor air quality and acoustics topics, a procedure is presented to determine user needs for the design process. User-activity combinations with various diurnal, weekly, monthly and annual schedules, named user-activity modules, are aggregated into functional spaces and accommodated in the total building layout. The translation of needs starts at the level of the building as a whole, moving down to building spaces, then to building parts and systems, to components and connective details, and finally to materials and accessories.

In the ICC building performance code, one starts with the objectives (or user needs) via the so-called user groups and performance groups related to user risks of building and facilities. Then functional statements (qualitative statements addressing the physical building features that should be considered in order to fulfil the objectives) and performance requirements are considered.

Most of these models use physical, chemical or even biological parameters serving as performance indicators to translate user needs into performance requirements. Moreover, these indicators are used for computational analysis to predict performance in the design phase. Statistical data on health and comfort, as well as on human response to the effects of the physical and chemical parameters on perception of building performance and satisfaction, are not available for all. Even if they were available, it is questionable whether prediction is possible due to the complexity of the factors acting together. As stated earlier, threshold levels for certain factors or parameters are only relevant if a one-on-one health risk has already been determined. In addition, psycho-social factors are also significant.

At present, there is no consensus about performance indicators and metrics integrating the end users' demands and wishes, although some standards and guidelines are available on physical and chemical parameters (ASHRAE, 2004b; ISO, 2005). What is most stunning is that all of these indicators are estimated or derived performance indicators and are not evaluated by or with the end users during the design and construction phase of a building.

It is clear that end users need to be involved somehow in the design process to make their wishes and demands more clear. Some notes to be made, however, are:

- The end user of the building does not always say what he or she means: we are simply not educated to do so.
- The end user cannot oversee the consequences of certain demands when they come together.
- The end user learns and can point out during the process, through experience, what he or she actually means or wants.

The end user can be involved in different ways:

- *Theoretical approach*, using theories and data that have been gathered in the past (i.e. PeBBu – see www.pebbu.nl), resulting in models and simulation programmes. The objective performance of the environment measured in terms of physical quantities (temperature, decibel, lux, etc.) can be part of this.
- *Commonsense approach* (Iacobucci, 2001), using human panels or groups who discuss and/or evaluate trends, options, products, 'designs', etc. (common marketing approach for product introduction). The use of consumer panels is very common particularly in the food and perfume industry (Kramer and Twigg, 1970); but the car industry also makes use of such panels. With regards to evaluating the indoor environment, human perception and assessment can be expressed by a person with so-called subjective environmental performance indicators, such as control of the environment or specific items (ventilation, noise, light, etc.), acceptability of the environment or specific items (air quality, thermal comfort, colour, etc.), and complaints or symptoms related to the environment (irritated eyes, skin, headaches, etc.), and many other factors.

So, several techniques are available to determine end users' wishes and demands: modelling, observation of behaviour, questionnaires or surveys, evaluation of prototypes, and end users involved in the design team.

It is difficult to pinpoint one single method as the best. Depending upon the end goal, one selects methods to suit the problem and the people, and not vice versa. These methods are generally complementary rather than mutually exclusive. One has to learn when, where and how to gain information. One does not use a printed questionnaire with migrant workers; on the other hand, this is most efficient for college students, while for children, direct observation supplemented by interviews (both individual and group) after the observations seems to work well (Sommer, 1969).

8.3.1 Modelling

Predicting how people feel or how people like an indoor environment has generally been focused on modelling one environmental aspect, particularly thermal comfort (see section 6.1.1 in Chapter 6). Some investigations have been undertaken in a laboratory set-up to determine the effect of different parameters on the acceptance of the indoor environment (Clausen and Wyon, 2005). Studies performed by Berglund and Cain (1989) demonstrated that perceptions of indoor thermal conditions and air quality are closely linked.

Most research in the last decades has been focused on epidemiological studies in which different parameters are monitored while occupants are questioned on the acceptance of the indoor environment. From these studies only some indicative relations and/or risk factors have been found (see section 6.2.2 in Chapter 6).

What is not always realised in these studies, although often taken into account via the so-called confounding factors, is that evaluative responses have cognitive (thoughts), affective (feelings) and behavioural (actions) components, which are correlated with another. Our evaluations or appraisals depend upon an array of factors, some derived from our sensory experience and some based on our past experiences mediated by culture and our subjective norms. In the evaluation of indoor spaces, we should allow for emotive as well as cognitive components of appraisal. For example, we may like a restaurant for its peaceful lighting, comfortable temperature, location, aesthetic quality, tasty food, hospitable services, etc.

Design, a problem-solving activity, aims to create spatial and facilitating solutions to respond to human habitual needs, which may appear in the form of physical, technical, social, managerial or functional constraints. Technology is used to facilitate the functions and performance of activities. Often, one concentrates only on the latter in simulation models. Farshchi and Fisher (2000) tried to develop a conceptual model that includes all of these confounding factors, based on the basic assumption that preference of a person depends upon the individual differences (such as gender, age, education and individuals' physical characteristics), as well as social factors (status, social role, cultural values and subjective norms, goal/purpose and motivation).

In the European HOPE project, an attempt was made to identify relations between perceived indoor environmental characteristics and the well-being of occupants at an individual level (i.e. to take into account several of these confounding factors) (Roulet et al, 2006b).

8.3.2 Observation of behaviour

Observing people without them knowing it can reveal a lot of information. The disadvantages of this technique comprise the uncontrollability of the situation; therefore, it is possible that the situation one wants to observe does not occur. In addition, because the variables under investigation cannot be influenced, it might be difficult to make an objective conclusion on the causes of the behaviour observed. With user testing (Perner, 2007) consumers are observed during the try-out of a new product. These consumers can also keep a diary, which can be very useful.

According to Sommer (1969), methods of biological sciences, particularly animal biology and ecology, which rely heavily upon observation and field experimentation over long periods, are more applicable to the design fields than the single-variable laboratory experiments characteristic of physics and chemistry. Participant observation where the observer shares the daily lives of the people under study, observing things that happen, listening to what is said, and questioning people over some length of time, produces data that are often strikingly different from those obtained through interview or casual observation methods. Living and working in the situation will assist the researcher in distinguishing between reactions to the present situation, memories of the past and hopes for the future.

In an initiative of the University of Wageningen, The Netherlands, and several companies, consumers of food are observed during their meal in the so-called restaurant of the future (Futurum) (see Box 8.6).

Box 8.6 Restaurant of the Future

The Restaurant of the Future, in the Futurum building of Wageningen University in the Netherlands, comprises a real restaurant, in which 'real-life' and 'real-time' effects of several types of food and products, packaging, lighting, smell, etc. on the behaviour and preferences of the visitor to the restaurant can be investigated (and filmed!). The initiators want to widen and intensify insights on product choice and eating behaviour of consumers, and want to anticipate future wishes and demands by developing new products and concepts within the restaurant sector, the food industry and the retail sector. Examples are products that comply better with those wishes and at the same time can promote healthier eating patterns. In cooperation with others, special target groups in special circumstances, such as schoolchildren in a classroom or the elderly in a nursing home, are investigated.

Important elements of the restaurant of the future are:

- the development kitchen, in which new products and concepts can be developed through a fast and direct feedback of the visitors in the restaurant;
- the product innovation kitchen, in which products are developed together with the client and, if necessary, with a chef or another expert and in interaction with a group of consumers;
- the sensory laboratory, the 'analytical heart' of the restaurant of the future, where trained panellists are used as human measuring devices and products are evaluated on appearance, smell, taste and texture;
- the 'mood rooms', in which diverse situations can be simulated, and controlled stimuli can be added to determine the effects on mood and behaviour of the guest or consumer;
- the 'body and mind lab', in which the integration of smell and taste in the brain and chew and swallow behaviour are studied;
- the 'experience lab', in which it is possible to simulate different environments with lighting and furniture;
- the real restaurant, in which not only the effect of the products with or without product information and the set-up of products can be tested, but also the actual eating behaviour (e.g. the number of bites or spoonfuls during a set time);
- the control rooms.

Source: www.restaurantvandetoekomst.nl

Figure 8.7 *Restaurant of the Future*

8.3.3 Questionnaires or surveys

It is possible to gain an insight into people's (dis)satisfaction with their existing situation through questionnaires or interviews (see Box 8.7), although determining what their expectations and wishes for the future are is difficult with this technique since people will always focus on what it is that is missing from their lives, forgetting to appreciate the good elements. Nevertheless, through questionnaires, it is possible to present a list of aspects that people can evaluate and prioritize in terms of their value.

As a result of years of investigations through questionnaires, it is clear that the link between objective aspects and satisfaction is ambiguous, as well as the link between objective aspects and people's

---

Box 8.7 The HOPE questionnaires

Within the European research project HOPE, 97 apartment buildings and 67 office buildings were investigated using checklists addressing the buildings' characteristics, and self-administered questionnaires asking occupants about their comfort (thermal, visual, acoustical and indoor air qualities) and health (sick building syndrome (SBS) symptoms and allergies) A total of 2703 valid questionnaires were collected in dwellings and 5992 in offices.

One hundred questions were posed to occupants in office buildings and 130 questions to those in homes on the following issues:

*   Location in building; orientation of main windows.
*   Background information such as age and gender; working hours spent in the building; type of job; possibility of opening windows, views from windows; number of people in the same office room; diseases such as asthma, hay fever, etc.; smoking habits.
*   Perceived well-being through SBS symptoms (dry or itchy eyes; blocked, stuffy or runny nose; dry throat; lethargy or tiredness; headaches; irritated skin) – questions for each symptom included:
    *   In office buildings: 'Do you have more than two episodes during the past 12 months? If yes, was it better out of the building and how frequent was the symptom?'
    *   In dwellings: 'How often have you suffered when in this flat?' and 'Do you think that this is because of the environment inside your flat?'
*   Perceived health with regard to allergies:
    *   In office buildings: 'Have you ever been diagnosed for asthma, hay fever, allergic rhinitis, eczema and other skin conditions?'
    *   In apartments buildings: 'Have you suffered from bronchitis, wheezing, other chest conditions and migraine?'
*   Absenteeism attributed to environmental conditions.
*   Perceived summer and winter comfort, including thermal comfort, air quality, lighting and glare problems, noise, vibration and acoustical comfort, perceived productivity.
*   Other aspects: perceived control of temperature, ventilation, shading, lighting and noise; layout and decor; cleanliness; speed and effectiveness of responses to requirements for improving HVAC or other aspects of the environment. Perceived comfort and environment quality is evaluated by the respondent on a seven-point scale from 1 (satisfactory) to 7 (unsatisfactory).

Additional questions for homes included:

*   During summer and winter, are there annoying smells and draughts and what are their origins?
*   How do you feel about the heating and air-conditioning systems; are there any problems?
*   What is your employment?

Source: Cox et al (2005)

experience. On the other hand, the relationship between experience and satisfaction is much clearer.

One problem with surveys is that people may unconsciously make false statements (Schultz and Schultz, 2006). On the other hand, if performed well, surveys of at least 100 well-selected respondents, with a good response rate, can lead to results that can be generalized. With surveys it is possible to measure people's desires, but not why people have them. Care should be taken not to ask questions that are too direct, which can lead to answers that you can predict beforehand (Perner, 2007).

The method of asking questions is important: do you ask them to give points on a scale from 1 to 10 for certain aspects, or do you ask them to divide 100 points between the same aspects? Both have advantages and disadvantages, depending upon the respondents selected. An alternative is the method of conjoint analysis, in which one has to score total products on several aspects. One can compare, for example, a car with moderate safety, low reliability and average economy with a car with moderate safety, high reliability and low economy, and with other combinations of cars with the same aspects. Through statistical analysis, one can determine which aspects are more or less important (statistically significant) (Perner, 2007). One disadvantage is that many respondents are required to obtain accurate results with this method.

A comparison of the results of two questionnaires showed that different phrasing on the same line of questioning may yield different results and that responses obtained may differ significantly owing to a variety of other factors within the questionnaire and its administration (Grimwood et al, 2002). Factors affecting response included:

- routing within the questionnaires and the use of filter questions;
- question wording and the options given for responses;
- interviewer coding instructions;
- use of show cards;
- focus of questions on specific noise sources or general categories of noise;
- interview technique;
- questionnaire structure and the order of questions.

In an attempt to capture user needs and to relate them to technical features of building components, knowledge-based systems using questionnaires and checklists were developed at several levels in the building cycle. An example of such a knowledge-based system is the TOBUS tool, an evaluation tool for the assessment of retrofitting needs of office buildings in compliance with improved energy performance and indoor environment (Caccavelli et al, 2000) (see Plate 16, centre pages, and Box 8.8).

Box 8.8 The TOBUS method

In TOBUS, the general state of an office building is diagnosed and the actions for improvement are defined. The decision-making procedures are applied at the retrofitting scenario level. The result of the TOBUS method is a proposal for a refurbishment strategy, the corresponding global actions along with their typical cost and impact on energy savings, and the improvement of indoor environmental quality (IEQ). One interesting aspect of TOBUS is the basic division of a building into building objects or elements (see Table 9.1). After the application of the tool and the TOBUS methods, for each of these elements several actions are presented. These actions will help the building manager, the architect or the engineer to improve this element (or replace it) according to:

- the physical state of degradation of building elements;
- functional obsolescence of building services;
- energy consumption;
- indoor environmental quality: based on an inventory of occupants' complaints about IEQ, as well as an inventory of building characteristics and the characteristics of the HVAC system, if possible, actions to solve the problems

are provided. Besides thermal comfort, indoor air quality, lighting and noise, work-related factors, personal characteristics and ergonomics (mainly with respect to chairs, desks and personal computers) are included.

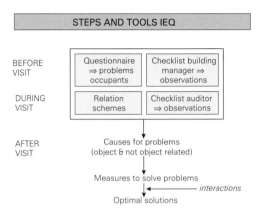

Source: adapted from Bluyssen and Cox (2002)

Figure 8.8 *TOBUS's indoor environmental quality (IEQ) methodology*

The approach comprises three types of data collection (see Annex A):

*   *Checklist for the building manager:* to collect information on building structure and services before the diagnosis of the building.
*   *Questionnaire for occupants:* to collect information on perceived comfort and complaints.
*   *Checklist for auditor:* with information to be collected by the auditor(s) during the visit to the building.

Based on relations between characteristics of the buildings and systems and the use of the building, different possible causes for the problems are identified; possible actions for improvement are then selected:

*   Object-related actions:
    *   observation: annoyance caused by traffic noise via natural ventilation openings (e.g. grills);
    *   action: use sound attenuation in grills.
*   Non-object related actions:
    *   observation: stuffy/bad smell inside due to smoking (smoking permitted in all rooms);
    *   recommendation: use separate smoking zones with good exhaust or ban smoking.

8.3.4 Evaluation of prototypes

Another method of determining occupants' future wishes and demands is to ask a panel of potential end users to evaluate a prototype. This prototype can have different forms: a first drawing of a design (very difficult for most people unless they are trained as an architect); a virtual reality tool (mostly visually oriented and not very useful for other sensors of the human body); a scale model or a one-to-one prototype of the space to be constructed. With current computer-aided design (CAD) systems capable of handling sophisticated geometry, it is possible to generate photo-realistic images and render models according to elaborate shading algorithms. These systems have the possibility of storing other information beyond geometric data, such as materials, electrical and heating systems, different types of doors, windows, roofs, etc.

And the 3D design representation can be automatically generated and updated from 2D drawings. It is even possible to 'walk' inside the design and analyse different interior details. Nevertheless, these systems are not easy to understand (yet) for end users and miss the physical aspect. Bartolo and Bartolo (2001) suggest adding rapid prototyping, a very fast manner of producing prototypes using the appropriate software.

In other industries, such as the car and food industries, prototyping is a common way of testing new products. Questions such as 'How does this taste?' should be used instead of 'How do you think this will taste?'; 'What do you find the best?' is preferable to 'What do think you will find the best?'

Focus groups can be used for this methodology: a fairly small group of people (approximately 8 to 12) who are paid to give their opinion on a certain topic. A moderator is present to lead the process and keep the discussion going and focused. From a quality point of view, the results can be good.

Nevertheless, quantitative results cannot be compared (Scheuren, 2004) and cannot be translated to a population's behaviour. Behavioural aspects can be determined by observing, for example, how the focus group members use or test a product or prototype. This is very interesting when testing the user friendliness of certain products. Sessions can be filmed. But be careful: people can say or do things that they assume others want to hear or see (Schultz and Schultz, 2006).

The use of focus groups is suitable for the first phase of an investigation. Based on the results, questions can be set up for a survey (e.g. to test a hypothesis). Conversely, focus groups can help to explain the outcome of a survey.

A technique that should provide information on future 'needed' products (months or years away) is the selection and application of *lead users* (von Hippel, 1986). This technique is especially valuable for fast-moving fields. Lead users are:

- users who present strong needs that will become general in a market place months or years in the future;
- users who can provide new product concepts and design data as well because they often attempt to fill the need they experience;
- users who are positioned to benefit significantly by obtaining solutions to those needs.

It is important to note that a lead user does not need to have an affinity with all of the attributes of the new 'product', and that a lead user can often be found among users of analogous industrial goods. For example, in the case of an identified trend towards lighter and stronger materials in the building industry, a lead user could be a manufacturer of composite materials in the aerospace industry, but could also be an industrial designer of furniture. It is therefore important to select the group of lead users carefully – this group is not, in fact, that different from the design team discussed in the following section.

8.3.5 End users involved in the design team

The most logical method seems to be to involve the end user in the design process: in other words, take them on board the design team. This approach was used in the OMNIUM project, which bases its ideas on the earlier introduced Ecospace® concept (Bluyssen et al, 2006).

To determine the system boundaries in the OMNIUM project, a preliminary screening (Adan and Bluyssen, 2004) was carried out with housing corporations and their clients about their wishes and demands for housing in 2030. In this context, the end user comprises two types: the owner (housing corporations, bank, investor, etc.) and the occupant (the individuals who actually live/work in the building).

For housing corporations it is important to realize lower exploitation costs during the whole life cycle of their housing stock. This means not only a reduction in initial costs, such as the use of prefabricated components, but also 'lighter' materials and constructions, which result in cheaper foundations. Moreover, it means reducing costs during the occupation of the building, such as less or more efficient maintenance and a higher flexibility of use.

The occupant is not always conscious about his wishes for his living environment. This environment should, of course, be healthy, comfortable and safe; but the road to innovative housing incorporates 'real' demands and requirements, such as buildings that are:

- healthy, comfortable and safe;
- energy neutral (perhaps energy-producing buildings);
- flexible, both from the outside and inside;
- maintenance free;
- lightweight in construction;
- integrates systems (air, water) in the building envelope.

For office buildings, the same requirements could be used, including *controllability of the indoor environment*.

In the first of the OMNIUM concurrent design sessions (see section 8.2.2), these wishes and demands were elaborated into the following requirements using the boundary conditions inventoried:

- *Requirement 1*: the building has to be energy neutral over its total life cycle and during use (preferably energy positive).
- *Requirement 2*: cost has to be positive (at least neutral) over the whole life cycle.
- *Requirement 3*: the building has to be sustainable during its whole life cycle.
- *Requirement 4*: design for a complete independent OMNIUM building in 2030 (meaning not linked to an external network for energy, water, sewage, etc.).
- *Requirement 5*: flexibility in functions in building and in type of occupants, but still a sparkling concept (Plate 17, centre pages).
- *Requirement 6*: the primary structure has to be maintenance free for a minimum of 50 years.
- *Requirement 7*: the technological guarantee of any equipment of the OMNIUM building has to span at least 30 years.
- *Requirement 8*: the building should be 10 per cent of the weight of a traditional building.
- *Requirement 9*: the indoor environment should be comfortable (and healthy) for the occupants.

Some of these requirements were still very vague and were made more tangible in the next sessions by applying the concurrent design methodology.

9

The Individual Interactions

The top–down approach presented in Chapter 8 only works well if the interactions taking place at several levels and places are well understood. Therefore, in this chapter the interactions occurring in, with and between the indoor environment and human beings are described. It becomes clear that no single parameter of the indoor environment can be evaluated on its own. The different environmental parameters interact and influence the perceptions and behaviour of people. Standards and guidelines for the indoor environment should take account of this.

9.1 Interactions

The goal should be: a pleasant state of physiological, psychological and physical harmony between human body and the environment. (Slater, 1985)

In the indoor environment, the following interactions essentially take place (see Figure 9.1):

- interactions at the human level: physical, psychological/neurological and between human beings;
- interactions at the indoor environmental parameter level: between and in;
- interactions at the building level: between elements of the building and between the building and the environment.

All of these interactions eventually determine how well you feel, how healthy you are and how comfortable you are at a certain moment in time, and determine your interaction with your environment over time.

9.2 Interactions at the human level

Receptors in our nervous system receive sensory information (as sensations via the eyes, ears, nose and skin), while effectors transmit motor information

(e.g. movements of the muscles). Sensations are the data of perception, although sensing and perceiving an object are not the same things. Previous experiences – errors through intelligent leaps of the mind – leading to illusion, can influence perception and therefore raise the question of what is objective and what is subjective (Taylor, 2006).

In addition to the stimuli that can be processed by our sensory system, the environment affects us in other ways, which are not immediately recognisable to us. The latter stimuli can cause changes in our psychological state, of which we apparently do not have to know the cause (no conscious experience), but can also be harmful to our physical state of well-being (e.g. invisible light, gases, chemical compounds, radiation etc.).

So it seems that the received information (sensations) can be looked upon from the physiology of the body and/or from a psychological point of view. In both, interactions take place. In addition, the interactions taking place between human beings should not be forgotten. They also have major effects on the physical and mental state of a human being in an indoor environment.

9.2.1 Physiological interactions

Human exposure to environmental factors (chemical, physical or biological) occurs through the senses (ears,

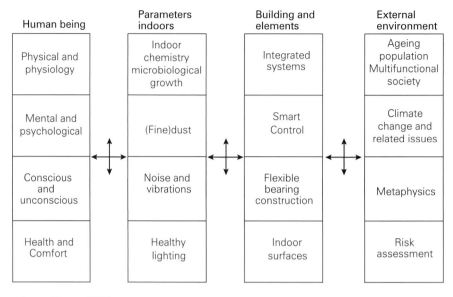

Source: Bluyssen (2008)

Figure 9.1 *Interactions at different levels*

eyes, etc.) enhanced by bodily processes such as inhalation, ingestion and skin contacts. All routes of exposure have to be taken jointly into account. Interactions may occur between stimuli in complex real-life mixtures as well as between various body responses to exposure. Some stimuli cause only nuisance; others can give serious health problems. Some have short-term effects, others long term. Our senses perceive individually, but interpretation occurs together.

Chapter 2 describes how, for *comfort-related complaints*, most of the senses are very good instruments to report on matters such as smell, noise, heat, cold, draught, etc. In some cases, when the stimulus goes over certain limits, these senses can also be used to report *health symptoms* (rashes on the skin caused by allergic reactions to certain pollutants; sunburn; hearing loss; eye damage due to too bright light, etc.). And for certain health symptoms the respiratory tract (including the lungs) is important, such as for sick building syndrome (SBS) symptoms and other allergic reactions. Allergy is a local or systemic inflammatory response to allergens.

All of these responses and symptoms mentioned above are produced, regulated and sometimes 'killed' by several systems in the body: the nervous system, the immune

system and the endocrine system (see Chapter 2). The health effects of our human body to stimuli from the environment are controlled (or better fought against) by the immune system, while our emotions and evaluations are controlled by our limbic system and other parts of the brain (see Figure 9.2). Additionally, the endocrine system provides boundary conditions for 'control' of environmental stimuli by our immune as well as our limbic system. So they are pretty much intertwined.

Several interactions take place between the three systems involved. A major interaction takes place via the *complex neurohormonal regulation mechanism* described in section 2.1 of Chapter 2. In this mechanism, neurohormones of the hypothalamus (part of the central nervous system) regulate the hormones of the pituitary gland (part of the endocrine system), which regulate the target glands. The hormone excretion of these target glands regulate not only the activities of certain target organs, but also provide feedback to the pituitary and hypothalamus, controlling levels of pituitary hormones and neurohormones. The *pituitary gland* (hypophysis) is the main link between the nervous and the endocrine system. The posterior lobe of the pituitary gland is, in fact, an extension of the hypothalamus.

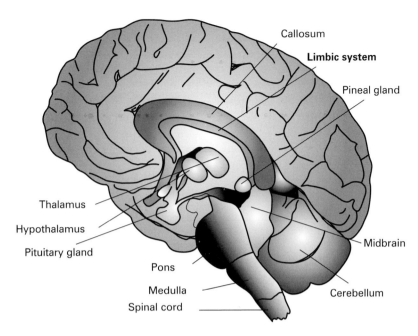

Callosum

Limbic system

Pineal gland

Thalamus

Hypothalamus

Pituitary gland

Pons

Medulla

Spinal cord

Midbrain

Cerebellum

Source: Wikipedia.org

Figure 9.2 *Limbic system, endocrine system (pineal and pituitary glands), brainstem and other parts of the brain*

Two examples for such control mechanism, resulting in a dynamic control and adjusting its operation to the needs of the body, are (Kapit, et al, 2000):

1   Long-term changes in environmental temperature can result in an adjustment of the basal metabolic rate and heat production by altering the thyroid secretion via increasing the thyrotropin-releasing hormone (TRH) by the hypothalamus (which initiates release of the thyroid-stimulating hormone (TSH) by the pituitary gland, which in its turn stimulates the thyroid gland).
2   In response to various stresses, an increase of the secretion of anti-stress glycocorticoids (cortisol) from the adrenal cortex takes place via the increase of corticotropin by the hypothalamus.

Interactions between the endocrine system and the immune system are also not uncommon. Hormones can modulate the sensitivity of the immune system. Examples include the following (Kapit, et al, 2000):

- *Female sex hormones* are known to stimulate both the adaptive and innate immune responses. By contrast, androgens such as testosterone seem to suppress the immune system.
- Other hormones appear to regulate the immune system as well, most notably the *growth hormone and vitamin D$_3$*. A progressive decline in hormone levels with age is thought to be partially responsible for weakened immune responses in ageing individuals.
- The *thymus gland* produces hormones to help B-lymphocytes in their defence against pathogens intruding upon the human body, and also works as a lymph gland of the immune system. It processes cells from the bone marrow to make T-lymphocytes.

Conversely, some hormones are regulated by the immune system, such as the thyroid hormone activity.

External stress factors influence all three systems and can result in both mental and physical effects.

Considering the diseases and disorders of the human body that can originate from an 'unhealthy indoor environment', the following division applies:

- *Those which are stress induced by external stress factors and which are 'handled' by the cooperation between the brain and the endocrine system, but can be influenced by the status of the immune system:*
  - direct noticeable comfort-related complaints by senses: such as smell, noise, heat, cold, draught, etc.;
  - systemic effects such as tiredness, poor concentration, depression, etc.
- *Those which are induced by external noxious effects and are 'handled' by the cooperation between the immune system and the endocrine system, but the handling can be influenced by the nervous system:*
  - irritation, allergic and hyper-reactive effects: irritation of mucous membranes on skin and respiratory tract, asthma, rashes on skin caused by allergic reactions to certain pollutants, sunburn, hearing loss, eye damage due to too bright light, etc.;
  - infectious diseases such as Legionnaires' disease;
  - toxic chronic effects: slowly increasing or appearing (such as cancer).

Starting with the second category, it begins with an inflammation, one of the first responses of the immune system to infection. The symptoms of inflammation are redness and swelling, which are caused by an increased blood flow to a tissue (see section 2.1 in Chapter 2). The first local responses are induced by locally produced hormones and proteins. If the infection is not relieved by these local responses, the centrally produced B-lymphocytes or even the T-lymphocytes become involved in the defence mechanism. It is interesting to note that most brain disorders are related to the functioning of the central nervous system synapses. *Synapses* are obviously crucial for the mental and physical state of the body.

In the first category, several examples can be given. An example that has been recently discovered is the effect that light as a stress factor (or stimuli) can have on the production of the hormone melatonin by the pineal body in the brain. Under the influence of light (specifically the blue-green part), the hypothalamus signals the pineal body to produce melatonin, a hormone that makes us want to sleep, following a day–night rhythm (the brain's biological clock). If exposed to light during the night, the production of melatonin immediately ceases (Brainard et al, 2001; Hoof and Schoutens, 2007).

The effect of the elevation of temperature on the secretion of hormones from the thyroid gland, which increases metabolic rate and results in a higher blood pressure, is another example. And a further example is the exposure to external stress factors (physical and/or mental). Too much stress can cause short-term illness and long-term physical and mental health problems. Hormones play an important role in response. In the short term, the brain signals to the adrenal medulla to produce epinephrine and to prepare the body for action. In the long term, the brain signals via an increase of corticotropin to the pituitary gland, which signals the adrenal cortex to produce anti-stress glycocorticoids (cortisol). Excessive cortisol may have detrimental and harmful effects: atrophy of lymphatic nodes, reduction of white blood cells, hypertension and vascular disorders, and possible stomach ulcers. On the other hand, high, short doses may have therapeutic effects against inflammations produced by wounds, allergies or rheumatoid arthritis (joint disease) (Kapit et al, 2000).

The identified health risks of exposure to noise (mostly traffic noise during the night), identified by the World Health Organization (WHO) (Berglund et al, 1999; WHO, 2003) are a good example of long-term stress (see section 6.1.4 in Chapter 6).

Besides the effect of external stress, the performance of the human senses (internal stress factor) can also have a major influence on the first category of complaints. Deterioration of the eyes, ears, olfactory bulb, etc., usually occurring with age, is an example of this. For instance, in terms of vision and ageing, blue light (wavelength of 450nm) is perceived less with age. This is due to the decrement of the pupil size and to the decreasing transparency of the lens and the vitreous body (Hoof and Schoutens, 2007). Deterioration of the immune system also increases with age.

The production of hormones in the human body can result in proteins that are mainly determined by our DNA and its messenger RNA, or it results in enzymes via intercellular messages. As a result, a major part of what is produced is genetically determined and can be changed by alterations to the cell DNA (e.g. via external influences such as radiation).

9.2.2 Psychological interactions

The way in which we evaluate our environment (perception) and the way in which we respond to our environment (behaviour) are two different processes. According to Vroon (1990), this can be explained by the fact that the part of the brain that evaluates the environment is not the same as the part of the brain that controls the behaviour of a human being. This might explain why there are often discrepancies between what people tell us they need or want and what their behaviour tells us, or what they tell us is the cause of certain complaints and what the real problem is.

In fact, the uses of the brain or mind can be divided into two categories (Taylor, 2006):

1 *Mental or cognitive activities*: perceiving, thinking, remembering, imagining, planning, reasoning and speaking and understanding words said to us.
2 *Emotional experience and unconscious processing*: this takes up about 90 per cent of the processing space in the brain and often wins when conflicts occur. An example is smoking cigarettes: the immediate reward wins out over the long-term consequences.

Perception consists of a complex process through which we recognize, organize and make sense of the sensations we receive from environmental stimuli. In normal conscious experience there a number of divisions: direct sensory experiences (smelling a rose), remembering something from the past, thinking hard about doing something (i.e. writing a book), or being in a strong emotional state (such as extreme anger or sorrow). The human brain appears to have no localized centre of conscious control. The brain seems to derive consciousness from interactions among numerous systems within the brain (Taylor, 2006):

- The neural codes in parts of the *brain stem* are the basis of early experience (reflexes) and are used to develop a higher level and more complex response system from infancy on.
- *Drives* ensure that primitive needs are met and are coded in various brain stem and hypothalamic sites. These are initially encoded genetically, but then are modified at higher-level codes in the cortices to develop the groups of stimuli that can provide satisfactions for each of these drives (such as food and liquid).

- *Limbic system (value maps):* when actions are made and primary drives are responded to by further actions and objects, values (also negative) are attached to the various objects (e.g. red-hot objects as a cause of pain). These reward maps are located in the orbito-frontal cortex, just above the eyes (in the orbit) and are crucial for making the most rewarding and effective autonomous decisions in response to certain situations. The more primitive value maps are located in the amygdale. Both maps appear to act independently of attention, explaining why emotions tend to be immune to cognitive control.
- *The memory system (episodic memories)* involves memories of self-interaction with other objects and persons and is located in the hippocampus. These memories are thought to be played back outside the hippocampus and finally merge with other object and action memories as semantic memories (with no relation to the self).
- *Attention control* is the highest control system in the brain, including the speed-up and monitoring involved in consciousness. The modules of the system are located in the parietal and prefrontal cortices. According to Taylor (2006), there is evidence that stimuli are processed up to a high level of meaning without being attended to or becoming conscious. The 'attentional blink' shows that of lot of processing occurs at an unconscious level in the brain – in other words, a certain amount of time is required to process a stimulus. During this time, no other stimuli can be attended to.

Over the years, several approaches have been presented to explain how our mind works. In these approaches *consciousness* is applied and/or defined differently. The following generalization in these approaches, which are, in fact, compatible, can be made from '*inside to outside*' and from '*outside to inside*', the main difference being that consciousness is considered as contents; data (consciousness of) versus consciousness is treated as part of the inner self.

From inside to outside

In this approach the focus is on high-level cognitive processes, existing knowledge and prior expectations (e.g. physics-based and dynamic models). There can only be consciousness of; there cannot just be consciousness. Discussion is limited to the contents of consciousness. The mind comprises neurons, not an inner self. These approaches have led to several dynamic models in which the components of the system interact with each other in a complex manner, using equations of interacting neurons, alongside behavioural data (past experiences) (Taylor, 2006) (see Box 9.1). Neural networking models have developed into dynamic system concepts with detailed simulations. Even artificial brains have been experimented with (TRI, 2007) (see Box 9.2 and Figure 9.3).

From outside to inside

Stimuli are categorized and organized into concepts in this approach, represented, for example, by the Gestalt view and Eastern mysticism. According to these two philosophies, there are two worlds: one inner mental world and one physical world. Mind and matter coexist in two parallel universes. The mental universe is just a mirror of the physical world (they do not interact).

Internal representation of external objects and surfaces is not anchored to the tissue of the brain, but is free to rotate coherently relative to the neural substrate. Eastern mysticism goes even further; it explores only the inner experience rather than its effect on human behaviour and the brain. Meditation training can ultimately lead to a state of consciousness termed 'pure', which is empty of content, but is not empty (Taylor, 2006).

According to the Gestalt view, the objects we experience as being in the world around us are the products or 'output' of our consciousness rather than the 'input' to it (Lehar, 2003) (see Figure 9.4). Immanuel Kant (1781) suggested two worlds of reality: the nouminal and phenomenal worlds, the nouminal world being the objective external world (source of light that stimulates the retina) and the phenomenal world defined as the internal perceptual world of conscious experience, which is, in fact, a copy of the external world of objective reality constructed in the brain on the basis of the image received from the retina. The Gestalt view believes that we perceive the world in three-dimensional space, not two-dimensional

---

Box 9.1 Inside to outside approaches

Physics based models:

- Quantum approach: sub-neuron processes to detect the way in which various quantum effects are studied (wave function coherence, collapse of the wave function or suggested quantum gravity effects).
- 40 Hz model: the 40 Hz signal is a necessary brain activation mechanism, but is not enough for consciousness, which achieves the binding of different features of an object split across different regions of the cortex.

Neural network models: an artificial neural network comprises a large number of interconnected elements that are analogous to neurons and are tied together with weighted connections, analogous to synapses. The processing or interpretation model uses a collection of mathematical models and is capable of learning, but, in general, does not use real-time learning (e.g. back propagation and self-organization map models; see Grossberg, 1998). Pattern recognition is an important application.

Dynamic system concepts can quantitatively simulate the neurophysiologically recorded dynamics of identified cells in known anatomies and the behaviours that they control, using real-time learning. Complementary computing uses such a dynamic system concept. It is (Grossberg, cited in TRI, 2007):

- Non-linear: the brain can deal with rapid changes in processing load that require non-linear compensation, at the receptor level or at a higher information processing level.
- Non-local: the brain uses widespread interactions that frequently connect their neurons, which are in different parts of the brain.
- Non-stationary feedback systems: the brain is continuously changing its structure through fast development and learning in order to adapt successfully to changing and unpredictable environmental contingencies.

Box 9.2 Example of an artificial brain

The artificial brain has the functions of vision (two cameras or retina chips), auditory (two microphones or cochlear chips), cognition and behaviour (one speaker). It has four functional modules:

1   *Vision module*: with sub-modules for feature extraction in the object path, stereo vision in the spatial path, and image recognition in the attention path.
2   *Auditory module*: also with feature extraction in the object path, binaural processing in the spatial path (to locate sound and reduce noise) and speech recognition in the attention path.
3   *Inference module*: all sensory information is integrated within the inference module, which provides learning, memory and decision-making functions. It performs knowledge acquisition (autonomous), emotional transition and user adaptation. Active learning improves the knowledge by asking proper questions.
4   *Action module*: signals for required sensory motor controls are generated. It consists of a speech synthesizer and facial representation controller, with capabilities of emotional representation.

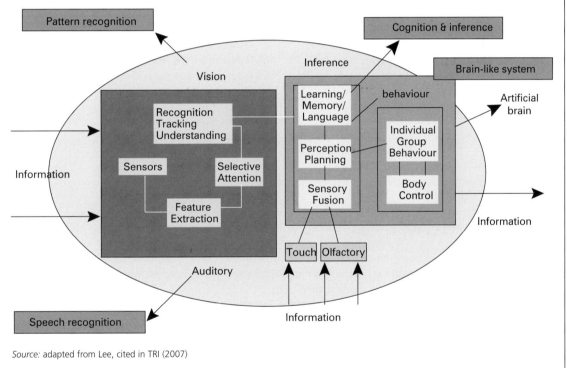

Source: adapted from Lee, cited in TRI (2007)

Figure 9.3 *Four functional modules in brain-inspired intelligent systems*

(according to sensory input). The lowest level of conscious experience contains a great deal more explicit information than that present at the sensory surface. Based on the Gestalt view and on the assumption that a bidirectional causal connection in the brain between different representational maps exist, Lehar introduced his *harmonic resonance theory* (see Box 9.3).

For both approaches, arguments and evidence have been presented. It is a challenge to use both approaches and to achieve complete understanding of

Source: Bluyssen

Figure 9.4 *Gestalt view: Internal perceptual world of conscious experience is a copy of the external world in the brain*

consciousness, alongside detailed experimental data. Taylor (2006) made an attempt with his *attention copy model* (see Box 9.4), which, for the moment, is a theoretical attempt. In this model consciousness is the ultimate controller, allowing us to focus attention on specific stimuli. Consciousness goes beyond attention: attention is not enough for awareness – there must be something extra. Attention acts as a filter; the brain will then be able to properly handle the selected components and make an efficient response.

One of the reasons that brains are so hard to understand is that one must simultaneously study multiple levels of the brain (neuron, network and behaviour) in order to understand how the brain works. Without a link between brain and behaviour, the mechanisms of the brain have no functional significance and the functions of behaviour have no mechanistic explanation.

Strong interactions are known to occur between perceptual qualities. For example, changes in perceived form or colour can cause changes in perceived motion,

---

Box 9.3 Harmonic resonance theory

The Gestalt view characterizes perception according to the following properties:

- The principle of emergence: the global configuration of a stimulus is often perceived in the absence of its local component features; no computational algorithm has ever been devised to handle this type of visual ambiguity. 'The whole is more than the mere sum of its parts' suggests some kind of magical mystical process whereby perceptual structure appears out of nowhere.
- *Reification*: a filling in of a more complete and explicit perceptual entity based on a less complete visual input (to regard something abstract as a material thing).
- *Multi-stability*: for example, the drawings of Escher and Salvador Dali.
- *Invariance*: how the essential structural character of an object is recognized immediately and effortlessly when presented according to a great variety of different aspects and viewing conditions.

These properties are different aspects of a single unified dynamic mechanism, which must be reflected in the perceptual model. Based on these properties of perception and based on the assumption that a bidirectional causal connection in the brain between different representational maps exists, Lehar (2003) introduced the *harmonic resonance theory*, in which he hypotheses that besides neural systems (from long-period circadian rhythms, to the medium-period rhythmic movements of limbs, to the very rapid rhythmic spiking of the single cell), harmonic resonance is also active in neurocomputation.

Synchronous oscillations are related to the integration of conscious experiences. If a local point in the brain is subjected to an electrical oscillation at a particular frequency, the tissue responds by 'dancing to that rhythm', generating an amplified oscillation at that same frequency and waveform. It's like throwing a stone in a pond, causing waves, but then rather than a single frequency as seen in the rings in a pond, a range of spatial and temporal frequencies is generated. The brain is a resonator of this sort, whose natural frequency of oscillation as a whole is observed in the global oscillations detected in the electro-encephalogram. Perception operates by generating a reified signal that is tuned to replicate and elaborate upon the pattern of regularity picked up by the sensory organ from the environment; this pattern is expressed in terms of harmonic resonance representation.

Source: Lehar (2003)

Box 9.4 Attention copy model

The attention copy model introduced by Taylor (2006) assumes that it involves the presence of the one who has the experience: the owner. This conscious experience can be transparent (we can look through our experiences to see the 'object' beyond, and not see our own processing getting in the way); ineffable (arises from the intrinsic, inexplicable nature of each of our conscious experiences); unique (one only has one conscious experience at a time); binding (different features of objects – their shape, colour, motion and so on – all fuse effortlessly in our final conscious experience of the objects); and has inner perspective. The latter has no properties of any standard form; by some it is called the pre-reflective self since it cannot be observed by any self-monitoring or reflective process. It is to the pre-reflective self that consciousness belongs (the inner self). For a conscious experience, the following process takes place according to Taylor (2006) (analogous to an engineering model).

The attention movement control signal generator produces an attention movement control signal, under either external or internal goal guidance. A copy of this attention movement signal is simultaneously generated and sent to its own specialized buffer site in order to be available for rapid checking of any expected error by the monitor. Simultaneously, the attention copy supplies a wake-up signal to the buffer site, from the attention copy buffer to the sensory buffer; simultaneous inhibition of possible distracter activity on the sensory buffer is activated by this attention copy signal. In the meantime, the attention movement signal from the attention movement signal generator reaches the posterior cortex and amplifies the relevant stimulus activity there representing the goal, and inhibiting it for distracters.

Therefore, all consciousness requires the precursor signal to move one's attention, and then to achieve the movement of attention, creating the ability to sense whatever it is out there that one wanted to sense. Emotions allow us to ascribe rewarding or penalizing values to various elements in the outside world. Emotions are roused when goals that are being attempted are achieved (leading to elation, happiness or joy) or prevented (frustration or anger). They can involve unconscious bodily responses (increased heart rate or sweaty palms) and the resulting conscious experience related to these physical components.

Consciousness has two components: ownership and contents. The contents arise from the activity in certain sensory buffer sites, coupled with brain activities coding for detailed features of the stimuli making up that content. Ownership is created when the attention copy signal is held on its own buffer site for use in speeding up attention and making it more robust against a variety of errors. It is held until the experience of presence, the attention movement signal itself, arrives (hundreds of milliseconds later).

Source: Taylor (2006)

---

and conversely; and changes in perceived brightness can cause changes in perceived depth, and conversely. How and why do these qualities interact? An answer to this question is needed to determine the functional and computational units that govern behaviour as we know it.

Behaviour (conscious and unconscious) is organized into perception/cognition/emotion/action cycles. Only by understanding the interactions of the brain with its environment, cyclically through time, can real-time behaviour be understood.

9.2.3 Interactions between human beings

Interactions between human beings also play an important role in how one perceives and/or reacts within a certain indoor environment. The most likely interaction to occur is physical contact, but even if physical contact does not occur, the presence of one or more individuals can have an effect. These effects can be:

- the transfer of viruses, bacteria and other particulates via sneezing and talking;
- exposure to the consequences of activities performed by others (e.g passive smoking when smokers are present, or exposure to emissions from photocopy machine when copies are being made in the vicinity, etc.);
- mental (psychological) effects, such as feeling discomfort (irritation) because of crowding, too little privacy or too much noise, or unconscious psychological effects as a result of interactions with other individuals because of their personality (dominating, etc.) or group processes.

9.3 Interactions at the indoor environmental parameter level

At the environmental parameter level, interactions can take place with the indoor environment and/or with the outdoor environment. The interactions considered to be important at the indoor parameter level are 'indoor chemistry', the chemical reactions among pollutants in the air and at surfaces, and microbiological growth at indoor surfaces. In addition, indoor environmental parameter interactions with the outdoor environment that are considered important (and discussed below) are outdoor noise, (fine) dust and biological lighting.

9.3.1 Indoor chemistry

Reactions between pollutants in the air and on a surface affect the indoor air quality to which people are exposed (Weschler, 2004). Emissions of products/materials can be significantly changed by surface chemistry, and the products of such reactions might dominate materials' long-term emissions (see Box 9.6). Indoor air chemistry influences indoor air quality. The mix of pollutants in indoor environments can be transformed due to

chemical reactions, which are the reason for short-lived, highly reactive compounds indoors.

According to Weschler (2004), reactions between ozone (in ventilation air) and terpenes (such as limonene, α-pinene and styrene) present in indoor environments frequently dominate indoor chemistry. Hydroxyl radicals (OH) are formed in these reactions, which in turn react with other products and form oxidized products (for information of ions see Box 9.6). Indoor conditions such as relative humidity and volatile organic compound (VOC) concentration influence these reactions in an unpredictable way. Ozone reactions, hydroxyl radical reactions, as well as other radical reactions (e.g. nitrate radical: NO_3) occur in the indoor environment. Secondary products that are formed comprise formaldehyde, aldehydes and NO_2. The concentrations of free radicals are not well known and are needed to advance indoor chemistry modelling.

Surface reactions may have a greater influence on the chemical composition of indoor air compared with outdoor air because, for a given volume of air, there are far more surfaces indoors. It appears that reactions on surface can increase the concentration of products in room air. However, ventilation rate influences surface and gas-phase processes: with very high ventilation rates, surface processes are favoured over gas-phase processes (reactions in the air).

From the above, it seems reasonable to assume that the products of ozone-initiated indoor chemistry may contribute to comfort and health complaints, although the magnitude of these effects still needs to be explained (Weschler, 2004). Indoor and source surface chemistry create 'new' and fairly unknown components.

9.3.2 Microbiological growth

Microbiological growth on indoor surfaces can be a problem. Substances given off may be irritating or allergenic, and health effects include respiratory problems as well as general malaise and headaches. Micro-organisms may even cause constructional problems (e.g. *Serpula lacrymans*). In a meta-analysis of the associations of respiratory health effect with dampness and mould in homes performed by Fisk et al (2007), it was found that building dampness and mould are associated with increases of 30 to 50 per cent in a variety of respiratory and asthma-related health outcomes.

Box 9.5 Examples of surface chemistry

Organic compounds that react with ozone on the surface of a used filter are transformed to more highly oxidized species. If oxidized chemicals are released fast enough compared with the airflow through the filter (organic compounds diffuse through the filter to the surface), they can thus influence the air quality downstream of the filter. In one study formaldehyde was found (Hyttinen et al, 2003).

Many esters are used in indoor products/materials, such as plasticizers (phthalate esters, phosphates, sebacates, etc.) and flame retardants (halogenated phosphate esters, aryl phosphates, etc.), and therefore become part of the indoor environment (Weschler, 2004). These esters are susceptible to hydrolysis, especially under basic (high pH) conditions, a reaction that is slower than oxidation reactions and therefore insignificant in the gas phase (too little time for the reaction to occur before the molecules are ventilated from the space). But on the surface these reactions are more likely to occur when the surfaces are moist. Moisture also facilitates the disproportionate nature of NO_2 in aqueous surface films, leading to increased levels of nitrous acid (HONO) in indoor air.

Box 9.6 Ions

An ion is an atom or molecule that has lost or gained one or more electrons, making it positively or negatively charged:

- Anions are negatively charged ions (there are more electrons associated with them than there are protons in their nuclei).
- Cations are positively charged ions (fewer electrons than protons).
- Dianions are a species that have two negative charges on it (e.g. the aromatic dianion pentalene).
- Radical ions are ions that contain an odd number of electrons and are generally very reactive and unstable.

Ions are essential to life. Sodium, potassium, calcium and other ions play an important role in the cells of living organisms, particularly in cell membranes. They are used in smoke detectors and ion engines, and negative ions are used in ion therapy, which utilizes a special electronic device that generates negatively charged particles.

Moulds grow on practically any organic material provided that there is enough water. Some yeasts, or yeast-like fungi, arise primarily from tap water, humidifiers and outdoor air. With rare exceptions, these require liquid water for growth. Fungi can produce spores, mycotoxins (toxic to humans), synergizers (increase potency of most obvious toxins) and volatile organic compounds (the dominant VOC in moulds is ethanol, which itself is a potent synergizer of many toxins). Mycotoxins are chemicals manufactured by fungi, some of which are extremely toxic to humans and animals (Schmidt-Etkin, 1994). When moulds make them, they also make synergizers: substances that can enhance the potency of other toxins in the environment. Some of these compounds may not be toxic, but become toxic when combined with other substances. Fungi also emit volatile organic compounds, which are responsible for their odour. More than 500 VOCs have been identified from different fungi.

Next to other factors, the amount of water available to a fungus determines foremost whether it will grow. Availability of water does not necessarily mean the presence of liquid water. Water activity (AW) describes the effective concentration of moisture in a substrate in equilibrium with relative humidity. The AW that will support the growth of a given mould is affected by temperature and available nutrients. The availability of water in the indoor environment and/or in construction products is influenced by several factors:

thermal performance of a building envelope, ventilation and *material characteristics*. The latter is the primary reason for microbial growth (Adan, 1994; IUMS, 2005). *The material constituents and moisture retention characteristics of a product determine the risk of microbial growth*:

- *Constituents*: if a product comprises organic materials, the risk of growth is higher than for completely inert materials. The trend towards eco-friendlier products has thus increased the potential growth risks (e.g. the use of water-based paints instead of oil-based). Organic dirt on inert material can also increase the risk, making the 'cleanability' of a product an important characteristic.
- *Moisture retention*: in general, during a short period of time in bathrooms and kitchens, substantial amounts of water vapour are produced. This water vapour condenses on surface areas and is retained on or in the surface layer of the material. Surface moistening and storage cannot be avoided with high ventilation rates, so the material will generally have enough moisture for growth until the next shower and the process starts again. On average, the relative humidity of the air in the bathroom is low, but the moisture retained by the surface areas can be high and thus the conditions for growth can be favourable all the time (see Figure 9.5).

At present, an increased resistance against microbial attack, and therefore the prevention of mould growth, requires the addition of biocides, with paints being the main application area. Because the actual period of time of biocides activity is short (maximum of one to two years), research is being performed to encapsulate the biocides; when moulds are present, the encapsulation breaks and slow release of the biocide occurs. A current problem is that most traditional biocides (e.g. mercury compounds) are under prohibitive rules – European Union Biocides Product Directive (BPD) (EU, 1998) – or will be. Eco-friendlier and less toxic alternatives are needed.

9.3.3 Biological lighting

The main needs of people for lighting in and around their home are safety, mood enhancement and comfort, and visual performance for various activities. Current lighting products, guidelines and standards are therefore based on

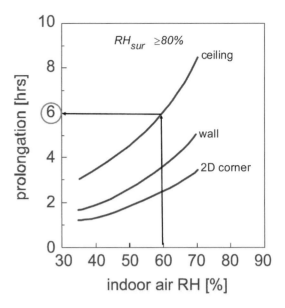

Note: The average relative humidity of the air is hardly affected by this and is clearly below any risk level.

Source: Adan (1994)

Figure 9.5 *Relative humidity in the indoor air versus the time of high relative humidity (>80%) at the surface is prolonged as a result of ten minutes of showering – the time of wetness (TOW): This is caused by moisture storage in the thin (maximum 1mm) finishing layer*

the principles of providing task lighting (e.g. cooking, reading, etc.) and of creating a pleasant atmosphere.

Research on biological lighting demands (the influence of light on the production of melatonin controlling the biological clock) shows, however, the need for lighting solutions that are completely different from current practice (LHRF, 2002). The amount of light entering the eye affects the biorhythm; improper lighting can lead to sleep distortions, trends of (winter) depression and loss of concentration. These findings introduce a new dimension to lighting principles.

In order to achieve so-called psychobiological lighting, the installation should be capable of more than providing light for the visual task. It must also bring a sufficient amount of light into the eye in order to stimulate biological and physiological processes in a proper way. Using daylight must be the first step towards good solutions, but there is a need for new light sources and design procedures.

Available sources and tools are incapable of achieving the right solution in a cost-effective and energy-efficient way. Therefore, a new technology is needed where new sources are capable of creating lighting that will satisfy the conventional criteria oriented towards illumination of the visual task, as well as the newly introduced biological, physiological and psychological demands. These demands include (Aries, 2005):

- visual comfort for conventional tasks (sufficient illumination of task, lack of glare, etc.);
- sufficient retinal illuminance to provide biological stimulus;
- adaptability in order to create biological regimes (variations over time, spatial and spectral distribution, colour temperature, etc.).

As a result, integrating health with the lighting principles of task and atmosphere provision, and balancing natural daylight design with adaptable and modular artificial lighting are crucial. For daylight, the major challenge is to control the direct solar radiation and to improve the distribution of daylight in the spaces behind the façades (IEA, 2000). Energy savings from daylighting systems depend upon the system designed as part of an integrated strategy that includes daylight-responsive lighting controls.

With respect to artificial lighting, light-emitting diode (LED) lighting can help (see Plate 18, centre pages). With LEDs, it is possible to include part of the lighting in the building structure (walls, ceilings, etc.), which makes different directions of (vertical and horizontal) illuminance at different locations possible without losing the strength of the light. The characteristics of LEDs (i.e. a large range of colours and dimming possibilities) make them suitable for lighting application.

9.3.4 (Fine) dust

Particles and semi-volatile organic compounds (SVOCs) may be considered as markers of combined exposure to other indoor stressors (WHO, 2006c). Many compounds that are generated in the indoor environment are semi-volatiles such as phthalates, flame retardants, polycyclic aromatic hydrocarbons (PAHs), chlorophenols, pesticides, organotins and

metals, and may adsorb to particulate matter present in the indoor air and to house dust. These particles may be inhaled or ingested, depending upon their size. Particulate air pollutants have very diverse chemical compositions that are highly dependent upon their source, and they are also diverse in terms of particle size. Figure 9.6 illustrates the range of sizes (on a logarithmic scale), together with the ranges where certain important components are typically encountered. It also shows the PM_{10}, $PM_{2.5}$ and ultra-fine particle fractions, which are typically those measured within the ambient (outdoor) air.

Until now, the most frequently used indicator for suspended particles in the air has been PM_{10} (particles with an aerodynamic diameter <10μm); $PM_{2.5}$ is an important indicator of risk to health from particulate pollution, and might also be a better indicator than PM_{10} for anthropogenic suspended particles in many areas. Ultra-fine particles are usually formed by nucleation, which is the initial stage of the process by which gas becomes a particle. These particles are a few nanometres in size but can grow up to 1μm, either through condensation (when additional gas condenses onto the particles) or through coagulation (when two or more particles combine to form a larger particle).

Current evidence suggests that the effects of ambient particulate matter (PM) may be manifested through several, probably interrelated, pathways involving oxidative stress and inflammation. Oxidative stress has been hypothesized to be a common factor in a range of adverse effects of air pollution on respiratory and cardiovascular systems, such as respiratory toxicity, reproductive effects and cancer. Additionally, the toxicological evidence does provide an indication that aspects of PM other than mass alone determine toxicity (WHO, 2006c).

The amount of air pollution penetrating from outdoors to indoors depends upon the penetration coefficient, the ventilation rate and the decay rate. The penetration factor lies between 0.5 and 0.9, being greatest for fine particles ($PM_{2.5}$) and lowest for coarse (PM_{10}) and ultra-fine particles (UFPs) (Weichenthal et al, 2007).

For PM, however, the composition of particles of outdoor origin can be very different from that of particles from indoor sources. The majority of UFPs indoors are produced indoors (50 to 80 per cent) (Weichenthal et al, 2007). Indoor sources of UFPs are home cooking and heating appliances, tobacco smoke,

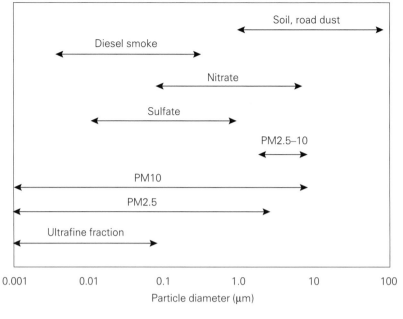

Source: WHO (2006c)

Figure 9.6 *Size ranges of airborne particles*

burning candles, vacuuming, natural gas clothes dryers and other household activities.

Non-ambient (indoor) particle exposure has not been associated with any of the health outcomes of ambient exposures, which does not imply that non-ambient exposures cannot have health effects of their own in other settings. In fact, in a literature study performed by Wiechenthal et al (2007), it was found that UFPs (mainly in animal studies and in vitro studies) can:

- cause oxidative stress and inflammation in lungs;
- promote the formation of reactive oxygen species and move coarse particles in alveolar epithelial and macrophage cells, contributing to inflammatory processes characteristic of asthma;
- prolong the effects of other pollutants (probably related to their ability to increase intercellular calcium levels which, in turn, inhibit phagocytosis and promote activation of transcription factors for pro-inflammatory genes);
- also contribute to 'airway remodelling' (changes caused by recurrent cycles of airway inflammation)

(e.g. thickening of airway wall and inhibition of cell repair);
- potentially promote a Th2 (T-helper type 2 lymphocyte)-type immunity response;
- increase the permeability of a alveolar-capillary barrier, which may allow UFPs to access smooth cells and directly influence airway hyper-responsiveness.

It was also found that UFP composition is an important determinant for biological effects. Results from human studies are inconsistent. A study performed by Allerman et al (2007) on the potency of dust related to the prevalence of building-related symptoms shows that work is being performed to obtain more information on the effects of dust (and particles) on human beings. Mølhave (2008) concluded in his review of five human provocation experiments in climate chambers in which people were exposed to office dust for up to five hours that exposure to normal office dust may cause health effects, such as decreased tear stability or break-up time and increased number of eosinophil cells in nasal lavages, as well as a decreased general well-being and increased general irritation in the eyes, nose and throat.

9.3.5 Noise and vibrations

As discussed in section 5.1.4 in Chapter 5, noise can cause serious health effects, especially noise from traffic during the night. Noise from traffic can interact with the indoor environment via several routes: directly via leaks in the envelope and indirectly via contact sound transmission or vibrations. Reviews of current research (Defra, 2006) have concluded that the percentage of time during which a disturbance is present (or the length of time during which a 'level of quiet' is regarded as acceptable) is generally more important than the actual noise level. In addition to these acoustical criteria, criteria on the sounds perceived in a certain context relating to positive or negative feelings are also important.

Vibration is, in general, experienced by fewer people than noise. However, where significant vibration occurs, it can be a cause of nuisance (or disturbance or complaint); and/or a cause of health effects (e.g. sleep disturbance) (Defra, 2007). The international standards ISO 2631 Part 1 (ISO, 1997) and Part 2 (ISO, 2003b) provide a protocol to measure vibrations between 1Hz and 80Hz on a subject-oriented axial system (z, y, z axes). Protocols for associated effects such as the level of structural and airborne noise, rattling and visual clues are also included. Advice is not provided on assessment indicators or criteria values (these are left to national standards). At the national level, for example in the UK, Germany and Scandinavia, these standards are applied, but differences exist with respect to the location of the measurements (in the building) and the weighting factor applied for the frequencies measured, which both influence the outcome. Based on literature study and previous work, Department for Environment, Food & Rural Affairs (Defra) (2007) concluded that the translation of the measurements to values as evaluated by occupants (i.e. dose–response relations) is not yet clear. In addition, the effect of (the evaluation of) noise on (the evaluation of) vibration and vice versa is still a topic of research.

As a result, a study was performed by the Defra to establish how people in residential environments respond to vibration from external sources (Defra, 2007). The vibration sources considered were those affecting residents outside their control (e.g. road, rail, industrial, construction and same building sources, such as neighbouring gyms, heating systems, washing machines, etc., but not domestic sources within the same residence). A measurement protocol and questionnaire was developed and trialled through a pilot study of 100 case studies. The pilot study aimed to test the proposed methods, confirm the quality of the data derived and validate them as far as possible, with the aim of applying them in a future project, encompassing a much larger study area (in terms of geography, demography, etc.) to evaluate the community exposure-response relationships for vibration emitted from different sources. Significant correlations between annoyance and three measures of vibration magnitude (the primary effect of feeling train vibrations, and secondary effects of annoyance from hearing and seeing vibrations) provide some confidence that residents' annoyance generally increased with increasing vibration magnitude.

9.4 Interactions at the building (element) level

9.4.1 Building elements

Traditionally, a building can be divided into a bearing structure (including the foundation and the skeleton with or without the envelope), its systems (ventilation, heating, cooling, light, etc.) and the surfaces (walls, floors and windows). The aim of the bearing structure, below (foundation) and above the ground, is to provide a construction that can resist natural and man-made forces up to a certain limit (water, wind, fire and sun) and is able to carry the loads without breaking down. The surfaces and the envelope of the building are meant to protect the occupants from unwanted intrusions such as rain, snow, noise, cold, heat and solar radiation, but also to provide comfort, security and privacy. The systems are often treated as something to be added.

From this division in three main parts, the building can be divided into elements, as was done in the European TOBUS project (Caccavelli et al, 2000) (see Table 9.1).

Three interactions of the building and its environment can be distinguished:

1   interaction of the building with the surface upon which it rests, referring to the foundation of the building (not discussed in this chapter);

Table 9.1 *Building elements of an office building that were applied in the TOBUS method*

Bearing structure	Surrounding
	Structure
	Roof superstructures
	Roof structure
	Gutters, sheet, metal work, etc.
	Balconies and galleries
Building envelope	External walls
	Roof covering
	Roof lights
	External windows
	Entrance doors
	Roof-thermal insulation
	Façade thermal insulation
	Ground-floor thermal insulation
Indoor surfaces	Partitions (non-load bearing)
	Wall finish
	Floor finish
	Ceiling finish
	Entrance
	Stairways, landings and ramps
	Interior doors and windows
	Fire-proof and emergency doors
HVAC systems	Heat production plant
	Cooling production plant
	Heating and cooling distribution
	Heating and cooling terminal units
	Air handling unit
	AHU humidifiers
	Fans
	Heat recovering
	Air distribution network
	Air terminal units
	Supply and exhaust air devices
	Control system for heating and cooling
	Control system for mechanical ventilation
Systems	Solar shading devices
	Controls for solar shading
	Toilets
	Sanitary hot water production
	Sanitary booster pump
	Sanitary water distribution
	Sewage system
	Fire protection system
	Smoke exhaust system
	Electrical power supply
	Uninterruptible power supply
	Wireless system
	Security Lighting
	Electrical power distribution
	Lighting system
	Lighting control
	PBAX (low current)
	Computer network
	VDI
	Radio paging system
	Building management system
	Public address system
	Time distribution system
	Video watching system
	TV distribution system
	Fire-detection system
	Anti intrusion system
	Standby diesel generator
	Lifts
	Transportation systems
	Mail transportation
	Cleaning services

2 interaction of the outdoor environment with the building, referring to the protection and transmission characteristics of the building's envelope;

3 interaction of the building with the indoor environment, referring to the maintenance and emission of the indoor surfaces and the systems for lighting, heating, cooling and ventilation integrated or not within the envelope.

9.4.2 Interactions of the building with the indoor environment

Elements and interactions

Interactions of the building with the indoor environment are related to the combinations of elements used. Changes made in or on these elements – for instance, by improving the effect of a certain environmental parameter on people – can influence or interact with another environmental parameter or other parameters considered important (such as energy consumption, degradation and functional obsolescence).

For example:

• When opening an external window in contact with a noisy outdoor environment, acoustic comfort is sacrificed for the benefit of the improvement of thermal comfort or air quality.

• When using solar protection to avoid overheating in an office, visual discomfort may occur because of the daylight reduction and blocking of views. Enlarging the glazing area to increase daylight improves visual comfort but can deteriorate thermal comfort (draught risks in winter and overheating risks in summer).

Table 9.2 provides some examples of measures aimed at improving an indoor environmental parameter, which can lead to discomfort or annoyance on another indoor environmental parameter. Indoor environmental quality measures can also affect other aspects, such as energy aspect, and vice versa (see Table 9.3). Note that interference may not be limited to one parameter: one measure or one action can lead to a chain of combined effects. For example, 'Increasing outdoor air supply rate' might improve the indoor environmental quality (IEQ), but leads to higher energy use for heating, and consequently can result in unsatisfactory temperature conditions if no measure is taken to reduce supplementary ventilation heat losses. Thus, whereas this action was initially designed to improve indoor air quality, a deterioration of thermal comfort can result from it as well as an increase in energy use.

Table 9.2 *Measures and effects of improvements to parameters that influence indoor environmental quality (IEQ)*

Measures taken on:	Leading possibly to failures in:
INDOOR AIR QUALITY	THERMAL QUALITY
Increased ventilation rate	Potential draughts
Reduced humidity to reduce micro-organisms' growth	Inadequate humidity levels
INDOOR AIR QUALITY	ACOUSTIC QUALITY
Increased air supply rate	Inadequate noise levels
Elimination of many synthetic materials	Reduction of available sound-absorbing materials
THERMAL QUALITY	INDOOR AIR QUALITY
Reduced infiltration to improve thermal comfort	Inadequate outdoor air rate
Use of humidifier	Growth of potential micro-organisms
THERMAL QUALITY	VISUAL QUALITY
Use of solar protection to reduce overheating	Decreased daylighting efficiency
VISUAL QUALITY	THERMAL QUALITY
Increased glazed surfaces	Potential overheating
VISUAL QUALITY	ACOUSTIC QUALITY
Use of glazed partitions	Potential sound reflecting
ACOUSTIC QUALITY	INDOOR AIR QUALITY
Use of sound attenuation in air inlets	Insufficient fresh airflow rate

Source: adapted from Bluyssen and Cox (2002)

Table 9.3 presents some examples of measures aimed at improving the quality of the indoor environment, which can lead to discomfort or annoyance on another indoor environmental parameter (e.g. energy, degradation, functional obsolescence), and vice versa.

In the European TOBUS project, an interaction scheme was developed that deals with both indoor environmental interactions and interferences between the indoor environment and other aspects (Bluyssen and Cox, 2002).

Computer simulation, building automation and commissioning

In computer simulation and building automation and commissioning of systems, interactions between the different systems used in a building are very important. Building automation in the occupational phase is the next step to computer simulation in the design phase (see section 5.1.3 in Chapter 5). Commissioning is the process that should guarantee the quality of the building systems (Soethout and Peitsman, 2007). In a building automation system, systems take care of managing, protecting and maintaining the technical systems and, therefore, the facility process (services) within a building. Technical systems comprise ventilation, heating and cooling, lighting, security and access systems.

Clearly, 'correct input' is crucial for a model, system and/or process to work properly. Everyone wants to contribute to a better built environment (Hensen, 2006); therefore the boundary conditions and type of input used (evaluation criteria and parameters) should be able to reach a definition of integral quality, which has many aspects and interactions, as shown above. In addition to those aspects, the dynamic aspect should not be forgotten. According to Rooijakkers (2006), prediction of dynamic building performance (the purpose of building simulation) requires a dynamic approach and should not be based on only a few measurement points, as is done now to evaluate those building simulation programmes.

Table 9.3 *Measures and effects of IEQ improvements on other parameters*

Measures taken on:	Leading possibly to failures in:
INDOOR ENVIRONMENTAL QUALITY	ENERGY
Increased ventilation rate	Excessive energy use
INDOOR ENVIRONMENTAL QUALITY	DEGRADATION
Chilled floor to improve thermal comfort	Potential damage in floor due to condensation
Increased humidity for health	Increased condensation potential, corrosion, fungus
INDOOR ENVIRONMENTAL QUALITY	FUNCTIONAL OBSOLESCENCE
Isolation of pollution-emitting equipment (printers, copiers, etc.)	Reduced flexibility, less convenient adjacencies
Isolation of polluters (smokers, etc.)	Reduced communication
ENERGY	INDOOR ENVIRONMENTAL QUALITY
Reduced infiltration heat losses	Inadequate fresh air rate
Minimization of outside air intake	Less outdoor air renewal
Air handling unit with re-circulated air	Inadequate outdoor air rate
Materials selected for insulation	Potential chemical emission
ENERGY	DEGRADATION
Minimization of outside air intake	Increased condensation potential, corrosion, fungus
DEGRADATION	INDOOR ENVIRONMENTAL QUALITY
Regular cleaning, maintenance of interior finishes	Possible chemical emission
Treatment of wood for preservation (against termites, fungus, etc.)	Possible chemical emission and toxic effects
FUNCTIONAL OBSOLESCENCE	INDOOR ENVIRONMENTAL QUALITY
Integration of pollution-emitting equipment	Pollution build-up
Movable partitions	Change internal acoustics of the room
Open vertical and horizontal connections between spaces	Potential pollution migration

Source: adapted from Bluyssen and Cox (2002)

As was discussed in section 8.1.1 of Chapter 8, the current design guidelines and standards are not enough to serve as a base for simulation or continuous control of building performance, as evaluated by the end user. The same can be said for the current applied performance criteria (such as temperature and humidity).

A building automation system only works with the 'correct' data input. This information is analysed and then used to provide automated decisions. An automated building system does not only take care of technical issues, such as the registration of the hours that a pump is running or a dirty filter report (related to maintenance issues); an automated building system is also involved in the primary organizational process. It can assist in making integral decisions using information from different systems, such as starting the cooling system and/or pulling down the solar shading with a certain outdoor air temperature, the position of the sun and the radiative power of the sun during the day (automatic interaction between different systems using a network protocol such as the Building Automation and Control network (BACnet; see www.big-eu.org), or LONworks (www.konmark.org) or KNX (www.konnex.org)).

In a building automation system, several disciplines meet each other, such as climatology and studies of electricity, as well as technical studies and facility management. The system integrates different functionalities, such as individual control of climate:

- self-diagnosis of the system in which the required maintenance is identified and communicated;
- efficient fault diagnosis and handling;
- adaptability to changes in the use of buildings.

However, in reality, not all of these functionalities are possible due to the fact that the information required is not complete and not possible to communicate (caused by the enormous amount of possible combinations of software and hardware) (compatibility) and due to the missing knowledge level of the stakeholders involved at the conceptual level (Bakker et al, 2006). In addition, 70 per cent of the systems do not operate optimally, which causes, on average, 25 per cent more energy use (Elkhuizen and Rooijakkers, 2006). Good commissioning can help to prevent this: continuous commissioning in which the end user informs the 'system' what he or she wants over time.

9.4.3 Interactions of the building with the outdoor environment

The main interactions that the building has with the outdoor environment are related to the building envelope with or without the systems responding to external environmental conditions such as temperature, sun, storms, etc., and the bearing construction.

The building envelope

The building envelope has basic roles of protection with respect to the local external climate, intrusions, air pollution and noise (the biological first skin), but today can also include active, reactive and adaptive systems of energy production (simultaneous production of hot/cold water and photovoltaic electricity) and distribution (assisted natural ventilation and lighting) (clothes, the second skin). It is even possible that the building envelope of tomorrow will tend towards an 'intelligent third skin': active, reactive and adaptive, removable and recyclable. It will be considered as a whole entity requiring an integrated design approach that will aim at the synthesis of many solutions facing many constraints (technical, economic, aesthetic, comfort, environmental, energy saving, safety, regulations), with the need to continuously improve its performances.

Since heating and cooling loads remain the most important energy consumers in buildings, the reduction of energy demand in buildings will essentially be accomplished through optimization of the thermal behaviour of the building envelope (e.g. reduction of heat losses, increase of thermal mass, management of solar gains, and development of daylighting technologies). The additional energy demand could be partially covered by renewable energies using equipment such as solar collectors integrated within the envelope (roofs and façades). From a simple 'skin', the envelope will become a multipurpose system (see example in Plate 19, centre pages). This technological breakthrough in the building envelope design can become a reality due to the massive integration of new materials and intelligent components (active, adaptive and multifunctional), enabling energy autonomy ('zero-energy building'), even energy production ('energy-positive-building') and respect for the environment ('green-building'), while meeting the comfort criteria of users and interacting with the surrounding mediums.

Bearing construction

The bearing construction interacts with the outdoor environment via forces that can influence the function of bearing:

- natural forces such as wind speeds, vibrations, flooding, extreme temperature changes, hail, etc. (predicted to increase in strength and occurrence as a result of climate change);
- manmade forces such as terrorist attacks, accidents and fires.

Current bearing constructions of buildings are, in general, made of heavy materials, resulting in significant dimensions of the structure itself and the foundation. These structures are not flexible in the face of changes caused by these forces. A flexible bearing construction is therefore important to consider. Heavy materials are, in general, not flexible; therefore lightweight elements, meeting fire safety requirements, could be a solution.

During the last decade, composites have found application in the construction sector in areas such as bridges, roofs, structural strengthening and stand-alone components. However, many practical aspects need to be addressed before composite technology is fully adopted by the construction industry. The main consideration is the performance of the materials in a fire. Composites usually contain a high proportion of fibres and fillers, neither of which support combustion. Epoxy resin is not normally fire resistant; but it can be mixed with fire-retardant additives, particularly nano-clay, to make the matrix self-extinguishing, with low smoke emissions. Other barriers could also limit the development of composites in construction, such as the lack of

knowledge about the health impacts and aesthetics. In a building, composite materials present a negative image of 'plastic stuff'; thus, important developments are needed so that the surface is more similar to materials perceived as traditional (wood, stone, brick, ceramic, etc.).

Composite materials are a possibility that need to be investigated because composites exhibit a higher strength-to-weight ratio than steel or aluminium and can be engineered to provide a wide range of tensile, flexural and impact strength properties (see Table 9.4). Composites can be corrosion resistant to most chemicals, do not suffer from electrolysis and incorporate long-term benefits such as weather ability and ultraviolet (UV) stability, which substantially reduces maintenance costs and extends product lifetime, while their lightweight nature leads to savings in transportation and installation costs. Major savings in assembly costs can be achieved by designing a single composite part to replace a multiple-part assembly of alternative materials.

Composite materials consist of two or more materials combined in such a way that the individual materials are easily distinguishable. A common example of a composite is concrete. It consists of a binder (cement) and reinforcement (gravel). Most modern engineering composites comprise a thermosetting resin matrix in combination with a fibrous reinforcement. Some advanced thermoplastic resins are also used, while some composites employ mineral filler reinforcements, either alone or in combination with fibrous types. Cellular reinforcements (foams and honeycombs) are also used to impart stiffness in conjunction with an ultra lightweight composition.

During the concurrent design sessions of the OMNIUM project (see section 8.2.2 in Chapter 8), it was discovered in a trade-off of several options for load-bearing materials that fibre-reinforced polymer materials are the best option for 2030, taking all the previous requirements into account (see Table 9.5).

Table 9.4 *Advantages of composites*

Key features	Design features	Optional features	Cost benefits
High strength with low weight	Flexibility in design	Fire retardant	Installation
Corrosion resistant	Dimensionally stable	Anti-static conductivity	Transportation
Longevity	Bonding capability	Abrasion resistant	Maintenance

Source: adapted from www.netcomposites.com

Table 9.5 *Trade-off for load-bearing materials for 2030*

General criteria	Sustainability	Cost	Comfort	Design (sparkling)	TRL	Energy
Weight factor	0.30	0.15	0.00	0.05	0.10	0.00
Fibre-reinforced polymer materials	++	++	0	++	0	--
(Steel)-reinforced concrete	--	--	0	--	0	++
Masonry	--	--	0	--	0	++
Wood composites	0	-	0	+	0	0
Bamboo composites	++	+	0	+	0	-

Specific criteria	Mass/volume	Strength/weight	Energy/strength	Weathering
Weight factor	0.10	0.10	0.10	0.10
Fibre-reinforced polymer materials	++	++	+	++
(Steel)-reinforced concrete	--	+	-	0
Masonry	0	-	0	+
Wood composites	+	+	0	-
Bamboo composites	++	++	++	0

	Total	
Fibre-reinforced polymer materials	4.7	Best
(Steel)-reinforced concrete	1.8	
Masonry	2.0	
Wood composites	3.0	
Bamboo composites	4.4	

Notes: In this matrix the general criteria for comfort and energy are not taken into account and therefore the weight factor is set at 0.0; TRL = Technology Readiness Level; ++ = excellent (5); + = good (4); 0 = neutral (3); - = insufficient (2); -- not to be considered (1).
Source: Bluyssen

9.5 Interactions of people with their environment

Finally, interactions between people (the end users) and their environment can be seen from the environmental or the human viewpoint: from inside to outside or from outside to inside.

9.5.1 From inside to outside

As discussed in section 9.2, the interactions of people with their environment can occur consciously or unconsciously and perhaps also in between.

For both conscious and unconscious interactions, some sort of control is performed on the environmental parameters in reactions with human behaviour and demand: manual (self-control) and automated control. For both type of controls, in order to function, the following components are required:

- *Sensors and signals*: registering environmental parameters and anticipating human signals.

- *Linking sensors and actuators*: acquiring and transferring signals to systems that react accordingly.
- *Actuators and local control*: anticipating and reacting to human behaviour and demands (manual or not).

Sensors and signals

Sensors and signals are elements that anticipate human demands and behaviour. Sensors are no more than systems that measure signals from the environment and/or people. Sensors for most environmental parameters are available, except for indoor air quality.

Numerous sensors, also named artificial noses, have been developed, but still none of them is able to specifically detect odorous air pollutants at low levels (ppt to ppb) as the nose can. Moreover, making the step of quantitative detection to integrated perception as the nose does is far more difficult. Indoor air consists of thousands of compounds. Neural networks have been applied to simulate the perception of the nose. For some individual compounds, this has been successful, but not for the cocktail of pollutants that is encountered in indoor spaces.

Emission sources comprise building and furnishing materials, heating, ventilating and air-conditioning (HVAC) systems, and people and their activities. Measuring these emissions is still a problem. Moreover, comparison of the emission effect on air quality is a major point of discussion. Labelling systems do exist, but the usability of these labelling systems is questionable.

From sensors to actuators

The internet is now attaining a level of resilience and capacity that is enabling it to support new embedded services, ranging from home security and entertainment, through comfort and health monitoring, to e-banking and other professional services. These services can be tailored to individual needs and delivered directly to the recipients. This will allow citizens to impose unprecedented levels of control on their home, work and travel environments.

Many companies in Europe, the US, Japan and Korea are developing capabilities for providing new services using broadband connections, mostly focused on the telecommunications, home entertainment and security markets. Much of this effort is fragmented and proprietary.

As with building automation systems, defining service in terms of the data required by service providers and implementation and user interfacing is the key issue – in other words, user requirements for the different human–environment interactions, followed by demonstrations on how the technology can be applied in an acceptable way to individuals in their home, work and travel environments.

Actuators and local control

The same can be said of actuators and local control (see Figure 9.7). The starting points are the end users' wishes and demands and the application of the control in reality (can/does the end user use the controls provided, or should the control be automatic: these are basic questions to be answered). In some cases automatic control is a must – for example, in an increased risk of infectious disease transmission. But in other situations, manual control or perhaps

Source: TNO

Figure 9.7 *Local control*

personalized automated control is a much better option since people, in general, like to take control in their own hands. There is a need for local systems allowing individual control of environmental conditions in the vicinity of a person (Melikov et al, 2002).

With respect to the components (actuators) of such a system, the latest research indicates that both new air cleaning and new lighting technologies (see section 9.3.3) are primarily required. The European AIRLESS project (Bluyssen et al, 2003) proved among other things that current filter systems, based on passive principles, collecting airborne particles, are the main potential pollution source of an HVAC system. The alternatives of biologically active (enzymes or bacteria; e.g. in the space technology) or chemically active air cleaning (using polymer technology) seem to show good results (ASHRAE, 2007).

9.5.2 From outside to inside

The external factors (stakes at different levels) presented and discussed in Chapter 6 (social, technological, political–legal and economical stakes, summarized in Plate 8, centre pages), are the factors from the outside that can interact with the wishes and demands of the end user (human being). These factors are influenced by forces upon which we (human beings) have no (direct) influence as well as forces that we can influence or manipulate. The field of *environmental metaphysics* presents the 'science' with which both types of forces are incorporated to design and build living environments that are in harmony with these forces. In the field of *risk assessment*, these forces are also taken as the basis for estimating or calculating risks for certain forces or factors, forming the base for making certain decisions or taking certain actions. In both fields, calculations and equations are applied, as well as common sense, in combination with 'expert'-based advice and assumptions.

Environmental metaphysics

In the field of environmental metaphysics, although several schools exist, they all have one thing in common: designing and building living environments

that are in harmony with physical and metaphysical forces. In China, this is called *feng shui*, in India *vaastu shastra*, in Japan *kaso* and in Europe, Geomancy. They all refer to a method of living life in a harmonious relationship with the Earth's environment and with its energy lines, and are a mixture of mystical beliefs, astrology, folklore and common sense. Essentially, it comes down to the belief that there are good and bad places in which to live and there are methods and tools to identify them. Because feng shui seems to be the school that has attracted the most followers in Western countries, it is discussed here.

Feng shui

Feng shui means 'wind and water' (Too, 1996). The laws of feng shui are used to differentiate between auspicious and inauspicious energy lines, and they provide instructions for positioning homes and designing room layouts in ways that promise to

---

Box 9.7 Schools of feng shui

- *Form school*: according to 9th century master Yang's principles (written in the book of changes *I Ching*), it is crucial to avoid inauspicious lines that represent 'killing breath' (*shar chi*) or 'poison arrows', and to create auspicious locations where the cosmic breath or *sheng chi* (breath of dragon) can be created and accumulated. Poison arrows are caused by the presence of sharp pointed objects or structures that channel bad feng shui (e.g. straight roads, a single tree, sharply pointed angles of roof lines, edges of a tall building, a cross or any object that has a threatening appearance). Good feng shui is associated with certain objects because of their colours, material or name (e.g. the elephant symbolizes wisdom; the crane, bamboo and pine trees symbolize longevity and good health).
- *Compass school*: this school uses the *pa kua*, an eight-sided symbol (see Plate 20, centre pages) around which symbolic hexagrams and trigrams are placed, resulting in the *luo pan* compass. It contains clues and symbols that indicate good and bad feng shui. Calculations and equations are used together with the compass:
  - Trigram: made out of three straight lines that are either broken or complete. They collectively symbolize heaven (upper), earth (lowest) and man (middle), and have their own multiple sets of meanings, corresponding to a cardinal point and compass directions, representing one of the elements (fire, wood, water, metal and earth) and epitomizing a specific member of the family.
  - Some feng shui formulas are based on the *lo shu* magic square: by adding the numbers together in any direction the result is always 15.

4	9	2
3	5	7
8	1	6

- One of the compass formulas is based on definition of eight types of houses and eight types of good and bad locations in a house using the compass directions and the five elements.

Source: Too (1996)

enhance the quality of their owner's life (good health, sound relationships, prosperity, good reputation, etc.). Bad feng shui brings illness and disaster, accidents, financial loss and unhappiness. In China, feng shui has been practised since at least 618 to 907 AD. By the late 19th and early 20th centuries, two major schools begin to emerge. Today, there are many combinations of the two schools, but irrespective of formulas, all symbols and tools are the same. It is only the interpretation that can differ (see Box 9.7).

All of these philosophies have the goal of creating *chi*: a balance between heaven (beyond our control), earth and man, which *requires constant adaptation to manmade and natural changes*. It is necessary to learn astronomy and astrology and to study the *I Ching* and various topographical features, and to understand social, political and religious forces, the hierarchical structure of society, and moral objectives of both society and individuals.

The two cosmic forces of *yin* and *yang*, which together form a balanced whole (known as Tao, or the way in which the internal principle of heaven and earth are in harmony) continually interact, creating change. Good auspicious feng shui can only be created when there is balance and harmony between yin and yang; without yin there is no yang (and vice versa); without death there is no life, without hot there is no cold, etc

(e.g. greenery and stone; shade and sunlight; light-coloured walls and dark furniture).

Risk assessment

Making choices and determining wishes and demands is all about risk management, consciously and unconsciously. Risk is a chance that something adverse will happen. To take a risk is to deliberately incur that chance; estimating a risk involves defining it precisely and finding a way of calculating how often it is likely to happen in particular circumstances. (HSE, 1992).

Traditional decision-making is solely based on the consequences (likelihood and severity) of possible choice alternatives. It is a cognitive activity and takes into account *anticipated* emotions (expected to be experienced in the future), but does not take into account *anticipatory* emotions (immediate visceral reactions; e.g. fear, anxiety and dread) to risks and uncertainties at the time of decision-making. Lupton (1999) named this the *cognitive science perspective*, which defines risk as the product of probability and the consequences (magnitude and severity) of an adverse event (i.e. a hazard). It is founded on rational behaviour, and accuracy of causal or predictive models are the main topic of discussion. Minimum indoor levels for carcinogens are established in this way (see Box 9.8).

Box 9.8 Health risk assessment approaches for air pollutants

- *For carcinogens*: air concentrations of carcinogenic air pollutants associated with an excess lifetime cancer risk of 1 per 10,000, 1 per 100,000 and 1 per 1 million are provided. For example, for tobacco smoke, the unit risk of cancer associated with lifetime environmental tobacco smoke (ETS) exposure in a home where one person smokes is approximately 1×10^{-3}, at levels of $1-10\mu g/m^3$ nicotine (WHO, 2000c). These levels are mainly based on animal bioassay data.

- *For non-carcinogens* (but sometimes also for carcinogens): for each chemical or pollutant, a no-observed adverse-effect level (NOAEL) or a lowest-observed adverse-effect level (LOAEL) if no NOAEL is available, is selected from a suitable animal or human study and divided by a series of multiplicative uncertainty factors.

- *Several effects*: this is the most commonly used approach and involves the application of uncertainty factors to occupational exposure levels (OELs). Typical OELs used are recommended exposure levels (RELs), threshold limit values (TLVs) and permissible exposure limits (PELs). The latter consider not only health effects but also other issues such as economic and technical feasibility. TLVs may be based on human and animal experimental data, industrial experience or chemical analogy based on similar structure, and are intended to prevent or minimize a given effect in workers who are generally healthy individuals and exposed for 40 hours a week.

Source: Calabrese and Kenyon (1991)

People are considered isolated objects who are ignorant of the threat to which they may be exposed to and/or miss self-efficacy in feeling able to do something about a risk. An example is the *health belief model*, which relies on a linear relationship between knowledge of a risk, developing the attitude that one is at risk and adopting a practice to prevent the risk from happening to oneself. In the cognitive science approach, the following steps have to be followed before individuals take steps to protect themselves from a health threat (Lupton, 1999):

- see themselves as vulnerable to the threat;
- must perceive the threat as having serious consequences;
- must believe that taking preventive actions will be effective;
- must believe that the benefits of that action will outweigh the costs.

But according to Loewenstein et al (2001), people react to the prospect of risk at two levels: they evaluate the risk cognitively and they react to it emotionally. Therefore, fear of the disease can cause more damage than the disease itself. Response to risky situations (including decision-making) results, in part, from direct (i.e. not cortically mediated) emotional influences, including feelings such as worry, fear, dread and anxiety. People often experience a discrepancy between the fear they experience for a particular risk and their cognitive evaluations of the threat posed by that risk, possibly leading to a feeling of interpersonal conflict.

This is partly explained by the fact that elements influencing emotional reactions are different from elements influencing cognitive evaluations of risk (probabilities of outcomes, severity assessments). Emotional reactions are not sensitive to probability variations as with cognitive evaluations: the fear is either there or not – the possibility of occurrence rather than the probability of negative consequences.

In addition, people can have an affective reaction to a stimulus before they know what it is that they are reacting to. For example, a sudden unexpected noise can cause fear well before the source of noise is determined. This effect also has been neurologically proven (e.g. stimulating the fear sites in the brain electrically or by intravenous injections of procaine fear can be evoked without cognitive evaluation).

The factors or attributes influencing emotional reactions during risk management (decision-making) can be approached from different angles, depending upon the risk to be evaluated. One can approach this for example from:

- *The socio-cultural perspective*: where mainly the socio-cultural context determines the way in which risks are defined and dealt with (behaviour according to social norms and values) (Lupton, 1999). This can range from micro-scale (e.g. bodily control as an expression of social control) to macro-social processes, such as individualism and breaking down of traditional norms and values, causing changes in the meanings of risks.
- *The governmental perspective*: is focused on risk in the context of discipline and regulation of populations, with, for example, norms of behaviour (Lupton, 1999). Expert knowledge providing guidelines and advice lead to normalization, methods by which norms of behaviour or health status are identified in populations and subgroups of populations. This approach is very common in indoor environmental assessments (e.g. percentage of dissatisfied and the predicted mean vote for thermal comfort).
- *The personal perspective*: is focused on the separation of emotions (feelings) and cognitive evaluation. This can range from emotions treated as being complementary, to emotions treated as departing from what individuals view as the best course of action (cognitive evaluation). Factors influencing the emotions are (Loewenstein et al, 2001):
  - Vividness and, thus, the strength of anticipatory emotions, through which consequences can be imagined. This depends upon individual differences in mental imaging ability (and the resulting visceral response, such as an increase in heart rate, blood pressure, etc.) and affective reactions such as anger and fear, but also upon the situational factors, such as how an outcome is described.
  - Personal experience plays a role as well (e.g. knowing a victim) or having had no relation whatsoever with a possible risk (e.g. flooding).
  - The reluctance to accept a risk, such as a woman's anticipatory anxiety about breast cancer, prevents them from examining themselves.

- Evolutionary preparedness causing contradictory reactions:
  - People are likely to react with hardly any fear to certain dangerous stimuli that evolution has not prepared them for, such as guns, hamburgers, automobiles, smoking and unsafe sex, even when they recognize the threat at a cognitive level.
  - Types of stimuli that people are evolutionary prepared to fear, such as spiders, snakes and heights, evoke a visceral response even when, at a cognitive level, they can recognize them to be harmless.
- Feedback process: can cause a panic attack. For example, the idea that fearful thoughts (induced by a focus on internal bodily sensations) produce bodily sensations intensifies fear, which increases physiological reactions, and so on. At a societal level, this can happen when sudden explosions of public concern about a problem occur, unconnected with the underlying risk.
- 'Heart before head': if danger approaches, the emotional system always wins when the two move in opposite directions.

In general, people evaluate risky activities according to much more than only the seriousness of possible damage (such as death), but a whole range of aspects (or attributes) are taken into account. Death per year is probably the simplest measure of risk. The disadvantage is that it cannot distinguish between earlier death of an older sick patient during exposure to smog, and the death of a young father with children in an accident. With lost years of a healthy life, non-fatal damage can be taken into account, but with disability-adjusted life years (DALY), for example (see section 5.3.4 in Chapter 5), sick people count less than healthy people, so this is also not an ideal measure (Hollander and Hanemaaijer, 2007).

For the health and comfort created by an indoor environment, extensive risk assessments have been made for certain air pollutants, varying from risks of death and certain illnesses to risks of discomfort, resulting in different types of 'allowable' levels. In section 6.3 in Chapter 6, several performance indicators for the indoor environment and/or individual indoor environmental parameters have been presented. What is missing in these indicators or risk measures is the individual 'emotions' part. Attempts are

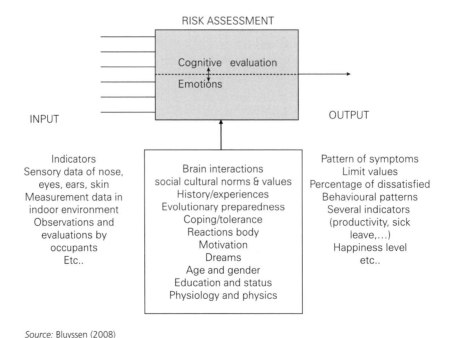

Source: Bluyssen (2008)

Figure 9.8 *Evaluation of risk assessment input parameters and output indicators*

always made, in a more or less governmental way, to somehow normalize behaviour. Besides the question of whether the correct risk measures are applied in this normalization, this (i.e. emotional attributes) can partly explain the deviations encountered in practice between what the 'norm' says the end user wants and what the end user wishes for.

The attributes or factors influencing behaviour are a combination of emotional and cognitive factors, which differ per situation and per individual, and can have different scores that can change over time.

Considering the above, it can be concluded that one universal measure for risk is not realistic, which makes comparison of risks difficult. The choice of a measure always has to consider the seriousness and extent of the problem to be analysed, the probability of occurrence, the complexities and uncertainties involved, and last, but not least, the extent of societal interest. Even if from a technical point the risk is small, the social implication of risk can become enormous with no relation to the loss of health, ecology or goods (as happened with severe acute respiratory syndrome, or SARS).

So, each risk assessment has to be treated uniquely. In practice, one can collect information on emotional reactions to risks, in addition to such traditional measures as probabilities and outcome values, Ideally, such measures would include physiological measures as well as self-reports and gender- and age-related changes in risk.

For an assessment of the indoor environment, the values or measures given to that indoor environment (OUTPUT) as a result of the different exposures (INPUT) are shown in Figure 9.8.

10

Summary and Conclusions

Over the past 100 years, much effort has been put into managing the indoor environment with the goal of creating healthy and comfortable conditions for the people living, working and recreating in it. Nevertheless, enough health problems and comfort complaints still occur to justify more research and development.

In this book the indoor environment is described by so-called environmental factors or (external) stressors, without downgrading the dimensions and aesthetics of shapes and spaces: indoor air quality, thermal comfort, acoustical quality and visual or lighting quality. Besides the systems of the human body (the nervous system, the immune system and the endocrine system), the human senses considered are the human skin, eyes, nose, ears and the respiratory tract. In Part I of this book some facts on this indoor environment are presented, as well as some insights on how the human body might respond to that indoor environment.

Environmental stimuli produced/caused by the environmental parameters (external stress factors) provide the input for our bodily sensations. Via the three major regulation and control systems of the human body (nervous system, immune system and endocrine system), both mental (e.g. memories, anxiety, etc.) and physical effects (escape, fight, protect, symptoms, etc.) are created. Depending upon internal stress factors such as degradation of performance of senses and immune system with age, as well as genetic aspects (such as colour blindness) and psychosocial aspects (context, history), our bodily responses, consciously or unconsciously, can differ in quality, quantity and over time.

In general, these responses can be divided into health-related or comfort-related evaluations, responses, complaints and symptoms. It is difficult to separate the two, but the following division can generally be made:

- *For comfort: those responses that are stress induced by external stress factors and that are 'handled' by the cooperation between the nervous system and the endocrine system, but which can be influenced by the status of the immune system,* such as:
  - direct noticeable comfort-related complaints by the human senses (e.g. smell, noise, heat, cold, draught, etc.);
  - systemic effects such as tiredness, poor concentration, etc.;
  - psychological effects such as not being in control, depression, anxiety, etc.
- *For health: those responses that are induced by external noxious effects and are 'handled' by the cooperation between the immune system and the endocrine system, although the handling can be influenced by the nervous system,* such as:
  - irritation, allergic and hyper-reactive effects: irritation of the mucous membranes of the skin and respiratory tract, asthma, rashes on skin caused by allergic reactions to certain pollutants, sunburn, hearing loss, eye damage caused by too bright light, etc.;
  - infectious diseases such as Legionnaires' disease;
  - toxic chronic effects: slowly increasing or appearing (such as cancer).

Over the years, control of indoor environmental factors has focused on the prevention or cure of the different related observed physical effects in a largely isolated way, trying to find solutions for thermal comfort, lighting quality, sound quality and air quality separately, with models that strictly consider only physical conditions.

In Part II of this book, the history of the definition of health and comfort in the indoor environment is sketched for indoor environmental parameters: thermal comfort, acoustical quality, and visual or lighting quality. Much time was spent on identifying objective relations between indoor environmental parameters and the human physical reactions (dose–response) in a laboratory environment, resulting in mostly quantitative environmental indicators, expressed in (assumed) acceptable numbers or ranges. Many control strategies for these parameters have been identified in order to minimize or prevent possible diseases and disorders of the human body and its components linked to these parameters (mainly focused on one specific parameter at the time). Only in the last decades of the 20th century was an attempt made through epidemiological studies to approach the indoor environment in a holistic way. The scientific approach towards evaluating and creating a healthy and comfortable indoor environment developed from a component-related to a bottom-up holistic approach (by trying to simply add the different components). Performance concepts and indicators, including not only environmental parameters, but also possible linked variables such as characteristics of building, emerged; methods of investigating indoor environmental quality from different perspectives were introduced. Nevertheless, control strategies were still focused on a component basis.

Even though these control strategies are currently being applied, complaints and symptoms related to the indoor environment still occur. How the human body and its systems receive, perceive and respond to certain environmental conditions seems a very important question to answer. Part III shows that not every person receives, perceives and responds in the same way due to physical, physiological and psychological differences, but also due to differences in history, context and situation. Next to the human drivers and the influence of time on environmental parameters, external drivers such as economics and regulatory issues, as well as the interactions occurring between aspects, need to be considered. Current performance indicators or risk measures for health and comfort, trying to normalize behaviour by capturing a number of these attributes, generally miss the individual 'emotions' and the time parameter (dynamic versus static). This can at least partly explain the deviations encountered, in practice, between what the 'norm' says the end user wants and what the end user 'wishes' for.

Part II presents climate change as an important driver of health and comfort in the indoor environment, as well as several social, economic and regulatory drivers. Innovative ways of managing the indoor environment with respect to climate change effects and changing end-user needs (which are not the same as 100 years ago) have an effect on the design of buildings, materials used, services and control systems. The enclosure of the building will (more than ever) need to integrate the different functions of a building, complying with climate change imperatives (e.g. saving energy), and providing comfort and health for the end users in the form of:

- control of entering daylight (for lighting quality as well as thermal comfort and energy purposes),
- clean outdoor air (most likely in combination with air-conditioning systems that are capable of cleaning and cooling the air as well);
- being noise and vibration free (controllable noise-reducing openings in the façade and construction details that can handle vibrations from the inside and outside); and
- having as low primary and secondary emissions as possible (depending upon the choice of materials as well as conditions of the indoor and outdoor environment).

However, saving energy, together with creating a healthy and comfortable indoor environment, is more than just providing an efficient and sustainable building envelope. The control of indoor environment parameters over time is very important as well. This control should be focused on anticipating the conscious and unconscious needs of different end users in relation to different activities. This anticipation can vary from complete central control to individual manual control of an individual's personal space (e.g. performance on demand, adaptability and flexibility, but within certain boundaries of the demands and wishes of the end user in question). Sensors and signals are key issues in anticipating human demands and behaviour. Sensors are no more than systems that measure signals from the environment and/or from individual people. However, if the determinants or indicators of a certain wish or demand are unknown, it will be difficult to pinpoint the sensor required for providing control. Without knowledge of cause and effect, an indicator will just provide a wild guess.

Besides these end users' requirements, the translation of these requirements into the technical and design requirements of a building appears to be another reason for the problems and complaints observed. In order to translate the end users' requirements in the appropriate way, communication between the stakeholders involved is important. In the traditional design and construction process, the stakeholders often use over-the-bench methodology, leading to misunderstandings and poor translation. Next to this communication process, understanding the needs and requirements of the end users in an integral way, before thinking about individual solutions, is crucial (Figure 10.1).

Part III argues that, in order to establish end users' wishes and demands (requirements and needs), as well as the communication process required to facilitate the design, construction, maintenance and occupation of an indoor environment, an interactive top–down approach is required. This 'top–down' approach may be complementary to the traditional bottom–up approach used to determine end users' needs. The system engineering management approach used in other industries could be a solution. For this top–down approach to function properly, it is important to understand:

- the end users' wishes and needs, both in the present and in the future;
- the context (social, economical, political-legal and technological), whether at the global or local level, and associated attributes;
- the stakeholders responsible and involved in the realization of the indoor environment, and the required communication processes;
- the people–indoor environment–building–outdoor environment interactions and all their interfaces.

Thus, new 'drivers', new insights and changing end-user requirements, as well as the observed discrepancy between current standards and end-users' needs, require a different approach towards managing health and comfort in the indoor environment. It is clear that, somehow, end users need to be involved in the design process to make their wishes and demands more clear. It is also evident that these wishes and demands are not always clear to the end users themselves.

In order to determine these end-user requirements for the indoor environment, a risk assessment procedure is needed in which the traditional bottom–up approach is used next to the top–down approach. Statistical models with parameters and anticipated quantitative relations already exist. Together with translation frameworks, such as the performance framework developed in PeBBu and the earlier established patterns of symptoms and complaints

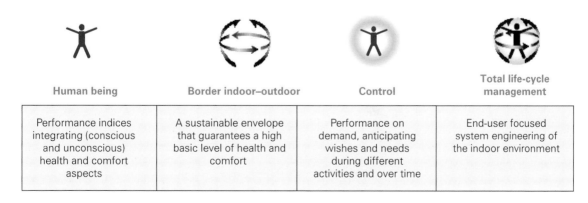

Human being	Border indoor–outdoor	Control	Total life-cycle management
Performance indices integrating (conscious and unconscious) health and comfort aspects	A sustainable envelope that guarantees a high basic level of health and comfort	Performance on demand, anticipating wishes and needs during different activities and over time	End-user focused system engineering of the indoor environment

Figure 10.1 *Framework for health and comfort*

related to certain indoor environmental characteristics, indications or certain indices can be established. However, it should always be realized that these established relations and indices are context related and should not be used to generalize the behaviour or health symptoms of large groups of people, unless policy-makers are attempting, for example, to make a decision on certain issues (e.g. in the case of a smoking ban in all public places) or unless a clear link between cause and effect has been established.

This does not mean that all methods, control strategies and models found so far have no meaning. On the contrary, we are just beginning. As Cain (2002) informed us, well over 100,000 studies have been published by PubMed (US National Library of Medicine) for the common diseases of breast cancer and diabetes since the mid-1960s. For rare diseases, fewer than 10,000 studies have been conducted, while for human comfort, only a few hundred. We still have lots of work to do.

Annex A
TOBUS

A.1 Questionnaire IEQ TOBUS

INSTRUCTIONS FOR COMPLETING THE QUESTIONNAIRE

Please attempt to answer all the questions. It is important that you record your own views, without talking to colleagues. Do not take too much time over your answers. Just give your initial response.

Questions 1–8

You can fill in completely.
We ask for your office number to have information from where in the building the questionnaires are coming in order to select offices to visit and to follow up any important comments.

Question 9–23

Some of these questions comprise two parts. In the first part you can give only one answer (tick the box), while in the second part more answers are possible (circle the possibilities). Additional information for the possibility 'other' can be given on the last page.

For example:
Part 1: If you are bothered how often do you feel annoyed by draught? (one answer possible)
    ☐ often   ☐ regularly
    ☐ sometimes   ☐ never

Part 2: From/where? (more than one answer possible)
1. Windows/ 2. stairways and landings/ 3. office door/ 4. external wall 5. ventilation system/ 6. heating system/ 7. ceiling/ 8. other (**circle possibilities**)

Questions 24–34

One answer per question (tick one box).

For example:
    If you are at the office for more than 4 hours, do you experience any of the following symptoms?
        ☐ often   ☐ regularly
        ☐ sometimes   ☐ never

Question 35–38

These questions comprise two parts. In the first part you can give only one answer (tick the box), while in the second part more answers are possible (you circle the possibilities). Additional information for the possibility 'other' you can give on the last page.

For example:
Part 1: How do you find the electrical services at your office and in the building?
        ☐ acceptable   ☐ not acceptable
Part 2: Reason: too few electrical sockets/bad lay out of electrical sockets/other (circle possibilities)

Question 39–41 and 43–46

One answer per question.

Question 42:

More answers are possible (you circle the possibilities). Additional information for the possibility 'other' you can give on the last page.

Question 47:

    Space for additional information (please add question number), comments and remarks.

During the completion of the questionnaire, you can take into account all your experiences of the last years.

QUESTIONNAIRE FOR OCCUPANTS

Survey number:

General information

1. Age: ......　　　　2. Sex: □ Male　□ Female　　　3. Office no: ......
　　　　　　　　　　　　　　　　　　　　　　　　　　　　(floor/room number)

4. What is the biggest part of the work you do? Please tick a box
　□ Managing people or resources
　□ Using specialist skills (e.g. legal, medical, engineering, scientific)
　□ Doing clerical, secretarial or administrative work
　□ Other, please write in ....

5. How long have you been working in this room?　　　　.....years　.... months
6. How many days per week do you normally spend in the building?　　.....days
7. How many hours per day do you normally work at your desk?　.....hours
8. How many hours per day do you normally operate a PC at work?　.... hours

---

How often do you feel annoyed by the following? (tick one box)

	often	regularly	sometimes	never
9.　Dry and/or stuffy air	□	□	□	□
10.　Stuffy/bad smell	□	□	□	□

From/where:　1. Outside/ 2. inside/ 3. stairways and landings/ 4. toilets/
5. heating system/ 6. Ventilation system/ 7. other (**circle possibilities**)

	often	regularly	sometimes	never
11.　Static electricity	□	□	□	□
12.　Draught	□	□	□	□

From/where:　1. Windows/ 2. stairways and landings/ 3. office door/ 4. external wall/
5. ventilation system/ 6. heating system/ 7. ceiling/ 8. other (**circle possibilities**)

	often	regularly	sometimes	never
13.　Too cold	□	□	□	□

When:　1. Winter/ 2. spring/ 3. summer/ 4. autumn (**circle possibilities**)

14.　Too warm	□	□	□	□

When:　1. Winter/ 2. spring/ 3. summer/ 4. autumn (**circle possibilities**)

	often	regularly	sometimes	never
15.　Temperature changes during a working day	□	□	□	□
16.　Cold feet	□	□	□	□
17.　Warm surface	□	□	□	□

Where:　1. Ceiling/ 2. outer wall/ 3. windows/ 4. floor (warm feet)/
5. other (**circle possibilities**)

18.　Too much or too strong light	□	□	□	□

Why:　1. too much artificial light/ 2. too much daylight/ 3. other (**circle possibilities**)

19.　Insufficient light	□	□	□	□

Why:　1. too little artificial light/ 2. bad quality of lighting system/
3. too little daylight/ 4. other　(**circle possibilities**)

20.　Reflections or glare	□	□	□	□

Caused by:　1. windows/ 2. lighting system/ 3. other (**circle possibilities**)

21. Unacceptable view   ☐   ☐   ☐   ☐
22. Feeling closed in   ☐   ☐   ☐   ☐
23. Noise   ☐   ☐   ☐   ☐

From: 1. Outside/ 2. adjacent rooms/ 3. offices below/ 4. offices above/ 5. toilets/ 6. stairways and landings/ 7. heating system/ 8. ventilation system/ 9. lifts/ 10. escalators/ 11. mail elevators/ 12. automatic distribution system/ 13. cleaning system/ 14. colleagues in office/ 15. equipment in office/ 16. machinery in buildings/ 17. other (**circle possibilities**)

How much control do you feel you have over the following? (tick one box)

	not enough	little	reasonable	enough
24. Temperature	☐	☐	☐	☐
25. Ventilation	☐	☐	☐	☐
26. Light	☐	☐	☐	☐

If you are at the office for more than 4 hours, do you experience any of the following symptoms? (tick one box)

	often	regularly	sometimes	never
27. Dry/watering eyes	☐	☐	☐	☐
28. Blocked/runny nose	☐	☐	☐	☐
29. Dry/irritated throat	☐	☐	☐	☐
30. Chest tightness	☐	☐	☐	☐
31. Dry/irritated skin	☐	☐	☐	☐
32. Headaches	☐	☐	☐	☐
33. Lethargy/tiredness	☐	☐	☐	☐
34. Pain in neck, shoulders or back	☐	☐	☐	☐

How do you rate the following services at your office and in the building? (tick one box)

	Acceptable	Not acceptable
35. Electrical services (hardware)	☐	☐

Reason: 1. too few electrical sockets/ 2. bad lay out of electrical sockets/ 3. other (**circle possibilities**)

	Acceptable	Not acceptable
36. Telephone services (hardware)	☐	☐

Reason: 1. too few telephone sockets/2. bad lay out of telephone sockets/ 3. other (**circle possibilities**)

	Acceptable	Not acceptable
37. Computer services	☐	☐

Reason: 1. network goes down often/ 2. slow network connection/ 3. no network available/ 4. not enough network sockets/ 5. other (**circle possibilities**)

	Acceptable	Not acceptable
38. Water services	☐	☐

Reason: 1. taps usually leak/ 2. taps are difficult to turn off/ 3. water-leaks from water-closet/ 4. no hot water in restrooms/ 5. takes too long to have hot water/ 6. takes too long to have cold water/ 7. other (**circle possibilities**)

About your room

39. How many other people normally share the room
    where you work?   ☐☐ people

40. Do you smoke while in the office?   ☐ yes   ☐ no

41. Do other people smoke in your immediate working
    environment at work?   ☐ yes   ☐ no

42. Which of the following equipment/items are present in your office room?
    (laser)printer/copier/humidifier/ioniser/plants/other (**circle possibilities**)

About yourself

43. Have you ever suffered from hay fever or other allergic reactions?   ☐ yes   ☐ no
44. Have you ever had asthmatic problems?   ☐ yes   ☐ no
45. Have you ever suffered from eczema?   ☐ yes   ☐ no

46. Do you mind us visiting your office?   ☐ yes   ☐ no

47. If you have comments or remarks you can put them here.

_____
_____
_____
_____
_____
_____
_____
_____
_____
_____
_____
_____
_____
_____
_____
_____
_____
_____
_____
_____

If questionnaires are collected at end of day:

Thank you very much for your time!!!
The questionnaires will be collected at end of the day.

If questionnaires have to be sent back by mail:

Thank you very much for your time!!!
Now you can send the questionnaire back in the enclosed envelope.
For questions, you can call: *telephone number.*

A.2 TOBUS checklist for building managers

1 Surroundings
In direct vicinity of building are present (more than one answer possible):
- ☐ high rise buildings
- ☐ parking
- ☐ industrial plant
- ☐ wastewater treatment
- ☐ cooling tower
- ☐ power plant
- ☐ other _____

2 Traffic
Building located at (more than one answer possible):
- ☐ motorway
- ☐ busy through road
- ☐ busy crossroad
- ☐ moderate busy road
- ☐ quiet road
- ☐ railroad
- ☐ airport
- ☐ other_____

3 Asbestos
a. Is asbestos used in the building?   ☐ yes
                    ☐ no   ☐ don't know
b. If yes, where is asbestos present?
- ☐ façade panelling
- ☐ partitioning walls
- ☐ resilient flooring (backing)
- ☐ ceiling panelling
- ☐ roof
- ☐ ducts
- ☐ insulation steel construction
- ☐ other _____

4 Recent works
Have there been works during the last year on:

Flooring	☐ yes	☐ no
Walls	☐ yes	☐ no
Ceiling	☐ yes	☐ no
Windows	☐ yes	☐ no
Heating system	☐ yes	☐ no
Ventilation system	☐ yes	☐ no

5 Leakage/flooding
a. Has there been major leakage or flooding in the last year?   ☐ yes   ☐ no
b. If yes, where:
- ☐ roof
- ☐ façade
- ☐ basement
- ☐ windows
- ☐ sanitary rooms
- ☐ pipes (HVAC, sprinkler)
- ☐ other _____

6 Ventilation
a. Ventilation rate of office rooms (please give air change per hour or outdoor air supply in $l/s.m^2$) Air change rate (average value for supply of outdoor air):
- ☐ less than 1 air changes per hour
- ☐ 1–2 air changes per hour
- ☐ 2–3 air changes per hour
- ☐ more than 3 air changes per hour

Outdoor air supply in $l/s^{-1}m^2$
- ☐ less than 0.75 $l/s^{-1}m^2$
- ☐ 0.75–1.5 $l/s^{-1}m^2$
- ☐ 1.5–3 $l/s^{-1}m^2$
- ☐ more than 3 $l/s^{-1}m^2$

b. Required outdoor flow rate per person:
- ☐ less than 8 l/s^{-1} per person
- ☐ 8–12 l/s^{-1} per person
- ☐ 12–16 l/s^{-1} per person
- ☐ more than 16 l/s^{-1} per person

7 Natural ventilation
Only applicable if grilles for natural ventilation are present. The question should be answered taking into account the majority of rooms in the building.
a. Can grilles be opened and closed by occupants?
                    ☐ yes   ☐ no
b. Distance from base of grille to floor?
    ☐ less than 1.8m   ☐ more than 1.8m

Only applicable if windows can be opened by occupants.
c. Can operable windows be fixed in different positions?   ☐ yes   ☐ no
d. Distance from base of window opening to floor?
    ☐ less than 1.8m   ☐ more than 1.8m

8 Mechanical ventilation
Only applicable in case of mechanical ventilation
a. Night ventilation (for cooling purposes)
                    ☐ yes   ☐ no
b. Filter type:
- ☐ bag
- ☐ cassette
- ☐ electrostatic
- ☐ other _____
c. Filter class
- ☐ G4 or less
- ☐ F5
- ☐ F6
- ☐ F7
- ☐ F8 or higher
d. Replacement of filters:
- ☐ twice a year or more
- ☐ once a year
- ☐ once every two years
- ☐ less than once every two years
- ☐ no regular period for replacement

e. Duct material
- ☐ steel   ☐ PVC
- ☐ fabric   ☐ asbestos cement
- ☐ other _____

f. Duct insulation
- ☐ none   ☐ external
- ☐ internal   ☐ both

9 *Maintenance of HVAC systems*

Type of maintenance:
- ☐ planned preventive   ☐ condition based
- ☐ on breakdown only

10 *Type of majority of office rooms*
- ☐ cellular   ☐ landscape
- ☐ other _____

11 *Density*

Average floor area per person in majority of office rooms:
- ☐ 8m^2 or less   ☐ 8–10m^2
- ☐ 10–12m^2 ☐ 12–16m^2
- ☐ 16m^2 or more

12 *Equipment*

a. number of VDUs per person (majority of workplaces):
- ☐ none   ☐ 1 VDU/person
- ☐ 1–2 VDUs/person   ☐ 2 VDUs/person or more

b. laser printers in office rooms
- ☐ yes   ☐ no

c. copiers in office rooms   ☐ yes   ☐ no

13 *Smoking policy*
- ☐ permitted in all rooms
- ☐ permitted in designated rooms
- ☐ permitted at own work place
- ☐ allowed in rooms if not shared with someone else
- ☐ not allowed
- ☐ other _____

14 *Activities in building other than office activities*
- ☐ Industrial
- ☐ Laboratory
- ☐ Garage
- ☐ Kitchen, canteen staff restaurant
- ☐ Apartments
- ☐ other _____

15 *Furniture*

a. Furniture is mainly made of:
- ☐ solid wood   ☐ veneered chip board
- ☐ metal
- ☐ other _____

b. Do chairs and desk comply with national regulations/guidelines with regard to ergonomics?
- ☐ yes   ☐ no

16 *Cleaning*

a. Vacuum cleaning of floor in offices:
- ☐ daily   ☐ twice a week
- ☐ once a week   ☐ less than once a week

b. Vacuum cleaning of floors in corridors, stairways and landings:
- ☐ daily   ☐ twice a week
- ☐ once a week   ☐ less than once a week

c. Cleaning of horizontal surfaces (desk, table, cupboards)
- ☐ daily   ☐ twice a week
- ☐ once a week   ☐ less than once a week

Only applicable in case of smooth floor in offices (resilient floor covering)

d. How often is floor waxed or polished?
- ☐ once a week   ☐ 1–3 times a month
- ☐ once a month   ☐ less than once a month

Only applicable in case of smooth floors in corridors, stairways and landings (resilient floor covering):

e. How often is floor waxed or polished?
- ☐ once a week
- ☐ 1–3 times a month
- ☐ once a month
- ☐ less than once a month

A.3 TOBUS checklist for auditors

Office rooms

1 Ceilings
Is thermal mass of structure accessible?

☐ yes ☐ no

(minimum of 10% of structure has to be free of covering material – sound absorption, suspended ceiling)

2 Air supply
Are there obstacles to air diffusion in the office rooms?

☐ yes ☐ no

3 Moulds
a. Is there visible mould growth in the office
    rooms? ☐ yes ☐ no
b. Where: ☐ walls ☐ ceiling ☐ floor
c. Are there damp spots on walls/ceiling/floor?

☐ yes ☐ no

4 Cleanliness
Impression of cleanliness of rooms?

☐ good ☐ moderate ☐ poor

5 Condensation
Are there (traces of) condensation on windows (e.g. mould growth at base of glass area)?

☐ yes ☐ no

6 Odours
a. Is there a mould odour in the office rooms?

☐ yes ☐ no

b. Is there another kind of odour in the office rooms?

☐ yes ☐ no

c. If yes, how would you describe that?

☐ carpet ☐ human odour
☐ food ☐ smoke

7 Items in office rooms?
Which items are present in most office rooms?

☐ humidifier ☐ ioniser
☐ plants ☐ printer
☐ copier

HVAC Installations

8 Traces of leakage
Are there traces of water leakage in the central HVAC installation room?

☐ yes ☐ no

9 Humidifier
Does the humidifier have traces of mould?

☐ yes ☐ no

10 Filters
a. How, in your opinion, do the filters look?

☐ dirty ☐ clean

b. Pressure difference exceeding limit value?

☐ yes ☐ no

Annex B
Sensory Evaluation by the Human Nose

B.1 General techniques and attributes

The attributes that can be measured though sensory evaluation by the nose are the same as for all other sensory modalities:

- detection (the limit value for absolute detection);
- intensity (odour intensity, sensory irritation intensity);
- quality (value judgement, such as hedonic tone or acceptability).

In a discrimination evaluation, a subject is asked to compare an air sample with another and express this comparison in 'greater, smaller or equal than', depending upon the attribute evaluated (pleasantness, strength, etc.). For this type of evaluation several techniques are available.

Detection

The classical threshold theory assumes the existence of a momentary absolute sensory threshold. However, in real life, there is no fixed odour or irritation threshold of absolute detection for a particular individual or a particular pollutant, but rather a gradual transition from total absence to definitely confirmed sensory detection. Therefore, in the theory of signal detectability (Engen, 1972), the same repeated signal is assumed to have a defined distribution; thus, each sensory evaluation by a subject is executed on a probability basis. Berglund and Lindvall (1979) have used this signal detection approach to test a few single compounds and building investigations.

In the classical methods, the detection threshold level is defined as the level at which 50 per cent of a given population will detect the odour. One of these methods is the threshold method that is standardized in many countries for the evaluation of outdoor air (CEN, 1994). In this threshold method an air sample is diluted stepwise (by a factor of 2 for each step) with clean (odour-free) air to determine the dilution at which 50 per cent of a panel of eight people can no longer distinguish the diluted air from odour-free air. This number of dilutions, expressed in odour units per cubic metre of air at 20°C (o.u./m^3), is the numerical value for the odour concentration of the original air sample.

Some measurements using the classical threshold level method have been made on indoor air, ventilation systems and building materials (Berglund and Lindvall, 1979; Bluyssen and Walpot, 1993). The absolute detection threshold varies widely with chemical substances, as is shown by the large spread in literature-reported odour thresholds for single compounds (Devos et al, 1990). This is caused, in part, by the procedure used, purity of chemical substance, equipment applied and sample of subjects.

Recognition threshold values (concentration at which a certain chemical is recognized) are usually measured in the same way as detection levels. Both use either the method of limits or the method of constant stimuli (ECA, 1999). In the method of limits, the chemical substance is presented in alternating ascending and descending series, starting at different points to avoid having the subject fall into a routine. The subject is asked to report whether the sample can be detected or not. The method of constant stimulus is based on the assumption that the momentary individual threshold value varies from time to time and that this variation has a normal distribution. The chemical substance is usually presented in a random selection of concentrations.

For both methods, no training is required, although subjects may be selected on their sensitivity to the chemical substances tested.

Intensity

The intensity of odours or irritants can be obtained by several methods: equal-intensity matching, magnitude estimation or direct-scaling methods (ECA, 1999). The latter is the most common in indoor air quality studies and uses, for example, visual semantic scales (e.g. no odour, weak odour, moderate odour, strong odour, very strong odour and overpowering odour). With equal intensity matching, the subject matches the intensity of, for example, two different odorants.

Magnitude estimation techniques generate magnitude estimates of intensity resulting from direct numerical estimations by subjects. The perceived intensity of an odour is established by rating the intensity of that odour on a magnitude scale, using reference odours or not. The technique from the American Society of Testing and Measurement (ASTM, 1981), for example, uses samples of 1-butanol vapour presented at varying concentrations, and the master scale unit method (Berglund and Lindvall, 1979) uses five concentrations of pyridine that are jointly measured with indoor air samples.

The assessment of decipol levels using trained panels of individuals of the air in office buildings in the European Audit project (Bluyssen et al, 1996) is an example of magnitude estimation with memory references. The same method with references (using numerical values) nearby to compare is an example of magnitude estimation with several references. This method that was applied in several European projects, such as the European Audit (Bluyssen et al, 1996), Database (Oliveira Fernandes and Clausen, 1997), MATHIS (Oliveira Fernandes, 2001) and AIRLESS (Bluyssen et al, 2001a) projects.

Quality

A value judgement of indoor air quality can be given in several ways. One can make a classification (e.g. yes/no), such as is used by the American Society of Heating, Refrigerating and Air Conditioning Engineers (ASHRAE, 2004b) (is the air acceptable or not?), resulting in a percentage of dissatisfied, or one can use a list of descriptors to describe a chemical substance. The latter is mainly used in the food and perfume industry from which many classification systems of odours have been developed.

For the evaluation of the acceptability of an air sample (percentage of dissatisfied persons), several methods have been applied. Besides the yes/no classification ('acceptable' or 'not acceptable'), the continuous acceptability scale (Gunnarsen and Fanger, 1992) is used. The middle of the scale is indicated as the transition between just acceptable and just not acceptable. With both methods, however, large panels (depending upon the statistical relevance required) of untrained individuals are required.

Two units – olf and decipol – were introduced to quantify sensory source emissions and perceived air quality (Fanger, 1988). Emission rates are measured in olf, where 1 olf is defined as the emission rate causing the same level of dissatisfaction as bio-effluents from one seated person at any airflow. Concentration or 'perceived air quality' is measured in decipol. One decipol is defined as the concentration of pollution causing the same level of dissatisfaction as emissions from a standard person diluted by a clean airflow of 10l/s. In this context, 'perceived air quality' signifies dissatisfaction with or acceptability of indoor air quality.

With these units the so-called decipol method was developed. The decipol method comprises a panel of ten or more individuals who are trained to evaluate the perceived air quality in decipol or an untrained panel of at least 50 people (Gunnarsen and Bluyssen, 1994). A method to train a panel to evaluate perceived air quality in decipol has been developed (Bluyssen, 1990; Bluyssen, 1991). Research indicates, however, that this method does not evaluate the acceptability, but the intensity, of the air sample (Bluyssen and Cornelissen, 1998).

Most interesting is that in a study performed by Ramakrishnan et al (1999) of a survey of 320 subjects in six indoor environments in Western Australia, a strong correlation was found between perceived air pollution and occupants' perception of the indoor spaces studies. The authors suggested that office occupants can be satisfactorily used for olfactory assessment of their working environments instead of or besides independent panels.

B.2 Trained panel method

Figure B.1 *Trained panel member evaluating the quality of air in the room*

In the context of the European Framework for Research and Technology Development (RTD), some projects have been launched since 1991, aimed at identifying the main causes of indoor air pollution and defining methodologies, such as the European Audit project (Bluyssen et al, 1996a), the Database project (Oliveira Fernandes and Clausen, 1997), MATHIS (Oliveira Fernandes, 2001) and AIRLESS (Bluyssen et al, 2003a). The use of human perception was central in these projects; therefore, the trained panel method was applied, using a reference gas, a scale, special equipment, and selection and training procedures (Bluyssen, 1998) (see below).

Reference gas and scale

When a panel has to be trained to evaluate perceived air pollution, a reference is required. A reference gas that is easy to measure and to produce i: 2-propanone (Bluyssen, 1998) The production of this reference source is based on passive evaporation and is introduced to the human nose by a constant airflow coming out of the so-called perceived air pollution

(PAP) meter (formerly named decipol-meter) (see the following sub-section).

The linear relation between 2-propanone concentration in air ($C_{2\text{-propanone}}$) and the PAP value is used to set a scale from 1 to 20 (Bluyssen, 1990):

$$\text{PAP value} = 0.84 + 0.22 \times C2\text{-propanone [ppm]} \quad [B.1]$$

Five different 2-propanone concentrations generated by five PAP meters can be used as the milestones for the training. These milestones have the following concentrations of 2-propanone in the top of the cone of the PAP meter:

- 0 ppm: assigned value 1 (no odour);
- 5 ppm: assigned value 2;
- 19 ppm: assigned value 5;
- 42 ppm: assigned value 10;
- 87 ppm: assigned value 20.

Equipment and reference gas production

The equipment required to select and train a panel of individuals comprises approximately 15 PAP meters, equipment for the production of 2-propanone (reference gas) and an air-conditioned room. The PAP meter consists of a 3 litre jar made of glass covered with a plastic cap, a fan and a diffuser (see Figure B.2). The cap has two holes; in one of them the fan is placed to suck the air through the jar. On top of the fan, a cone diffuses the exhausted air. The angle of the cone was chosen to be 8° to avoid mixing with room air. The diameter of the top of this cone was chosen to be 8cm, convenient to situate the nose in the middle. The cone is made of glass, supported by a stainless steel stand. The small fan was selected to produce at least 0.9 l/s, several times higher than the highest airflow during inhalation. The person therefore exclusively inhales air from the jar, undiluted by room air.

The 2-propanone gas can be generated in the PAP meter by means of passive evaporation. By placing one or more 30ml glass bottles filled with 10ml 2-propanone and making different holes in the caps of these bottles, different 2-propanone concentrations can be established. The steady-state concentration of 2-propanone in the top of the diffuser depends upon the level of the liquid in the small bottles (which is standardised at 10ml), the location of the small bottles in the jar of the PAP meter, the ambient temperature and the variation of this temperature (standardized at 22°C), and the size of the holes in the caps of the small bottles through which the 2-propanone diffuses.

The time it takes to reach a steady-state concentration depends upon several factors: the time and temperature of 2-propanone before it is put in the small bottles; the movement of bottles before they are placed in the jar; the transportation of the bottles; and the time before the over-caps are removed from the bottles. The following strategy is therefore recommended. Fill the bottles at least one hour before the test with 2-propanone (that has been conditioned at 22°C the day before); place the bottles at the correct position in the jar and leave the over-caps off. Activate the fan (6 volts required). After 30 minutes, a steady-state level with less than 3 per cent variation should be reached.

Additional recommendations are to keep the:

- environmental temperature as constant as possible (<0.5°C variation);
- small bottles at the same location in the jars;
- combination of jar, fan, cone and small bottles the same if one wants to create the same stead-state level again;
- fan voltage at 6 volts.

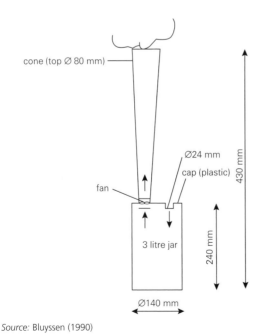

Source: Bluyssen (1990)

Figure B.2 *The perceived air pollution (PAP) meter*

If only one small bottle, placed on the left side of the two openings in the cap (see Figure B.2), is used to establish a certain concentration, the relation between diameter of hole and the 2-propanone concentration in the top of the cone is approximately:

$$C_{\text{2-propanone}} \text{ (ppm)} = 3 \times \text{diameter [mm]} \qquad \text{[B.2]}$$

where:

- diameter ≤ 8mm;
- standard deviation of 2-propanone = circa 3 per cent.

Combinations of several bottles in general give a higher concentration then the addition of the concentrations of the individual bottles would provide. Furthermore, if a combination of bottles or bottle-hole is placed in another PAP meter, concentrations can vary slightly. Once the milestones are calibrated, it is therefore important to keep the same PAP meters with the same bottles at the same location in the jar.

The unknown levels to be used for training should vary from 1 to 20, e.g. 1, 1.5, 2, 2.5, 3, 3.5, 4, 4.5, 5, 6, 7, 8, 9, 10, 11, 12, 13, 14, 15, 16, 17, 18, 19 and 20. Each level can be established by putting one to four bottles with a specific diameter hole, filled with 10ml 2-propanone in the PAP meter. The location of the bottles should be noted and always be at the same location. For different amounts of bottles, the recommended locations are shown in Figure B.3. The unknown concentrations used during the training should, if possible, be measured every day before the training starts to exactly determine the concentration that occurs with the PAP meter used that day. The concentration might vary, although the same bottles at the same locations are applied.

The position of the small bottles in the PAP meter is of great importance. To make it easier to reproduce the positions of small bottles, a scale glued at the bottom of the PAP meter is a possibility. Furthermore, a sign on the cone of the PAP meter and the 3 litre jar of the PAP meter is handy to keep them together.

The training of the panel should take place in a well-ventilated, temperature-controlled space with low-emitting and low-absorbing/adsorbing/desorbing materials.

A critical point in the use of the PAP meter, as an instrument to produce different 2-propanone levels to

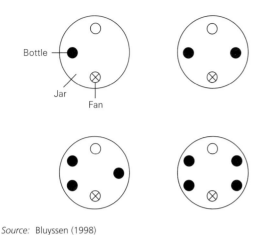

Source: Bluyssen (1998)

Figure B.3 *Recommended locations of small bottles in the PAP meter*

train a panel to evaluate perceived air quality, is the establishment of the low 2-propanone values (i.e. values below 1 on the scale). A zero level cannot be established by the PAP meter as such. The PAP meter without any 2-propanone results in a PAP level of circa 0.8. To prevent this deficiency from increasing, it is therefore of utmost importance that the training takes place in a room with a very low background level.

The space where the sensory panel is trained has to fulfil certain criteria. Preferred spaces are temperature controlled and feature 100 per cent outdoor ventilation, a filtration unit (e.g. active carbon), a Teflon layer on the walls, floor and ceiling, and displacement ventilation (from floor to ceiling) or local exhaust.

Acceptable spaces have an empty room (no smoking); the walls, floor and ceiling could be covered with a Teflon layer or cleaned with a non-smelling agent. It should also feature a mechanical air supply with filtered air, and mixing ventilation with a certain minimum ventilation rate. The minimum criterion for a space where the sensory panel is trained is a background level of 2-propanone expressed in a maximum allowable concentration. This maximum allowable concentration is 1 ppm.

Selection and training procedure

A panel of 12 to 15 subjects will be selected for the training. The subjects should be selected from a group of at least 50 applicants of ages ranging from 18 to approximately 35 years old. There is no restriction on distribution of gender or smoking habits.

Each of the applicants will participate in a selection test. The subjects will be asked before the selection test to refrain from smoking and drinking coffee for at least one hour before the test. In addition, they are asked not to use perfume, strong-smelling deodorants or make-up, and not to eat garlic or other spicy food the day before the test and on the day of the test.

In the selection test, the applicants will one by one be given a short introduction in how to use the milestones and in how to put their nose in the cone of the PAP meters. They are then asked to assess eight different concentrations of 2-propanone using the milestones as the reference. The applicants will be instructed to have at least two inhalations of unpolluted air in between each exposure to a 2-propanone concentration. The following question is then asked:

> How strong is the air that you perceive? Give a number on a scale from 1 to 20, but refer this number always to the numbers on the milestones 1, 2, 5, 10 and 20. One is equal to no smell (you perceive nothing), 20 is equal to extremely strong smell.

During the test, the applicants are allowed to go back and forth between the eight different unknown concentrations and the milestones as often as needed. Five of the concentrations are evenly distributed in the range of 1 to 10, while the last three concentrations are in the range of 10 to 20. For each person the sum of the numerical errors (differences between the voted and the correct values) in the eight assessments is calculated. The 12 to 15 subjects with the lowest sum of errors are then selected.

The 12 to 15 subjects will be trained for three to five days in smaller groups of three or four individuals. Each day they will receive approximately one hour of intensive training. In the first two days of the training the panel will be trained to assess the PAP of concentrations of 2-propanone unknown to them by making comparisons with the milestones. On the third to fifth day, training will comprise 2-propanone concentrations and other sources of pollution.

Before the training starts, and if necessary this will also be stressed during the training, the panel members will be asked again to refrain from smoking and drinking coffee for at least one hour before the test. In addition, they are asked not to use perfume, strong-smelling deodorants or make-up, and not to eat garlic or other spicy food the day before the test and on the day of the test.

On the first day of training, the panel members will receive an instruction about the training procedure and the experiments. During the refreshment time (or waiting time in between), the panel members are placed in a well-ventilated room where they can talk together but are not allowed to converse about the experiments at all. The instruction they received during the selection will be repeated and it will be emphasized that they will always take two inhalations of unpolluted air before they are exposed to another source to prevent getting used to the smell.

The panel members will be instructed in how to use the milestones and the scale correctly. They will be taught how to rate the intensity of the test concentration based on a scale of 0 to 20 by making a comparison with the intensity of the milestones. The panel members are allowed to go back and forth between the milestones and the unknown concentration or source, but they will be instructed to have at least two inhalations of unpolluted air between each exposure to avoid adaptation. After the evaluation of each unknown concentration of 2-propanone, the panel members will be given the correct answer and the performance of the panel members will be discussed with the experiment leader. The panel members will write their vote on a form where it is possible to follow their performance during the training.

The panel members will be exposed to 6 to 12 2-propanone concentrations during each training session. From the second day of training the panel members will furthermore be trained to assess air polluted with samples of building materials or other sources. Since the pollutants have a different character than 2-propanone, it is of great importance that the panel members understand that they are evaluating the intensity by comparing the intensity of the milestones. For the assessments of air samples of other sources than 2-propanone, the perceptions cannot be compared to any expected result, but the assessments can be discussed with each panel member separately.

On the third day of training the panel members are exposed to a performance test (see the following sub-section). The panel members assess the concentrations as during the previous training except that no feedback is given on the assessment deviations. If the votes do not meet the requirements, the panel member does not qualify and should be trained for at least one more day before taking the exam once more. Another option is to exclude the panel member from the panel.

On each experimental day, the panel members will be retrained for approximately 15 to 20 minutes per group of three to four individuals. During this training the panel members will be exposed to two or three different concentrations of 2-propanone and two different materials, which they will receive feedback on.

In addition, on each experimental day, the panel members will be exposed to six different concentrations of 2-propanone corresponding to the values 1, 3, 7, 12, 16 and 19. The concentrations of 2-propanone will be measured just before the sensory assessments of each group of panel members. These exposures make it possible to compare different sensory panels and to calculate performance factors (see the following sub-section).

The panel members will be placed in a well-ventilated waiting room. During each round of assessments, the panel members will, one by one, assess the intensity of the PAP of the air sample (from a material in a PAP meter, in a walk-in climate chamber, air from a ventilation system, etc.) by making comparison to the intensity of the milestones. The panel members will be allowed to go back and forth between the milestones and the polluted air sample. The panel members will write down their assessment on a voting sheet, which they will hand over to the experimental leader before making the next assessment.

The time between each panel member's assessments should not be less than 3 minutes. An experienced panel member can assess an air sample within 30 to 45 seconds. With a panel of 12 subjects, the time between assessments for a panel member will be approximately 9 minutes, and for a group of four panel members, 3 minutes.

Performance

The training level can be determined by using the given votes compared to correct votes for the 2-propanone levels and by using the repeated votes and/or the standard deviation on the panel vote for the unknown sources.

Performance with 2-propanone. On each training day a panel evaluates a certain quantity of (for them) unknown 2-propanone levels. A linear regression of all given votes versus the correct votes for each panel member or the whole panel (the ideal relation – i.e. a perfectly trained panel member — is then voted = correct) can then be determined. On the basis of these lines, each individual panel member can be instructed on how to adjust his or her votes.

The difference between the correct and the voted level shows how the vote lies towards the line voted = correct. A panel member can have an almost perfect relation between the voted and the correct level, but still have large differences between the correct and the voted level. It is therefore important to take the relative difference between the correct and the voted level into consideration. This can be defined by the so-called performance index:

$$PF = (voted-correct) \times 100/correct \text{ [%]} \qquad [B.3]$$

where:

- PF = performance index (%);
- voted = voted level;
- correct = correct level.

In order to determine the training level per day, the mean of all performance indices of all given votes that day can be calculated, together with the standard deviation of the performance index. A panel member with a PF of 9 per cent with a standard deviation of 60 per cent performs worse than a panel member with a mean performance index of –20 per cent and a standard deviation of 10 per cent. The second panel member is more consistent in his or her votes than the first one.

Each day the panel members can be ranked according to their best performance by adding the square root of the quadratic performance index to the standard deviation. The best panel member is the one with the lowest result. Another way to determine the training level of a panel is to calculate the standard deviation of a single vote given to the unknown levels of 2-propanone. The mean standard deviation for all evaluated levels per day then presents a training level. This statement assumes, however, that the standard deviation is independent of the evaluated level.

Individual panel member exam. For the individual panel exam, each individual panel member must evaluate six 2-propanone levels with the values of 1, 3, 7, 12, 16 and 19 in a randomized order. The votes have to meet certain requirements. If the votes do not meet these requirements, the panel member does not qualify and should be trained at least one more day before he or she is allowed to take the exam once more. Another option is to exclude the panel member from the panel. The requirements for the individual exam are shown in Figure B.4. In this figure the individual performance factor is shown for each combination of voted and correct level (Bluyssen and Elkhuizen, 1994; Bluyssen, 1996).

Individual Performance Factor

For comparison between panel members of different panels, the individual performance with 2-propanone concentrations can be described by the individual performance factor (IPF). The IPF is defined as:

$$IPF = voted\ error/allowed\ error = (voted-correct)/(A \times correct + B) \qquad [B.4]$$

where:

- voted error = voted minus correct;
- allowed error = allowed difference between voted and correct;
- A = tangent of angle difference between lines;
- B = intersection with Y-axis;
- for PAP <5: A = –3/28 and B = +59/28;
- for PAP >= 5: A = +4/28 and B = +24/28.

Note that the values for A and B originate from experience with trained panels in the European Audit project and are related to perceived air quality evaluations in decipol.

For this performance method the ideal vote (voted = correct) as index = 0 is taken. An allowed maximum and minimum error (both level dependent) are also defined as index +1 and –1. With this approach the index should theoretically be independent of the chosen level (if the error limits are chosen correctly) and result in information about the voted error related to the allowed error (0 = perfect; < |1| = allowed; > |1| = bad). The mean value of the IPF and the standard

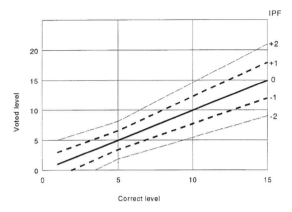

Note: For the individual exam the following counts — votes in the area between the fat line and the fat dashed line — are accepted. One in four votes is accepted in the area between the fat dashed line *and the thin dashed line.*

Source: Bluyssen (1998)

Figure B.4 *Required precision of an individual panel member vote when assessing the perceived air quality of 2-propanone concentrations*

deviation of the IPF give an indication of the quality of the panel member related to 2-propanone concentrations. If the allowed errors change, the coefficients A and B in the formula also change.

Panel performance factor (PPF). The same approach is possible for the whole panel. The mean IPF value of the performance for the whole panel is called the panel performance factor (PPF). The mean value of the PPF and the standard deviation give an indication of the quality of the whole panel related to 2-propanone concentrations.

Performance with other sources. The performance of the whole panel for other sources than 2-propanone can be shown by the standard error of the mean votes given to the perceived air quality caused by other sources than 2-propanone, and by the reproducibility for replicas (standard deviation of the replicas).

Several judgements of the same pollution source provide information on the reproducibility of a panel. The standard deviation around the mean of the two or more replicas of a source divided by the mean vote of that source determines the reproducibility.

FORM FOR SELECTION

You are kindly requested to fill this in

Date: ...../..../....
Name: ....
Address :   ....
Zip code: ....
City: ....
Phone: ....
Sex: man/woman
Age: ....
Smoker: yes/no

Personal number: [*number given by experimental leader to applicant*]

SELECTION TEST

How strong is the air that you perceive? Provide a number on a scale from 1 to 20, but always refer this number to the numbers on the milestones 1, 2, 5, 10 and 20. One is equal to no smell (you perceive nothing), 20 is equal to extremely strong smell.

Sample	Value
1	
2	
3	
4	
5	
6	
7	
8	

VOTING SHEET FOR EXPERIMENTS

Personal number	
Date	
Time	
Sample number	
Vote	

How strong is the air that you perceive? Provide a number on a scale from 1 to 20, but always refer this number to the numbers on the milestones 1, 2, 5, 10 and 20. One is equal to no smell (you perceive nothing), 20 is equal to extremely strong smell.

FORM FOLLOWING THE PERFORMANCE DURING THE TRAINING

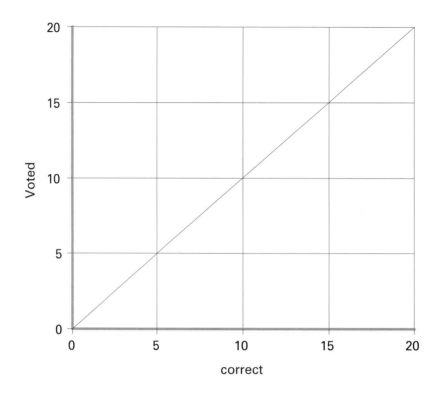

Sample	1	2	3	4	5	6	7	8
Voted								
Correct								

Sample	9	10	11	12	13	14	15	16
Voted								
Correct								

Personal number:-   Date:-

Annex C
Current Standards and Regulations

C.1 Thermal comfort

While some existing standards specify only one level of comfort, such as ASHRAE 55 (ASHRAE, 2004a), others, such as ISO EN 7730 (ISO, 2005), CR 1752 (CEN, 1998) and EN15251 (CEN, 2005), recommend three categories, as shown in Table C.1. Each category prescribes a maximum predicted percentage of dissatisfied (PPD) for the body as a whole and for each of the four types of local discomfort. The three categories in Table C.1 apply to spaces where people are exposed to the same thermal environment.

For a given conditioned space there exists an optimum operative temperature corresponding to PMV = 0, depending upon the activity and the clothing of the occupants. The number of dissatisfied people in Table C.2 is not additive. Some of the same people experiencing general thermal comfort (PMV–PPD) may be the same as the people experiencing local thermal discomfort. Table C.2 provides examples of recommended operative temperatures in some typical spaces.

For local discomfort parameters, ISO 7730 (ISO, 2005), ASHRAE 55 (ASHRAE, 2004a) and EN15251 (EN, 2005) give similar recommendations (see Tables C.3 to C.5).

For adaptive comfort (mainly in naturally ventilated buildings), ASHRAE (2004a) recommends the ranges found in Figure C.1 and CEN (2005) recommends the ranges found in Figure C.2, in which a running weekly mean outdoor temperature is used instead of a monthly average.

Table C.1 *Three categories of thermal comfort*

Category	Thermal state of the body as a whole			Local discomfort Percentage of dissatisfied due to:		
	Predicted percentage of dissatisfied (PPD) (%)	Predicted mean vote (PMV)	Draught (DR) (%)	Vertical air temperature difference (%)	Warm or cool floor (%)	Radiant asymmetry (%)
A	<6	$-0.2<PMV<+0.2$	<15	<3	<10	<5
B	<10	$-0.5<PMV<+0.5$	<20	<5	<10	<5
C	<15	$-0.7<PMV<+0.7$	<25	<10	<15	<10

Source: CEN (2005)

Table C.2 *Example criteria for operative temperature and mean air velocity for typical spaces: Relative humidity is assumed to be 60% for summer (cooling season) and 40% for winter (heating season)*

Type of Building/ space	Clothing		Activity	Category	Operative temperature		Mean air velocity	
	Cooling season (summer) clo	Heating season (winter) clo	met		Cooling season (summer) °C	Heating season (winter) °C	Cooling season (summer) ms⁻¹	Heating season (winter) ms⁻¹
Office	0.5	1.0	1.2	A	24.5 ± 0.5	22.0 ± 1.0	0.18	0.15
				B	24.5 ± 1.5	22.0 ± 2.0	0.22	0.18
				C	24.5 ± 2.5	22.0 ± 3.0	0.25	0.21
Cafeteria/ restaurant	0.5	1.0	1.4	A	23.5 ± 1.0	20.0 ± 1.0	0.16	0.13
				B	23.5 ± 2.0	20.0 ± 2.5	0.20	0.16
				C	23.5 ± 2.5	20.0 ± 3.5	0.24	0.19
Department store	0.5	1.0	1.6	A	23.0 ± 1.0	19.0 ± 1.5	0.16	0.13
				B	23.0 ± 2.0	19.0 ± 3.0	0.20	0.15
				C	23.0 ± 3.0	19.0 ± 4.0	0.23	0.18

Source: CEN (2005)

Table C.3 *Vertical air temperature difference between head and ankles (1.1m and 0.1m above the floor) for the three categories of the thermal environment*

Category	Vertical air temperature difference (°C)
A	<2
B	<3
C	<4

Source: ASHRAE (2004a), CEN (2005), ISO (2005)

Table C.4 *Range of floor temperature for the three categories of the thermal environment*

Category	Range of surface temperature of the floor (°C)
A	19–29
B	19–29
C	17–31

Source: ASHRAE (2004a), CEN (2005), ISO (2005)

Table C.5 *Radiant temperature asymmetry for the three categories of the thermal environment – valid for low ceiling spaces*

Category	Radiant temperature asymmetry (°C)			
	Warm ceiling	Cool wall	Cool ceiling	Warm wall
A	< 5	< 10	< 14	< 23
B	< 5	< 10	< 14	< 23
C	< 7	< 13	< 18	< 35

Source: ASHRAE (2004a), CEN (2005), ISO (2005)

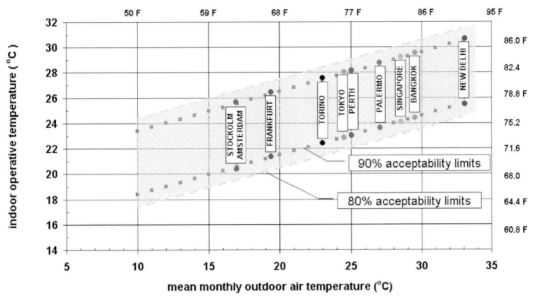

Source: ASHRAE (2004a); B. Oleson, Technical University of Denmark

Figure C.1 *Acceptable operative temperature ranges for naturally conditioned spaces according to ASHRAE 55-2004: Range is shown for different climatic areas*

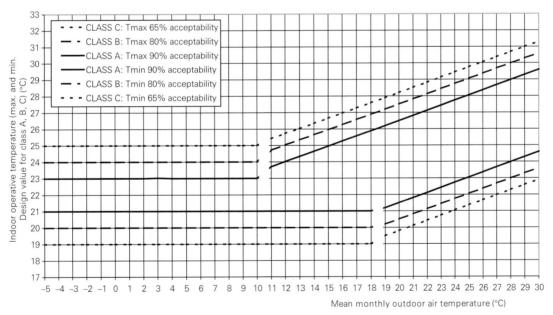

Notes: The formulae of the lines in Figure C.2 (right part) are as follows:

Class A: upper limit: $T_{i\ max} = 17.8 + 2.5 + (0.31\ T_o)$ [C1a]

     lower limit: $T_{i\ min} = 17.8 - 2.5 + (0.31\ T_o)$ [C1b]

Class B: upper limit: $T_{i\ max} = 17.8 + 3.5 + (0.31\ T_o)$ [C1c]

     lower limit: $T_{i\ min} = 17.8 - 3.5 + (0.31\ T_o)$ [C1d]

Class C: upper limit: $T_{i\ max} = 17.8 + 4.2 + (0.31\ T_o)$ [C1e]

     lower limit: $T_{i\ min} = 17.8 - 4.2 + (0.31\ T_o)$ [C1f]

• where T_i = acceptable indoor temperature (°C);

• T_o = mean monthly outdoor temperature (°C).

Source: CEN (2005); B. Oleson, Technical University of Denmark

Figure C.2 *Design values for the indoor operative temperature for buildings without mechanical cooling systems*

C.2 Lighting quality

EN 12464-1 (CEN, 2002a) provides recommendations for lighting level of task, the unified glare rating (UGR) and the colour index (R_a). The lighting level may be lower than the lighting level in the direct environment, but not lower than the values presented in Table C.6. The task area has to be lighted as homogeneously as possible. The homogeneity factors are also given in Table C.6.

Blinding caused by a lighting system can be determined with the use of a table from the CIE Unified Glare Rating method in which the values are calculated with Equation 3.33 (see section 3.3.2 in Chapter 3). The minimum required protection angles are presented in Table C.7.

Recommended luminance ratios for critical views and frequent changes of view are:

- For a visual task and the direct environment (a view angle of circa 20°): not higher than 3.
- For a visual task and the rest of the environment (periphery): not more than 10.

In general, 1:20 for direct and 1:30 for periphery are acceptable. If the reflectance for the furnishing and space surface areas is not known, the following is assumed:

- The diffuse reflectance of the work tables lies between 0.3 and 0.5.
- The diffuse reflectance of the walls lies between 0.3 and 0.7.
- The diffuse reflectance of the floor has to be at least 0.2.

Lamps with a colour index lower than 80 should not be used in indoor environments where people stay or work for a longer period. For some locations and/or activities, exceptions can be made (e.g. lighting in high spaces); but additional measures need to be taken to guarantee lighting with a higher colour index at permanent occupied workplaces and at locations where security colours need to be recognized. Table C.9 presents general requirements for the colour index.

NEN 2057 provides recommendations for daylight openings of buildings and how to determine them. Essential information to know about a lighting system is as follows (CEN, 2004b):

- Dimensions for a lamp:
  - luminous flux;
  - lamp lumen maintenance factor (LLMF);
  - lamp survival factor (LSF);
  - general colour rendering index (R_a);
  - correlated colour temperature (T_{cp});
  - facultative: nominal lamp wattage and lamp energy efficiency class (LEEC).
- For a luminary:
  - the normalized intensity table;
  - normalized luminance table: normalized to a total bare lamp flux in the luminary of 1000 lm in cd/klm – this is the light output ratio (LOR) of the luminary;
  - unified glare rating (UGR) table;
  - glare rating (GR);
  - correction factors: to modify the luminaries' data to those of similar luminaries;
  - shielding angle: angle between the horizontal plane and the first line of sight at which the luminous parts of the lamps in the luminary are directly visible.

Table C.6 *Homogeneity and ratio between light level of the environment and the task area*

Lighting level of task (lux)	Lighting level of direct environment (lux)
≥750	500
500	300
300	200
≥200	E_{task}
Homogeneity ≥0.7	Homogeneity ≥0.5

Source: CEN (2002a)

Table C.7 *Minimum required protection angles for different lighting system intensities*

Lighting system intensity (kcd/m²)	Minimum protection angle required (°)
20 to <50	15
50 to <500	20
≥500	30

Source: CEN (2002a)

Table C.8 *Summary of ISO 9241-3*

Topic	Aspect	Requirements
Recognition: the visual characteristics of some letters and symbols should be easily recognized	• View distance • Height of letter • Thickness/height ratio of letter • Width/height ratio of letter • Matrix • Screen luminance • Luminance contrast • Homogeneity luminance	• >400mm • >16bgmin • 1/6 to 1/12 • ½ to 1/1 • Numeric and capital: ≥5 x 7 • > 35cd/m² • Contrast ratio ≥3 • Mean screen luminance from middle to border: ≤1.7:1
Readability: groups of letters should be easily distinguished, recognized and interpreted	• Letter distance • Word distance • Line distance	• ≥ thickness letter or 1 pixel • ≥ letter width • ≥ 1 pixel
Coding: has to attract attention and/or be readable	• Luminance coding • Colour coding	• Luminance ratio ≥ 1.5 • See EN-ISO 9241-8
Visual comfort: screen view should be stable and free of flickering	• Temporal instability	• Free of flickering for >90% of users

Source: ISO (1992b)

Table C.9 *Required general colour index R_a related to the visual task*

Requirements for colour impression	R_a minimum
Accurate colour evaluation and colour comparison is possible	90
Natural colour impression is required	80
Colour impression is of little importance	50
Colour impression is not important	–

Source: CEN (2002a)

C.3 Indoor air quality

Ventilation rates

In all current ventilation standards (CEN, 1998; ASHRAE, 2004b; CEN, 2005) a *prescriptive method* (for comfort) and *an analytical procedure* (for health) is included.

Prescriptive procedure

For the prescriptive method, a minimum ventilation rate per person and a minimum ventilation rate per square metre of floor area are required. The two ventilation rates are then added. The person-related ventilation rate should take care of pollution emitted from the person (odour) and the ventilation rate based on the person's activity and the floor area should cover emissions from the building, furnishings, heating, ventilating and air-conditioning (HVAC) system etc.

The design outdoor airflow required in the breathing zone of the occupied space or spaces in a zone (i.e. the breathing zone outdoor airflow (V_{bz})) is determined in accordance with the equation:

$$V_{bz} = R_p P_z + R_a A_z \qquad [C.2]$$

where:

- A_z = zone floor area: the net occupied floor area of the zone (m^2);
- P_z = zone population: the greatest number of people expected to occupy the zone during typical usage; note: if P_z cannot be accurately predicted during design, it may be an estimated value based on the zone floor area and the default occupant density listed in Table C.10;
- R_p = outdoor airflow rate required per person: these values are based on adapted occupants;
- R_a = outdoor airflow rate required per unit area.

Table C.10 shows the required ventilation rates from recent standards such as EN15251 (CEN, 2005), ASHRAE 62.1 (ASHRAE, 2004a) and CR 1752 (CEN, 1998). There are, however, quite substantial differences between the European recommendations and those listed by ASHRAE (Table C.11). One major reason is that ASHRAE requirements are minimum code requirements, where the basis for design is adapted people, whereas the European recommendations are based on unadapted people.

Table C.10 *Smoking-free spaces according to CR1752 and EN15251*

Type of building/ space	Occupancy (person/m²)	Category (CEN)	Minimum ventilation rate (l/s person)	Additional low polluting (l/sm²)	Additional not low-polluting (l/sm²)	Total (l/sm²)
Single office (cellular office)	0.1	A	10	1.0	2.0	2
		B	7	0.7	1.4	1.4
		C	4	0.4	0.8	0.8
Landscaped office	0.07	A	10	1.0	2.0	1.7
		B	7	0.7	1.4	1.2
		C	4	0.4	0.8	0.7
Conference room	0.5	A	10	1.0	2.0	6
		B	7	0.7	1.4	4.2
		C	4	0.4	0.8	2.4
Classroom	0.5	A	10	1.0	2.0	6
		B	7	0.7	1.4	4.2
		C	4	0.4	0.8	2.4
Kindergarten	0.5	A	12	1.0	2.0	7
		B	8.4	0.7	1.4	4.9
		C	4.8	0.4	0.8	2.8

Source: CEN (1998, 2005)

Table C.11 *Smoking-free spaces according to ASHRAE 62.1*

Type of building/ space	Occupancy (person/m²)	Minimum ventilation rate (l/s person) (R_p)	Additional ventilation for building (l/sm²) (R_a)	Total (l/sm²)
Single office (cellular office)	0.1	2.5	0.3	0.55
Landscaped office	0.07	2.5	0.3	0.48
Conference room	0.5	2.5	0.3	1.55
Classroom	0.5	3.8	0.3	2.2
Kindergarten	0.5	5.0	0.9	3.4

Source: ASHRAE (2004b)

Analytical procedure

All of the listed standards also have an analytical procedure, either in the standard text or in an informative appendix. In this procedure the required ventilation rate is calculated on a comfort basis (perceived odour and/or irritation) as well as on a health basis. The highest calculated value, which in most cases will be the comfort value, is then used as the required minimum ventilation rate. The basis for the calculation is in all standards based on a mass balance calculation.

The required ventilation rate is calculated as:

$$Q = \frac{G}{(C_i - C_o) \cdot E_v} \qquad 1\,s^{-1} \qquad [C.3]$$

where:

- G = total emission rate (mg/s);
- E_v = ventilation effectiveness;
- C_i = concentration limit (mg/l);
- C_o = concentration in outside air (mg/l).

In all of the standards, however, knowledge concerning emission rates (G) and concentration limits (C_i) from a health point of view is very limited. Within the next few years, knowledge will increase and data will be available from ongoing research projects and from testing by manufacturers of building materials and furnishing.

Relative humidity

While ISO 7730 (ISO, 2005) recommends keeping the *relative humidity* between 30 and 70 per cent (the upper limit of 70 per cent to reduce the survival chances of bacteria and viruses, and the lower limit of 30 per cent to prevent static electricity effects), ASHRAE 55 (2004a) recommends a range of relative humidity between 30 and 60 per cent. These limits are based on complaints related to dry skin, eye irritation, respirable health, microbiological growth and other humidity-related processes.

Exposure limits for air pollutants

Table C.12 *Health effects and exposure limits for air pollutants*

Pollutants	Possible sensitivity/effect	Recommended exposure limits
Organic gases		
Formaldehyde $(CH_2O)^*$	Short term: irritation of the eyes, nose and throat, together with concentration-dependent discomfort, lachrymation, sneezing, coughing, nausea, dyspnoea and, finally, death. Long term: upper and lower airway irritation and eye irritation in humans; degenerative, inflammatory and hyperplastic changes of the nasal mucosa; nasopharyngeal cancer.	Non-carcinogenic no-effect level: $30\mu g/m^3$. Pending on IARC revision of formaldehyde: a guideline should be as low as reasonably achievable.
Benzene $(C_6H_6)^*$	Aplastic anaemia and acute myelogenous leukaemia, carcinogen.	As low as reasonably achievable; should not exceed outdoor concentrations.
Naphthalene $(C_{10}H_8)^*$	Sensitivity of certain subpopulations to naphthalene toxicity, including infants and neonates. Haemolytic anaemia caused by deficiency in glucose-6-phosphate dehydrogenase (G6PD).	Long-term guideline value is $10\mu g/m^3$.
Acetaldehyde $(C_2H_4O)^*$	Short term: irritation of the eyes and respiratory tract and altered respiratory function. Long term: eye and upper respiratory tract irritation with the possibility of chronic tissue damage and inflammation in the respiratory tract; considered a probable human carcinogen: upper respiratory tract cancer (smoking).	$200\mu g/m^3$
Toluene $(C_7H_8)^*$	Short term: dysfunction of the central nervous system and narcosis; irritation of the skin, eye and respiratory tract. Inhalational abuse of toluene. Long term: progressive and irreversible changes in brain structure and function.	$300\mu g/m^3$ Acute $15,000\mu g/m^3$
Xylenes (C_8H_{10}) meta (m-), para (p-) and ortho (o-)*	Short-term inhalation: irritation of the eyes, nose, and throat, gastrointestinal effects, eye irritation, and neurological effects. Chronic (long-term) inhalation: central nervous system (CNS) effects, such as headache, dizziness, fatigue, tremors, and lack of coordination; respiratory, cardiovascular and kidney effects have also been reported.	$200\mu g/m^3$ Short term: $20\mu g/m^3$
Styrene $(C_8H_8)^*$	Short term: irritates the eyes and mucous membranes and may be toxic to the central nervous system Long term: central nervous system (CNS) and peripheral nervous system effects. Possibly carcinogenic.	Long term: $250\mu g/m^3$
Limonene $(C_{10}H_{16})^*$	Low acute toxicity.	$450\mu g/m^3$
α-pinene $(C_{10}H_{16})^*$	Irritating effects to the eyes, nose and throat.	$450\mu g/m^3$
CO*	Deaths and acute poisonings (intoxication) symptoms (similar to those associated with viral illness or clinical depression).	$10mg/m^3$ (8 hours) and $30mg/m^3$ (1 hour).
CO_2	Tightness of chest, suffocation.	≤ 800 ppm
TVOC	Irritation, intoxication, cancer, allergy.	TVOC $<0.2mg/m^3$ Allergic people: effects possible with much lower concentrations.

Table C.12 *Health effects and exposure limits for air pollutants (Cont'd)*

Pollutants	Possible sensitivity/effect	Recommended exposure limits
Inorganic gases		
Nitrogen dioxide (NO_2)*	No clear evidence for a concentration–response relationship for NO_2. Asthmatics and persons with chronic obstructive pulmonary disease (COPD) are the most susceptible populations to acute changes in lung function, airway responsiveness and other respiratory symptoms.	$40\mu g/m^3$ (1 week) and $200\mu g/m^3$ (1 hour)
Sulphur dioxide (SO_2)**	Short term: reduction in ventilatory capacity, increases in specific airway resistance, and symptoms such as wheezing or shortness of breath. Long term: airway symptoms, chronic obstructive pulmonary disease.	$500\mu g/m^3$ (10 minutes) $125\mu g/m^3$ (24 hours) $50\mu g/m^3$ (yearly average)
Ozone (O_3)**	Decrements in lung function, airway inflammatory changes, exacerbations of respiratory symptoms and symptomatic and functional exacerbations of asthma in exercising susceptible people.	$120\mu g/m^3$ (8 hours) (see Table C.14)
Ammonia (NH_3)*	Short term: site-of-contact lesions primarily of the eyes and the respiratory tract; eye, nose and throat irritation, coughing, and narrowing of the bronchi. Long term: respiratory distress.	Short term: $70\mu g/m^3$ Long term: $100\mu g/m^3$
Radon	Radon is a known human carcinogen (classified by IARC as group 1 with genotoxic action). A lifetime lung cancer risk below about 1×10^{-4} cannot be expected to be achievable because natural concentration of radon in ambient outdoor air is about 10 Bq/m^3.	No guideline value for radon concentration is recommended.
Particulate matter		
PM_{10}** $PM_{2.5}$**	Short term: eye irritation, conjunctivitis, reduced lung function. Long-term exposure to particulate matter is associated with reduced survival, and a reduction of life expectancy in the order of one to two years. Prevalence of bronchitis symptoms in children and of reduced lung function in children and adults.	Effects have been observed at annual average concentration levels below $20\mu g/m^3$ (as $PM_{2.5}$) or $30\mu g/m^3$ (as PM_{10}) (see Table C.13)
Manmade vitreous fibres (MMVF)**	MMVF of diameters greater than $3\mu m$ can cause transient irritation and inflammation of the skin, eyes and upper airways. IARC classified rock wool, slag wool, glass wool and ceramic fibres in Group 2B (possibly carcinogenic to humans) while glass filaments were not considered classifiable as to their carcinogenicity to humans (group 3).	Refractory ceramic fibres: for lifetime risks of 1/10,000, 1/100,000 and 1/1 million: 100, 10 and 1 fibre/l, respectively. Other MMVF: no adequate data.
Bio-aerosols		
Pollen (10–$100\mu m$) and mite products***	Allergic asthma, allergic rhinitis, conjunctivitis, constitutional eczema.	10–25 pollen per m^3 100–500 mites/g house dust
Bacteria (0.4–$5\mu m$), endotoxins	Intoxication, inflammation.	–
Moulds (10–$30\mu m$), mycotoxines	Intoxication, allergy.	–

Source: * INDEX report (Kotzias et al, 2005);** WHO guidelines (WHO, 2000b) *** ECA (1991)

Table C.13 *WHO air quality guideline and interim targets for particulate matter, mean annual and 24-hour levels*

Mean level	PM$_{10}$ (µg/m³)	PM$_{2.5}$ (µg/m³)	Basis for the selected level
Annual			
Interim target 1	70	35	Estimated to associate with 15% higher long-term mortality than at AQG levels.
Interim target 2	50	25	In addition to other health benefits, these levels lower risk of premature mortality by approximately 6% compared to interim target 1.
Interim target 3	30	15	In addition to other health benefits, these levels lower risk of premature mortality by approximately another 6% compared to interim target 2.
Air quality guidelines (AQGs)	20	10	Lowest levels at which total cardiopulmonary and lung cancer mortality have been shown to increase with more than 95% confidence in response to PM$_{2.5}$. Use of PM$_{2.5}$ guideline is preferred.
24 hour			
Interim target 1	150	75	Based on published risk coefficient from multicentre studies and meta-analysis (about 5% increase in short-term mortality over AQGs).
Interim target 2	100	50	Based on published risk coefficient from multicentre studies and meta-analysis (about 2.5% increase in short-term mortality over AQGs).
Interim target 3	75	37.5	About 1.2 increase in short-term mortality over AQGs.
Air quality guidelines (AQGs)	50	25	Based on a relation between 24-hour and annual PM levels.

Note: The epidemiological evidence indicates that the possibility of adverse health effects remains even if the guideline value is achieved. For this reason, some countries might decide to adopt lower concentrations than the World Health Organization (WHO) guideline values as national air quality standards. In addition to guideline values, interim targets are given. Progress towards the guideline values should, however, be the ultimate objective of air quality management and health risk reduction in all areas.

Source: WHO (2006c)

Table C.14 *WHO ozone air quality guideline and interim target*

	Daily maximum (8-hour mean)	Effects at the selected ozone level
High level	240µg/m³	Significant health effects; substantial proportion of vulnerable population affected.
Interim target 1	160µg/m³	Important health effects; an intermediate target for populations with ozone concentrations above this level. Does not provide adequate protection of public health. Rationale: • Lower level of 6.6-hour chamber exposures of healthy exercising young adults that show physiological and inflammatory lung effects. • Ambient level at various summer camp studies showing effects on health of children. • Estimated 3–5% increase in daily mortality (based on findings of daily time series studies).
Air quality guideline	100µg/m³	This concentration will provide adequate protection of public health, though some health effects may occur below this level. Rationale: • Estimated 1–2% increase in daily mortality (based on findings of daily time series studies). • Extrapolation from chamber and field studies based on the likelihood that real-life exposure tends to be repetitive and chamber studies do not study highly sensitive or clinically compromised people or children. • Likelihood that ambient ozone is a marker for related oxidants.

Source: WHO (2006c)

C.4 Regulatory and voluntary schemes

Regulatory

Currently, the DIBt Principles for health assessment of construction products used in interiors comprise the only regulatory assessment for volatile organic compound (VOCs) and semi-volatile organic compound (SVOC) emissions of a construction product (more specifically, flooring materials) indoors. The assessment concept has two stages:

1   registration and assessment of the constituents of the construction product;
2   determination and assessment of VOC and SVOC emissions and, where appropriate, of further emissions from the construction product.

The flowchart for this assessment in stages is set out in Figure C.3.

In addition to the applicable legislative regulations (such as the order banning certain chemicals), usage bans or restrictions must also be adhered to. The current version is published in the DIBt journals and, where applicable, on the DIBt website (see www.dibt.de).

Voluntary schemes

In addition to this regulatory scheme in Germany, there are a number of voluntary schemes available. Most of these voluntary schemes apply the newly developed EN or ISO standards (EN-13419 parts 1 to 4 and the CEN ISO 16000 parts 3, 6, 9, 10, 11), or very similar methods for emission testing and analysis. Most schemes, or labels, apply a short-term test for

	Construction product		
Stage 1	↓		
	Determination of the constituents (formula/analysis)		
	↓		
	Exclusion criteria apply	→ Yes →	Rejection
	↓ No ↓		
	Knowledge of health tolerability/comparison with similar products which have been positively assessed	→ Yes →	Requirement met
Stage 2	↓ No ↓		
Test 1 after 3 days	$TVOC_3 \leq 10$ mg/m^3?	→ No →	Rejection
	↓ Is the sum of all detected carcinogens ≤ 0.1 mg/m^3?	→ No →	Rejection
Test 2 after 28 days	↓ $TVOC_{28} \leq 1.0$ mg/m^3?	→ No →	Rejection
	↓ Σ SVOC$_{28} \leq 0.1$ mg/m^3?	→ No →	Rejection
	↓ Is the sum of all detected carcinogens ≤ 0.001 mg/m^3?	→ No →	Rejection
	↓ Assessable substances: When taking into account all VOCs with a concentration of > 0.005 mg/m^3, does $R = \Sigma \ C_1/LCI_1^* \leq 1$ apply?	→ No →	Rejection
	↓ Non-assessable substances: Is the sum of VOCs for which no LCI* applies Σ VOC$_{28no\ VOC} < 0.1$ mg/m^3?	→ No →	Rejection
	↓ Requirement met		

Note: * LCI = lowest concentration of interest (DIBt, 2005).

Source: www.dibt.de

Figure C.3 *Flowchart for the health assessment of construction products*

initial emissions after one to three days, and all labels apply a test for characterizing long-term emissions after 28 days – or even earlier (after ten or even three days) if the initial emissions of all covered products decrease rapidly.

In Report 24 (*Harmonisation of Indoor Material Emission Labelling Systems in the EU: Inventory of Existing Systems*) of the European collaborative action Urban Air, Indoor Environment and Human Exposure – Environment and Quality of Life (ECA, 2005), the following labelling systems and concepts have been inventoried, compared and discussed:

- ECA Report 18: a concept for a global scheme for evaluating VOC emissions from building materials, established by a European working group (ECA, 1997);
- AgBB scheme (AgBB, 2005);
- AFSSET (previously entitled CESAT – evaluation of environmental and health-based properties of building products) (France);
- M1: Emission Classification of Building Materials (Finland);
- Indoor Climate Label (ICL-Denmark);
- LQAI scheme (Portugal);
- Natureplus (Germany and Europe);
- The Blue Angel (Germany);
- Ecolabel scheme (Austria);
- GUT for carpets (Germany and Europe);
- Emicode system by GEV for adhesives and related material (Germany and Europe).

The intention of the 1997 Report 18 of the European collaborative action *Indoor Air Quality and its Impact on Man* (*Evaluation of VOC Emissions from Building Products*) was to serve as a guideline and has, in fact, laid good grounds for harmonizing systems.

Only some labels apply an odour test: the M1 and the Danish ICL, and documentation on reliability and reproducibility of such tests is still lacking. A large variety of odour testing methods are applied. These tests are mainly based on either desiccator tests or on dynamic chamber tests, as described in the European database project (Bluyssen et al, 2000), Nordtest Standard (Hansen et al, 1999) and ECA Report 20 on sensory evaluation (ECA, 1999). A number of labels do not include any odour testing at all. Some of the schemes include control of labelled

products according to certain frequency intervals. Most labels require involved testing laboratories to apply for approval. Only some labels organized round-robin tests for checking the quality of the testing labs.

The M1 labelling system, established in 1995, is the oldest system and is regarded as one of the voluntary schemes with most experience today. The system uses the emission scenario as defined in the CEN ISO 16000 series (based on more than 20 years of research). The M1 was developed before the CEN ISO 16000 series was available and is based on testing protocols developed in the European EDBIAPS, MATHIS and AIRLESS projects:

- EBDIAPS (1994–1997): focused on building and furnishing materials (Oliveira Fernandes and Clausen, 1997);
- AIRLESS (1998–2000): concerned with HVAC systems and components (Bluyssen et al, 2003);
- MATHIS (1998–2001): created the SOPHIE database (Sources of Pollution for a Healthy Indoor Environment) (Oliveira Fernandes, 2001);
- VOCEM (1996–1998): developed a measurement protocol for VOCs from construction products (together with MATHIS, this formed the basis for the ISO 16000 series developed in WG7 of CEN TC 264) (Cochet, 1998);
- CEN TC 264 WG7: developed a measurement VOC protocol resulting in the ISO 16000 series;
- ISO TC 146 SC6 development of analytical procedures to the CEN ISO 16000 series;
- *European Collaborative Action Indoor Air Quality and Its Impact on Man, Environment and Quality of Life*, Report 18: evaluation of emission of flooring materials (this report forms the base for most evaluation schemes used today) (ECA, 1997).

The M1 system measures the emissions of TVOC (all VOCs between C6–C16 in toluene equivalent) according to 16000-6; 200 µg/m^3 is the limit, at 28 days. In practice, this does the job with regards to reducing the possible health effects from building product chemical emissions, according to the Finnish experience. More than 1000 products have been given the M1 label and research has shown that the indoor air environment has clearly improved (lower TVOC concentrations: one fifth of before).

C.5 Acoustical quality

In Table C.15 specific noise limits have been set for each health effect, using the lowest noise level that produces an adverse health effect. The time base for LAeq for daytime and night time is 12 to 16 hours and 8 hours, respectively. No time base is given for evenings, but typically the guideline value should be 5dB to 10dB lower than in the daytime. Precautions should be taken for vulnerable groups and for certain noises (e.g. low frequency components, low background noise).

Standards and regulations for building elements

Regulatory – The Netherlands Building Decree (VROM, 2007)

- Protection against noise from the outside: the façade should have a certain sound insulation not smaller than the difference between the limit value according to the Noise Annoyance Law for a certain area and the limit value of the sound level in the occupied space, with a minimum of 20dB(A). For a space meant to be occupied, the limit value to be taken lies 2dB(A) under the limit value according to the Noise Annoyance Law. For aircraft noise-sensitive areas, different requirements are set (only applied in The Netherlands).

- Protection against noise from service systems: a service system (toilet, mechanical ventilation system, elevator, etc.) may not cause a sound level in other dwellings of more than 30dB(A). This means that protection against the noise of service systems in one's own dwelling is not protected.

- Noise insulation between spaces with the same function: has to be at least 20dB(A) for both contact and air sound transmission. This requirement does not hold for spaces in contact with each other through a door or located on the same floor.

Table C.15 *Guideline values for specific environments*

Specific environment	Critical health effect(s)	L_{Aeq} (dB(A))	Time base (hours)	L_{Amx} fast (dB)
Outdoor living area	Serious annoyance, daytime and evening	55	16	–
	Moderate annoyance, daytime and evening	50	16	–
Dwelling, indoors	Speech intelligibility and moderate annoyance, daytime and evening	35	16	
Inside bedrooms	Sleep disturbance, night-time	30	8	45
Outside bedrooms	Sleep disturbance, window open (outdoor values)	45	8	60
School class rooms and pre-schools, indoors	Speech intelligibility, disturbance of information extraction, message communication	35	During class	–
Pre-school bedrooms, indoors	Sleep disturbance	30	Sleeping time	45
School, playground, outdoors	Annoyance (external source)	55	During play	–
Hospitals, ward rooms, indoors	Sleep disturbance, night-time	30	8	40
	Sleep disturbance, daytime and evenings	30	16	–
Hospitals, treatment rooms, indoors	Interference with rest and recovery	Alap[1]		
Industrial commercial shopping and traffic areas, indoors and outdoors	Hearing impairment	70	24	110
Public addresses, indoors and outdoors	Hearing impairment	85	1	110
Music and other sounds through headphones/earphones	Hearing impairment (free-field value)	85	1	110
Impulse sounds from toys, fireworks and firearms	Hearing impairment (adults)	–	–	140[2]
	Hearing impairment (children)	–	–	120[2]

Notes: 1: as low as possible; 2: at 100mm from the ear.

Source: Berglund et al (1999)

- Reduction of echo: in non-common spaces to prevent echo in adjoining corridors, staircases, etc. a sound absorption of at least one eighth of the volume of the space for each of the isofones with middle frequencies of 250Hz, 500Hz, 1000Hz and 2000Hz is required.
- Noise insulation between spaces with different functions: between occupied spaces of different

dwellings the air sound insulation should be not lower than 0dB and the contact sound insulation should be not lower than 5dB. Between enclosed spaces such as a bathroom of different dwellings, these values are respectively −5dB and 0dB. Between an enclosed space and an occupied space of different dwellings, the values are the same as if it concerns both occupied spaces.

Voluntary: Example in The Netherlands

Table C.16 *Classes of noise insulation related to percentage of those dissatisfied*

Noise insulation class	Description	Percentage dissatisfied (indication) (%)
I	High protection and quietness. Noises from outside are hardly noticeable. Loud speech is, in general, not understandable, normal speech and music cannot be perceived, loud music and parties can be perceived but are not annoying. Walking sounds are not disturbing and service system noise is hardly disturbing.	<5%
II	Under normal conditions a good protection without many limitations for behaviour of occupants; normal speech can not be perceived, louder speech and music are sometimes perceivable but not understandable. Very loud speech, music and parties can be perceived but not understandable. Walking sounds are not disturbing, service system noise is sometimes disturbing.	5–10%
III	Protection against unacceptable interruption, assuming consideration is taken of others. Speech is sometimes perceivable, but not understandable. Very loud speech is understandable; loud music can be perceived. Walking sounds are sometimes disturbing. Unacceptable disturbance from service systems noise is, in general, prevented	10–25%
IV	Regulatory disturbance even with adjusted behaviour. Speech and music are often perceived. Very loud speech is understandable and music is disturbing. Walking sounds are often disturbing. Regulatory disturbance from service system noise.	25–50%
V	No protection against noise. Normal speech is often understandable; music and loud speech, walking sounds and service system noise are often disturbing.	> 50%

Source: NEN (1999)

Table C.17 *Relation classes of noise insulation and building decree*

Noise insulation class	Characteristic air sound insulation (dB)	Contact sound insulation (dB)	Characteristic service system sound level (dB(A))	Limit sound level value in dwelling for determination of characteristic sound insulation (dB(A))
I	+10	+15	20	25
II	+5	+10	25	30
III[1]	0	+5	30	35
IV	−5	0	35	40
V	−10	−5	40	45

Note: 1: Minimum performance requirements of Building Decree.

Source: ISSO/SBR (2006)

Annex D
Some Attributes and Factors

D1. Building quality assessment (BQA) checklist

1 **Corporate attribute:** the overall requirements of an organization purchasing or renting a facility, concerned with what the building achieves or intends to achieve rather than how, and with the procurement of the building and its broad functions ratherthan with the details of physical building design. *Factors of concern:* corporate objectives, serviceability, image, tenure, code compliance, time, initial cost, life cost, rent, operating cost, refurbishment, disposal, security.

2 **Site attribute:** those items concerned with the site, regardless of the building that is on it; the location of the site and the environment (built and climatic) in which the building is located or will be constructed. *Factors of concern:* access, built environment, micro-climate, local services, site, conditions.

3 **Construction attribute:** all those items which make up the physical building, and that support it and define its shape, spaces and materials. Depending upon the extent of the refurbishment and fit-out options, the construction factors provide the basis and ultimately the limitations on the performance that can be obtained from a building. *Factors of concern:* structure safety, structure adaptability, overall dimensions, shell geometry, structural layout, cladding materials, access, security.

4 **Space attribute:** those factors and items which ensure that the building provides spaces for all the functions required of it and can be adapted with a reasonable flexibility to changing requirements in the future. *Factors of concern:* major zones, office spaces, other personnel space requirements, keeping the building functioning, storage, circulation space, stairs, social, ease of finding one's way, staff amenities, space use flexibility and quality, space able to be sublet, potential to redecorate, finishes, furnishings and fittings.

5 **Internal environment attribute:** those items whose main function is to modify the environment and to provide an enclosed or semi-enclosed space for particular activities and materials. For office buildings, the principal requirement is to provide an environment that enhances occupants' well-being and facilitates their productivity. The quality of the internal environment is both objective and subjective. *Factors of concern:* air quality, ventilation, thermal comfort, noise, lighting, special areas, ambience.

6 **Building services attribute:** those items which play an essential part in the quality of the internal environment created by the building. They facilitate communications within the building and with the external world and support the functionality of the building as a whole. In all areas of building services, an assessment of current and likely future needs is essential.
Factors of concern: flexibility (possibility for change) of the systems to user needs, maintenance costs, heating, ventilating and air-conditioning (HVAC) systems, HVAC distribution, electrical services, information technology, vertical transport, water services, fire protection, costs of services.

Source: adapted from Bruhns and Isaacs (1996)

D.2 Serviceability tools and methods (STM) – topics of serviceability scales

A.1	**Support for office work**	A.8.7	Systems of secure waste
A.1.1	Photocopying	A.8.8	Security of key and card control systems
A.1.2	Training rooms, general		
A.1.3	Training rooms for computer skills	**A.9**	**Facility protection**
A.1.4	Interview rooms	A.9.1	Protection around building
A.1.5	Storage and floor loading	A.9.2	Protection unauthorized access to site/parking
A.1.6	Shipping and receiving	A.9.3	Protective surveillance of site
A.2	**Meetings and group effectiveness**	A.9.4	Perimeter of building
A.2.1	Meeting and conference rooms	A.9.5	Public zone of building
A.2.2	Informal meetings and interaction	A.9.6	Facility protection services
A.2.3	Group layout and territory		
A.2.4	Group workrooms	**A.10**	**Work outside normal hours/conditions**
		A.10.1	Operation outside normal hours
A.3	**Sound and visual environment**	A.10.2	Support after hours
A.3.1	Privacy and speech intelligibility	A.10.3	Temporary loss of external services
A.3.2	Distraction and disturbance	A.10.4	Continuity of work (during breakdowns)
A.3.3	Vibration		
A.3.4	Lighting and glare	**A.11**	**Image to public and occupants**
A.3.5	Adjustment of lighting by occupants	A.11.1	Exterior appearance
A.3.6	Distant and outside views	A.11.2	Public lobby of building
		A.11.3	Public spaces within building
A.4	**Thermal environment and indoor air**	A.11.4	Appearance/spaciousness of office spaces
A.4.1	Temperature and humidity	A.11.5	Finishes and materials in office spaces
A.4.2	Indoor air quality	A.11.6	Identity outside building
A.4.3	Ventilation air (supply)	A.11.7	Neighbourhood and site
A.4.4	Local adjustment by occupants	A.11.8	Historic significance
A.4.5	System capability and controls		
		A.12	**Amenities to attract and retain staff**
A.5	**Typical office information technology**	A.12.1	Food
A.5.1	Office computers and related equipment	A.12.2	Shops
A.5.2	Power at workplace	A.12.3	Daycare
A.5.3	Building power	A.12.4	Exercise room
A.5.4	Data and telephone systems	A.12.5	Bicycle racks for staff
A.5.5	Cable plant	A.12.6	Seating away from work areas
A.5.6	Cooling		
		A.13	**Special facilities and technologies**
A.6	**Change by occupants**	A.13.1	Group or shared conference centre
A.6.1	Disruption due to physical change	A.13.2	Video teleconference facilities
A.6.2	Illumination, HVAC and sprinklers	A.13.3	Simultaneous translation
A.6.3	Minor changes to layout	A.13.4	Satellite and microwave links
A.6.4	Partition wall relocations	A.13.5	Mainframe computer centre
A.6.5	Lead time for facilities group	A.13.6	Telecommunications centre
A.7	**Layout and building features**	**A.14**	**Location, access and way finding**
A.7.1	Influence of HVAC on layout	A.14.1	Public transportation (urban sites)
A.7.2	Influence of sound/visual features on layout	A.14.2	Staff visits to other offices
A.7.3	Influence of building loss features on space needs	A.14.3	Vehicular entry and parking
		A.14.4	Ease of finding one's way to the building and lobby
A.8	**Protection of occupants' assets**	A.14.5	Capacity of internal movement systems
A.8.1	Control of access from building public zone to occupant reception zone	A.14.6	Public circulation/ease of finding one's way in the building
A.8.2	Interior zones of security		
A.8.3	Vaults (secure rooms)	**B.1**	**Structure, envelope and grounds**
A.8.4	Security of cleaning service systems	B.1.1	Typical office floors
A.8.5	Security of maintenance service systems	B.1.2	External walls and projections
A.8.6	Security of renovation outside active hours		

B.1.3	External windows and doors		B.3.2	Competences of in-house staff
B.1.4	Roofs		B.3.3	Occupant satisfaction
B.1.5	Basement		B.3.4	Information on unit costs and consumption
B.1.6	Grounds			
			B.4	**Cleanliness**
B.2	**Manageability**		B.4.1	Exterior and public areas
B.2.1	Reliability of external supply		B.4.2	Office areas (interior)
B.2.2	Anticipated remaining service life		B.4.3	Toilets and washrooms
B.2.3	Ease of operation		B.4.4	Special cleaning
B.2.4	Ease of maintenance		B.4.5	Waste disposal for building
B.2.5	Ease of cleaning			
B.2.6	Janitor's facilities		**C.1**	**Fire and life safety**
B.2.7	Energy consumption		C.1.1	Egress facilities; building has a sprinkler system
B.2.8	Energy management and controls		C.1.2	Egress facilities; building does not have a sprinkler system
			C.1.3	Exits, number and design
B.3	**Management of operations and maintenance**		C.1.4	Fire protection, active
			C.1.5	Fire protection, passive
B.3.1	Strategy and programme for operations and maintenance		C.1.6	Fire department support

Source: adapted from Davis and Szigeti (1996)

D.3 Housing Health and Safety Rating System

A dwelling, including the structure, the means of access, any associated outbuildings and a garden, yard and/or other amenity space should all provide a safe and healthy environment for the occupants and any visitors. In order to satisfy this principle a dwelling should be free from unnecessary and avoidable hazards; where hazards are necessary or unavoidable, they should be made as safe as reasonably possible.

The Housing Health and Safety Rating System is designed to rate the severity of hazards; the higher the hazard score, the greater the threat to health and safety. A hazard is the effect that may result from a fault and which has the potential to cause harm. A fault is a failure of an element to meet the ideal. The ideal is the currently perceived model for an element which defines the functions and safest performance criteria that can be expected of that element. An element is any component or constituent part, facility or amenity of a dwelling, such as a wall, a window, a staircase, a bath, means of lighting, and means of space heating.

The assessment involves judging each element of a dwelling against an ideal for that particular element. Any faults identified are then assessed for their potential to cause harm.

To generate a hazard score, the surveyor provides information on:

- The likelihood of an occurrence over the following 12-month period which could result in major harm. This involves taking into account features which may increase or reduce the likelihood. The likelihood is given as a ratio (e.g. 1 in 10, 1 in 200, etc.).
- The spread of health outcomes or harm which could from such an incident to a person vulnerable to that particular hazard (e.g. gaps to balustrades are judged in relation to a young child).

The possible harms (or health outcomes) which may result from an occurrence are categorized according to the perceived severity:

- *class I extreme*, including death, permanent paralysis below the neck, regular severe pneumonia, and 80 per cent burns;
- *class II severe*, including chronic confusion, regular and severe fever, loss of a hand or foot, and serious fractures;
- *class III serious*, including chronic severe stress, regular and persistent dermatitis, loss of a finger, severe concussion, and serious strain or sprain injuries;
- *class IV moderate*, including chronic or regular skin irritation, benign tumours, slight concussion, moderate cuts to face or body, and regular serious coughs or colds.

A weighting is given to each class of harm to reflect the degree of incapacity of each class: class I:

10,000; class II: 1000; class III: 300; and class IV: 10. Although a single harm (or health outcome) is the most likely, other outcomes are possible, which may be more or less severe. For example, there may be a 60 per cent chance or a class III harm, with a 30 per cent chance of a class IV harm and a 10 per cent chance of a more serious class II harm. From the judgements made by the surveyor, a hazard score is generated using the formula in the following table.

Formula for calculating a hazard score								
Class of harm weighting			**Likelihood (1 in ...)**		**Spread of harm (%)**			
I	10,000	÷	100	X	0	=	0
II	1000	÷	100	X	10	=	100
III	300	÷	100	X	30	=	90
IV	10	÷	100	X	60	=	6
				Hazard score		=	196

Source: adapted from Office of the Deputy Prime Minister (2004)

References

Adan, O. C. G. (1994) *On the Fungal Defacement of Interior Finishes*, PhD thesis, Technical University of Eindhoven, The Netherlands

Adan, O. C. G. and Bluyssen, P. M. (2004) *(Ver)huren in de nabije toekomst: verkennende studie naar toepassingsmogelijkheden van ruimtevaarttechnologie voor innovatie van wonen in de context van energie* [*Renting in the Near Future: An Inventory of Possibilities to Apply Space Technology to Innovate Ways of Living in the Context of Energy*], TNO report, Delft, The Netherlands

AgBB (2005) *Health-Related Evaluation Procedure for Volatile Organic Compounds Emissions (VOC and SVOC) from Building Products*, Committee for Health-Related Evaluation of Building Products, Berlin, Germany

Allerman, L., Pejtersen, J., Gunnarsen, L. and Poulsen, O. M. (2007) 'Building-related symptoms and inflammatory potency of dust from office buildings', *Indoor Air*, vol 17, pp458–467

Amoore, J. E. (1964) 'The stereochemical theory of odour', *Scientific American*, February, pp64–101

Ang, K. I., Hendriks, L. W. J. L and van Zanten, J. H. (1995) *Werken met prestatiecontracten bij vastgoedontwikkeling* [*Working with Performance Contracts in Project Development*], VROM publication 8839/138, The Hague, The Netherland.

Apte, M. G., Fisk, W. J. and Daisey, J. M. (2000) 'Associations between indoor CO_2 concentrations and sick building syndrome symptoms in US office buildings: An analysis of the 1994–1996 BASE study', *Indoor Air*, vol 10, no 4, pp246–257

Aries, M. B. C. (2005) *Human Lighting Demands: Healthy Lighting in an Office Environment*, PhD thesis, Technical University of Eindhoven, The Netherlands

ASHRAE, (1991) 'Control of gaseous contaminants of indoor air', in *ASHRAE Handbook – HVAC Applications*, American Society of Heating, Refrigerating and Air-Conditioning Engineers, Atlanta, GA, US, Chapter 40

ASHRAE (1992) 'Air cleaners for particulate contaminants', in *ASHRAE Handbook – HVAC Systems and Equipment*, American Society of Heating, Refrigerating and Air-Conditioning Engineers, Atlanta, GA, US, Chapter 25

ASHRAE (2004a) *ASHRAE Standard 55-2004: Thermal Environment Conditions for Human Occupancy*, American Society of Heating, Refrigerating and Air-Conditioning Engineers, Atlanta, GA, US

ASHRAE (2004b) *ASHRAE Standard 62.1-2004: Ventilation for Acceptable Indoor Air Quality*, American Society of Heating, Refrigerating and Air-Conditioning Engineers, Atlanta, GA, US

ASHRAE (2007) *HVAC Applications*, CD ROM, American Society of Heating, Refrigerating and Air-Conditioning Engineers, Atlanta, GA, US

ASTM (1981) *Standard Practices for Referencing Supra Threshold Odour Intensity*, Annual book for ASTM standards E544-75 (reapproved 1981), Pennsylvania, US, pp32–44

ASTM (2000) *ASTM Standards on Whole Building Functionality and Serviceability*, Pennsylvania, US

Auliciems, A. (1981) 'Towards a psycho-physiological model of thermal perception', *International Journal of Biometeorology*, vol 25, no 2, pp109–122

Axel, R. (1995) 'The molecular logic of smell', *Scientific American*, October, pp130–137

Baird, G. (ed) (1996) *Building Evaluation Techniques*, Centre for Building Performance Research, Victoria University of Wellington, McGraw-Hill, US

Baldwin, R., Yates, A., Howard, N. and Roa, S. (1998) *BREEAM 98 for Offices*, Building Research Establishment Ltd, Watford, UK

Baker, N. and Steemers, K. (2002) *Daylight Design of Buildings*, ISBN 1 873936885, James & James Ltd, London, UK

Baker, N. V., Fanchiotti, A. and Steemers, K. (eds) (1993) *Daylighting in Architecture: A European Reference Book*, James & James Ltd for the Commission of the European Communities, London, UK

Bakker, L. G., Soethout, L. L. and Elkhuizen, P. A. (2006) 'Moderne gebouwautomisering en regulering' ['Modern building automation and control'], *TVVL Magazine*, vol 35, no 11, pp82–93

Banham, R. (1984) *The Architecture of the Well-Tempered Environment*, second edition, University of Chicago Press, Chicago, US

Bartolo, P. J. S. and Bartolo, H. M. G. (2001) *Concurrence in Design: A Strategic Approach through Rapid Prototyping*, CIB World Building Congress, Wellington, New Zealand, paper INF 05

Beck, E. M. (1990) 'Filter facts', in *Indoor Air '90*, Toronto, Canada, July–August, vol 3, pp171–176

Bedford, T. (1936) *The Warmth Factor in Comfort at Work*, Medical Research Council Industrial Health Research Board, Report 36, London, UK

Berglund, B. and Lindvall, T. (1979) 'Olfactory evaluation of indoor air quality', in *Indoor Climate '78*, Danish Building Research Institute, Copenhagen, pp141–157

Berglund, B. and Lindvall, T. (1990) 'Sensory criteria for healthy buildings', in *Proceedings of INDOOR AIR '90*, Toronto, Canada, vol 5, pp65–78

Berglund, B., Berglund, U. and Lindvall, T. (1976) 'Psychological processing of odour mixtures', *Psychology Review*, 83, pp432–441

Berglund, B., Lindvall, T. and Schwela, D. H. (1999) *Guidelines for Community Noise*, WHO, Geneva, Switzerland

Berglund, B., Gunnarsson, A. G. and Nilsson, U. E. (2000) 'Weighted descriptor profiles as an alternative method to measure the sick building syndrome', in *Proceedings of Healthy Buildings 2000*, Helsinki, Finland, vol 1, pp597–602

Berglund, L. G. and Cain, W. S. (1989) 'Perceived air quality and the thermal environment', in *Proceedings of IAQ 89*, ASHRAE, Atlanta, GA, US

Bergsma, S. (2007) 'De eindgebruiker beter af?, PPS-renovatie Financiën nader uitgelegd' ['The end user better off? Finances of PPS-renovation explained'], *De Ontwerpmanager*, no 1, pp8–11

Bierre, S., Cunningham, C., Cunningham, M., Baker, M., Robinson, J., Kennedy, M., Sansom, A. and Howden-Chapman, P. (2004) *A Healthy Housing Index: A Collaborative Approach to Measuring Housing Condition*, WHO International Housing and Health Symposium, Vilnius, Lithuania, pp93–103

Billings, J. S. (1883) 'Ventilation and heating', *The Engineering Record*

Billings, J. S., Mitchell, S. W. and Bergey, D. H. (1898) *The Composition of Expired Air and Its Effects upon Animal Life*, Smithsonian Contributions to Knowledge, Washington, US

Blanchard, B. S. (2004) *System Engineering Management*, third edition, John Wiley & Sons, Inc, New Jersey, US

Bluyssen, P. M. (1990) *Air Quality Evaluated by a Trained Panel*, PhD thesis, October, Laboratory of Heating and Air Conditioning, Technical University of Denmark, Lyngby

Bluyssen, P. M. (1991) 'Air quality evaluated with the human nose', *Air Infiltration Review*, vol 12, no 4, pp5–9

Bluyssen, P. M. (1992) 'Indoor air quality management: A state of the art review and identification of research needs', *Indoor Environment*, 52, no 1, pp326–334

Bluyssen, P. M. (1994) *Het sorptiegedrag van materialen in het binnenmilieu* [*Sorption Behaviour of Materials in the Indoor Environment*], TNO report 94-BBI-R0170, Delft, The Netherlands

Bluyssen, P. M. (1996) *Methods and Sensors to Detect Indoor Air Pollutants Perceived by the Nose*, TNO report 96-BBI-R0873, Delft, The Netherlands

Bluyssen, P. M. (1998) *AIRLESS DOC 1.10 Protocol for Sensory Evaluation of Perceived Air Pollution with Trained Panels*, October, Delft, The Netherlands

Bluyssen, P. M. (2001) *State-of-the-Art on Performance Concepts and Tools for Buildings*, TNO report 2001-GGI-R100, Delft, The Netherlands

Bluyssen, P. M. (2004a) 'Sensory evaluation of indoor pollution sources', in P. Pluschke (ed) *The Handbook of Environmental Chemistry, Part 4.F: Indoor Air Pollution*, Springer-Verlag, Berlin and Heidelberg, Germany, pp179–217

Bluyssen, P. M. (2004b) *A Clean and Energy-Efficient Heating, Ventilating and Air-Conditioning System: Recommendations and Advice*, February 2004, TNO, The Netherlands

Bluyssen, P. M. and Adan, O. C. G. (2006) 'Marketing the indoor environment: Standardization or performance on demand?', *Proceedings of Healthy Buildings 2006*, Lisboa, Portugal, June 2006, vol 5, pp275–280

Bluyssen, P. M. (2008) 'Management of the indoor environment: from a component related to an interactive top-down approach', *Indoor and Built Environment*, vol 17, no 6, pp483–495

Bluyssen, P. M. and Cornelissen, H. J. M. (1998) *AIRLESS DOC 1.1 Evaluation of Perceived Air: How to Proceed?*, June, Delft, The Netherlands

Bluyssen, P. M. and Cornelissen, H. J. M. (1999) 'Addition of sensory pollution loads – Simple or not, that is the question', in *Design, Construction and Operation of Healthy Buildings*, ASHRAE, Atlanta, GA, US, pp161–168

Bluyssen, P. M. and Cox, C. (2002) 'Indoor environment quality and upgrading of European office buildings', *Energy & Buildings*, vol 34, no 2, February, pp155–162

Bluyssen, P. M. and Elkhuizen, P. A. (1994) *Sensory Evaluation of Air Quality: Training and Performance, Part II*, TNO report 94-BBI-R1664, Delft, The Netherlands

Bluyssen, P. M. and Lemaire, T. (1992) 'The distribution of the perceived air quality in an office space', Paper presented to the Third International Conference on Air Distribution in Rooms, ROOMVENT '92, Aalborg, Denmark, 2–4 September

Bluyssen, P. M. and Loomans, M. G. L. C. (2003) 'A framework for performance criteria of healthy and energy-efficient buildings', in *Proceedings of Healthy Buildings*, Singapore, pp446–452

Bluyssen, P. M. and Walpot, J. (1993) 'Sensory evaluation of perceived air quality: a comparison of the threshold and the decipol method', in *Proceedings of INDOOR AIR '93*, Helsinki, Finland, vol 1, pp65–70

Bluyssen, P. M., Oliveira Fernandes, E. de, Groes, L., Clausen, G. H., Fanger, P. O., Valbjørn, O., Bernhard, C. A. and Roulet, C. A. (1996a) 'European Audit project to optimize indoor air quality and energy consumption in office buildings', *Indoor Air Journal*, no 6, pp221–238

Bluyssen, P. M., Cornelissen, H. J. M., Hoogeveen, A. W., Wouda, P. and van der Wal, J. F. (1996b) 'The effect of temperature on the chemical and sensory emission of indoor materials', in *Proceedings of INDOOR AIR '96*, 21–26 July 1996, Nagoya, Japan, vol 3, pp619–624

Bluyssen, P. M., Oliveira Fernandes, E. de and Molina, J. L. (2000) 'Database for sources of pollution for healthy and comfortable indoor environment (SOPHIE): Status 2000', in *Proceedings of Healthy Buildings 2000*, Helsinki, Finland, vol 4, pp385–390

Bluyssen, P. M., Opstelten, I. J., Cox, C. W. J. and Brand van den, G. J. (2001) *Prestatie-Index: Interviews en Projectvoorstellen* [*Performance Index: Interviews and Project Proposals*], TNO report 2001-GGI-109, Delft, The Netherlands

Bluyssen, P. M., Seppänen, O., Oliveira Fernandes, E. de, Clausen, G., Müller, B., Molina, J. L. and Roulet, C. A. (2003a) 'Why, when and how do HVAC-systems pollute the indoor environment and what to do about it', *Building and Environment*, vol 38, issue 2, pp209–225

Bluyssen, P. M., Cox, C., Boschi, N., Maroni, M., Raw, G., Roulet, C. A. and Foradini, F. (2003b) 'European project HOPE (Health Optimization Protocol for Energy Efficient Buildings)', in *Healthy Buildings 2003*, Singapore, vol 3, pp76–81

Bødker, S. and Grønbaek, K. (1991) 'Cooperative prototyping: Users and designers in mutual activity', *Journal of Man–Machine Studies*, vol 34, no 3, pp453–478

Boer, J. B. and Rutten, A. J. F. (1974) *Algemene verlichingskunde* [*General Lighting*], Dictate 7.815, Technical University Eindhoven, The Netherlands

Bonnefoy, X. R., Annesi-Maesona, I., Aznar, L. M., Braubachi, M., Croxford, B., Davidson, M., Ezratty, V., Fredouille, J., Ganzalez-Gross, M., van Kamp, I., Maschke, C., Mesbah, M., Moisonnier, B., Monolbaev, K., Moore, R., Nicol, S., Niemann, H., Nygren, C., Ormandy, D., Röbbel, N. and Rudnai, P. (2004) *Review of Evidence on Housing and Health*, Fourth Ministerial Conference on Environment and Health, Budapest, Hungary, 23–25 June 2004

Bornehag, C.-G., Sundell, J., Weschler, C. J., Sisgaard, T., Lundgren, B., Hasselgren, M. and Hägerhed-Engmann, L. (2004) 'The association between asthma and allergic symptoms in children and phthalates in house dust: A nested case-control study', *Environmental Health Perspectives*, vol 112, pp1393–1397

Bornehag, C.-G, Sundell, J., Hägerhed-Engmann, L. and Sigsgaard, T. (2005) 'Association between ventilation rates in 390 Swedish homes and allergic symptoms in children', *Indoor Air*, vol 15, pp275–280

Boschi, N. and Pagliughi, L. M. (2002) 'Quality of life: Meditations on people and architecture', *Proceedings of INDOOR AIR 2002*, Monterey, California, US, pp953–958

Brainard, G. C, Hanifin, J. P., Greeson, J. M., Byrne, B., Glickman, G., Gerner, E. and Rollag, M. D. (2001) 'Action spectrum for melatonin regulation in humans: evidence for a novel circadian photoreceptor', *Journal of Neuroscience*, August, vol 21, pp6405–6412

Bron-van der Jagt, S. (2007) *Sound Transmission through Pipe Systems and into Building Structures*, PhD thesis, Eindhoven, The Netherlands

Bruckman, H. W. L (1994) *Kunsstof CO-sensor* [*Artificial CO-Sensor*], TNO report 0795/U94, Delft, The Netherlands

Bruhns, H. and Isaacs, N. (1996) 'Building quality assessment', in G. Baird (ed) *Building Evaluation Techniques*, Centre for Building Performance Research, Victoria University of Wellington, McGraw-Hill, US

BSRIA (1994) *Environmental Code of Practice for Buildings and Their Services*, Bracknell Berkshire, UK

Buck, L. and Axel, R. (1991) 'Odorant receptors and the organization of the olfactory system', *Cell*, vol 65, pp175–187

Burge, H. A. (1987) 'Bioaerosols: Guidelines for assessment and sampling of saprophytic bioaerosols in the indoor environment', *Applied Industrial Hygiene*, vol 2, ppR10–16

Burge, S., Hedge, A., Wilson, S., Bass, J. H. and Robertson, A. (1987) 'Sick building syndrome: A study of 4373 office workers', *Annals of Occupational Hygiene*, vol 31, no 4A, pp493–504

Caccavelli, D., Balaras, C., Gügerli, H., Allehaux, D., Witchen, K., Rasmussen, M. H., Bluyssen, P. M. and Flourentzous, F. (2000) 'EPIQR–TOBUS: A new generation of decision-aid tools for selecting building refurbishment strategies', Paper presented to the Second International Conference on Decision Making in Urban and Civil Engineering, Lyon, France, November

Cain, W. S. (1989) 'Perceptual characteristics of nasal irritation', NIVA course, Copenhagen, October

Cain, W. S. (2002) 'The construct of comfort: A framework for research', in *Proceedings of INDOOR AIR 2002*, Monterey, California, US, vol II, pp 12–20

Cain, W. S. and Cometto-Muniz, J. E. (1993) 'Irritation and odour: Symptoms of indoor air pollution', *Proceedings of INDOOR AIR '93*, vol 1, pp21–31

Cain, W. S., Leaderer, B. P., Isseroff, R., Berglund L. G., Huey, R. J., Lipsitt, E. D. and Perlman, D. (1983) 'Ventilation requirements in buildings: Control of occupancy odor and tobacco smoke odor', *Atmospheric Environment*, vol 7, no 6, pp1183–1197

Cajochen, C., Zetzer, J. M., Czeisler, C. A. and Dijk, D.-J. (2000) 'Dose–response relationship for light exposure and ocular and electroencephalographic correlates of human alertness', *Behavioural Brain Research*, vol 115, pp75–83

Calabrese, E. J. and Kenyon, E. M. (1991) *Air Toxics and Risk Assessment*, Lewis Publishers, Inc, US

Campagno, A. (1999) *Intelligent Glass Facades*, fourth edition, Birkhauser, Basel, Switzerland

Carrothers, T. J., Graham, J. D. and Evans, J. (1999) 'Putting a value on health effects of air pollution', *IEQ Strategies – Managing Risk*, October, vol 3, no 10

Carslaw, N. and Wolkoff, P. (2006) 'Guest editorial 2006', *Indoor Air*, vol 16, p4–6

CEC (1996) *Daylight II Final Report JOU2-CT92-0144, Vol 1: Availability of Daylighting in Europe and Design of a Daylighting Atlas*, CEC, Brussels, Belgium

CEN (1994) *Dynamic Olfactometry to Determine the Odour Threshold*, Draft European preliminary standard, CEN TC264/WG2, European Committee for Standardization, Brussels, Belgium

CEN (1998) *CR 1752: Ventilation for Buildings – Design Criteria for the Indoor Environment*, European Committee for Standardization, Brussels, Belgium

CEN (2002a) *EN 12464–1 Light and Lighting – Lighting of Work Places; Part 1. Indoor Work Places*, European Committee for Standardization, Brussels, Belgium

CEN (2002b) *EN 12665: Light and Lighting – Basic Terms and Criteria for Specifying Lighting Requirements*, European Committee for Standardization, Brussels, Belgium

CEN (2003) *EN 12354-6, Building Acoustics – Estimation of Acoustic Performance of Buildings from the Performance of Elements; Part 6. Sound Absorption in Enclosed Spaces*, European Committee for Standardization, Brussels, Belgium

CEN (2004a) *EN 13032-2, Light and Lighting – Measurements and Presentation of Photometric Data of Lamps and Luminaries; Part 2: Presentation of Data for Indoor and Outdoor Work Places*, European Committee for Standardization, Brussels, Belgium

CEN (2004b) *EN 717, Wood-based Panels – Determination of Formaldehyde Release; Part 1. Formaldehyde Emission by the Chamber Method; Part 2. Formaldehyde Release by the Gas Analysis Method; Part 3. Formaldehyde Release by the Flask Method*, European Committee for Standardization, Brussels, Belgium

CEN (2005) *EN 15251: Criteria for the Indoor Environment including Thermal, Indoor Air Quality, Light, and Noise*, European Committee for Standardization, Brussels, Belgium

CEN–IEC (2003) *Electroacoustics – Sound Level Meters*, Brussels, Belgium

CEN–ISO (2001a) *EN ISO 14257, Acoustics – Measurements and Parametric Description of Spatial Sound Distribution Curves in Workrooms for Evaluation of Acoustical Performance*, European Committee for Standardization, Brussels, Belgium

CEN–ISO (2001b) *EN ISO 16000 – Part 3: Determination of Formaldehyde and other Carbonyl Compounds. Active Sampling Method*, European Committee for Standardization, Brussels, Belgium

CEN–ISO (2003) *EN ISO 354 Acoustics – Measurement of Sound Absorption in a Reverberation Room*, European Committee for Standardization, Brussels, Belgium

CEN–ISO (2004) *EN ISO 16000 – Part 6: Determination of Volatile Organic Compounds in Indoor and Test Chamber Air by Active Sampling on Tenax TA Sorbent, Thermal Desorption and Gas Chromatography using MS/FID*, European Committee for Standardization, Brussels, Belgium

CEN–ISO (2005) *EN ISO 10052 Acoustics – Field Measurements of Airborne and Impact Sound Insulation and of Service Equipment Noise – Survey Method*, European Committee for Standardization, Brussels, Belgium

CEN–ISO (2006a) *EN ISO 18233, Acoustics – Application of New Measurement Methods in Building and Room Acoustics*, European Committee for Standardization, Brussels, Belgium

CEN–ISO (2006b) *EN ISO 16000 – Part 9: Determination of the Emission of Volatile Organic Compounds from Building Products and Furnishing – Emission Test Chamber*, European Committee for Standardization, Brussels, Belgium

CEN–ISO (2006c) *EN ISO 16000 – Part 10: Determination of the Emission of Volatile Organic Compounds from Building Products and Furnishing – Emission Test Cell Method*, European Committee for Standardization, Brussels, Belgium

CEN–ISO (2006d) *EN ISO 16000 – Part 11: Determination of the Emission of Volatile Organic Compounds from Building Products and Furnishing – Sampling, Storage of Samples and Preparation of Test Specimens*, European Committee for Standardization, Brussels, Belgium

CEN–ISO (2007) *EN ISO 16000 – Part 5: Sampling Strategy for VOC*, European Committee for Standardization, Brussels, Belgium

CIB (1982) *Working with the Performance Approach in Building*, CIB Report Publication 64, International Council for Research and Innovation in Building and Construction Rotterdam, The Netherlands, www.pebbu.nl

CIE (1988) 'Malignant melanoma and fluorescent lighting', *CIE Journal*, vol 7, pp29–33

CIE (1995) *CIE 117: Discomfort Glare in Interior Lighting*, International Commission on Illumination, Vienna, Austria

Clausen, G. and Wyon, D. P. (2005) 'The combined effects of many different indoor environmental factors on acceptability and office work performance', in *Proceedings of INDOOR AIR 2005*, pp351–356

Clausen, G., Pejtersen, J. and Bluyssen, P. M. (1993) *Final Research Manual of European Audit project to Optimize Indoor Air Quality and Energy Consumption in Office Buildings*, Technical University of Denmark and TNO-Building and Construction Research, Lyngby, Denmark

Clements-Croome, D. (2002) (ed) *Creating the Productive Workplace*, E&FN Spon, London and New York

Clinch, J. P. and Healy, J. D. (2000) 'Housing standards and excess winter mortality', *Journal of Epidemiology and Community Health*, 54, pp719–720

Cochet, C. (1998) *VOCEM, Further Development and Validation of a Small Test Chamber Method for Measuring VOC Emissions from Buildings Materials and Products*, Final report, CSTB, Paris, France

Cohen, R., Standeven, M., Bordass, B. and Leaman, A. (2000) 'Assessing building performance in use 1: the Probe process', *Building Research and Information*, vol 29, no 2, pp85–102

Committee on Indoor Pollutants (1981) *Indoor Pollutants*, National Academy Press, Washington, DC, US

Coniglio, W. A. and Faglinno, J. (1990) 'Urinary excretion of chromium, an index of exposure', in *Proceedings of INDOOR AIR '90*, Toronto, vol 2, pp139–144

Cox, C. (2005) *European Project HOPE (Health Optimization Protocol for Energy-Efficient Buildings)*, Final report, Delft, The Netherlands

Cunefare, K. (2004) 'Active noise control', Presented to 75th anniversary meeting of the Acoustical Society of America (ASA), New York

Davis, G. and Szigeti, F. (1996) 'Serviceability tools and methods' in G. Baird (ed) *Building Evaluation Techniques*, Centre for Building Performance Research, Victoria University of Wellington, McGraw-Hill, US

de Dear, R. (2004) 'Thermal comfort in practice', *Indoor Air*, vol 14, supplement 7, pp32–39

de Dear, R. and Brager, G. S. (1998) 'Developing an adaptive model of thermal comfort and preference', *ASHRAE Transactions*, vol 104, no 1a, pp145–167

de Dear R. and Brager, G. (2002) 'Thermal comfort in naturally ventilated buildings: revisions to ASHRAE standard 55', *Energy and Buildings*, vol 34, no 6, pp549–561

de Dear, R. J., Knudsen, H. N. and Fanger, P. O. (1989) 'Impact of air humidity on thermal comfort during step-changes', *ASHRAE Transactions*, vol 95, part 2, pp236–350

Defra (2007) *Human Exposure to Vibration in Residential Environment*, Department for Environment, Food and Rural Affairs, NANR172, London, UK

Devos, M., Patte, F., Ronault, J., Laffort, P. and van Gemert, L. J. (1990) *Standardised Human Olfactory Thresholds*, IRL Press, New York, and Oxford University Press, UK

DIBt (2005) *Principles for Health Assessment of Construction Products Used in Interiors*, Notification no 2005/255/D, Berlin, Germany

Dol, C. P. and Haffner, M. E. A. (2001) *House Statistics in the European Union 2001*, Finish Ministry of Environment, Helsinki, Finland

Dorgan, C. B. and Dorgan, C. E. (1999) 'Commissioning green buildings', in *Proceedings of INDOOR AIR '99*, Edinburgh, Scotland, vol 4, pp531–536

Dorgan Associates (1993) Productivity and Indoor Environmental Quality Study, National Management Institute Alexandria, VA, US

ECA (1989) *Strategy for Sampling Chemical Substances in Indoor Air*, Report no 6, Community COST – Concertation Community COST project 613, Environment and Quality of Life, Luxembourg

ECA (1991) *Effects of Indoor Pollution on Human Health*, Report no 10, European Concerted Action Indoor Air Quality and Its Impact on Man, Luxembourg

ECA (1994) *Sampling Strategy for Volatile Organic Compounds (VOCs) in Indoor Air*, Report no 14, European Collaborative Action, Indoor Air Quality and Its Impact on Man, EUR 16051 EN, Ispra, Italy

ECA (1997) *Evaluation of VOC Emissions from Building Products – Solid Flooring Materials*, Report no 18, European Concerted Action, Indoor Air Quality and Its Impact on Man, EUR 17334 EN, Ispra, Italy

ECA (1999) *Sensory Evaluation of Indoor Air Quality*, Report no 20, European Collaborative Action, Indoor Air Quality and Its Impact on Man, EUR18676EN, Ispra, Italy

ECA (2005) *Harmonisation of Indoor Material Emission Labelling Systems in the EU: Inventory of Existing Systems*, Report no 24, European Collaborative Action Urban Air, Indoor Environment and Human Exposure – Environment and Quality of Life, EUR 21891 EN, Ispra, Italy

Elkhuizen, B. and Rooijakkers, E. (2006) 'De kwaliteit van installaties in gebouwen' ['The quality of systems in buildings'], *Verwarming en ventilatie*, April

Elma, K., Yokoyama, M., Nakamoto, T. and Moriizumi, T. (1989) 'Odour-sensing system using a quartz-resonator sensor array and neural network pattern recognition', *Sensors and actuators*, vol 18, pp291–296

Encyclopaedia Britannica (1991a) 'Light' and 'Lighting and lighting devices', in *Macropaedia vol 23*, 15th edition, Chicago, US, pp1–28, 29–38

Encyclopaedia Britannica (1991b) 'Human sensory reception', *Macropaedia, vol 27*, 15th edition, Chicago, US, pp163–221

Encyclopaedia Britannica (1991c) 'Energy conservation', in *Macropaedia, vol 18*, 15th edition, Chicago, US, pp332–339

Encyclopaedia Britannica (1991d) 'Respiration and respiratory systems', *Macropaedia, vol 26*, 15th edition, Chicago, US, pp725–757

Engen, T. (1972) 'Psychophysics, discrimination and detection', in J. W. Kling and L. A. Riggs (eds) *Woodworth and Schlosberg's Experimental Psychology, Vol 1: Sensation and Perception*, Holt, Rinehart and Winston, New York, pp11–46

Engström, D., Thompson, S. and Oostra, M. (2007) 'Building manufacturing: Architecture, whatever you thought, think again', in A. S. Kazi, M. Hannus, S. Boudjabeur and A, Malone (eds) *Open Building Manufacturing, Core Concepts and Industrial Requirements*, Manubuild, Finland, pp111–131

Esposito, G. (2005) *Reliability Aspects of Perception of Wind Induced Vibrations in Tall Buildings*, TNO report 2005-CI-R0152, Delft, The Netherlands

EU (1970) *Council Directive 70/157/EEC of 6 February 1970 on the approximation of the laws of the Member States relating to the permissible sound level and the exhaust system of motor vehicles*, OJ L 42, 23.2.1970 as subsequently amended, in particular by Council Directive 92/97/EEC of 10 November 1992, OJ L 371, 19.12.1992

EU (1988) *European Council Directive of 21 December 1988, 89/106/EEC on the approximation of laws, regulations and administrative provisions of the Member States related to construction products*, European Commission, Brussels, Belgium

EU (1989) *Council directive 89/391/EEC of 12 June 1989 on the introduction of measures to encourage improvements in the safety and health of workers at work*, European Commission, Brussels, Belgium

EU (1991) *Council Directive 91/322/EEC of 29 may 1991 on establishing indicative limit values by implementing Council Directive 80/1107/EEC on the protection of workers from the risks related to exposure to chemical, physical and biological agents at work*, European Commission, Brussels, Belgium

EU (1996a) *Future Noise Policy*, Green paper COM(96) 540, European Commission, Brussels, Belgium

EU (1996b) *Directive 96/61/EC of 24 September 1996 concerning integrated pollution prevention and control*, OJ L 257, 10.10.1996, European Commission, Brussels, Belgium

EU (1996c) *Council Directive 96/48/EC of 23 July 1996 on the interoperability of the trans-European high-speed rail system*, OJ L 235, 17.9.1996, European Commission, Brussels, Belgium

EU (1997) *Directive 97/24/EC of the European Parliament and of the Council of 17 June 1997 on certain components and characteristics of two or three-wheel motor vehicles*, OJ L 226, 18.8.1997, European Commission, Brussels, Belgium

EU (1998) *European Parliament and Council Biocides Products Directive 98/8/EEC*, European Commission, Brussels, Belgium

EU (2000) *Directive 2000/14/EC of the European Parliament and of the Council of 8 May 2000 on the approximation of the laws of the Member States relating to the noise emission in the environment by equipment for use outdoors*, OJ L 162, 3.7.2000, European Commission, Brussels, Belgium

EU (2001) *Directive 2001/43/EC of the European Parliament and of the Council of 27 June 2001 amending Council Directive 92/23/EEC relating to tyres for motor vehicles and their trailers and to their fitting*, OJ L 211, 4.8.2001, European Commission, Brussels, Belgium

EU (2002a) *6th Environment and Health Action Plan (2004–2008)*, European Commission, Brussels, Belgium

EU (2002b) *European Directive 2002/91/EC 2002 on the energy performance of buildings*, European Commission, Brussels, Belgium

EU (2002c) *Directive 2002/30/EC of the European Parliament and of the Council of 26 March 2002 on the establishment of rules and procedures with regard to the introduction of noise-related operating restrictions at Community airports*, OJ L 85, 28.3.2002, European Commission, Brussels, Belgium

EU (2002d) *European Union Directive 2002/49/EC 2002 on the assessment and management of environmental noise*, European Commission, Brussels, Belgium

EU (2002e) *Directive 2002/44/EC on the minimum health and safety requirements regarding the exposure of workers to the risks arising from physical agents (vibration)*, European Commission, Brussels, Belgium

EU (2003a) *Directive 2003/44/EC of the European Parliament and of the Council of 16 June 2003 amending Directive 94/25/EC on the approximation of the laws, regulations and administrative provisions of the Member States relating to recreational craft*, OJ L 214, 26.8.2003, European Commission, Brussels, Belgium

EU (2003b) *European Directive on the minimum health and safety requirements regarding the exposure of workers to the risks arising from physical agents (noise)*, Directive 2003/10/EC, European Commission, Brussels, Belgium

EU (2004) *COM 160 final, Report from the commission, to the European Parliament and the council concerning existing Community measures relating to sources of environmental noise, pursuant to Article 10.1 of Directive 2002/49/EC relating to the assessment and management of environmental noise*, Geneva, Switzerland

EU (2005) *M/366, Development of horizontal standardised assessment methods for harmonised approaches relating to dangerous substances under the construction products directive (CPD), Emission to indoor air, soil, surface water and ground water*, European Commission, Brussels, Belgium

EU (2006) *Regulation (EC) No 1907/2006 of the European Parliament and of the council of 18 December 2006 concerning the Registration, Evaluation, Authorisation and Restriction of Chemicals (REACH), establishing a European Chemicals Agency, amending Directive 1999/45/EC and repealing Council Regulation (EEC) No 793/93 and Commission Regulation (EC) No 1488/94 as well as Council Directive 76/769/EEC and Commission Directives 91/155/EEC, 93/67/EEC, 93/105/EC and 2000/21/EC*, European Commission, Brussels, Belgium

EU (2007a) *Together for Health: A Strategic Approach for the EU: 2008–2013*, White paper, COM(2007) 630 final, Brussels, Belgium

EU (2007b) *Improving Quality and Productivity at Work: Community Strategy 2007–2012 on Health and Safety at Work*, COM(2007) 62 final, Brussels, Belgium

European Parliament (2000) *Presidency Conclusions*, Lisbon European Council, 23–24 March

Fanger, P. O. (1982) *Thermal Comfort*, Robert E. Krieger Publishing Company, Florida, US

Fanger, P. O. (1988) 'Introduction of the olf and the decipol units indoors and outdoors', *Energy and Buildings*, vol 12, 1988, pp1–6

Fanger, P. O. and Berg-Munch, B. (1983) 'Ventilation requirements for the control of body odor', in *Proceedings of Engineering Foundation Conference on Management of Atmospheres in Tightly Enclosed Space*, ASHRAE, Atlanta, GA, US

Farshchi, M. A. and Fisher, N. (2000) 'Emotion and the environment: The forgotten dimension', in D. Clements-Croome (ed) *Creating the Productive Workplace*, E&FN Spon, London, UK, Chapter 5, pp51–70

Finnegan, H. J., Pickering, C. A. C. and Davies, P. S. (1985) 'Factors affecting the development of precipitating antibodies in workers exposed to contaminated humidifiers', *Clinical Allergy*, vol 15, pp281–282

FiSIAQ (2001) *Classification of Indoor Climate 2000 – Target Values, Design Guidance and Product Requirements*, FiSIAQ Publications 5E, Espoo, Finnish Society of Indoor Air Quality and Climate

Fisk, W. J. (2000) 'Review of health and productivity gains from better IEQ', in *Proceedings of Healthy Buildings 2000*, Helsinki, Finland, August, vol 4, p22–34

Fisk, W. J., Lei-Gomez, Q. and Mendell, M. J. (2007) 'Meta-analysis of the associations of respiratory health effects with dampness and mould in homes', *Indoor Air*, vol 17, no 4, pp284–296

Flatheim, G. (1998) 'Value of indoor air quality to productivity', CIB World Congress 1998, Gaevle, Sweden, paper no B181

Foliente, G. C., Leicester, R. H. and Pham, L. (1998) *Development of the CIB Proactive Program on Performance-Based Building Codes and Standards*, BCE Doc 98/232, CSORI Building, Construction and Engineering, Highett, Australia

Fontana, D. (2007) *Verborgen taal van symbolen* [*The Secret Language of Symbols*], Librero, The Netherlands

Fontoynont, M. (1999) *Daylight Performance of Buildings*, James & James Ltd, London, UK

Gardner, J. W. and Bartlett, P. N. (ed) (1992) *Sensors and Sensory Systems for an Electronic Nose*, Kluwer Academic Publishers, Dordrecht, The Netherlands, NATO ASI Series: Applied Science vol 212

Gardner, J. W., Bartlett, P. N., Dodd, G. H. and Shurmer, H. V. (1990) 'The design of an artificial olfactory system', in D. Schild (ed) *Chemosensory Information Processing*, vol H39, Springer-Verlag, Berlin, Heidelberg, Germany, pp131–173

Geldard, A. (1972) 'The sense of smell' in *The Human Senses*, John Wiley & Sons, second edition, New York, Chapter 5

Gore, A. (2006) *An Inconvenient Truth: The Planetary Emergency of Global Warming and What We Can Do About It*, Bloomsbury, UK

Government of Japan (2000) *Law No 98 of 1968: Latest Amendment by Law No 91 of 2000*, Ministry of Environment, Japan

Grancqvist, C. G. (ed) (1991) *Materials Science for Solar Energy Conversion Systems*, Pergamon, Oxford, UK, pp106–167

Grimwood, C. J., Skinner, C. J and Raw, G. J. (2002) 'The UK National Noise Attitude Survey 1999/2000', Paper presented to Noise Forum Conference, 20 May, UK

Groes, L., Raw, G. J. and Bluyssen, P. M. (1995) 'Symptoms and environmental perceptions for occupants in European office buildings', in *Proceedings of Healthy Buildings '95*, Milano, 1995, vol 3, pp1293–1298

Gunnarsen, L. and P. M. Bluyssen (1994) 'Sensory measurements using trained and untrained panels', in *Proceedings of Healthy Buildings '94*, Budapest, Hungary, vol 2, pp533–538

Gunnarsen, L. and Fanger, P. O. (1992) 'Adaptation to indoor air pollution', *Environment International*, vol 18, pp43–54

Hansen, V., Larsen, A. and Wolkoff, P. (1999) *Round Robin – Chemical Emission Testing by Use of Flec*, Nordtest report TR438, approved 1999–10, Denmark

Harber, L. C., Whitman, G. B., Armstrong, R. B. and Deleo, V. A. (1985) 'Photosensitivity diseases related to interior lighting', *Ann.N.Y.Acad.Sci.*, vol 453, pp317–327

Harper, R., Smith, E. C. D. and Land, D. G. (1968) *Odour Description and Odour Classification*, J&A Churchill, London, UK

Hartman, D. L. (1993) 'Radiative effects of clouds on Earth's climate', in P. V. Hobbs (ed) *Aerosol–Cloud–Climate Interactions*, Academic Press Inc, San Diego, US

Hasselaar, E. (2004) 'Checklist healthy housing for tenants and home owners', Paper presented to WHO International Housing and Health Symposium, Vilnius, Lithuania, pp93–103

Hawkes, D. (1982) 'The theoretical basis of comfort in the "selective" control of environments', *Energy and Buildings*, vol 5, no 2, 127–134

Hawkes, D. (2008) *The Environmental Imagination, Technics and Poetics of the Architectural Environment*, Routledge, Taylor & Francis Group, UK

Hensen, J. L. M. (2006) 'Gebouwsimulatie' ['Building simulation'], *TVVL Magazine*, vol 35, no 2, p5

Hersoug, L.-G. (2005) 'Viruses as the causative agent related to "dampness" and the missing link between allergen exposure and onset of allergic disease', *Indoor Air*, vol 15, pp363–366

Hill, S. M. (1997) *Intelligent Tools for Strategic Performance Evaluation of Office Buildings*, Internal report, Eindhoven University of Technology, Eindhoven, The Netherlands

Hodgson, A. T., Desaillats, H., Sullivan, D. P. and Fisk, W. J. (2007) 'Performance of ultraviolet oxidation for indoor air cleaning applications', *Indoor Air*, vol 17, pp305–316

Hollander, A. G. M. and Hanemaaijer, A. H. (2007) 'Nuchter omgaan met risico's' ['Handling risks with common sense'], *TVVL Magazine*, vol 35, no 11, pp60–67

Hollander, A. G. M. and Melse, J. M. (2006) 'Valuing the health impact of air pollution', in J. Ayres, R. Maynard and R. Richards (eds) *Air Pollution and Health, Air Pollution Reviews*, vol 3, Imperial College Press, London, UK

Hoof, J., van and Schoutens, A. M. C. (2007) 'Verlichting voor de ouder wordende samenleving' ['Lighting for the ageing society'], *TVVL Magazine*, vol 35, no 5, pp42–45

Houghton, J. (2004) *Global Warming, the Complete Briefing*, third edition, Cambridge University Press, Cambridge, UK

Hout, van den F. (1989) *Kleur en uitzicht* [*Colour and View*], Technical University of Eindhoven, The Netherlands

Howkins, J. (2001) *The Creative Economy: How People Make Money from Ideas*, Penguin, UK

HSE (1992) *The Tolerability of Risk from Nuclear Power Stations*, Health & Safety Executive, UK

Humphreys, M. A. (1978) 'Outdoor temperature and comfort indoors', *Building Research and Practice*, vol 6, no 2, pp98–105

Humphreys, M. A. and Nicol, J. F. (1998) 'Understanding the adaptive approach to thermal comfort', *ASHRAE Transactions*, vol 104, no 1, pp991–1004

Hunt, R. W. (1998) *Measuring Colour*, third edition, Fountain Press, England

Hyttinen, M., Pasanen, P., Salo, J., Björkroth, M., Vartianen, M. and Kalliokoski, P. (2003) 'Reactions of ozone on ventilation filters', *Indoor and Built Environment*, vol 12, no 3, pp151–158

Iacobucci, D. (2001) *Kellog on Marketing*, John Wiley & Sons, Inc, US

ICC (2003) *2003 ICC Performance Code for Buildings and Facilities*, International Code Council, US

IEA (2000) *Daylighting in Buildings: A Source Book on Daylighting Systems and Components*, Report of the International Energy Agency, SHC Task 21/EBCS Annex 29, Paris, France

Institute of Medicine (2000) *Cleaning the Air: Asthma and Indoor Exposures*, Committee on the Assessment of Asthma and Indoor Air, National Academy Press, Washington DC, US, p438

IPCC (2007) *Climate Change 2007: The Physical Science Basis*, Summary for Policy Makers, Intergovernmental Panel on Climate changes Geneva, Switzerland, www.ipcc.ch

ISIAQ–CIB (2004) *Performance Criteria of Buildings for Health and Comfort*, CIB no 292, Taskgroup TG42, Rotterdam, The Netherlands

ISO (1984) *ISO 6897 Guidelines for the evaluation of the response of occupants of fixed structures, especially buildings and offshore structures, to low-frequency horizontal motion (0.063 to 1 Hz)*, International Organization for Standardization, Geneva, Switzerland

ISO (1990) *Acoustics – Determination of occupational noise exposure and estimation of noise-induced hearing impairment*, International Organization of Standardization, Geneva, Switzerland

ISO (1992a) *ISO 6242, Building construction – Expression of users' requirements – Part 1: Thermal requirements, Part 2: Air purity requirements, Part 3: Acoustical requirements*, International Organization for Standardization, Geneva, Switzerland

ISO (1992b) *ISO 9241-3, Ergonomic requirements for office work with visual display terminals (VDIs) – Part 3: Visual display requirements*, International Organization for Standardization, Geneva, Switzerland

ISO (1997) *ISO 2631-1 Mechanical vibration and shock – Evaluation of human exposure to whole-body vibration – Part 1: Vibration in buildings (1Hz to 80Hz)*, International Organization for Standardization, Geneva, Switzerland

ISO (1998) *EN ISO 7726, International Organization for Standardization, Instruments for measuring physical quantities*, Geneva, Switzerland

ISO (2003a) *ISO 9921, Ergonomics – assessment of speech communications*, Geneva, Switzerland

ISO (2003b) *ISO2631– 2 Mechanical vibration and shock – Evaluation of human exposure to whole-body vibration – Part 2: Vibration in buildings (1Hz to 80Hz)*, second edition, International Organization for Standardization, Geneva, Switzerland

ISO (2004) *EN ISO 8996, Ergonomics – Determination of metabolic heat production*, International Organization for Standardization, Geneva, Switzerland

ISO (2005) *EN ISO 7730, Moderate thermal environments – Determination of the PMV and PPD indices and specification of the conditions for thermal comfort*, International Organization for Standardization, Geneva, Switzerland

ISO (2006a) *EN ISO 9920, Estimation of the thermal insulation and evaporative resistance of a clothing ensemble*, International Organization for Standardization, Geneva, Switzerland

ISO (2006b) *ISO/TS21929 Building construction – sustainability in building construction – sustainability indicators – Part I: Framework for the development for indicators for buildings*, International Organization for Standardization, Geneva, Switzerland

ISSO/SBR (2006) *Geluidwering in woningen* [*Sound Reduction in Dwellings*], Handbook Healthy Buildings, Rotterdam, The Netherlands

ISSO/SBR (2007) *Gezonde verlichting in gebouwen* [*Healthy Lighting in Buildings*], Handbook Healthy Buildings, Rotterdam, The Netherlands

IUMS (2005) *Statements and Recommendations from the Second International Workshop on Fungi in Indoor Environments: Towards Strategies for Living in Healthy Buildings*, International Union of Microbiological Sciences, International Commission on Indoor Fungi, Utrecht, The Netherlands, 17–19 March 2005

Jager, de, C. (2007) 'De zon actiever dan ooit' [The sum more active then ever'], *TVVL Magazine*, vol 36, no 10, pp52–54

Jansen, C. A., Rooijakkers, G. W. J. and Kerdèl, J. F. P. G. (2007) 'Gebouwbeheerssystemen aan de rand van een nieuw tijdperk' ['Building management systems on the verge of a new era'], *TVVL Magazine*, vol 26, no 12, pp8–15

Janssen, J. E. (1999) 'The history of ventilation and temperature control, the first century of air conditioning', *ASHRAE Journal*, October, pp48–70

Jantunen, M. J., Hänninen, O., Katsouyanni, K., Knöppel, H., Keunzli, N., Lebret, E., Maroni, M., Saarela, K., Sram, R. and Zmirou, D. (1998) 'Air pollution exposure in European cities: The "Expolis study"', *JEAEE*, vol 8, no 4, pp495–518

Jasuja, M. (ed.) (2005) *PeBBu International State of the Art Report*, EUR 21989, October, CIB, Rotterdam, The Netherlands

Jenkins, L., Phillips, T. J. and Mubog, E. J. (1990) 'Activity patterns of Californians: Use and proximity to indoor pollutant sources', in *Proceedings of INDOOR AIR '90*, Toronto, vol 3, pp465–470

Johnson, C. (1989) 'Aeroallergens', NIVA Course on The Sick Building Syndrome, Copenhagen, October

Johnson, C. R., Albrechtsen, O., Nielsen, P. A., Nielsen, G. D. and Frank, C. (1990) 'Controlled human exposure to building materials in climate chambers, Part I: Performance and comfort', *Proceedings of INDOOR AIR '90*, Toronto, vol 1, pp269–274

Jung, C. G. (1966–1976) *The Collected Works of C. G. Jung*, vol 1–18, Princeton University Press, US

Jurado, S. R. (2006) 'Indoor pollutants, microbial concentrations and thermal conditions influence student performance', in *Proceedings of Healthy Buildings 2006*, Lisbon, Portugal, vol 1, pp277–282

Kapit, W. and Elson, L. M. (2002) *The Anatomy Coloring Book*, third edition, Benjamins/Cummings Science publishing, CA, US

Kapit, W., Macey, R. I. and Meisami, E. (2000) *The Physiology Coloring Book*, 2nd edition, Benjamins/Cummings Science publishing, CA, US

Kendall, S. and Jonathan, T. (2000) *Residential Open Building*, Part III, E&FN Spon, London and New York, p301

Kirchner, S., Pasquier, N., Cretier, D., Gauvin, S., Golliot, F., Pietrowski, D. and Cochet., C. (2002) 'The French permanent survey on indoor air quality – survey design in dwellings and schools', *Proceedings of INDOOR AIR 2002*, Monterey, California, pp349–354

Kjaegaard, S. (1992) 'Assessment of eye irritation in humans', *Ann. N.Y. Acad. Sci.*, vol 641, pp187–198

Klein, S. (2006) *The Science of Happiness*, Marlowe, New York

Kotler, P. (1997) *Marketing Management: Analysis, Planning, Implementation and Control*, ninth international edition, Prentice Hall, New Jersey, US

Kotzias, D., Koistinen, K., Kephalopoulos, S., Schlitt, C., Carrer, P., Maroni, M., Jantunen, M., Cochet, C., Kirchner, S., Lindvall, T., McLaughlin, J., Mølhave, L., Oliveira Fernandes, E. de and Seifert, B. (2005) *The Index Project, Final Report: Critical Appraisal of the Setting and Implementation of Indoor, Exposure Limits in the EU*, EUR 21590 EN, Joint Research Centre, ISPRA, Italy

Kramer, A. and Twigg, B. A. (1970) 'Fundamentals: Taste testing', in *Quality Control for the Food Industry*, third edition, vol 1, AVI Publishing Company, Inc, Westport, Connecticut, US, Chapter 9, pp121–154

Lammers, J. T. H. (1982) *Natuurkunde van het binnenmilieu II* [*Physics of the Indoor Environment II*], no 7.303.0, Technical University of Eindhoven, The Netherlands

Leaman, A. (1996) 'Building in use studies', in G. Baird (ed) *Building Evaluation Techniques*, Centre for Building Performance Research, Victoria University of Wellington, McGraw-Hill, US

Lehar, S. (2003) *The World in your Head: A Gestalt View of the Mechanism of Conscious Experience*, Psychology Press, UK

Lemaire, A. D. (1990) 'A numerical study of the air movement and temperatures in large atria and sunspaces', Paper presented to Roomvent '90 Conference, Oslo, Norway

Levy, J. I., Nishioka, Y. and Spengler, J. D. (2003) 'The public health benefits of insulation retrofits in existing housing in the United States', *Environ Hlth*, vol 2, p4

LHRF (2002) *Proceedings of Symposium Healthy Lighting*, Light and Health Research Foundation, Eindhoven, The Netherlands

Lichtenberg, J. (2002) *Development of Project-Independent Building Products*, PhD thesis, Technical University of Delft, The Netherlands

Loewenstein, G. F., Weber, E. U., Hsee, C. H. K. and Welch, N. (2001) 'Risk as feelings', *Psychologic. Bull.*, vol 127, pp267–286

Lupton, D. (1999) *Risk*, Routledge, London, UK

Madigan M., Martinko J. and Parker, J. (eds) (2005) *Brock Biology of Microorganisms*, 11th edition, Prentice Hall, New Jersey, US

Maslow, A. (1943) 'A theory of human motivation', *Psychological Review*, vol 50, pp370–396

McCarthey K. and Nicol, J. F. (2002) 'Developing an adaptive control algorithm for Europe: Results of the SCATs project', *Energy and Buildings*, vol 34, no 6, pp623–635

McIntyre, D. A. (1980) *Indoor Climate*, Applied Science, Publishers LTD, Essex, UK

Meerdink, G., Rozendaal, E. Z. and Witteveen, C. J. E. (1988) *Daglicht en uitzicht in kantoorgebouwen [Daylight and View in Office Buildings]*, Directoriaat-Generaal van de Arbeid, Voorburg, S 51, The Netherlands

Melikov, A. K. (1989) 'Quantifying draught risk', *Technical Review*, Bruel & Kjaer, no 2, Denmark

Melikov, A. K., Cermak, R. and Majer, M. (2002) 'Personalized ventilation: Evaluation of different air terminal devices', *Energy and buildings*, vol 34, pp829–836

Mendell, M. J. (2007) 'Indoor residential chemical emissions as risk factors for respiratory and allergic effects in children: A review', *Indoor Air*, 2007, vol 17, pp259–277

Millen, P. (2002) 'Communicating performance', *Manufacturing-Engineer*, vol 81, no 3, pp119–122

Milton, D. K., Glencross, P. M. and Walters, M. D. (2000) 'Risk of sick leave associated with outdoor air supply rate, humidification, and occupant complaints', *Indoor Air*, vol 10, pp212–221

Mitchell, C. T. (1995) 'Action, perception and the realisation of design', *Design studies*, vol 16, pp4–28

Mølhave, L. (1990) 'Volatile organic compounds, indoor air quality and health', in *Proceedings of INDOOR AIR '90*, Toronto, Canada, vol 5, p15–33

Mølhave, L. (2008) 'Inflammatory and allergic responses to airborne office dust in five human provocation experiments', *Indoor Air*, vol 18, pp261–270

Monk, P. M. S., Mortimer, R. J. and Rosseinnsky, D. R. (1995) *Electrochromism: Fundamentals and Applications*, VCH, Weinheim, Germany

Murray, C. J. L. and Lopez, A. D. (eds) (1996) *The Global Burden of Disease: A Comprehensive Assessment of Mortality and Disability from Disease, Injury and Risk Factors in 1990 and Projected to 2020*, vol I, Harvard University Press, Harvard, Massachusetts, US

MVROM (1990) *Kunstlicht en gezondheid [Artificial Light and Health]*, VROM, Rijksgebouwendienst, Directie Advisering en Onderzoek, Techniek en Kwaliteitszorg, TKZ 11053.01, The Netherlands

Mygind, N. (1986) *Essential Allergy: An Illustrated Text for Students and Specialists*, Blackwell Scientific Publications, London

Nakamoto, T., Fukunishi, K. and Moriizumi, T. (1990) 'Identification capability of odour sensor using quartz-resonator array and neural-network pattern recognition', *Sensors and Actuators*, vol B1, pp473–476

NCA (1988) *Noise Pollution and Abatement Act of 1972*, Public Law No 92-574, 86 Stat. 1234, codification amended at 42 U.S.C. 4901-4918, US

NEN (1997) *NEN 3087, Ergonomics, visual ergonomics in relation to lighting – principles and applications*, Delft, The Netherlands

NEN (1999) *NEN 1070, Noise control in buildings – specifications and rating of quality*, Delft, The Netherlands

NEN (2001) *NEN 2057, Daylight openings of buildings – Determination method of the equivalent daylight area of a space*, Delft, The Netherlands

Nicol, J. F. and Humphreys, M. A. (1972) 'Thermal comfort as part of a self-regulating system', in *Proceedings of the CIB Symposium on Thermal Comfort*, Building Research Establishment, Watford, UK

Nielsen, G. D. (1985) 'Exposure limits for irritants', *Ann.Am.Conf.Ind.Hyg.*, vol 12, pp119–135

Nielsen, G. D., Larsen, S. T., Olsen, O., Løvik, M., Poulsen, L. K., Glue, C. and Wolkoff, P. (2007) 'Do indoor chemicals promote development of airway allergy?', *Indoor Air*, vol 17, no 3, pp236–235

Niemann, H. and Maschke, C. (2004) *Noise Effects and Morbidity*, WHO LARES final report, Bonn, Germany

NIOSH (2004) *Worker Health Chartbook 2004*, NIOSH publication 2004-146, Cincinnati, Ohio, US

NKB (1995) *Tenax as a Collection Medium for Volatile Organic Compounds*, Report 06E, Nordic Committee on Building Regulations, Indoor Climate Committee, Helsinki, Finland

NPR (2007) *NPR 3438, Ergonomics – Noise at the Workplace: Determination of the Amount of Disturbance of Communication and Concentration*, Delft, The Netherlands

NRC (1981) *Indoor Pollutants*, National Research Council, National Academy Press, Washington, DC

NRC (2001) *Climate Change Science: An Analysis of Some Key Questions,* National Academy Press, Washington, DC, US

NRC (2005) *Managing VOCs and Indoor Air Quality in Office Buildings: An Engineering Approach*, Washington DC, US

Office of the Prime Minister (2004) *Housing Health and Safety Rating System*, Guidance (version 2), London, UK

Oliveira Fernandes, E. de (2001) *MATHIS Publishable Final Report*, Joule III Programme, EC, Porto, Portugal

Oliveira Fernandes, E. de and Clausen, G. (1997) *European Database on Indoor Air Pollution Sources*, Final Report, Porto, Portugal

Ott, J. N. (1973) *Health and Light*, Ariel Press, Ohio, US

Padmos, P. (1988) *Gezondheidsschade door TL-verlichting? [Health Damage by Tube Lighting?]*, TNO-IZF Report no 1988 C-31, Soesterberg, The Netherlands

Pallasmaa, J. (2005) *The Eyes of the Skin*, Academic Editions, London, 1996; revised edition, Wiley Academy, Chichester, UK

Palladio, A. (1570) *The Four Books of Architecture*, translated by I. Ware (1738), Dover Publications, New York, 1964 edition

Parker, S. (2003) *Hormones, Injury, Illness and Health*, Heinemann Library, Chicago, US

Perner, L. (2007) *San Diego State University*, www.consumerpsychologist.com

Persily, A. (2005) 'What we think we know about ventilation', *Proceedings of INDOOR AIR 2001, volume 1*, Beijing, China, pp24–35

Preller, L., Zweers, T., Boleij, J. S. M. and Brunekreef, B. (1990) *Gezondheidsklachten en klachten over het binnenklimaat in kantoorgebouwen [Health Symptoms and Complaints on Indoor Climate in Office Buildings]*, Directoraat-Generaal van de Arbeid, Ministerie van Sociale Zaken en Werkgelegenheid, S83, Voorburg, The Netherlands

Ramakrishnan, K., Cena, K. and Taplin, R. H. (1999) 'Indoor thermal climate, air contaminants and sensory perception in the assessment of indoor air quality (IAQ) or indoor environmental quality (IEQ) and sick building syndrome (SBS)', in *Proceedings of INDOOR AIR 1999*, Edinburgh, Scotland, vol 5, pp408–413

Raw, G. J., Roys, M. S. and Leaman, A. (1990) 'Further findings from the office environment survey: productivity', in *Proceedings of INDOOR AIR 1990*, Toronto, Canada, vol 1, pp231–236

Raw, G. J., Coward, S. K. D., Llewellyn, J. W., Brown, V. M., Crump, D. R. and Ross, D. I. (2002) 'Indoor air quality in English homes – introduction and carbon monoxide findings', in *Proceedings of INDOOR AIR 2002*, Monterey, California, US, vol 4, pp461–466

Ree, H. van, Meel, J. van and Lohman, F. (2007) *Better Briefing for Better Buildings*, An Innovative Modelling Tool for Specifications Management, www.icop.nl

REN (1991) *Real Estate Norm, norm voor de beoordeling van kantoorlokaties en kantoorgebouwen [Real Estate Standard, Standard for Evaluation of Office Locations and Buildings]*, Stichting Real Estate Norm Nederland, Nieuwegein, The Netherlands

REN (1992) *Real Estate Norm, Methode voor de advisering en beoordeling van kantoorlocaties en kantoorgebouwen [Real Estate Standard, Method for Advising and Evaluation of Office Locations and Buildings]*, Stichting Real Estate Norm Nederland, Nieuwegein, The Netherlands

Revkin, A. (2005) 'A new measure of well-being from a happy little kingdom', *The New York Times*, 4 October

Rgd (1991) *Methode voor de beoordeling van het thermisch binnenklimaat [Method for Evaluation of the Thermal Indoor Climate]*, Rgd report, TKZ 11117.01, The Hague, The Netherlands

Rooijakkers, E. (2006) 'Visie op gebouwprestatiesimulatie' ['Vision on simulation of building performance'], *TVVL Magazine*, no 2, vol 35, pp12–19

Rohr, A. C. (2001) 'Methods for assessing irritation effects in IAQ field and laboratory studies', in J. D. Spengler et al (eds) *Indoor Air Quality Handbook*, McGraw-Hill, US, Chapter 26

Rossow, W. B., Walker, A. W., Beuschel, D. E. and Roiter, M. D. (1996) *Documentation of New Cloud Datasets*, International Satellite Cloud Climatology Project (ISCCP), World Meteorological Organization, Geneva, Switzerland

Roulet, C.-A. (2008) 'Measurement and visualisation of air movements', in H. B. Awbi (ed) *Ventilation System, Design and Performance*, Taylor & Francis, Oxon, UK, pp400–438

Roulet, C.-A., Flourentzou, F., Foradini, F., Bluyssen, P. M., Cox, C. and Aizlewood, C. (2006a) 'Multi-criteria analysis of health, comfort and energy-efficiency of buildings', *Building Research Information*, vol 34, pp475–482

Roulet, C.-A., Bluyssen, P. M., Cox, C. and Foradini, F. (2006b) 'Relations between perceived indoor environment characteristics and well-being of occupants at individual level', in *Proceedings of Healthy Buildings 2006*, Lisbon, Portugal, vol 3, pp163–168

Rowland, I. D. and Howe, T. N. (2007) *Vitruvius: Ten Books on Architecture*, Cambridge University Press, Cambridge, UK

Rust, W. N. J., Seyffert, F., den Heijer, A. C. and Soeter, J. P. (1995) *Vastgoed financieel [Real Estate Financial]*, Vlaardingen, The Netherlands

Rutten, P. G. S. and Trum, H. M. G. J. (1998) *Prestatiegericht ontwerpen en evalueren [Performance Oriented Design and*

Evaluation], Faculty of Management, Technical University Eindhoven, The Netherlands

Sandberg, M., and Sjöberg, M. (1984) 'The use of moments for assessing air quality in ventilated rooms', *Building and Environment*, vol 18, pp181–197

Saarela, K. and Tirkonen, T. (2004) *M1, Emission Classification of Building Materials: Protocol for Chemical and Sensory Testing of Building Materials*, The Building Information Foundation RS, Finland, version 15

Scharpf, S. M. (1999) 'ERP & MES: Framing a new information architecture', *PIMA's–Papermaker*, vol 81, no 4, pp33–36

Scheuren, F. (2004) 'What is a survey', American Statistical Association, www.whatisasurvey.info

Schmidt-Etkin, D. (1994) 'Biocontaminants in Indoor Environments', *Indoor Air Quality Update*, Cutter Information Corp, US

Scholten, N. P. M. (2001) *Technische en juridische grondslagen van de technische bouwregelgeving Woningwet en Bouwbesluit* [*Technical and Legal Foundations of the Dutch Technical Building Regulations*], PhD thesis, Delft, The Netherlands

Schultz, D. P. en Schultz, S. E. (2006) *Psychology and Work Today*, Pearson Education International, ninth edition, New Jersey, US

Silver, W. L. and T. E. Finger (1991) 'The trigeminal system', in T. V. Getchell, R. L. Doty, L. M. Bartoshuk and J. B. Snow Jr (eds) *Smell and Taste in Health and Disease*, Raven Press, New York, pp97–108

Sins, A. (1999) 'Second opinion – lowest price wins is still the norm in construction, but all that is about to change', *Building*, 26 February, p8

Skov, O., Valbjørn, O. and DISG (1987) 'The "sick" building syndrome in the office environment: The Danish town hall study', *Environmental International*, vol 13, pp339–349

Slater, K. (1985) *Human Comfort*, Thomas, Springfield, US

Smith, K. R. (2003) 'The global burden of disease from unhealthy buildings: preliminary results from a comparative risk assessment', in *Proceedings of Healthy Buildings 2003*, Singapore

Soethout, L. L. and Peitsman, H. C. (2007) 'Intelligent diagnosticeren van gebouwinstallaties' (Intelligent diagnosis of building systems), *TVVL Magazine*, vol 26, no 12, pp32–35.

Sommer, R. (1969) *Personal Space: The behavioral basis of design*, Prentice Hall, inc., Englewood Cliff, New Jersey, US

Spengler, J. D., Samet, J. M. and McCarthy, J. F. (eds) (2001) *Indoor Air Quality Handbook*, McGraw-Hill, US

Stevens, S. S. (1957) 'On the psycho-physical law', *Psychol Review*, vol 64, pp153–181

Sundell, J. (2000) 'Building related factors and health, Increase asthma and allergies', in *Proceedings of Healthy Buildings 2000*, Helsinki, Finland, vol 1, pp22–34

Svendsmark, H. (2007) 'Cosmoclimatology: A new theory emerges', *Astronomy and Geophysics*, Royal Astronomy Society, London, vol 48, pp1.18–1.24

Svendsmark, H. and Calder, N. (2007) *The Chilling Stars: A New Theory of Climate Change*, Icon Books Ltd, London, UK

Taylor, J. (2006) *The Mind: A User's Manual*, John Wiley & Sons Ltd, England

The New Economics Foundation (2006) *Happy Planet Index*, www.happyplanetindex.org.

Tirkkonen, T., Mrouch, U.-M. and Orko, I. (1995) 'Tenax as an adsorption medium in indoor air and material emission on measurements – a review', in *Proceedings of Healthy Buildings 1995*, Milan, Italy, vol 2, pp813–819

Tissen, R., Andriessen, D. and Lekanne Deprez, F. (1998) *Value-Based Knowledge Management: Creating the 21st Company: Knowledge Intensive, People Rich*, Addison Wesley Longman, Amsterdam, The Netherlands

TNO (1979) *TNO-daglichtdiagrammen* [*TNO-Daylight Diagrams*], Institute for Environmental Hygiene and Health Technique, Delft, The Netherlands

Tol, van A. (1984) *Jellema, Bouwkunde 7a*, Waltman, Delft, The Netherlands

Too, L. (1996) *The Complete Illustrated Guide to Feng Shiu*, HarperCollins Publishers, London, UK

TRI (2007) *Tri Society Newsletters*, vol 5, no 2, www.inns.org

US Department of Commerce (2000) *Ageing in the Americas into the XXIth Century*, National Institute on Ageing, US

VDI (1986) *VDI-Richtlinien, VDI 3881, Blatt 1/part 1, Olfactometry, Odour Threshold Determination: Fundamentals*, Düsseldorf, Germany, May

Veenhoven, R. (2007) *World Database of Happiness, Trend in Nations*, Erasmus University Rotterdam, www.world databaseofhappiness.eur.nl/trendnat

Vischer, J. C. (1989) *Environmental Quality in Offices*, Van Nostrand Reinhold, New York, US

Visser, R. (1992) *Verlichting en interieur* [*Lighting and Interior*], Dekker v.d Bos & Partners BV, Amersfoort, The Netherlands

Vitruvius (100 BC) *Ten Books of Architecture*, Morgan MH (translation), Dover, NY, 1961, Chapter 1

VROM (2007) *Building Decree*, www.vrom.nl/bouwbesluit

Von Hippel, E. (1986) 'Lead-users: A source of novel product concepts', *Measurement science*, vol 32, no 7, pp791–805

Vroon, P. A. (1990) *Psychologische aspecten van ziekmakende gebouwen* [*Psychological Aspects of Building Related Illness*], Ministry of Housing, Planning and Environment, The Netherlands

Vijverberg, G. (1999) 'Methoden voor kwaliteitsmeting kantoorgebouwen' ['Methods for quality assessment office buildings'], *Facility Management Magazine*, March, pp42–45

Wagenberg, A. F. and Wilmes, R. (1989) 'Gebruik en beleving van de werkplek in kantoororganisaties (1), (2)

en (3)' ['Use and experience of the workplace in office organizations (1), (2) and (3)'], *Gebouwmanagement*, March, pp48–51, May, pp57–63, and September, pp24–29

Wal van der, J. W. (1990) *Stof in het binnenmilieu* [*Dust in the Indoor Environment*], Seminar, Maastricht, The Netherlands

Wallace, L., Pellizari, E. and Gordon, S. (1990) 'The use of breath analysis to determine accent or long–term exposure to indoor sources of volatile organic chemicals', in *Proceedings of INDOOR AIR 1990*, Toronto, vol 2, pp127–132

Wargocki, P., Wyon, D., Sundell, J., Clausen, G. and Fanger, P. O. (2000) 'The effects of outdoor air supply rate in an office on perceived air quality, sick building syndrome (SBS) symptoms and productivity', *Indoor Air*, vol 10, no 3, pp222–236

Weichenthal, S., Dufresne, A. and Infante-Rivard, C. (2007) 'Indoor ultrafine particles and childhood asthma – exploring a potential public health concern', *Indoor Air*, vol 17, no 2, pp81–91

Weschler, C. J. (2004) 'Chemical reactions among indoor pollutants: What we've learned in the new millennium', *Indoor Air*, 14 (Supplement 7), pp184–194

WHO (1989) *Indoor Air Quality: Organic Pollutants*, EURO reports and studies no 11, WHO Regional Office for Europe, Copenhagen, Denmark

WHO (2000a) *The Right to Healthy Indoor Air*, European HEALTH21 Targets 10.13, Report EUR/00/5020494, World Health Organization Europe, Copenhagen, Denmark

WHO (2000b) *Air Quality Guidelines for Europe*, second edition, World regional publication European series no 91, World Health Organization, Geneva, Switzerland

WHO (2002) *Active Ageing: A Policy Framework*, Contribution of the World Health Organization to the Second United Nations World Assembly on Ageing, Madrid, Spain

WHO (2003a) *Climate Change and Human Health – Risks and Responses*, World Health Organization, Geneva, Switzerland

WHO (2003b) *WHO Technical Meeting on Exposure–Response Relationships of Noise on Health*, 19–21 September 2002, Bonn, Germany

WHO (2006a) *Housing and Health Regulations in Europe*, Final report, July 2006, Bonn, Germany

WHO (2006b) *Electromagnetic Fields and Public Health: Base Stations and Wireless Technologies*, Fact sheet no 304, www.who.int.

WHO (2006c) *Air Quality Guidelines: Global Update 2005, Particulate Matter, Ozone, Nitrogen Dioxide and Sulphur Dioxide*, WHO Regional office for Europe, Denmark

WHO (2007) *Electromagnetic Fields and Public Health: Exposure to Extreme Low Frequency Fields*, Fact sheet no 322, www.who.int.

WHO (2008) *Chronic Obstructive Pulmonary Disease (COPD)*, Fact sheet no 135, www.who.int

Wilby, R. B. (2007) 'A review of climate impacts on the built environment', *Built Environment*, vol 33, pp31–45

Wilke, O., Jann, O. and Broedner, D. (2004) 'VOC and SVOC emissions from adhesives, floor coverings and complete floor structures', *Indoor Air*, vol 14, Supplement 8, pp98–107

Wilkins, A. J., Nimmo-Smith, I., Slater, A. I. and Bedocs, L. (1989) 'Fluorescent lighting, headaches and eyestrain', *Lighting Research Technology*, vol 21, no 1, pp11–18

Wilson, S. and Hedge, A. (1987) *The Office Environmental Survey: A Study of Building Sickness*, Building Use Studies, London, UK

Wolkoff, P. and Nielsen, P. A. (1996) 'A new approach for indoor climate labelling of building materials – emission testing, modelling, and comfort evaluation', *Atmospheric Environment*, vol 30, pp2679–2689

Wolkoff, P. and Nielsen G. D. (2001) 'Organic compounds in indoor air – their relevance for perceived air quality', *Atmospheric Environment*, vol 35, pp4407–4417

Wijk, M. and Spekkink, D. (1998) *Bouwstenen voor het PvE* [*Building Bricks for the Brief*], SBR publicatie 421, Stichting Bouwresearch, Rotterdam, The Netherlands

Wyon (1993) 'Healthy buildings and their impact on productivity', in *Proceedings of INDOOR AIR 1993*, Helsinki, Finland, vol 6, pp3–13

WMO/UNEP (2006) *Scientific Assessment of Ozone Depletion: 2006*, Executive Summary, Assessment Panel of the Montreal Protocol on Substances that Deplete the Ozone Layer, 18 August, ozone.unep.org

Yaglou, C. P. E., Riley, C. and Coggins, D. I. (1936) 'Ventilation requirements', *ASHVE Transactions*, vol 42, pp133–162

Yang, X., Chen, Q. and Bluyssen, P. M. (1998) 'Prediction of short-term and long-term volatile organic compound emissions from SBR bitumen-backed carpet under different temperatures', *AHSRAE Transactions*, vol 4, part 2, paper no TO-98-23-4

Yoshino, H., Netsu, K., Yoshida, M., Ikeda, K., Nozaki, A., Kakuta, K., Hojo, S., Amano, K. and Ishikawa, S. (2006) 'Long-term field survey on IAQ and occupants health in 57 sick houses in Japan', in *Proceedings of Healthy Buildings 2006*, Lisbon, Portugal, vol 3, pp315–320

Zuraimi, M. S., Naydenov, K., Hägerhed, L. E., Tham, K. W., Bornehag, C.-G. and Sundell, J. (2006) 'A study on dampness and its associations with asthma and allergies among 20,103 young children in Sweden, Bulgaria and Singapore', in *Proceedings of Healthy Buildings 2006*, Lisbon, Portugal, vol 1, pp147–150

Index